T0375198

Fixing the Fragmented University

Fixing the Fragmented University

Decentralization With Direction

Joseph C. Burke

Rockefeller Institute of Government

Editor

Anker Publishing Company, Inc.

Fixing the Fragmented University
Decentralization With Direction

ISBN 978-1-933371-15-3

Composition by Tanya Anoush Johnson
Cover design by Dutton & Sherman Design

Anker Publishing Company, Inc.
563 Main Street
P.O. Box 249
Bolton, MA 01740-0249 USA

www.ankerpub.com

Library of Congress Cataloging-in-Publication Data
Fixing the fragmented university : decentralization with direction /
Joseph C. Burke, editor.
        p. cm.
Includes bibliographical references and index.
    ISBN-13: 978-1-933371-15-3
    1. Public universities and colleges—United States. 2. Schools—
Decentralization—United States. 3. Educational change—United
States. I. Burke, Joseph C.

    LB2328.62.U6F59 2007
    378.050973—dc22

                                                            2006028943

Table of Contents

About the Authors

The Editor

Joseph C. Burke is director of the Higher Education Program and a Senior Fellow at the Nelson A. Rockefeller Institute of Government, and professor of higher education policy and management at the State University of New York. After receiving his Ph.D. in history from Indiana University, Dr. Burke taught for 12 years. He served as president of the State University of New York at Plattsburgh for 12 years, followed by 9 years as provost and vice chancellor for academic affairs and 1 year as interim chancellor of the State University of New York System. While provost, he also held the post of president of the State University of New York Research Foundation, the fiscal agent for all research grants and contracts in the SUNY System. Dr. Burke was also a consultant with the Center for Public Higher Education Trusteeship and Governance at the Association of Governing Boards of Universities and Colleges. In 2005, he served as an advisor to the State Higher Education Executive Officers National Commission on Accountability.

Dr. Burke has consulted, written, and lectured on a wide array of topics in higher education, including the role of college and university presidents, system governance, accountability and autonomy in higher education, outcomes assessment, and performance reporting, budgeting, and funding. He has published more than 60 books, monographs, and articles on these subjects. His most recent book, which he edited and coauthored, is *Achieving Accountability in Higher Education: Balancing Public, Academic, and Market Demands* (2005, Jossey-Bass). The Henry Luce Foundation, the Pew Charitable Trusts, and the Ford Foundation have awarded him grants for national studies of the budgeting, reporting, accountability, and performance of public university systems and state colleges and universities. The Ford Foundation supported the preparation of this present book.

The Contributors

Mayra E. Beers is executive director of the Center for Leadership at Florida International University and director of board of operations and associate corporate secretary to the university's board of trustees. Ms. Beers holds an M.A. in history from Florida International University and is a Ph.D. candidate in history. She holds graduate certificates in African–New World Studies and Latin American and

Caribbean Studies. Ms. Beers is the recipient of the Jay I. Kislak Foundation Prize in history and anthropology and the James R. Scobie Memorial Award in history. She completed her doctoral coursework under the auspices of a Mellon Foundation Doctoral Fellowship and a Ford Foundation grant for doctoral research.

Roger Benjamin, president of the Council for Aid to Education, was director of RAND Education from 1994 to 1999 and senior research scientist at RAND from 1990 to 2005. Previous to his appointment to RAND, he was a member of the Department of Political Science at the University of Minnesota from 1966 to 1983 and 1988 to 1990 and associate dean and executive officer of the university's College of Liberal Arts from 1980 to 1983, provost of the University of Pittsburgh from 1983 to 1986, and vice president for academic affairs and provost at the University of Minnesota from 1986 to 1988. Dr. Benjamin is the author or coauthor of more than 50 books, monographs, and articles on political change, comparative political economy, and public and higher education policy. He currently codirects a national initiative to assess student learning outcomes in undergraduate education.

Robert H. Bruininks is the 15th president of the University of Minnesota, where he previously served as professor, dean, and executive vice president and provost. He oversees a major strategic planning and positioning effort aimed at making the University of Minnesota one of the top public research universities in the world within a decade. Among his priorities are the continued improvement of the student experience, deepened culture of interdisciplinary scholarship, commitment to continuous improvement in the university's administration and management, and renewal of the university's public obligations as a land-grant institution. An educational psychologist by training, Dr. Bruininks has centered his academic career on human development and performance, policy research and development in education and social services, and strategic improvement and accountability in the fields of preK–12 and higher education. He has authored or coauthored more than 150 journal articles and book chapters, as well as several training materials.

Richard Cherwitz is founder and director of the Intellectual Entrepreneurship Consortium, a nationally acclaimed initiative at the University of Texas–Austin designed to educate citizen-scholars so as to promote interdisciplinary education and greater synergies between academe and society. He also serves as a professor in communication studies and in the division of rhetoric. In addition to numerous scholarly books and articles exploring the relationship between rhetoric and philosophy, Dr. Cherwitz has written about the need for reform in higher education and the necessity of increasing academic engagement at research institutions; these essays have appeared in *Change, Academe, Peer Review, Journal of Hispanic Higher Education, Black Issues in Higher Education, The Scientist,* and *College and University Journal.* Dr. Cherwitz has received the National Communication Association's Karl R. Wallace Memorial Award, the Douglas Ehninger Distinguished Rhetorical Scholar Award, the Woodrow Wilson National Fellowship Foundation's Innovation Award, the Conference of Southern Graduate Schools Outstanding Contribution to Graduate Education Award, the Ernest A. Lynton Award for Faculty Professional Service and Academic Outreach (New England Resource Center for Higher Education), and the National Speakers Association Outstanding Professor Award. Dr. Cherwitz served for seven years as a dean in the University of Texas Graduate School.

James J. Duderstadt is president emeritus and university professor of science and engineering at the University of Michigan. He is a graduate of Yale University and the California Institute of Technology. Dr. Duderstadt's teaching, research, and publishing activities include nuclear science and engineering, applied physics, computer simulation, science policy, and higher education. He has served on numerous National Academy and federal commissions including the National Science Board and the National Commission on the Future of Higher Education. He has received numerous awards, including the E. O. Lawrence Award for excellence in nuclear research, the Arthur Holly Compton Prize for outstanding teaching, the Reginald Wilson Award for national leadership in achieving diversity, and the National Medal of Technology for exemplary service to the nation. At the University of Michigan he currently directs the program in science, technology, and public policy in the Gerald R. Ford School of Public Policy, the Michigan Energy Research Council, and the Millennium Project.

Paul D. Gallagher is senior vice president and founding professor at Florida International University. He has served as senior vice president for business and finance, vice president for advancement, vice president for student affairs, and provost and vice president for academic affairs. Additionally, for more than a decade he was executive director of the University Foundation and led the university's successful $200 million campaign. Dr. Gallagher holds a Ph.D. in educational research from Florida State University and a B.S. in psychology from Pennsylvania State University. He has served on numerous community boards including the American Red Cross, WLRN Public Radio, Dade County

Exposition and Fair, and Parkway Regional Hospital. He is a member of the American Educational Research Association and past president of the Florida Educational Research Association.

E. Johanna Hartelius is a doctoral student in the Department of Communication Studies at the University of Texas–Austin, where she also serves as director of the Pre–Graduate School Internship for the university's Intellectual Entrepreneurship Consortium. Her publications include an article on rhetorical homologies and pedagogy in the winter 2006 issue of *Rhetoric Society Quarterly*. Her dissertation research focuses on the changing nature of expertise in American culture and politics; her other research interests include classical rhetorical theory and philosophy, digital and visual media, and the rhetoric of myth and collective memory.

Karen A. Holbrook, the 13th president of The Ohio State University, is committed to making the school one of the world's truly great research universities. Prior to this appointment, she served as senior vice president for academic affairs and provost at the University of Georgia. She helped create the Biomedical and Health Services Institute, three new colleges, the New Media Institute and Faculty of Engineering, and played a major role in developing the university's strategic plan. Before that, Dr. Holbrook served at the University of Florida–Gainesville as vice president for research and dean of the Graduate School and professor of anatomy, cell biology, and medicine. She spent the majority of her academic career as a professor of biological structure and medicine at the University of Washington School of Medicine, where she gained a national reputation for her expertise in human fetal skin development and genetic skin disease.

Richard (Tom) Ingram served as president of the Association of Governing Boards of Universities and Colleges from 1992 through 2005. Devoted to volunteer trustee education and board development in public and private higher education, AGB is a national organization in the service of college and university trustees, chief executives, and senior executive and academic officers totaling 34,000 individuals, 1,800 institutions, and 1,150 boards. Dr. Ingram has served on the boards of two private institutions and other enterprises including an insurance company and a private school. He is an active writer in the field and has conducted scores of workshops to assist boards of trustees with self-studies of their effectiveness. His *Ten Basic Responsibilities of Nonprofit Boards* (BoardSource, 2002) has sold more than one million copies. A native of the Pittsburgh area, he holds a Ph.D. in higher education administration from the University of Maryland.

George D. Kuh is chancellor's professor of higher education at Indiana University Bloomington, where he directs the Center for Postsecondary Research, home to the National Survey of Student Engagement. Since joining the IU faculty in 1976, he has held the positions of chair of the Department of Educational Leadership and Policy Studies, associate dean for academic affairs in the School of Education, and associate dean of the faculties. Dr. Kuh has written extensively about assessment, student engagement, institutional improvement, and campus cultures. He most recently coauthored the book *Student Success in College: Creating Conditions That Matter* (Jossey-Bass, 2005). A past president of the Association for the Study of Higher Education (ASHE), he currently serves on the editorial boards of *Change* and *Liberal Education*. Dr. Kuh has received awards for his research contributions from the American College Personnel Association, Association for Institutional Research, ASHE, Council of Independent Colleges, and National Association of Student Personnel Administrators. He also received the Virginia B. Smith Innovative Leadership Award from the National Center on Public Policy and Higher Education and Council for Adult and Experiential Learning, the Educational Leadership Award for teaching from St. Cloud State University, and Indiana University's prestigious Tracy M. Sonneborn Award for a distinguished record of scholarship and teaching.

C. Peter Magrath is currently senior advisor to the College Board. He served as president of the National Association of State Universities and Land-Grant Colleges from 1992 through 2005, originating many of the initiatives of that organization, including the Kellogg Commission on the Future of State and Land-Grant Universities. Dr. Magrath was president of three public universities, first at the State University of New York–Binghamton for 2 years, next the University of Minnesota for 10 years, and finally the University of Missouri system for 7 years. The author of numerous books, monographs, and articles on American constitutional law and history, higher education, and international affairs, he has been active on many national higher education commissions, task forces, and committees.

Modesto A. Maidique is the fourth President of Florida International University and the longest-serving university president in Florida. Maidique holds a Ph.D. in solid state electronics from the Massachusetts Institute of Technology and has served on the faculty at MIT, Harvard University, and Stanford University. He was cofounder of Analog Devices Semiconductor, served as CEO of Collaborative Research (now Genome Therapeutics), and as general partner of Hambrecht & Quist, a venture capital firm. Dr. Maidique authored numerous articles on the management of high-technology enterprises and coauthored or contributed to 10 books. Appointed by former President George H. W. Bush to his Education Policy Advisory Committee, Dr. Maidique was also appointed by President George W. Bush to the Education Transition Panel. He currently serves on the boards of directors of National Semiconductor and the Carnival Corporation and is a member of the Secretary of Energy's Advisory Board and President Bush's Presidential Scholars Commission.

William F. Massy received his B.S. from Yale University in 1956 with high honors and then an M.S. in management and Ph.D. in economics from the Massachusetts Institute of Technology. He spent most of his career at Stanford University as a professor, vice provost for research, and vice president for business and finance. In 1984, he joined the board of Diebold Inc., where he now chairs the Audit Committee. He has served on the Yale University Council and the Hong Kong government's University Grants Committee. Since 1995, he has consulted to colleges and universities on a worldwide basis through his firm, the Jackson Hole Higher Education Group. Dr. Massy received the Operations Research Society of America's Lanchester Prize for the best management science work in 1980 and the Society for College and University Planning's annual Career Award. He has written 20 books, more than 100 articles, and a large-scale computer simulation game.

Daniel James Rowley is professor of management at the University of Northern Colorado. He is the lead author of several scholarly articles on the subject of strategic planning, the lead author of five scholarly books and one workbook on strategic planning in higher education, and has coauthored a general textbook on strategic management. He was named the Monfort College Scholar of the Year and the University of Northern Colorado Scholar of the Year in 2004. Dr. Rowley received a baccalaureate degree at the University of Colorado–Boulder, a master's degree at the University of Denver, and a Ph.D. at the University of Colorado–Boulder. He has presented to national and international conferences and has done extensive consulting work with several colleges and universities in the United States and around the world.

Herbert Sherman is a professor in the Division of Business at Southampton College–Long Island University. In 1988, he received his Ph.D. in strategic management from the Union Institute. Dr. Sherman has published in several journals including *Journal of Management Science and Policy Analysis, Entrepreneurship and Regional Development, Management Development Forum, Business Case Journal, Journal of Behavioral and Applied Management, Journal of the International*

Academy for Case Studies, and *The Management Development Journal,* and has recently coauthored the book From *Strategy to Change: Implementing the Plan in Higher Education* (Jossey-Bass, 2001). He also has a book awaiting publication on academic planning and has been recently named the editor of *The Case Journal.* His research interests include business strategy, case writing and research, and education administration.

J. Fredericks Volkwein, a professor and senior scientist at Pennsylvania State University's Center for the Study of Higher Education, holds a B.A. from Pomona College and a Ph.D. from Cornell University. With scholarly interests in issues related to organizational effectiveness, his studies of accreditation, strategic planning, student outcomes assessment, state regulation, and institutional research have won him a national reputation. He has produced more than 100 journal articles, research reports, conference papers, and book chapters. He currently is the principal investigator or coprincipal investigator on projects in the areas of accreditation, engineering education, and training institutional researchers. Dr. Volkwein chaired the Middle States committee that produced the monograph *Framework for Outcomes Assessment* (1996), and he recently completed a 10-year term as editor in chief for the Jossey-Bass series *New Directions for Institutional Research.*

Ralph A. Wolff is executive director of the Accrediting Commission for Senior Colleges and Universities of the Western Association of Schools and Colleges. WASC accredits 150 institutions serving more than 750,000 students in California, Hawaii, Guam, and the Pacific Basin. Under his leadership, WASC received more than $2 million in grants to transform the accrediting process to become learning centered. This grant resulted in the development and implementation of an innovative three-stage model of accreditation focusing on educational effectiveness, student learning results, and organizational learning systems for all institutions. Prior to joining the commission staff, he was on the law faculty of the University of Dayton Law School and was a founder of the Antioch School of Law. He also has served as associate provost of Antioch College and dean of the Graduate School of Education. In addition, he founded the Institute for Creative Thinking, a think tank for higher education leaders in the West, and is a Fellow of the World Academy of Art and Science. He received a bachelor's degree in history from Tufts University and a J.D. degree, with honors, from the National Law Center of George Washington University.

Preface

On the eve of the millennium, public research universities in America appeared triumphant abroad but troubled at home. Academics welcomed the triumphs but wondered at the tribulations. Public universities had produced research and doctorates that were the wonder of the world, fueling economic development through high-tech graduates and cutting-edge research that made our nation's economy a model for the world. Why then the fall in public trust and support at home? What explains the mounting expectations from society, and yet the meager funding? How can government and business leaders increasingly see the source of so much good for states and society as a private benefit for paying customers rather than a public good for all Americans?

The answer is that every age produces its own imperatives. The challenge for public universities had changed by the final decade of the 20th century. In the decades following World War II, specialization through decentralization and departmentalization had mined the wealth of the knowledge explosion and met the burgeoning demand for access and specialties by creating the multiversity. The new era required a more unified university capable of integrating knowledge in multidisciplinary studies and generating comprehensive responses to societal problems. State accountability programs increasingly held presidents, provosts, and trustees responsible for student learning, graduation rates, school reform, economic development, and a host of other priorities. Unfortunately, these officials had little authority over the colleges, schools, and departments responsible for those results. By the mid 1990s, the time had clearly come to fix the fragmented university—to put unity back into the multi-university.

The Kellogg Commission

In 1996, the Kellogg Foundation and the National Association of State Universities and Land-Grant Colleges created a commission to deal with this dilemma. The Kellogg Commission had a tacit charge that was at once difficult and delicate. It had to respond to growing concerns about perceived declines in access and affordability, neglect of undergraduate education for faculty research, and pursuit of peer prestige more than public needs. The commission had to convince external critics that public universities could respond to their concerns without alienating university leaders who feared that change could erode their autonomy.

The Kellogg Commission responded to this dual challenge first by getting history on its side. Finding precedents in past traditions is the safest way to sell new directions. The titles of the commission's first five reports all begin with "Returning to Our Roots." Those roots reached back to the sacred covenant for public universities struck by Justin Morrill and Abraham Lincoln in the Morrill Act of 1862, which promised that state universities would offer the opportunity of liberal and practical education to all Americans and bring the benefits of research and service to every state. In return, public funds would support these public institutions in these public purposes.

The Kellogg commissioners, composed of 25 current or former presidents and chancellors of state universities, responded to external critics but with careful language that was least likely to alienate their campus colleagues. The reports denied the alleged conflict between research and teaching. They talked of redesigning, not rebalancing, the university mission of teaching, research, and service. Research would retain its exalted place, but the commission proposed raising teaching and public service to equal status. A "new kind of public university" would become a "great student" and publicly "engaged university" as well as a "great research university." Offering ideal images of what public universities could become seemed the softest way to state their current faults.

The five reports, issued from April 1997 to January 2000, discussed the *student experience, student access, engaged institutions,* the *learning society,* and *campus culture.* Two focused on students and two on public engagement. Noticeable by its absence was a volume on faculty research and graduate studies. The commission announced its purposes to campus colleagues in 1996 with a letter titled *Taking Charge of Change* (Kellogg Commission on the Future of State and Land-Grant Universities [Kellogg Commission], 1996).

The full reports started with *The Student Experience* (1997). The commissioners called on their colleagues at state universities "to put students first"—to make their campuses "student centered" "learning communities" tailored to student needs (pp. vii-viii). "This new university" would deliver "instruction anywhere, anytime, and to practically anyone who seeks it" (p. viii). The promises were aimed straight at the public university critics: to reinvigorate the college/school partnership, recommit to undergraduate education, relate to careers, restate learning objectives and assess results, raise the academic and personal development of students, and reconnect discovery and learning through undergraduate research. The second report—*Student Access*

(1998)—called access, affordability, and student diversity the defining issues for public universities in the 21st century. The report argued that access was empty unless graduation became equally achievable to all groups of Americans.

The third report—*The Engaged Institution* (1999a)—encouraged public universities to respond to society's needs and provide service-learning for students in the surrounding communities. It urged a two-way partnership as public engagement rather than the old one-way dictation of public service, which meant that universities gave communities what academics thought they needed. The next publication—*A Learning Society* (1999b)—claimed engagement should cover "life-long learning" in a society where the rate of knowledge creation required continuous reeducation. Learning would begin at early childhood and continue after college through interactive technology, with the public universities engaged at every stage.

The first four reports proposed the promises. The fifth presented the problems confronting public universities in meeting their obligations to students, states, and society. *Toward a Coherent Campus Culture* (2000b) confronted the fundamental problem of the fragmented university. The "knowledge explosion" and increasing specialization had transformed the "university" into the "multiversity," where the departments become so dominant that the university nearly disappeared:

> The *uni*-versity has become an institutionally fragmented aggregation of departments. The primary loyalties of scholars are increasingly directed away from their immediate colleagues, students, and institutions toward national and international societies and associations of their disciplinary peers. (Kellogg Commission, 2000b, p. 10)

Specialization spread divisions and encouraged the growth of disciplines, programs, enrollment, and research. In contrast, the new public demands for college/school partnership, student retention and learning, and response to societal and scientific problems required collective, multidisciplinary responses that only the university as a whole could provide.

The sixth report—*Renewing the Covenant* (2000a)—championed a new university grounded in old ideal. Unlike the other reports addressed to university colleagues, this one appealed to opinion leaders and the general public. The commissioners began with a "sense of urgency and concern" (p. 15). They spoke not as private pleaders from "a special interest group" (p. 9) but as champions of the public good. The future success of our nation in a knowledge and information era required renewing the "covenant" between state universities and the American people. The report deplored the growing trend in state capitols of seeing the teaching, research, and service of public universities as "private commodities" purchased by customers rather than public benefits paid for mostly by public funds. For its side of the covenant, the Kellogg Commission (2000a) promised to create

> A new kind of public institution, one that is as much a first-rate student university as it is a first-rate research university, one that provides access to success to a much more diverse student population as easily as it reaches out to "engage" the larger community. (p. 10)

The commissioners pledged "an open accounting of our progress toward achieving our commitment to the public good; and intensive, on-going monitoring of the progress of the Kellogg Commission's recommendations" (2000a, p. 11). The covenant challenged state universities to become again the "public's universities" proposed by Lincoln and Morrill.

Redirecting the services and redesigning the mission of the public universities required increased public resources. The federal government should adopt a Higher Education Millennial Partnership Act, a modern version of the original land-grant legislation. The Millennial Act would help fund university partnerships for K–12 reform and the creation of a "learning society" through the latest information and communication technology that could deliver knowledge to those who need it and where and when they wanted it. Federal tax policy should also encourage public/private research partnerships and assist parents and students, both part- and full-time, to save for higher education. The covenant asked the states to again provide the "lion's share" of public funding and to avoid "politics" and "patronage" in the appointment of trustees and administrators for public universities (Kellogg Commission, 2000a, pp. 9–11).

Great Ideas Require Good Implementation

Though the Kellogg Commission issued *Returning to Our Roots: Executive Summaries of the Reports* in January 2001 and made a considerable effort to sell the covenant, it received mixed response on most campuses and little interest in the state and national capitols. Spreading six reports on different subjects over three years undoubtedly explains some of this tepid response. But the mixed results had other reasons. The commission issued daunting challenges with great ideas but offered only scant strategies for fixing the fragmented university and changing campus cultures that honor decentralization and resist direction. Great ideas can inspire interest but they fade without planned implementation. Political scientists have long noted this policy malady, which seems especially virulent in academic settings. Great ideas are always abundant on campus, but good implementation is relatively rare.

Creating a "student" and "engaged" university that equaled the existing "research" university also required a change in campus culture in leading state universities. The strongest institutional link for colleges, schools, and departments at those institutions often came from their university's rating on national rankings, such as *U.S. News & World Report*. University reputation tended to provide a halo effect for program ratings. On too many campuses, pursuing the public good ran a distant second to achieving academic prestige. The Kellogg Commission left the biggest problem unexplored: how to transform the culture of many research universities from provider-driven prestige to public-centered engagement. Its reports delivered a glorious description of the goals for a new state university but failed to describe the means of achieving these ideals.

This Book

This book takes on the more mundane but meaningful task of discussing the methods for fixing the fragmented university and changing the campus culture. It brings together a group of national experts and asks each to describe how their particular part of the puzzle can help fix the fragmented university and assist it in becoming as devoted to undergraduate education and public engagement as it is to faculty research. Opening with an introduction, it is followed by four parts with related chapters and ends with two conclusions.

Chapter 1. In this introductory chapter, Joseph C. Burke describes the Kellogg Commission's analysis and discusses how and why the multiversity developed in the decades after World War II. This chapter argues that decentralization is in fact necessary for internal creativity and innovation, but there must also be direction to respond to external problems and issues. The greatest challenge for public universities is changing a campus culture that pursues peer prestige more than public needs.

Part I • The Participants

Chapter 2. Richard T. Ingram argues that trustees must reconcile societal needs and campus concerns. Trustees exercise their authority best not by providing answers and taking actions, but by posing tough questions about university priorities and performance and insisting on clear answers.

Chapter 3. James J. Duderstadt draws on his experience as president of the University of Michigan during difficult times. He laments that presidential authority falls far short of its responsibility. Still, he argues for caution as well as courage in presidents. They best bring unity to their campuses by articulating an inspiring vision that uses the university saga of traditional values to transform the university for a challenging future.

Chapter 4. Roger Benjamin brings the best of campus and policy worlds to this chapter in which he argues that faculty senates have become dormant. Most academic activities, especially research and graduate studies, are now too diverse and decentralized for direction by university-wide senates. Instead, these senates should take charge of general education and assessment programs, which require institutional direction.

Part II • Means and Methods of Cohesion

Chapter 5. Daniel James Rowley and Herbert Sherman argue that strategic planning often goes wrong before it begins. They stress the importance of the "planning to plan stage," which should yield agreement on the purpose of strategic planning and on who will be the participants in the process.

Chapter 6. William F. Massy insists that budgets should reflect priorities and argues for a combination of decentralized and centralized budgeting. The first encourages revenue generation by colleges and schools, while the second supports university goals and priorities.

Chapter 7. J. Fredericks Volkwein argues that quality assurance on student learning can connect classroom, program, and institutional activities and bring unity and direction to the university. This chapter also proposes special accreditation for general education programs to give them the same prestige that is provided to specialized academic programs.

Chapter 8. Ralph A. Wolf describes the shift of regional accreditation from accessing input resources to emphasizing student learning outcomes. Wolff suggests that universities should place accreditation documents prominently on their web sites to stimulate a dialogue on general education and assessing student learning.

Chapter 9. Joseph C. Burke proposes a limited list of common indicators for colleges, schools, and departments that align institutional and unit goals, while allowing unique measures that suggest unit strengths. This proposal would close the gap in institutional accountability by putting departments in the performance loop.

Part III • Redesigning the Mission

Chapter 10. George D. Kuh presents data from several years of the National Survey of Student Engagement to propose programs and approaches that can achieve the goal of making students matter.

Chapter 11. Richard A. Cherwitz and E. Johanna Hartelius insist that public engagement requires a rhetoric capable of convincing the faculty that research on public problems is as rigorous as traditional research.

Part IV • Making It Happen on Campus

Chapter 12. Robert H. Bruininks recounts the process of producing a comprehensive plan to raise a leading public research university to one of the "top three universities in the world" and persuading campus constituencies and external stakeholders to accept it.

Chapter 13. Karen A. Holbrook insists that building excellence in the land-grant mission of research, teaching, and engagement requires commitments from successive presidents. This chapter describes how three presidents pursued that common goal through continuous, connected initiatives.

Chapter 14. Mayra E. Beers, Paul D. Gallagher, and Modesto A. Maidique tell the astonishing story of the 35-year strategic transformation of a small upper-division college into a top urban research university.

Chapter 15. This first concluding chapter by C. Peter Magrath provides a retrospective look at the Kellogg Commission, including its strengths and its shortcomings, and suggests the continuing relevance of its recommendations to the future of state universities.

Chapter 16. Joseph C. Burke analyzes the ties that bind and those that continue to divide the public university. He also notes that the pull of markets and prestige is diminishing its public purpose and offers recommendations for putting unity, students, and public back into the state university.

Debts and Credits

This book owes a debt to those who have worked in the fields of public university management, planning, budgeting, and performance at both the policy and practical levels. Of course, my biggest debt goes to the exceptional group of experts and practitioners who put aside their own priorities to join in this project. Their participation underscores the importance of fixing the fragmented public university. Jiri Stocek, as graduate research assistant, eased my task as editor by assuming the difficult assignments of editing my contributions as well as formatting the manuscript. Tom McCord, formerly of the New York State Education Department, provided advice on the project and reviewed several chapters. Leif Hartmark, vice president for finance and management at Oneonta College and former Fellow of the Higher Education Program at the Nelson A. Rockefeller Institute of Government, previewed chapters and suggested revisions. Tom Moran, director of the Institute for Ethics in Public Life, reviewed the project from its initial concept to final manuscript and read and commented on my draft chapters. Special thanks go to the Ford Foundation and to Jorge Balan for supporting the work on this book. Finally, I can never say enough about the sustaining support of my wife Joan, last on the list but first in my life.

Joseph C. Burke
April 2006

References

Kellogg Commission on the Future of State and Land-Grant Universities. (1996). *Taking charge of change.* Washington, DC: National Association of State Universities and Land-Grant Colleges.

Kellogg Commission on the Future of State and Land-Grant Universities. (1997). *Returning to our roots: The student experience.* Washington, DC: National Association of State Universities and Land-Grant Colleges.

Kellogg Commission on the Future of State and Land-Grant Universities. (1998). *Returning to our roots: Student access.* Washington, DC: National Association of State Universities and Land-Grant Colleges.

Kellogg Commission on the Future of State and Land-Grant Universities. (1999a). *Returning to our roots: The engaged institution.* Washington, DC: National Association of State Universities and Land-Grant Colleges.

Kellogg Commission on the Future of State and Land-Grant Universities. (1999b). *Returning to our roots: A learning society.* Washington, DC: National Association of State Universities and Land-Grant Colleges.

Kellogg Commission on the Future of State and Land-Grant Universities. (2000a). *Renewing the covenant: Learning, discovery, and engagement in a new age and different world.* Washington, DC: National Association of State Universities and Land-Grant Colleges.

Kellogg Commission on the Future of State and Land-Grant Universities. (2000b). *Returning to our roots: Toward a coherent campus culture.* Washington, DC: National Association of State Universities and Land-Grant Colleges.

Kellogg Commission on the Future of State and Land-Grant Universities. (2001). *Returning to our roots: Executive summaries of the reports of the Kellogg Commission on the Future of State and Land-Grant Universities.* Washington, DC: National Association of State Universities and Land-Grant Colleges.

1

"The Fragmented University"

Joseph C. Burke

The Challenge of Change: From "Changer" to "Changed"

The 1996 letter *Taking Charge of Change* set the theme of the Kellogg Commission. Twenty-five present and former presidents and chancellors used the word *change* no less than 15 times in this four-page letter to colleagues at public universities. "Seismic shifts" in demography, technology, attitudes, and accountability put the future of public universities at risk. "Like dinosaurs, they risk becoming exhibits in a kind of cultural Jurassic Park: places of great interest and curiosity, increasingly irrelevant in a world that has passed them by. Higher education cannot let this happen" (Kellogg Commission, 1996, p. 1).

Change threatened the covenant of Justin Morrill and Abraham Lincoln in the Morrill Act of 1862: state universities provided a public good for all Americans and deserved public support. The Kellogg Commission reminded readers of this fundamental pact. Five of its six reports came under the umbrella of "Returning to Our Roots" and the sixth was about "Renewing the Covenant." For colleagues more interested in current happenings than old history, the opening letter pointed ominously to the restructuring forced by change in health care and business organizations. The commissioners had a tough but touchy task: to get reluctant colleagues to change their universities without being too critical of their current campus conditions.

Change was hardly new to public universities. The novelty came from the challenge "to take charge of change." The call must have surprised the many academics who thought universities already had that control. Had they not transformed American society and become the wonder of the world? Yet this challenge was different. It reversed the roles of society and university. Society became the agent and the university the object of change. In the past, academics decided—or at least thought they decided—how to change society. Now society seemed determined that universities must change to meet its demands. Public universities, especially their professors, appeared unlikely to relish an altered role from "changer" to "changed." They certainly would not welcome their university rather than their department, school, or college taking charge of change on campus. The real challenge posed by the Kellogg Commission—which many in the academy may have missed— was not so much about change as about who would direct it, how would it be accomplished, and, always important, who would pay for it?

Academics' attitude toward change confounds critics who often call us two-faced because we stand on both sides of change, proposing it abroad and opposing it at home. Academics' interest in change seems in direct proportion to its distance from the department, school, or university, in that order. Burton Clark (1983) claims that even internally, campuses combine change with conservatism. Academic attitudes stimulate disciplinary change but stifle it at the institutional level. Disciplines continually change as discoveries displace traditional truths with new theories. Departments differ on many matters but unite against institutional changes that may intrude on their autonomy and the freedom of individual faculty members.

Laissez-faire reigns on many campuses through a tacit bargain among faculty colleagues: "Do anything you want, just don't ask me, my department, school, or university to do it." Clark Kerr anticipated this development in 1963 when he wrote about the rise of the multiversity, where ". . . the professor's love of specialization has become the student's hate of fragmentation. A kind of bizarre version of academic-laissez-faire has emerged. . . The Modern University was born" (pp. 14–15). Thirty-three years later, when the Kellogg Commission met, the problem had worsened.

Dominant Departments and the Fragmented University

Not surprisingly, external critics charged that public universities were not interested in the changes needed by society. The Kellogg Commission's first full report—*The Student Experience* (1997)—

accepted the criticism but claimed that "organization," not "interest," hampered the desired changes in public universities.

> . . . we are poorly organized to deal with many of these issues. As the nature of knowledge changes, our departmental structure has difficulty responding. As the challenges facing our communities multiply, we find it hard to break out of the silos our disciplines create. The world has problems; universities have departments. (p. 21)

Departmental divisions not only prevented the university from responding to society's concerns, they also hindered efforts to address problems and issues in knowledge—both theoretical and applied—that increasingly fell in the gaps between the disciplines and required collaboration across them.

The commission's fifth report—*Toward a Coherent Campus Culture* (2000b)—focused on the fundamental problem—the fragmented university. A combination of disciplinary dominance and institutional indecision kept public universities from responding to—much less taking charge of—change. Governors, legislators, and the general public held presidents and chancellors, even trustees, responsible for university results on a series of societal concerns, such as student access and graduation, undergraduate knowledge and skills, and school reform and civic engagement (Burke & Minassians, 2002a). The Kellogg commissioners recognized that the fragmented university depended on those results from academic departments that were far more interested in faculty research, student selectivity, and program ratings than public concerns. Peer prestige outpulled public purpose in the fragmented research university.

If academic attitudes resisted responses to societal needs, departmental divisions also subverted institutional unity in confronting society's problems. "The *uni*-versity has become an institutionally fragmented aggregation of departments. The primary loyalties of scholars are increasingly directed away from their . . . institutions toward national and international . . . disciplinary peers" (Kellogg Commission, 2000b, p. 10). Despite these complaints, it was noted that "the departmental organization of academic life has been strangely absent from the reform conversation" (Kellogg Commission, 2000b, p. 31).

The fragmented university dominated by divided departments could never "take charge of change" and carried two related defects. First, institutional identity had diminished "as scholarly successes have transformed the uni-versity into the multi-versity. The second is the expectation that we can be all things to all people" (Kellogg Commission, 2000b, p. 19). A third defect went unmentioned. The discipline-dominated university encouraged the pursuit of peer prestige rather than public good. Departments and their universities had one united interest—the national ratings of their units and institutions based largely on peer perceptions of academic quality (Volkwein & Grunig, 2005).

From Additional to Reallocated Resources _____

As if campus change was not challenging enough, it had to come most-ly through reallocated, not additional, resources. The third commission report—*The Engaged Institution* (1999)—complained that state fund-ing for some state universities had plunged from "about 80% of the budget 20 years ago to 30% or less today" (p. 22). For top universities, state funding frequently fell to a far lower figure. The report included James Duderstadt's quip that during his presidency from 1988 to 1996 his description of the University of Michigan went from "state university," to "state assisted," to "state related," and, finally, to "state located" (Kellogg Commission, 1999, p. 22). By the time the commission began in 1996, state funding had improved from the recession early in the decade, but public higher education's share of state revenues never returned to previ-ous levels. Unfortunately, experience persuaded many academics to view funding increases as normal and constraints as aberrations.

Perhaps concern about provoking internal complaints explains the near silence of the Kellogg Commission on the need for reallocation. In its opening letter and six reports, the commission mentioned *realloca-tion* only twice. In the first, it softened the impact by raising the possi-bility of additional federal or state resources. It recommended, as one of five strategies, that "academic leaders secure stable funding to support engagement, through reallocation of existing funds or the establishment of a new Federal-state-local-private matching fund" (Kellogg Commission, 1999, p. 13). The second strategy mentioned reallocation but only in a sidebar confined to Penn State University (Kellogg Commission, 1999, p. 22). In the past, public universities largely sup-ported new programs demanded by states and society with additional funding. Now cuts in current programs had to fund new additions.

Arthur Levine (1997), former president of Columbia Teachers College, argued in *The Chronicle of Higher Education* a year after the commission began, that public universities had to do "less with less" rather than the much-heralded "more with less." Levine was only half right. Public universities had to do both less and more: "less" of what they wished and "more" of what the public wanted. And what the public wanted most was improved undergraduate education and public engagement, not the increased graduate studies and research that many professors preferred. The latter demanded decentralized diversity and departmental competition while the former required institutional direction and departmental cooperation. The Kellogg Commission (2000b) proposed dual loyalty to both departments and the institution, but left no doubt that the institution was the endangered half of the equation.

> . . . there is no more significant index of institutional effectiveness than the degree to which it hangs together as a coherent institution, secure in its sense of purpose, confident of its mission and values, and alert to the needs of all its constituents . . . (p. 44)

Despite this recommendation, the commission conceded that specialization and decentralization had gone so far that even the idea of an integrated institutional culture "seems somehow quaint and archaic today" (Kellogg Commission, 2000b, p. 21). The comprehensiveness of the public university mission contributed to the fragmentation. "Big size" and "broadest scope" became the signs of quality as public universities expanded undergraduate and graduate enrollments and added programs in every undergraduate area, as well as graduate degrees in all the arts and sciences and most professional fields. Society, business, and individuals contributed by demanding degrees, research, and service in new and ever more specialized areas. Leaders of public universities rarely said no to these external demands for expansion; and when they did, legislators at times insisted on adding unneeded programs. Governors and legislators criticized leaders of public universities for not cutting costs, but when the latter tried on rare occasions to cut programs, state officials often protested.

As enrollments grew by tens of thousands, departments and programs trebled, and colleges and schools multiplied, the university became a "holding company" for internal corporate units. Colleges and schools, departments and centers, all with their own management, revenues, and priorities, saw themselves as anything but subsidiary to their university (Muller, 1994, p. 119). By the mid-1990s, some public universities seemed little more than franchises for colleges, schools, and departments that used their university's brand name for prestige but set their own priorities. Private universities suffered less from these pressures.

Public universities became much bigger, more diverse, and less manageable, in part because their multiple publics made so many demands.

Hallowed Decentralization _____

Decentralization has a hallowed tradition in higher education. Leaders of public universities demanded autonomy from states and society and gradually granted it to their colleges, schools, and departments. As early as 1963, Clark Kerr lamented the loss of the university and the rise of the multiversity. By the early 1970s, theories emerged to explain, and even defend, the practices of the fragmented university under the rubric of decentralization. Academics are especially good at developing theories to justify our practices. In spite of constant complaints about importing notions from business to the university (Birnbaum, 2001, 2003), the writers in the 1970s described the fragmentation of the university based on the latest organizational theory of the day, drawn largely from business.

As usual, academics constructed the theories. But what was unusual was that they were adopted in the academy, rather than just exported to outside organizations. Ironically, the theories applied to universities questioned the rationality of decision-making drawn largely from distrusted business organizations. Cohen and March (1974) carried this thesis to its illogical extreme. They called colleges and universities—the self-proclaimed seats of rationality—"organized anarchies" characterized by problematic goals, unclear technologies, and fluid participation.

> The American college or university is prototypical organized anarchy. It does not know what it is doing. Its goals are either vague or in dispute. Its technology is familiar but not understood. Its major participants wander in and out of the organization. These factors do not make the university a bad organization, or a disorganized one, but they do make it a problem to describe, understand and lead. (Cohen & March, 1974, p. 3)

Cohen and March saw anarchy in universities as inevitable, perhaps even desirable. Academics have seen many of these problems in practice but few would subscribe to a description of universities as 1% organization and 99% anarchy. Those that saw some resemblance would immediately recognize the 1% organization coming from the central administration as intrusive and the 99% at the departmental level not as anarchy but as autonomy. Luckily, governors and legislatures did not read Cohen and March, or else the external problems of public universities would have started in the 1970s rather than the 1990s.

Karl Weick (1976) offered a more judicious explanation of decentralization and fragmentation in his article "Education as Loosely Coupled Systems." Writers on college and university organization invariably cite this work, even though it focuses on school systems and not higher education. The theory does appear much more applicable to colleges and universities, which are much more loosely connected than public schools. Weick wanted to suggest a concept of educational organizations that differed from the bureaucratic interpretation of the components that held business companies together. After rejecting "position" and "authority" in educational settings, he developed the concept of "loosely coupled systems." Weick debunked the effectiveness of planning because of the loose coupling between intention and action in all or most organizations, which inevitably bewilders managers. In a line seldom cited by proponents of the loosely coupled concept, Weick conceded, "It remains to be seen under what conditions loosely coupled systems are fragile structures because they are shored up by consensual anticipations, retrospections, and understanding that can dissolve, and under what conditions they are resilient structures" (p. 15).

By the time Weick wrote, the lush funding of public higher education in the decades after World War II that encouraged "loose coupling" and even "anarchy" had ended. The golden decade of the 1960s for funding of public universities had gone and the new depression of the 1970s had begun (Balderston, 1974; Cheit, 1971, 1973; Graham & Diamond, 1997; Rosenzweig, 1998). As often happens, writers of higher education in the 1970s, and to a lesser extent in the 1980s, developed theories of operations that reflected an earlier age when universities had sufficient resources to support both growing aspirations and decentralized governance. Organizational theorists call this "slack." Unfortunately, the "slack" was gone by the 1970s, but the theories lived on.

Roger Benjamin and his colleagues, writing in the 1990s during a real period of financial depression in higher education, noted that "the current governance system of incremental, decentralized decision-making" emerged during the post–World War II period (Benjamin, Carroll, Jacobi, Krop, & Shires, 1993, p. 23): "This approach served well in an era of stable growth. But it is poorly suited for setting priorities and reallocating resources" (p. 23). Nearly all the previous initiatives pushed from outside had carried much of their own funding, such as the GI Bill, sponsored research, and financial aid. As a result, universities could respond with additions. By the 1990s, external demands exceeded resources, a situation that required setting internal priorities among many possibilities and reallocation to achieve them. Only the institution as a whole could set university-wide priorities that demand reallocating resources. It is no coincidence that such loosely connected behemoths—as many public universities had become by the mid and late 1990s—might have trouble meeting state and student needs, especially in times of depressed public funding.

The 1990s: The Age of Accountability and Commissions

Restrained funding naturally brought new demands that public universities provide accountability and efficiency in meeting public needs. Those needs required raising student participation and graduation rates—including minority and disadvantaged groups; improving and assessing student learning in general education and academic majors; partnering in school reform; and increasing degree production in critical but less prestigious fields such as teaching and nursing (Burke & Associates, 2005; Burke & Minassians, 2002b). Expanding enrollments, programs, and research demanded diversity and decentralization. The new imperatives required unity and direction for the university as a whole.

The Kellogg Commission started after a new depression in higher education funding in the early 1990s had begun to recede and ended just before another began in 2001. It was only one of several commissions on higher education in the 1990s. In 1992, the Association of Governing Boards of Colleges and Universities (AGB) assembled a national panel on higher education. Its report—*The Trustees and Troubled Times in Higher Education*—warned colleges and universities that they must plan strategically to deal with restrained state funding and the need to serve more minority students. In 1996, another AGB Commission called for *Renewing the Academic Presidency: Stronger Leadership for Tougher Times*. It claimed, "Faculty loyalties and the faculty reward system increasingly focus on achieving eminence in (and protecting) a particular discipline rather than supporting the goals of the institution" (AGB, 1996, pp. 15-16). The report advocated more powerful presidents to push university purposes, manage their resources, and reshape shared governance to stress shared responsibilities. That commission rejected as outdated the notion of governance as a "zero-sum game where increasing presidential leadership diminishes the role of the board or the faculty" (AGB, 1996, p. x).

Four years later, the Kellogg Commission (2000b) used almost identical language to encourage cooperative action rather than shared governance, which accented conflicting claims of authority. Both commissions hoped to correct the anomaly of the university presidency, described by James Duderstadt (2000) as "a mismatch between responsibility and authority that is unparalled in other social institutions" (p. 249).

A year after the AGB report, still another commission addressed the crisis of higher education, in both funding and performance. It was cochaired by Joseph Dionne, former CEO of the McGraw-Hill Companies, and Thomas Kean, president of Drew University and former governor of New Jersey. Their report—*Breaking the Social Contract: The Fiscal Crisis in Higher Education* (1997)—proposed a "two-pronged strategy" to meet the crisis created by falling government funding and public confidence. It first recommended increased resources but warned that they would not come unless higher education followed "the health care industry" by restructuring to deal with "issues of cost, productivity, efficiency, and effectiveness."

As the Kellogg Commission later contended, the 1997 Dionne and Kean report also cited disciplinary departments as the problem.

> The academic department, for example, which is the heart of the current governance structure, is based on the assumption that faculty members should govern themselves . . . The continued sway of the department might be justified if departments were truly autonomous. In reality, however, they function as parts of a greater whole—one on which they are financially dependent.

Writers of the 1990s, many of them former university administrators, increasingly cited the fragmented university, composed of decentralized departments, as the real restraint on university responses to public demands (Keller, 1995; Kennedy, 1997; Munitz, 1995; Rhodes, 1999; Rosenzweig, 1998). "The current disciplinary-driven governance structure makes it difficult to deal with broader, strategic issues since universities are highly fragmented and decentralized . . . with little coordination or even concern about university needs or priorities" (Duderstadt & Womack, 2004, p. 163). Burton Clark, whose earlier work in 1983 had been more sympathetic to decentralized disciplinary departments, advocated increased activity at the steering core of his "entrepreneurial university."

If left in customary form, central direction ranges
between soft and soggy. Elaborated collegial authority leads to sluggish decision-making. . . . Evermore
complex and specialized, elaborate basic units—faculties, schools, and departments—tend to become
separate entities with individual privileges, shaping
the university into a federation in which major and
minor parts barely relate to one another. (Clark,
1998, pp. 131–132)

Robert Birnbaum remains the most thoughtful, eloquent, and persistent advocate of decentralization and minimal central leadership. He
believes the loosely linked units of American universities do very well
with little if any help from central administrators (Birnbaum, 1988).
Indeed, he claims the repeated efforts to introduce what he calls "management fads" into the academy always fail, because universities are
unique institutions (Birnbaum, 2001, 2003). Besides, they are unnecessary. Campuses develop feedback loops that keep them close to their
environment and generally self-correct when critical problems persist
(Birnbaum, 1988). Yet even Birnbaum concedes that funding problems
produce difficulties in loosely coupled systems.

The Dead End of Either/Or Thinking

All too often, arguments about university governance and management
suffer from either/or thinking. University organizations must be loose
or tight, decentralized or centralized, bottom up or top down in decision-making. The problem in large universities is that the bottom rarely
gets up and the top seldom gets down. The Kellogg Commission wanted to break out of this dichotomist thinking and find a new and better
way to manage, govern, and organize the modern state university.

The top-down corporate model, which could pose a
ready threat to academic freedom, and the loose feu-
dalism into which the university has now fallen and
which increasingly fragments the scholarly core of
the institution, both have formidable drawbacks. We
need new and fresh approaches capable of rebalancing our multiple purposes and of reintegrating the
increasingly atomized academy while respecting the
core functions and values that lie at the heart of its
mission. (Kellogg Commission, 2000b, p. 27)

Managerialism does not work in an academic setting and collegiality has become hollow not only at the department—as noted by Massy, Wilger, and Colbeck (1994)—but even more so at the institutional level. Alan Wolfe (1996) argues that real faculty power lies with professors whose research grants have transformed individuals into "independent revenue raisers" (p. 54). They want to maintain their independence, and faculty senates, no longer centers of influence, also tend to support the status quo. James Duderstadt (2000) claims, "We need to devise a system that releases the creativity of individual faculty members while strengthening the authority of responsible leaders" (p. 248).

Decentralization With Direction

The answer to the fragmented university is not to end decentralization, which is necessary for faculty creativity and innovation, but to add direction, which is essential for institutional responsiveness and accountability. Coupling decentralization with direction preserves the best and avoids the worst of bottom-up or top-down decision-making. The coupling should be loose enough to encourage department and faculty creativity yet tight enough to ensure institutional priorities and performance. Burton Clark (1998), studying five entrepreneurial universities in Europe, described the best way in practice as "centralized decentralization," where " . . . administrative backbone fused new managerial values with traditional academic ones" (p. 137). It required a strengthened "central core" with trusted academics taking more responsibility for institutional decisions and serving on institutional committees.

As early as 1958, David Riesman labeled American universities "directionless . . . as far as major innovations are concerned" (p. 64). Clark Kerr (1963) denied the charge but agreed that universities did not set their own directions.

> . . . universities . . . have been moving in clear directions and with considerable speed. But these directions have not been set as much by the university's visions of its destiny as by the external environment, including the federal government, the foundations, the surrounding and sometimes engulfing industry. (p. 122)

Kerr then warned more than 30 years before the Kellogg Commission that ". . . the present and future problems of the university would more require internal than external resolution and the university may . . . again need to find out whether it has a brain as well as a body" (p. 123).

Even a short list of external directions, beginning with the GI Bill and ending with financial aid, confirms the truth of Kerr's claim that the university's directions came largely from the outside. By the time the Kellogg Commission convened in 1996, the public university's body had grown beyond belief, but it still had not found a brain for direction.

Burton Clark makes the case for turning the fragmented university into a focused one. He quotes Charles Vest, a former president of the Massachusetts Institute of Technology, who characterized the modern research university as "overextended, underfocused, overstressed, [and] underfunded" (Clark, 1998, p. 146). Clark claimed the demand side of the university far exceeded its supply capacity, given funding restraints: "The loosely coupled universities have offered ad hoc, diffuse responses. Scattering their promises, and in many cases unable to cap their size, they will continue to tend to spread in a virtually uncontrolled fashion" (p. 146). Clark's entrepreneurial university called for more direction from the central core coupled with continued decentralization in the disciplinary departments. Unfortunately, he conceded that the five universities he studied enrolled from 6,000 to 13,000 students. He doubted whether his approach could work in the 30,000- to 50,000-student universities in the United States (Clark, 1998).

The Ratings Rule

Two goals compete for the allegiance of state research universities. One pulls toward provider prestige; the other pushes for public purposes. The first requires decentralization, the second demands direction. Three models of excellence exist for colleges and universities: resource and reputation, strategic investment, and client-centered focus (Burke & Associates, 2005; Burke & Minassians, 2002a). *Resource and reputation* represent a provider-driven model reflecting financial resources, faculty reputations, and student selectivity. *Strategic investment* involves a state-oriented model based on a cost/benefit of the results achieved from the resources received. The *client-centered* model focuses on student and other customer satisfaction. By calling for both a "student" and an "engaged university," the Kellogg Commission combined the state-oriented and the client-centered into a single public-purpose model.

The resource and reputation model rules the national ratings of colleges and universities. Lemming-like, many public universities—mimicking their private counterparts—flock to raise their institutional and program rankings on the *U.S. News & World Report* and other national ratings (Volkwein & Grunig, 2005). Their goals, even their purposes, seem the same—reaching that rarified realm of the top 5, 10, 20, or 50 universities, depending on their current rankings. "How many Top 10 or Top 50 universities can there be?" asked Mark Yudof (2003), chancellor of the University of Texas System. "If you believe all the university generated press releases, the answer seems to be something like 200."

U.S. News & World Report offers the most cited ratings for both institutions and programs. The National Research Council reports (Goldberger, Maher, & Flattau, 1995) represent the "gold standard" of program ratings, but reports issued only every decade fail to slake the craving for this year's, not last year's, ranking (Volkwein & Grunig, 2005). In addition to its yearly institutional rankings, *U.S. News & World Report* grades graduate programs in professional disciplines annually and in many other fields every two to five years.

In this age of ratings, the last thing a university wants is to appear different. Although *U.S. News & World Report* often changes its criteria, alterations are only a slight variation on the resource and reputation theme that grades all colleges, universities, and programs, whether public or private. To differ is to decline in rank. The "imitative university" has displaced the "distinctive university" as the goal of many presidents and provosts in public as well as private universities. The same holds true for academic deans and department chairs reaching for higher program rankings.

A relatively new entry in the ratings race for research universities is TheCenter, founded in 2000 by John Lombardi, former president of the University of Florida, an original member of the Kellogg Commission, and current president of the University of Massachusetts–Amherst. TheCenter issues an annual report that assesses the "Top American Research Universities" (Lombardi, Capaldi, Mirka, & Abbey, 2005; Lombardi, Capaldi, Reeves, & Gater, 2004; Lombardi, Craig, Capaldi, & Gater, 2000, 2002; Lombardi, Craig, Capaldi, Gater, & Mendonça, 2001; Lombardi et al., 2003). It avoids the ranking problem of slight differences in scores suggesting significant variations in quality by placing universities in the top 25 private and the top 25 public research universities. Its reports rate some 200 private and public research universities. Despite the disclaimer about ranking, universities can easily rank themselves by comparing the scores given in TheCenter's reports.

TheCenter's publications give their creators' opinions on the characteristics of great research universities and the criteria for rating them.

Research universities have two structures, an "academic core" and an "administrative shell" (Lombardi et al., 2001, pp. 7–10). The names alone tell the tale of importance and of fragmentation. "Faculty guilds" in each discipline form the critical academic core that controls and creates teaching and research. Professors in the local guilds work for the university but get their standards from, and owe their allegiance to, national and international guilds in their discipline. Outsiders immediately recognize the administrative shell of presidents, vice presidents, and deans, who are much less important than they appear or believe.

> Participants in the administrative shell typically demonstrate a fondness for public displays of institutional homogeneity, as expressed in the form of mission statements, strategic plans, and the like. These high-minded products generally have minor impact on the guilds and their work . . . (Lombardi et al., 2001, p. 10)

University management concentrates on "process" rather than "purpose . . . because of the highly fragmented nature of the academic guilds and their handicraft production methods" (Lombardi et al., 2004, p. 15). The academic core determines and does the work of research and teaching, while the administrative shell delivers the funding to the guilds and defends them from outside interference.

The following statement from TheCenter presents an apt description of a provider prestige-driven university.

> Some might say that the research university produces students, research products, economic development, and public service. While the university does produce these things, the delivery of goods and services to society is actually a secondary benefit from the university's primary pursuit of internal quality, as represented by research and students. (Lombardi et al., 2001, p. 10)

TheCenter insists that research universities, whether public or private, "exist to accumulate the highest level and the greatest amount of internal academic quality possible" (Lombardi et al., 2001, pp. 9–10). Then, as if this assertion were not bald enough, it continues, "Although the research university delivers a wide variety of products to external constituencies, such as graduates, technology, economic development, and public service, its primary focus is on the creation of internal quality" (p. 10).

One wonders what government and civic leaders would think of such a provider-driven notion of a public university purpose. This blunt description suggests that falling public funding may not be the only reason for the privatization of public universities. It indicates that some of their leaders put provider prestige ahead of public purpose. TheCenter's approach represents a classic case of the resource and reputation model of university excellence. Excellence depends more on what a university gets than what it does. Alexander Astin (1985), considering this very issue, questions whether "the pursuit of institutional self-interest through resource acquisition and reputation enhancement is compatible with the public university's mission of serving the public interest" (p. 73). He quickly mentions two public mandates that are not well served by this model—"the educating of undergraduate students and the expansion of opportunities for minority and low income-students" (p. 73).

One need not wonder what students would think of TheCenter's approach. One of its reports introduces the criteria for rating universities with following comment: "Any number of indicators serve this purpose, but most observers know that research matters more than anything else in defining the best institutions" (Craig, 2002, p. 5). TheCenter's performance indicators include only one measure related to students and undergraduate education. Not surprisingly, it is the median SAT score of students. The other eight include total research expenditures, federal research expenditures, endowment assets, annual giving, faculty members in the National Academies, faculty awards, doctorates awarded, and postdoctoral appointees (Lombardi et al., 2004). With such statements and criteria from a leading center evaluating "Top Research Universities," it is easy to understand the conflicts encountered by research universities that try to become "student-centered" universities (Geiger, 2004).

Given TheCenter's stress on the disciplinary guilds, it seriously slights the growing importance of cross-disciplinary research. "While many topics at the edges of these guild boundaries overlap, and produce such fields as biochemistry, the guilds define themselves by the center of their intellectual domains and not the edges" (Lombardi et al., 2004, p. 6). Here TheCenter missed the major growth area for research in institutes and centers, much of it performed by tenured faculty jointly appointed from academic departments.

It seems TheCenter has attracted considerable attention. Within a year and a half of its first report in 2000, its web site (http://thecenter.ufl.edu) received 57,000 unique visitors. The web site of the

Association of American Universities carries a link to TheCenter's home page. One of TheCenter's publications also claims that some universities used its annual reports for "strategic planning, public relations, and institutional research" (Craig, 2002, p. 4). Such a claim seems ironic for a center that saw small impact from such administrative shell activities. Several reasons explain the popularity of TheCenter's reports. They appear annually, use statistical criteria, avoid the reputation surveys of the other ratings, and offer the academic aura of coming from a university center rather than a commercial magazine.

Public Universities Pursue Public Purposes

In many ways, the Kellogg Commission anticipated and attempted to correct many of the assumptions in TheCenter's reports, which apparently had already gained currency in many public universities before TheCenter's creation. In *Renewing the Covenant*, the commission deplored the growing tendency to view the teaching and research of public universities more as private purchases than public benefits. It lamented the "blurring of the differences between private and public higher education":

> We find public institutions behaving more and more like private universities—replacing limited state sources of revenue with private dollars in the form of tuition increases, while mounting aggressive capital fundraising campaigns unprecedented in their scope and scale. At some indefinable point, these trends threaten the "public" character of our institutions because strategies focused on finances and market share, no matter how powerful, will never meet all public needs. (Kellogg Commission, 2000a, p. 18)

The commission concluded that the public character of their universities depended on student access and public service and cited the tests proposed by Robert M. Berdahl, then chancellor of the University of California–Berkeley.

> The legitimacy of the public university's claim as an instrument of progress in a democratic society hangs in balance on the question of access—and not only on access, but quality and purpose. Are we providing the broadest possible cross-section of America's population access to the best possible education? Are we excluding by any means anyone who has the right to

be included? Are we serving society—with our
research and by teaching people to serve as leaders
and citizens? (Kellogg Commission, 2000a, p. 18)

The commission tried to meet those tests by stressing student
access and public engagement. It proposed elevating student learning
to the same exalted status as faculty research. Its 1998 *Student Access*
report gingerly questioned the level of student selectivity in some public universities promoted in national ratings by suggesting that admission standards on some campuses may exceed the real requirement for
student success. The commission also attempted to reawaken the public purposes of state universities started by the Morrill Act with the concept of "public engagement." Of its five topical reports (the sixth proposed renewing the covenant with government), two centered on students (*Student Access* and *The Student Experience*) and two on public
service (*A Learning Society* and *The Engaged Institution*). The fifth—
Toward a Coherent Campus Culture—urged the public institutions to
become both "student" centered and publicly "engaged" universities
(Kellogg Commission, 2000b).

The Kellogg Commission carefully advocated raising the relative
importance of undergraduate education and public engagement without questioning doctoral studies and research. The commission dismissed the popular notion of conflict between these missions with the
comment that "a great deal of sterile discussion" argued that research
overwhelmed teaching and service on campus and in faculty evaluation
(Kellogg Commission, 2001, p. 29). After confirming its commitment
to all three roles, it urged redesigning, not rebalancing, the classic missions of teaching, research, and service. The commission used the late
Ernest Boyer's (1990) integrative model with its four branches of scholarship: discovery, integration, application, and pedagogy. Discovery
generally covered basic research; integration connected discoveries by
building bridges between the disciplines; application brought the benefits of scholarship to the public; and pedagogy or teaching used
research to improve instruction.

The Greatest Challenge

The Kellogg Commission challenged their colleagues to create "great
student universities" as well as "great research universities."

Many of the nation's public universities pride themselves on being "great research universities," national
and international centers of scholarship and inquiry;

they consider how faculty are to be rewarded, institutional self worth is to be measured, national rankings are to be assessed, and public budgets are to be
allocated. This Commission wants to suggest that it
is time our universities also preserve our commitment to be "great student universities." (Kellogg
Commission, 2000b, p. 53)

The commission realized this recommendation cut against the
grain of academic attitudes in the modern public research university.
"Too many of us have a tendency to define 'greatness' without reference
to students, undergraduate or graduate" (Kellogg Commission, 2000b,
p. 53). The term "great student university" was not only "unfamiliar,"
it makes "many of us" "a little uncomfortable" (p. 53). William
Richardson (1996), president of the Kellogg Foundation, which funded the commission, and former president of Johns Hopkins University,
stated the problem more bluntly in the year the commission convened:

There is little question that a research-as-king mindset has shaped the academic culture and hierarchy of
most American universities. And clearly, our ability
to change the status quo will pose yet another major
challenge for higher education . . .

The Kellogg Commission claimed that the destiny of public universities depended on achieving what some might see as an impossible
dream. In a single sentence, the commission coupled the creation of a
"great student university" with completion of its social compact of
serving society.

If public universities are to prosper in the future, they
must be great student universities as well as centers of
research, focusing on their most basic mission and
the social compact it embodies between institutions
on the one hand, and taxpayers, parents, students,
and public officials, on the other. (Kellogg
Commission, 2000b, p. 54)

What went unsaid was the worry of some academics that the goals
of a great student university and great research university were not just
uncomfortable but incompatible. Roger Geiger (2004) warns that student-centered universities can lead to student consumerism and loss of
faculty control over the curriculum. The Kellogg Commission credited
the idea of a "great student university" to an essay by William Cronon

(1999), a historian from the University of Wisconsin–Madison. He championed a "great undergraduate university," while the commission softened the call by including graduate as well as undergraduate students (Kellogg Commission, 2000a).

The commission's sixth report—*Renewing the Covenant*—advocated nothing less than a "new kind of public institution" (Kellogg Commission, 2000a, pp. 20). It would provide "access to success to a more diverse student body," "engage" society by serving its needs, offer "lifelong learning" to all, and provide scholarship to the states and the nation (Kellogg Commission, 2000a, p. 10). In describing the benefits of this new institution, the commissioners addressed many of the external complaints leveled at public universities. Available courses would allow students to graduate on time and encourage them to analyze, reflect, and think independently. The new university would provide personal and career counseling and offer every student the opportunity to know several professors well enough to receive personal references on graduation. Students would engage fully with campus life and community activities and benefit from service learning. Best of all, the new university would offer more students the opportunity to participate with professors in research.

Although the Kellogg Commission couched its challenges in careful language, *Renewing the Covenant* really recommended the transformation of the public research university. It championed the creation of "a student university" to complement the current "research university" and added an "engaged university" devoted to a new type of public service. The research university had flourished for a time with disciplinary decentralization. Now even the research mission demanded university-wide action to encourage cross-disciplinary research. All three missions required fixing the fragmented university, for they demanded institutional planning and priorities with aligned goals and objectives for colleges, schools, and departments and cooperation across the disciplines in research and teaching.

The Kellogg Commission presented current challenges and proposed awesome aspirations for public universities. Turning those challenges and aspirations into more than millennial rhetoric required more specific suggestions about how to achieve them. The commission did give examples of implementation, especially on engagement, at several universities (Kellogg Commission, 1999). In addition, *Toward a Coherent Campus Culture* proposed eight strategies: 1) start with values and mission, 2) foster institutional coherence, 3) reinvigorate academic governance, 4) develop administrative leadership, 5) define the nature of acceptable scholarly work, 6) reinforce the integrity of tenure,

7) align athletics and academics, and 8) end with values: put learning first (Kellogg Commission, 2000b, pp. 39–54).

Great Ideas Demand Good Implementation _____

Although the commissioners offered these strategies, they claimed the differences among public universities and supporting states prevented proposing implementation plans for their achievement. This reluctance may have been a mistake. First, the problems that face public universities in the knowledge and information era increasingly know no boundaries. Nearly every public university has to grapple with the same issues in the context of constrained state funding: access and affordability, retention and graduation, school reform and economic development, and increased attention to undergraduate education while maintaining momentum in research and graduate studies. Second, the campus culture that encouraged fragmentation and chased reputational ratings constituted a national phenomenon. Finally, reports that present daunting challenges and advocate grand aspirations without suggesting specific strategies for their achievement often go directly from the mail to the shelf. The policy graveyard is filled with great ideas followed by poor implementation (Mazmanian & Sabatier, 1981).

The Kellogg Commission appointed an Implementation Committee; annual meetings of the National Association of State Universities and Land-Grant Colleges discussed best practices; and The National Forum on Higher Education for the Public Good held three National Leadership Dialogues (Byrne, 2004).[1] These dialogues featured great discussions on whether pursuing the public good was a "moral" or "civic" duty or whether "the organizing" or "the service" model was the best method for its pursuit (Kellogg Forum on Higher Education for the Public Good, 2002a, 2002b, 2002c). The dialogues appeared devoid of practical approaches to fixing the fragmented university and changing a campus culture that pushed peer prestige more than public purpose. As the third dialogue drew to a close—a point where the meeting should have moved to summarizing potential plans of action—a sociology professor asked pertinent questions that were followed by disturbing answers:

> Have we clarified the mission? Well, there is no single mission at the University of Michigan that holds weight among all of its participants. Do we have a strategy? We have many strategies, but no *single* strategy at the institutional level. Are we organized? Well, ours is a loosely coupled federation of little villages

and only sometimes do our students pass between
them. Have we joined together in solidarity? It does
happen occasionally. But if your measure is cooperation, coordination, or even communication, we are as
likely—or more likely—to compete with each other
as we are to collaborate. (Kellogg Forum on Higher
Education for the Public Good, 2002b, pp. 13–14)

The leaders of the Kellogg Commission made a valiant effort to
disseminate its recommendations, including publishing the executive
summaries of all its reports in 2001. A flurry of publicity occurred with
the release of each of the commission's reports, but it soon subsided.
Just three years after the commission's last full report called for a
"Millennial Partnership Act" (Kellogg Commission, 2000a, p. 11), the
dean of forestry at Oregon State asked, "Where are we with the Higher
Education Millennial Partnership Act that Kellogg called for? Does
anyone know where that is?" (Salwasser, 2003, p. 5)? Though conced-
ing the divided attitudes in external society about public universities,
this dean added, "But not all of the Divides we face are 'out there.' We
also have some internal divides that must be conquered" (p. 3).

Conclusion

The reports of the Kellogg Commission represented more than millennial rhetoric. Telling universities—admittedly dominated by departments whose national reputations depended on research—that they
must "put students first" and "engage" public needs took considerable
courage. When champions call for change, it is always a good strategy
to get history on your side.

We start with students and invite you to join us. State
and land-grant universities were established to put
students first. In responding to change, we begin by
returning to our roots, because too many of us have
lost touch with much that was best in our past.
(Kellogg Commission, 1997, p. vii)

The Kellogg Commission challenged public universities across the
country to reorder their priorities, restructure their governance, and
redesign their missions. The first called for more attention to university-wide priorities and better alignment of department, school, and college goals with institutional purposes. The second argued for stronger
central leadership and more faculty concern for institutional priorities.
The third advocated making undergraduate education and public

engagement the equals of research and graduate studies in public university missions.

The commission claimed that change came "from setting forth a sense of vision, priorities, and possibilities for the future" (Kellogg Commission, 2000b, p. 46). But vision, priorities, and possibilities are the entrée, not the end of reform. The chapters that follow supply the missing link between the commission's aspirations and their campus applications by offering practical suggestions on how to implement them. This book is based on the belief that great recommendations all too often fail at the final and most critical stage of implementation. Special strategies become essential when the object of change is nothing less than changing the campus cultures of public research universities.

The Kellogg Commission's recommendations are too good to stay on the shelf. These statements of leading presidents and chancellors recall public universities to the purposes of their roots, pursuing public good, not provider prestige. Today with all the talk of privatization, public universities need to recall the commission's response to the question "What . . . does the term 'public university' mean today? The irreducible idea is that we exist to advance the common good" (Kellogg Commission, 2000a, p. 9). In the words of Abraham Lincoln, we should again become "the public's universities" (Kellogg Commission, 2000a, p. 15).

Endnotes

1) For the response to a survey on the impact of the commission recommendations on some universities, see Byrne (2006).

References

Association of Governing Boards of Universities and Colleges. (1992). *The trustees and troubled times in higher education.* Washington, DC: Author.

Association of Governing Boards of Universities and Colleges. (1996). *Report of the Commission on the Academic Presidency: Renewing the academic presidency: Stronger leadership for tougher times.* Washington, DC: Author.

Astin, A. W. (1985). Selectivity and equity in the public research university. In L. W. Koepplin & D. A. Wilson (Eds.), *The future of state universities: Issues in teaching, research, and public service* (pp. 67–83). New Brunswick, NJ: Rutgers University Press.

Balderston, F. E. (1974). *Managing today's university.* San Francisco, CA: Jossey-Bass.

Benjamin, R., Carroll, S., Jacobi, M., Krop, C., & Shires, M. (1993). *The redesign of governance in higher education.* Santa Monica, CA: RAND.

Birnbaum, R. (1988). *How colleges work: The cybernetics of academic organization and leadership.* San Francisco, CA: Jossey-Bass.

Birnbaum, R. (2001). *Management fads in higher education: Where they come from, what they do, why they fail.* San Francisco, CA: Jossey-Bass.

Birnbaum, R. (2003). *The end of shared governance: Looking ahead or looking back.* Retrieved August 10, 2006, from the University of Southern California, Rossier School of Education web site: www.usc.edu/dept/chepa/gov/roundtable2003/birnbaum.pdf

Boyer, E. L. (1990). *Scholarship reconsidered: Priorities of the professorate.* Princeton, NJ: Carnegie Foundation for the Advancement of Teaching.

Burke, J. C., & Associates. (2005). *Achieving accountability in higher education: Balancing public, academic, and market demands.* San Francisco, CA: Jossey-Bass.

Burke, J. C., & Minassians, H. P. (2002a). *New directions in institutional research: No. 116. Reporting higher education results: Missing links in the performance chain.* San Francisco, CA: Jossey-Bass.

Burke, J. C., & Minassians, H. (2002b). *Performance reporting: The preferred "no cost" accountability program.* Albany, NY: The Rockefeller Institute of Government.

Byrne, J. V. (2004). Taking charge of change: The Kellogg Commission on the Future of State and Land-Grant Universities. In B. D. Ruben, *Pursuing excellence in higher education: Eight fundamental challenges* (pp. 359–388). San Francisco, CA: Jossey-Bass.

Byrne J. V. (2006). *Public higher education reform five years after the Kellogg Commission on the Future of State and Land-Grant Universities.* Washington, DC: National Association of State Universities and Land-Grant Colleges.

Cheit, E. F. (1971). *The new depression in higher education: A study of financial conditions at 41 colleges and universities.* New York, NY: McGraw-Hill.

Cheit, E. F. (1973). *The new depression in higher education—Two years later.* Berkeley, CA: Carnegie Commission on Higher Education.

Clark, B. R. (1983). *The higher education system: Academic organization in cross-national perspective.* Berkeley, CA: University of California Press.

Clark, B. R. (1998). *Creating entrepreneurial universities: Organizational pathways of transformation.* Oxford, England: Elsevier Science.

Cohen, M. D., & March, J. G. (1974). *Leadership and ambiguity: The American college president.* New York, NY: McGraw-Hill.

Craig, D. D. (2002). *TheCenter Top American Research Universities: An overview.* Retrieved August 10, 2006, from the University of Florida, TheCenter web site: http://thecenter.ufl.edu/TARUChina.pdf

Cronon, W. (1999, Winter). Only connect: The goals of a liberal education. *Liberal Education, 85*(1), 6–13.

Dionne, J. L., & Kean, T. (1997). *Breaking the social contract: The fiscal crisis in higher education.* Retrieved August 10, 2006, from www.rand.org/pubs/aid_to_edu_docs/CAE100/index2.html

Duderstadt, J. J. (2000). *A university for the 21st century.* Ann Arbor, MI: University of Michigan Press.

Duderstadt, J. J., & Womack, F. W. (2004). *The future of the public university in America: Beyond the crossroads.* Baltimore, MD: Johns Hopkins University Press.

Geiger, R. L. (2004). *Knowledge and money: Research universities and the paradox of the marketplace.* Stanford, CA: Stanford University Press.

Goldberger, M. L., Maher, B. A., & Flattau, P. E. (Eds.). (1995). *Research-doctorate programs in the United States: Continuity and change.* Washington, DC: National Academies Press.

Graham, H. D., & Diamond, N. (1997). *The rise of American research universities: Elites and challengers in the postwar era.* Baltimore, MD: Johns Hopkins University.

Keller, G. (1995, Summer). The vision thing in higher education. *Planning for Higher Education, 23*(4), 8–14.

Kellogg Commission on the Future of State and Land-Grant Universities. (1996). *Taking charge of change.* Washington, DC: National Association of State Universities and Land-Grant Colleges.

Kellogg Commission on the Future of State and Land-Grant Universities. (1997). *Returning to our roots: The student experience.* Washington, DC: National Association of State Universities and Land-Grant Colleges.

Kellogg Commission on the Future of State and Land-Grant Universities. (1998). *Returning to our roots: Student access.* Washington, DC: National Association of State Universities and Land-Grant Colleges.

Kellogg Commission on the Future of State and Land-Grant Universities. (1999). *Returning to our roots: The engaged institution.* Washington, DC: National Association of State Universities and Land-Grant Colleges.

Kellogg Commission on the Future of State and Land-Grant Universities. (2000a). *Renewing the covenant: Learning, discovery, and engagement in a new age and different world.* Washington, DC: National Association of State Universities and Land-Grant Colleges.

Kellogg Commission on the Future of State and Land-Grant Universities. (2000b). *Returning to our roots: Toward a coherent campus culture.* Washington, DC: National Association of State Universities and Land-Grant Colleges.

Kellogg Commission on the Future of State and Land-Grant Universities. (2001). *Returning to our roots: Executive summaries of the reports of the Kellogg Commission on the Future of State and Land-Grant Universities.* Washington, DC: National Association of State Universities and Land-Grant Colleges.

Kellogg Forum on Higher Education for the Public Good. (2002a). *Higher education for the public good: Educating for the public good: Implications for faculty, students, administrators and community.* Ann Arbor, MI: Author.

Kellogg Forum on Higher Education for the Public Good. (2002b). *Higher education for the public good: Practical strategies for institutional civic engagement and institutional leadership that reflect and shape the covenant between higher education and society.* Ann Arbor, MI: Author.

Kellogg Forum on Higher Education for the Public Good. (2002c). *Higher Education for the public good: The role of public understanding, public support and public policy in reflecting and shaping the covenant between higher education and society.* Ann Arbor, MI: Author.

Kennedy, D. (1997). *Academic duty.* Cambridge, MA: Harvard University Press.

Kerr, C. (1963). *The uses of the university.* Cambridge, MA: Harvard University Press.

Levine, A. (1997, January 31). Higher education's new status as a mature industry. *The Chronicle of Higher Education,* p. A48.

Lombardi, J. V., Capaldi, E. D., Mirka, D. S., & Abbey, C. W. (2005). *The Top American Research Universities.* Gainesville, FL: University of Florida, TheCenter.

Lombardi, J. V., Capaldi, E. D., Reeves, K. R., Craig, D. D., Gater, D. S., & Rivers, D. (2003). *The Top American Research Universities*. Gainesville, FL: University of Florida, TheCenter.

Lombardi, J. V., Capaldi, E. D., Reeves, K. R., & Gater, D. S. (2004). *The Top American Research Universities*. Gainesville, FL: University of Florida, TheCenter.

Lombardi, J. V., Craig, D. D., Capaldi, E. D., & Gater, D. S. (2000). *The Top American Research Universities*. Gainesville, FL: University of Florida, TheCenter.

Lombardi, J. V., Craig, D. D., Capaldi, E. D., & Gater, D. S. (2002). *The Top American Research Universities*. Gainesville, FL: University of Florida, TheCenter.

Lombardi, J. V., Craig, D. D., Capaldi, E. D., Gater, D. S., & Mendonça, S. L. (2001). *The Top American Research Universities*. Gainesville, FL: University of Florida, TheCenter.

Massy, W. F., Wilger, A. K., & Colbeck, C. (1994, July/August). Overcoming "hollowed" collegiality. *Change, 26*(4), 10–20.

Mazmanian, D. A., & Sabatier, P. A. (Eds.). (1981). *Effective policy implementation*. Lexington, MA: DC Heath.

Muller, S. (1994). Presidential leadership. In J. R. Cole, E. G. Barber, & S. R. Graubard (Eds.), *The research university in a time of discontent* (pp. 115–130). Baltimore, MD: Johns Hopkins University Press.

Munitz, B. (1995, Fall). Wanted: New leadership for higher education. *Planning in Higher Education, 24*(1), 9–16.

Rhodes, F. H. T. (1999). The new university. In W. Z. Hirsch & L. E. Weber (Eds.), *Challenges facing higher education at the millennium* (pp. 167–174). Oxford, England: Elsevier Science.

Richardson, W. C. (1996). *A peacetime mission for higher education*. Retrieved August 10, 2006, from www.arl.org/newsltr/187/peace.html

Riesman, D. (1958). *Constraint and variety in American education*. Lincoln, NE: University of Nebraska Press.

Rosenzweig, R. M. (1998). *The political university: Policy, politics, and presidential leadership in the American research university*. Baltimore, MD: Johns Hopkins University Press.

Salwasser, H. (2003). *Bridging the divide: Roles and strategies for land grant universities*. Retrieved August 10, 2006, from the Oregon State University, College of Forestry web site: www.cof.orst.edu/cof/admin/deanspresentations.htm

Volkwein, J. F., & Grunig, S. D. (2005). Resources and reputation in higher education: Double, double, toil and trouble. In J. C. Burke & Associates, *Achieving accountability in higher education: Balancing public, academic, and market demands* (pp. 246–274). San Francisco, CA: Jossey-Bass.

Weick, K. E. (1976, March). Education as loosely coupled systems. *Administrative Science Quarterly, 21*(1), 1–19.

Wolfe, A. (1996, Winter). The feudal culture of the postmodern university. *The Wilson Quarterly, 20*(1), 54–66.

Yudof, M. (2003). *Remarks by Mark G. Yudof.* Retrieved August 10, 2006, from the University of Texas System, Office of the Chancellor web site: www.utsystem.edu/cha/speechesarticles/AGBFlorida1-22-03.htm

2

Governing Boards of Public Research Universities as Conflicted Necessities

Richard T. Ingram

Writing this chapter coincides with my retirement from the presidency of the Association of Governing Boards of Universities and Colleges (AGB) after 13 years in that position. Through my nearly 35 years overall at AGB, I have become very aware that trustees, regents, and governing boards must learn to cope with many ambiguities and paradoxes in the conduct of their part-time and voluntary responsibilities. Especially apparent in the public research university is the inherent conflict between ensuring *accountability* to the general public (much more than simply to and for "the government") and ensuring *advocacy* for its needs and enabling it to meet educational and other functions. This tug makes citizen governing boards "conflicted necessities." The Kellogg Commission called attention to the imbalance between these two pulls by urging public universities to become more student centered and more publicly engaged. Can the governing board and its lay members help to meet these challenges and help to put unity back into public universities?

All university trustees, public and private, are conflicted as they strive to balance public needs and desires and academic priorities and ambitions. Trustees of private universities feel some of the same pressures, but their governance is largely immune from the dictates of state capitols and certainly state coordinating or system governing boards. Governing boards are a necessity because they help to reconcile the natural tension between the university's missions to serve public needs and protect academic values. These two priorities are not mutually exclusive, of course, but the latter can, and often does, overwhelm the former.

With all their faults, colleges and universities would be poorer places without our unique system of citizen trusteeship. It is reasonable to conclude that any group that is consistently criticized by government officials and campus leaders (both administrators and professors) must be serving useful purposes. We all criticize trustees, but the problem begins closer to home. The eminent philosopher Pogo pointed to the real problem with trustees of public research universities when he proclaimed ungrammatically but truly, "We have met the enemy and they is us." At their best, trustees of public universities express the public's highest hopes for universities that convey learning, discover the unknown, and serve our society. At their worst—with constant pressures from us—trustees reflect our self-interests, wants, and divisions.

Higher education students from abroad wonder what part-time trustees who are neither learned educators nor government officials can bring of value to the governance of universities. The theory is, of course, that there is nothing like distance to diminish—if not disinfect—self-interest. Neither educators nor politicians (we hope), public trustees can distinguish between the legitimate interests of both campus and capitol. With a foot in both camps, these "outsider-insiders" can mediate between real public interests and realistic academic concerns. At their best, trustees can bring the outside in and the inside out by championing in their state the creation of a public agenda for higher education and their campuses that melds societal needs and academic values. No group is better positioned to ensure that campus leaders address the fragmented public research university by insisting on institutional priorities capable of creating truly great student-centered and publicly engaged research institutions.

Closing the External Gap and Meeting the Internal Challenge

Governing boards of public research universities must confront external and internal challenges at a time when their and their institutions' reputations are clouded. Trustees often appear two-faced to both outsiders from state capitols and insiders on their campuses (AGB, 1998). Governors and legislators frequently view them as captives of campus self-interests, who fail to resist incessant demands for higher appropriations and more autonomy yet do not confront their institutions' soaring costs, stagnant productivity, and generally weak performance in undergraduate education. Trustee reputation on campus is often not much better. Professors and administrators at more than a few public universities regard them as pawns of the political party in power, concerned mostly with cutting costs and undermining the faculty's voice in governance.

Given their task of mediating public and campus needs, it is not surprising that the actions of governing boards sometimes give credence to both characterizations. Moreover, at times and at one place or another, trustees have fallen under the spell of either campus rhetoric and the resistance of the faculty culture to needed change, or of political and partisan ideology from outside the institution from one or another special interest group or the present government in office.

Another characteristic of dysfunctional governing boards is when they fall to the extremes of inaction or intrusion. At one extreme there are some boards whose members patiently sit through endless show-and-tell sessions that recount successes or ambitions on national ratings involving mostly research and graduate studies. Talk about undergraduate education centers mostly on SAT or ACT score trends. They seldom or never ask about the problems of identifying the knowledge and skills that undergraduates should acquire or the difficulties of developing methods for assessing their achievement. At the other extreme are activist trustees who think they know exactly what knowledge and skills undergraduates should acquire because they are never wrong and seldom in doubt. Indeed, they are prepared to prescribe a ready-made curriculum in general education—without faculty participation. The worst of them see higher education as being fundamentally broken and in the control of the wrong people, meaning some group other than themselves.

This chapter advocates a middle way for trustees, one that plays to their collective strengths. It reflects the premise that trustees know society well enough to distinguish between its shifting demands and enduring needs, and that many of them have sufficient stature to stand up to governors and legislators who might try to impose their political influence on the university. Trustees should also know their university well enough to distinguish between real institutional strengths and mere desires—between realistic aspirations and unfocused ambitions. Only trustees are likely to see simultaneously in two directions—to perceive both inside out and outside in. Of course, not all governing boards—at least not enough of them—have and act on this perspective. The point is that no other group on or off campus is positioned to acquire such a balanced point of view of external needs and internal requirements. If governing boards do not act on this perspective, the clash between state demands and camp desires will undermine public support. It is arguable that the current debate about whether the public university should be *privatized* (an unfortunate term for several reasons not elaborated here) stems not just from the fall in state funding as a percentage of total revenue, but from the university's seeming detachment from ensuring that it addresses some of the public's most pressing problems.

Offered in this chapter are some practical suggestions for how the governing boards of public universities can close the gap between state capitols and public campuses. They can best do this by accepting the challenge of the Kellogg Commission to work to fix the fragmented university and to encourage institutional priorities that elevate undergraduate education and public engagement to levels that match the devotion to faculty research. Governing boards, with and through their presidents and provosts, and the best faculty leaders, should champion undergraduate education and public engagement. The latter requires attention and direction at the institutional level even as the research mission demands the kind of decentralization so prevalent on our campuses today.

The Kellogg Commission's Challenge _____

Public research universities cannot close the gap between campus and capitol without directing more attention to undergraduate education and to societal problems. Though both issues need particular programs and services from colleges, schools, and departments, they require collaboration and direction that only the university as a whole can provide. These demands are daunting, especially for public multiversities which have a complex mix of undergraduate, graduate, and professional programs. The influence of rating schemes on what seems to constitute quality in the public mind is perverse in the long term. Rather, faculties should be engaged in decisions that will keep the university nimble in adjusting to its many new realities and opportunities and steadfast in defending its academic values.

The Kellogg Commission's charge is correct: The modern university is "fragmented" and in desperate need of coherent governance. (Indeed, a fair question is whether university governance was ever really coherent. Has it ever been a pretty picture?) This chapter probes a few of the more typical solutions proposed thus far to address this very complex issue of institutional coherence, as governing boards with their presidential leaders have difficulty fostering substantive change in academic culture as we know it today.

Concluding on a positive note, this chapter argues that governing boards and chief executives can develop, in partnership with government, civic, and education leaders, a "public agenda" that can foster intra-institutional communication with the faculty expertise across colleges and departments capable of generating university priorities. This agenda can bring with it more cohesive internal governance and, ultimately, a strengthened public standing for public research universities.

Shared Governance, Severed Responsibilities_____

In 1966, AGB commended but did not formally "endorse" the American Association of University Professors' *Statement on Government of Colleges and Universities*. Interestingly, although the term *shared governance* is not used anywhere in the document, the statement soon became synonymous with that concept. According to the statement, trustees and presidents hold "primary responsibility" over missions and planning and to a somewhat diminished extent over budgets, while the faculty largely rules supreme over all academic matters.

The cooperative approvals required under this concept seemed to work well enough in the time of expansion after World War II, a period characterized by fairly steady demands for teaching and research programs and normally incremental funding from state governments. Steady demands for undergraduate programs and sponsored research and incremental funding from states forced few controversial decisions by trustees, administrators, and faculty. By the 1980s, diverse demands for teaching and research pushed for decentralized decisions at the college, school, and department levels. By the 1990s, diminishing public funding per student for public research universities furthered decentralization by increasing the importance of self-generated income from academic units, sponsored research, and student tuition.

Declining state support as a percentage of total revenue, shifting student demands, and targeted research funding splintered the faculty as a whole into those colleges, schools, and departments with rising student demand and research grant income and those without. The more fortunate programs and faculty favored responsiveness to external demands and funding opportunities, while the less well positioned feared the reallocations and reductions these developments would bring. Furthermore, faculty did not like being asked to make the hard choices that presidents, governing boards, and senior executives had to make and are making today. "Shared governance" and the viability of the traditional academic senate have suffered along with other consequences of the "fractured" university. What are governing boards, vested with ultimate responsibility and authority for the university as a whole, to do—and not do?

Stronger Presidents for Tough Times? _____

In 1996, when the Kellogg Commission issued *Taking Charge of Change* to presidents of public universities, an AGB Commission also published its report, *Renewing the Academic Presidency: Stronger Leadership for Tougher Times.* The latter had several recommendations for presidents and chancellors, including reducing the ambiguities in authority and decision-making processes, and resisting the academy's insatiable appetite for the kind of excessive consultation that can bring institutions to a standstill. It had recommendations for faculty as well, including calls for departures from tradition and a greater willingness to make painful decisions about individual professors or academic programs, to match commitment to academic disciplines with commitment to the institution. As a result of the governance deadlock at the university level, the action moved to the departments, schools, and colleges, each responding to its own favored demands. This decentralized decision-making raised costs, fractured priorities, and fragmented universities. The AGB Commission report pushed for strengthening presidencies and presidents, not trustees, to break this governance deadlock. It argued for expanding presidential authority even though the multiversity's growing complexity with its bewildering array of specialties seems too much for one person to comprehend, much less influence or lead.

Now that some professors and scholars are lamenting the emergence of strong chief executives on campus, we have forgotten how sad the condition of the college and university presidency was in the 1970s and 1980s. I remember a "Point of View" column in *The Chronicle of Higher Education* from the 1970s that depicted graphically the fallen state of the university presidency. At the top of the article appeared a picture of Clark Gable in academic regalia. Beneath the caption ran a line that read something like the following: "Since the faculty doesn't want its President to do anything, why not choose one who looks like a leader?" Cohen and March (1974) turned this imagery into scholarship with their book *Leadership and Ambiguity: The American College President*, which counseled presidents not to worry about their impotency, since they had little or no effect on the successes or stumbles of their institutions. They presided over "organized anarchies" that did not know what they were doing, where they were going, or why they acted as they did. The book excused presidential ineffectiveness and faculty recalcitrance as inherent and inevitable—and perhaps even desirable.

The independent Commission on the Academic Presidency proposed more effective presidencies as the antidote to "academic anarchy." It claimed that "Faculty loyalties and the faculty reward system

increasingly focus on achieving eminence in (and protecting) a particular discipline, rather than supporting the goals of the institution"
(AGB, 1996, pp. 15–16). The report advocated more powerful presidents to push university purposes, manage their resources, and reshape
shared governance to stress shared responsibilities. It sought to redress
the flaws of "shared governance" that gave the faculty a veto on nearly
every issue, including those where trustees and presidents presumably
hold "primary authority." Such a veto could not work when changing
conditions mean that universities have to reallocate positions and funds
from some colleges, schools, and departments with declining enrollments and research funding to areas with exploding demands. Colleges,
schools, and departments in the biomedical technology, engineering,
and professional fields rushed to respond to shifting external opportunities. But faculty and university senates, following a public posture
that all academic disciplines are equal, had and still have difficulty
approving university-wide decisions that mean reallocating limited
resources.

The commission's report called on trustees to seek presidents,
including nontraditional candidates who may not have had long
careers in the academy, who are "risk takers" and "change agents."
There were also some important messages for political leaders. It urged
merit selection of trustees for gubernatorial appointment and challenged governing boards to stand by presidents and chancellors publicly and effectively "when they are under siege by internal and external
constituents."

The commission's report rightly called for presidential leadership
in setting campus directions based on strategic planning that matched
societal needs with institutional strengths. Although well received by
presidents and trustees, the professorate's spokespersons in
Washington, DC, and elsewhere gave it less than enthusiastic response.
Subsequently, partly in response to the commission's urging, AGB's
Board of Directors released its own statement on institutional governance in 1998. It encouraged all governing boards and chief executives
to "examine the clarity, coherence, and appropriateness of their institutions' governance structures, policies, and practices and to revise them
as necessary" (p. 3). It offered some principles to guide faculty and
trustees engagement (and other internal and external stakeholders) in
the exercise of their responsibilities.

The report called for more specificity in determining who can
make what decisions, and in so doing, urged distinctions among the
three actions of "communication," "consultation," and "decision-making."

Some decisions, it argued, necessitated only communication of the decisions made; others required extensive consultation with faculty and students; still others required joint decision-making of all the traditional parties of trustees, presidents, faculty, and students.

Not surprisingly, faculty spokespersons reacted even more negatively to AGB's 1998 guidelines for its member boards and chief executives than to the original commission 1996 report, *Renewing the Academic Presidency.* The assertion that the faculty constituted one of several key stakeholder groups—along with trustees, administrators, and even students—proved particularly irksome to professors. After all, many of them believe the faculty is the institution. Furthermore, they asked, how can governing boards composed increasingly of imports from the corporate world understand university operations and faculty culture. Various articles in *The Chronicle of Higher Education* and the American Association of University Professors' *Academe* continue to rail against the use of external executive search consultants in presidential searches that allegedly oversteer the process and minimize the faculty's voice in presidential selection; the substantial increases in presidential compensation; the invasion of "corporate culture" into campus decision-making; the adoption of business concepts such as treating students as customers; and talk of institutional branding and "market positioning." This onslaught from business and industry clashes, they say, with the values and beliefs of the academy. The irony is that the same professors in public research universities who complain about such matters rush to improve their institutional and program positions in the national ratings—the academic version of branding. At many universities, sadly, the rage for climbing the national ratings remains one of the few shared beliefs of many professors, presidents, and trustees.

Despite this shared obsession, many within the professorate dismiss the conclusion of the Commission on the Academic Presidency that "Strengthening presidential leadership does not mean undermining the role of boards or compromising the integrity of faculty" (AGB, 1996, p. 10). Apparently, most professors fail to see the same threats as outsiders to the financial health, rigor, effectiveness, competitiveness, and reputation of universities—especially public research universities. Rather than perceiving a major mismatch between responsibility and authority in the academic presidency, some concerned faculty activists believe presidents and chancellors already have far too much authority. Furthermore, they do not consider the university as fragmented. For many professors, the power resides where it belongs, closest to them in their departments, and to a lesser extent in schools and colleges. Many of these departmental advocates view faculty and university senates as only marginally more trustworthy than trustees and presidents.

On the other hand, in more recent years, there are some indications of faculty resignation to the modest but continuing trend for governing boards to seek nontraditional candidates for the presidency, to tolerate presidential compensation well beyond what was the norm, and to forgo their stronger voice in setting institutional priorities. Professors from fields with increasing demands for enrollments and research in times of declining state support are beginning to see the need for change. The faculty posture on some governance fronts may be showing encouraging changes in attitude and perspective, but there is a long and bumpy road ahead for the academy.

Sharing Responsibilites

Other chapters in this book discuss the declining condition of faculty governance (i.e., active faculty leadership and participation in helping to shape the strategic directions of universities). There are many reasons why most university senates have become moribund and hidebound, of course, and there is plenty of blame to go around for their general malaise, including some to bullheaded trustees and presidents. Precisely at a time when the university needs to reexamine virtually everything that it does and how it does it, to be quick to seize new and fast-evolving opportunities, and to moderate the adverse consequences of specialization within academic disciplines, we seem to be stuck in the mud. And yet we know that faculty commitment to change is essential to make it a reality on campus.

One of the academy's sacred cows continues to be the notion of shared governance, an article of faith in the profession traceable to the 1960s that is too vague and bereft of real value to address what is facing the academy today. It is arguable that the term has become an unfortunate symbol of faculty denial that the university is failing to deal constructively with its new realities in a very different world. For many professors who want to be consulted more on the decisions required to rebalance their university's place in the modern world and marketplace, we respectfully urge that "shared" governance—first and foremost—be decoupled from the legitimate and timeless principle of academic freedom. We need to evolve a term of art that calls for a different kind of faculty engagement that is more precise, understood, and accepted in order to encourage rather than to discourage presidents (and, indirectly, governing boards) from consulting, collaborating, and communicating with faculty more than they typically do. That term must convey the sense that the faculty response will equal the external and internal challenges, or at least not ignore them.

To be sure, coherent and effective faculty participation in university governance is about accepting responsibility for the hard decisions about resource reallocation that must be made. Being all things to all people and satisfying every faculty desire for doctoral or research programs is no longer possible, even for largest and best endowed public universities. Exploring more effective ways of imparting knowledge less expensively for larger numbers of students is not an unreasonable demand imposed by misguided state officials. It is a necessity for controlling costs and bringing student learning in line with the latest technology, which many professors accept in their research but reject in their teaching. Teaching deserves the same creativity and technology lavishly allocated to research. It also deserves more of the problem-solving approaches across disciplines that increasingly characterize faculty research. Finally, faculty must become more willing to partner with presidents and provosts to keep their institutions competitive in a difficult environment, and to shape and act on an agenda that more compellingly addresses pressing public needs. Are faculties able and willing to undertake these tasks and others like them? If not, what will it take for them to do so?

A recent study of the relationship between the practice of tenure and the participation of senior professors in institutional governance reveals a general apathy toward faculty senates and university senates (Chait, 2002), arguing that we have a trilemma. One "lemma" is the apathetic or change-averse senior faculty in traditional fields; another consists of presidents who are reluctant to engage faculty in decision-making because professors are not held to anything like the standards of accountability expected of their presidents. In the middle of this stalemate are governing boards that often press for change without fully understanding its implications. Indeed, some governing boards are reluctant to change some of their own behavior, even where it is obviously needed. This conundrum becomes all the more difficult because not one of these three categories of players has the capacity by itself to make good things happen.

Revive the Academic Senate?

In Chapter 4, Roger Benjamin calls for recreating the faculty role in university governance. He concludes that the fragmentation of faculty into departments, schools, and colleges, isolated from and in competition with one another, "has led to the virtual collapse of governance in public universities." It is arguable that this statement also extends to the independent sector of higher education, particularly in its research universities. Benjamin calls for recognition that the university produces public, not private, goods, that teaching and learning should be differentiated from research, and that the key to improvement may be found in restoring faculty interest in undergraduate education to the institutional level (rather than retained at the departmental) led by faculty leaders in the arts and sciences. Unless this is done, he contends that "The whole of the university is no longer clearly more than the sum of its parts." Benjamin knows that it will take an extraordinary effort within the faculty ranks to enable academic senates to reclaim the center of university governance.

A 2005 article by friend and colleague Steve Trachtenberg, president of George Washington University, includes several vignettes about how presidential life is affected by relationships with faculties when everyone wants "their piece of the cake." In the article, Trachtenberg tells a story about proposing to the faculty that the university shift to a year-round calendar to make better use of time, effort, and facilities. He writes, "The faculty responded with 17—I counted them— 'whereas-es' condemning the idea as grotesque, heretical, smelly, fishy, unnatural, and loutish" (p. 12). He concludes that "they would not even entertain further *talk* on this unmentionable subject. Sometimes retreat is the best thing a leader can do—for the moment" (pp. 12–13).

Presidents find themselves in too many quandaries today to make retreat an option. Should presidents conclude that it is simply not possible or worth the effort to work with elected faculty leaders to restore a responsible faculty voice that willingly accepts accountability with more authority over painful resource allocations and the like? Or should they accept faculty distraction, preoccupation, or apathy as a mostly good thing and work around formal faculty governance mechanisms to get things done? Many more presidents seem to be making the second choice, as evidenced by their convening ad hoc commissions with faculty representation for planning and initiatives and seeking out only the most highly respected senior faculty for their opinion and help. With regard to inviting faculty engagement in institutional governance, presidents are understandably being much more careful about what they wish for. Is it possible the growing use of task forces and commissions of our most highly respected and broad-minded faculty is the new form of internal institutional governance?

In the end, it is arguable that neither unionized faculties nor, with many exceptions to be sure, those who generally make time to accept leadership positions in academic senates today are where trustees and administrators would like them to be on these matters. Thus we have trustee and presidential impatience with "process," and disappointment with everything from shortfalls in serious interdisciplinary work to missed opportunities for colleges and schools to work together in common cause on behalf of the university as a whole. If we accept the premise that the best predictor of future performance is past performance, then the prognosis for rejuvenating academic senates in their current forms to much higher levels of institutional commitment is not good. The answer may be more likely to be found down another road.

Whatever that road may be, trustees must insist that their universities put more weight on responding to societal and student needs that reflect outputs, outcomes, and results, rather than relying on resources and ratings that reflect inputs of student preparation, endowments, and faculty reputation. Trustees must help the other two partners make the shift from the pursuit of national ranking. They must push their colleagues to develop indicators that assess the value added in knowledge and skills acquired by students with help from faculty, along with the board, administrators, and students. Research universities should not continue down the path of merely recording SAT or ACT scores of entering students as *the* proxy for quality in undergraduate education.

Governing Boards Should Ask Rather Than Act _____

Perhaps part of the solution to the problems of public universities can come from trustees. After all, it might be reasoned, the governing board has the legal authority to do virtually anything it wishes! The American Association of University Professors' 1966 *Statement on Government of Colleges and Universities* concedes that the board has ultimate authority, even while condemning its use. But can and should governing boards use more of this latent authority as some trustees contend?

One complication is that some public universities have their own trustees, while others are part of multicampus systems and do not have institutional boards (courtesy of their state governments that like it that way). State leaders should ask educational leaders this intriguing question: If we really want first-tier public research universities in our state, are they more likely than not to have *their own* as opposed to system boards? Clearly, there are some top public research universities currently in system structures, but they are in the minority. Interestingly, the majority of research universities, either independent or public, have their own fully governing boards. There are some interesting implications in this observation as we ponder the possibility of a cause and effect relationship. Sophisticated research on this proposition may prove useful.

In an article by Derek Bok (2005) seemingly based on his then forthcoming book *Our Underachieving Colleges: A Candid Look at How Much Students Learn and Why They Should be Learning More* (2006), he states that it is time to ask that trustees and governing boards help to enhance student learning. The former president of Harvard University calls—rather surprisingly and no doubt causing much chagrin from sitting presidents—for trustees to "alter the incentives and rewards that currently influence academic leaders" (p. B12). He urges conscientious trustees not to worry about the inevitability of their being charged with "meddling" and the like, but to persist with asking their chief executives and academic leaders to respond to questions such as these:

- What efforts does the (institution) make to assess student progress toward generally accepted goals, such as critical thinking, quantitative skills, writing, and proficiency in a foreign language?
- Are funds available to enable instructors to experiment with new teaching methods, and are the results evaluated and publicized within the faculty?
- Is training in classroom teaching given to new faculty members? Does it include exposure to research findings on teaching and learning?
- What evidence of a candidate's teaching is collected in reviewing professional qualifications for appointment or promotion . . . ? (p. B12)

Two points in Bok's advice are especially interesting. First, he stresses the importance of emphasis on undergraduate, and especially general, education. Second, he suggests that trustees should become more engaged, not by acting, but by asking questions.

There is a way for trustees to become more active without being intrusive; intrusiveness is something that presidents, provosts, and professors understandably fear. Though governing boards (not individual trustees) have full legal authority, they should exercise that authority largely through the actions of others, especially the president. Their value added flows from the questions asked and the answers generated rather than from their own unilateral decisions. Asking questions about institutional priorities and performance results in public research universities is not for the faint of heart. Standing at the interface of the university and society, governing boards must protect the public character of the university by ensuring that it responds to societal needs while safeguarding institutional integrity by resisting political and especially ideologically driven pressures. These matters require trustees' persistence, patience, time, and consistent and very public support of their presidents and chancellors.

Only Bok knows whether he would have responded kindly and effectively to such inquiries from either of his two boards when he was in the presidency at Harvard, but one's perspectives often change after leaving the presidency. What is especially interesting is that this thoughtful and influential former president has apparently exhausted all other possibilities before calling on trustees and governing boards to help with necessary reform. I say better late than never. Now Interim President Bok has a second chance to implement his ideas at Harvard.

There is no question that governing boards can and should be much more active players in the quest for more coherent campus decision-making. They do need to get closer to the action without trying to micromanage faculty or the curriculum, or the president and the administration. It is important that trustees appoint and reappoint presidents who:

- Accept that there are priority problems that need addressing
- Have not already given up on their faculty's ability to participate responsibly in change management at the university
- Believe their boards will *publicly* support them over the long-term in the face of likely faculty resistance that may extend to, horror of horrors, votes of no confidence

The key function of trustees in this equation is to probe for and facilitate possible solutions, without themselves succumbing to that sinking conclusion that restoring responsible and cohesive faculty participation is impossible, or worse, that only trustee action can resolve the most perplexing of university problems.

One of the most important obstacles for boards to overcome is the understandable inclination to challenge presidents, provosts, deans, and professors to raise the position of their universities and their academic programs to the top of such national rankings as *U.S. News & World Report* or the "Top American Research Universities" at TheCenter at the University of Florida. The purpose here is not to belabor the problems with these ratings and how they have distorted institutional priorities and goals by distracting presidential, board, and faculty leadership. But it is to suggest in the strongest possible terms, reinforced by others in this book, that these ratings have become a very large part of the problem for universities. These institutions should seek to serve their broader public trust and to be more responsive to the needs of the people who support them and the students they teach, especially at the undergraduate level. These ratings, which put peer prestige ahead of public purpose, undermine the values of university community, collaborative governance, and institutional commitment to the public good.

One other board function may yet prove to be a powerful form of intervention that could stimulate more conversation on campus and result in a more cohesive and consequential internal governance structure. Governing boards should use their bully pulpits to insist that universities undertake a much more proactive and visible set of initiatives to meet real and pressing human needs within the state and region. Trustees should help shape and act on a public agenda.

In Pursuit of a Public Agenda

University plans should focus much more than they typically do on articulating and fulfilling an agenda that places it squarely in the service of meeting some of the most pressing human needs in their states and the educational needs of their undergraduate students. By doing so, it is possible that a more coherent sense of community and purpose within the university can be achieved. The spark of pursuing a very different kind of agenda can cause the kinds of conversations on campus that will rekindle cross-college cooperation, the application of interdisciplinary approaches to problem solving, more cohesive and coherent decision-making, and other positive results. Doing so will not help to move the institution into the next higher tier of peer group rankings, but it *will* help the university to counter those who believe that the university has lost its way and deserves less public support. It will also help to restore the university's standing in the court of public and public policymaker opinion.

In pre-Katrina Mississippi, the governor accepted the invitation of AGB to sponsor a statewide exploration of a public agenda. This brought leaders from higher and K–12 education and from business and government from both parties together in a common cause. As a first objective, they identified some of the most pressing needs in the state and then proposed how the state's educational and business enterprises could address them. Second, trustees from both public and private colleges and universities participated with government, civic, and K–12 leaders in preparing an explicit public agenda that addressed those issues. The results of that statewide effort are contained in a 2002 report published by AGB. The AGB Center stands ready to help similar initiatives in other states.

These initiatives can take place within all universities, public and private, if their presidents and governing boards want them to happen. There is no reason to doubt that most professors across the university will be eager to participate down to the departmental level. The central question to open the conversation would be something like this: How can our university bring its human and intellectual and physical assets to bear on the most pressing of the public's needs in our state and region? What are those needs, and what can we do to reach consensus on them and on strategies to address them? Who needs to be brought into our deliberations external to the university to provide public credibility and additional expertise? How can we manage and govern the university's long-term commitment to address them?

It may be naïve to hope such an effort shows a new way to enlist faculty commitment to broader university goals and objectives well beyond the self-interest inherent in their own disciplines, departments, and colleges. But given the fact there is little or no downside to this proposition, public research universities conceivably have the most to gain from trying. Such an initiative will help counter the attitude in state capitols that public universities are interested only in their own prestige and their "piece of the cake."

The governance oars of presidents, governing boards, and faculties are not pulling in the same direction as things now stand. It is time to try something different and challenging to accomplish ambitious and clearly defined goals that call for university-wide pursuit, effective intra-institution governance, and the possibility of earning even stronger public confidence in the university. It is not enough for those who labor in the academy's halls to rationalize that the pursuit of old agendas and ways of conducting ourselves somehow meet our obligations to the society that assists us through philanthropic support, tax appropriations, and tuition and fees.

Governing boards composed of nonacademic laypersons holding legal authority over college and universities represent a time-proven alternative to direct governmental control; such boards are an institution and a tradition unique to the United States. After nearly 35 years of working through frequent concerns about how citizen governing boards can be made more useful and effective, I have concluded that we would have to create them, if they did not exist. Higher education needs boards that truly govern in the center of the academic enterprise as an integral part of the system of checks and balances that keep the enterprise honest, accountable, and responsive to its public responsibilities.

Leading by Asking Rather Than Acting

Though trustees hold the legal power in theory and in law, they should exercise it in practice largely through the actions of others, especially the president. There is an important place for restraint in this equation. They should take a page from Derek Bok's book by exercising their authority mostly by asking rather than acting. Their value added arises from the questions asked and the answers acquired rather than the decisions they make and the actions they take. Asking questions about institutional priorities, especially performance results, in public research universities is, as noted earlier, not for weak-kneed trustees. Neither is standing at the interface of the university and society, protecting the public character of the university by ensuring that it responds to societal needs while safeguarding its integrity from those who would invade it.

Public research universities differ in many ways, but trustee queries will have a similar ring. Trustee questions should be few but powerful and probe for strategic directions, not programmatic details. Their queries should push for institutional direction and leave many details to provosts, deans, and faculty in colleges, schools, departments, and interdisciplinary centers. Their queries should strengthen, not undermine, the presidency as well as the president—who, we must remember, is always between the proverbial rock and hard place.

External Questions

- Has our board joined with trustees of other public colleges and universities and their alumni to encourage governors to establish and work with independent and bipartisan (or nonpartisan) nominating commissions to recommend candidates for trustees of public colleges and universities as proposed by AGB?
- Has our board worked with business, civic, and political leaders from political parties, trustees and officials from public and private colleges and universities, and public schools to create a public agenda of what our state needs most from higher education?
- Has our board advocated the needs of our universities to state officials and the general public and has it advocated on campuses the teaching, research, and service programs that respond to the needs of the citizens of our state?

Internal Questions

- Does the university's strategic plan approved by the board reflect both public needs and institutional strengths, hopefully adopted in response to a public agenda as just mentioned?
- Does that strategic plan identify university-wide priorities that are ambitious but realistic, specific, and measurable? Do they focus on performance results and not just resource inputs?
- Do those priorities emphasize campus strengths and state priorities over national rankings and ratings?
- Does our university mission statement show an appropriate balance among student learning, public engagement, and faculty research? Do the criteria for faculty promotion and tenure reflect this balance?
- Do our operating and capital budgets reflect these missions and priorities?
- Does the governing board periodically review university results on institutional priorities?
- Does the administration present its plans to raise performance in areas requiring improvement?
- Does the university have an assessment plan for undergraduate learning that identifies the knowledge and skills expected for all undergraduates in general education?
- Does it evaluate the extent of their achievement by graduates?
- Have academic departments done the same for their specialized programs?
- Does the board review periodically the assessment results, and how well do they measure up to the identified goals?
- Does the board insist that its university participate in the National Educational Survey of Student Engagement and review its comparative results with peer institutions?
- Does the board review carefully the campus accreditation self-studies and visiting team reports, and request reports on progress in addressing recommendations for improvement?
- Does the board consider these missions, priorities, and reviews when assessing the performance of a sitting president, and when it selects a new president?
- Do the explicit priorities and goals in the university's current or forthcoming fundraising campaign reflect these institutional priorities and goals?
- Does the board also ask tough questions about its own performance to set an example for the rest of the university and to strengthen its effectiveness?

Conclusion

Governing boards are a conflicted necessity, especially in public research universities. They stand at the interface of society and the university, which have mutual needs but conflicting interests. The critical function of governing boards is to manage that connection between public needs and educational values. Losing its strategic focus by allowing itself to be inundated with a succession of unconnected reports is the bane of an ineffective or dysfunctional governing board. Effective governing boards do not impose answers on complex academic matters beyond their competence; rather, as loving critics, they should challenge presidents, provosts, and faculty leaders to propose priorities that build on institutional strengths and focus on pressing societal needs.

Trustees need to keep their eyes on the prize—the responsiveness of their university in shaping a critical public agenda with as many appropriate partners as possible. Though governing boards legally possess ultimate institutional authority, they must act mostly through actions of academic leaders. Their success depends more on the quality and timeliness of the questions they ask than on the actions they take. In ancient times, Socrates queried Athenian youth about the connection between personal virtue and civic life (although he did ultimately pay a price for it). It's time for courageous and committed university trustees to ask the same question of ourselves, our administrators, and our professors.

References

American Association of University Professors. (1966). *Statement on government of colleges and universities*. Retrieved August 9, 2006, from www.aaup.org/statements/Redbook/Govern.htm

Association of Governing Boards of Universities and Colleges. (1996). *Report of the Commission on the Academic Presidency: Renewing the academic presidency: Stronger leadership for tougher times*. Washington, DC: Author.

Association of Governing Boards of Universities and Colleges. (1998). *Bridging the gap between state government and public higher education*. Washington, DC: Author.

Bok, D. C. (2005, December 16). The critical role of trustees in enhancing student learning. *The Chronicle of Higher Education*, p. B12.

Bok, D. C. (2006). *Our underachieving colleges: A candid look at how much students learn and why they should be learning more.* Princeton, NJ: Princeton University Press.

Chait, R. P. (Ed.). (2002). *The questions of tenure.* Cambridge, MA: Harvard University Press.

Cohen, M. D., & March, J. G. (1974). *Leadership and ambiguity: The American college president.* New York, NY: McGraw-Hill.

Kellogg Commission on the Future of State and Land-Grant Universities. (1996). *Taking charge of change.* Washington, DC: National Association of State Universities and Land-Grant Colleges.

Trachtenberg, S. J. (2005, July/August). Academic leadership is not a piece of cake. *Trusteeship, 13*(4), 8–13.

3

Fixing the Fragmented University: A View From the Bridge

James J. Duderstadt

This chapter addresses the challenge of unifying the fragmented university from the perspective of the university president. The contemporary university finds itself increasingly compartmentalized. The divisions arise from the specialization of academic departments and faculty interests, the decentralization of budgets and resources, the nomadic character of the faculty in a highly competitive marketplace, the technologies allowing the creation of scholarly communities detached from campuses, and the ever more numerous and complex missions demanded by a diverse multiplicity of clients and stakeholders. While this increasingly decentralized nature of the university allows it to function as a loosely coupled adaptive system, evolving in a highly reactive fashion to its changing environment, it can also undermine the ability of the university to respond effectively to the broader needs and demands of society, particularly in its core missions of student learning and social engagement.

While management tools and governance structures provide useful methods of unifying the university, budgets and organization can only accomplish so much. Far more important is leadership, particularly from the president, that is capable of embracing the values that pull a fragmented community together to address a common and public purpose.

After a brief review of the various forces driving fragmentation of the university and the impact of this decentralization on the institution's character and mission, this chapter turns to a discussion of possible remedies, drawing heavily from the experience of leading one of the nation's largest public universities during a period of significant transformation. Some consideration will be given to the traditional methods university leaders have used to pull together their institutions, for example, allocating resources, introducing faculty incentives, and modifying organizational structures. However, most attention will be devoted to bolder approaches aimed at enabling universities to better serve a rapidly changing society.

The Forces and Implications of Fragmentation _____

The intellectual fragmentation of the university was driven by the rapid evolution of the scientific method in the late 19th century, as specialization and new disciplines were needed to cope with the explosion of knowledge. Academic disciplines began to dominate the university by developing curriculum, marshaling resources, administering programs, and doling out rewards. Both the organization and the resource flows of the university became increasingly decentralized to adapt to the ever more splintered disciplinary structure. The increasingly narrow focus of scholarship created diverse faculty subcultures throughout the university—in the humanities, the natural and social sciences, the professional schools—widening still further the gap among the disciplines and shifting faculty loyalties away from their institutions and toward small peer communities that became increasingly global in extent.

Decentralization has also been driven by the rapidly changing nature of how universities are financed. In earlier times, the responsibility for generating the resources necessary to support the activities of the university was highly centralized. Public institutions were primarily supported by state appropriations, while private giving and student fees supported private institutions. Since these resources usually increased from year to year, institutions relied on incremental budgeting, in which the central administration simply determined how much additional funding to provide academic units each year. In today's brave new world of limited resources, battered by seriously strained state budgets and turbulent financial markets, the resources supporting most public and private universities are no longer collected centrally through appropriations or gifts. They are generated locally at the level of academic units and even individual faculty members, which compete in the marketplace for students (and hence tuition dollars), research grants and contracts (which flow to principal investigators), gifts (which are given to particular programs or purposes), and other auxiliary activities (clinical care, executive management education, distance learning, and entertainment—e.g., football). It is little wonder that most universities are moving toward highly distributed budget models in which authority and accountability for revenue generation and cost containment are delegated to individual academic and administrative units, further decentralizing the university (Duderstadt & Womack, 2003).

The growing pressures on faculty not only to achieve excellence in teaching and research but also to generate the resources necessary to support their activities are immense. Today's faculty members are valuable and mobile commodities in a highly competitive marketplace that enables them to jump from institution to institution in search of an optimal environment to conduct their research, teaching, and other professional activities. They are well aware that their careers—their compensation, promotion, and tenure—are determined more by their research productivity, publications, grantsmanship, and peer respect, than by other university activities such as undergraduate teaching and public service. This reward climate helps to tip the scales away from teaching and public service, especially when quantitative measures of research productivity or grantsmanship replace more balanced judgments of the quality of research and professional work. It is no surprise that faculty loyalties have shifted from their institutions to their disciplinary communities. Faculty careers have become nomadic, driven by the marketplace, hopping from institution to institution. As one junior faculty member exclaimed in a burst of frustration, "The contemporary university has become only a holding company for research entrepreneurs!"

The academic organization of the university is sometimes characterized as a creative anarchy. Faculty members possess two perquisites that are extraordinary in contemporary society: academic freedom, which allows faculty members to study, teach, or say essentially anything they wish; and tenure, which implies lifetime employment and security. Faculty members do what they want to do, and there is precious little administrators can do to steer them in directions where they do not wish to go.

More abstractly, the modern university has become a highly adaptable knowledge conglomerate, both because of the diversity of the needs of contemporary society and because of the varied interest, efforts, and freedom of its faculty. It is characterized by a transactional culture, in which everything is up for negotiation. Today the comprehensive university is managed effectively as a federation. The university administration sets some general ground rules and regulations, acts as an arbiter, raises money for the enterprise, and tries—with limited success—to keep activities roughly coordinated. But rarely does the university find strong vision or leadership from the top.

Although this frequently resembles organizational chaos to outsiders, in reality the entrepreneurial university has developed an array of structures to enable it to better interact with society and pursue attractive opportunities. Yet while this organization has proven remarkably adaptive and resilient, particularly during periods of social change, it all too frequently tends to drift without the engagement or commitment of its faculty, students, and staff to institution-wide priorities.

For example, many contend that today's university has diluted its core mission of learning, particularly undergraduate education, with a host of entrepreneurial activities. It has become so complex that few, whether on or beyond our campuses, can comprehend its reality. It has become sufficiently encumbered with processes, policies, procedures, and past practices so that its best and most creative people are frequently disengaged from institution-wide priorities.

More fundamentally, there is a growing concern that the fragmented university has lost the coherence of its educational, scholarly, and service activities. Clearly the undergraduate curriculum has acquired a shopping mall character, reflecting more what professors are interested in teaching than what students need to learn. Universities offer far too many courses and majors, again reflecting the deification of the disciplines at the expense of the more coherent objectives of a college education.

The integration of knowledge is not only key to the vitality of scholarship, but also to fulfilling the public purpose of the university. Perhaps E. O. Wilson (1998) put it best in his provocative book *Consilience*:

> Most of the issues that vex humanity daily cannot be solved without integrating knowledge from the natural sciences with that of the social sciences and humanities. Only fluency across the boundaries will provide a clear view of the world as it really is, not as seen through the lens of ideologies and religious dogmas or commanded by myopic response to immediate needs. (p. 13)

So how should university administrations—especially university presidents—approach the challenge of taming this fragmentation and unifying the university into a more coherent focus on its fundamental values, mission, and public purpose? First it is important to acknowledge several realities of the contemporary university.

The Realities

The contemporary university has become one of the most complex institutions in modern society—far more complex, for example, than most corporations or governments. It comprises many activities, some nonprofit, some publicly regulated, and some operating in intensely competitive marketplaces. It teaches students; conducts research for various clients; provides health care; preserves and distributes cultural richness; engages in economic development; enables social mobility; and provides mass entertainment (athletics). And, of course, the university also has higher purposes such as preserving our cultural heritage, challenging the norms and beliefs of our society, and preparing the educated citizens necessary to sustain our democracy.

The University of Michigan provides an excellent example of this complexity: With an annual budget of more than $4.5 billion, an endowment of $5 billion, and more than $10 billion under active investment management, the UM, Inc. would rank roughly in the middle of the Fortune 500 list. Beyond educating more than 55,000 students at any given time, the university also conducts more than $800 million of research each year, operates a massive health care empire treating more than 1.5 million patients each year, engages in knowledge services on a global basis, and provides entertainment to millions (think Michigan Wolverines).

Clearly no president or executive team nor governing board can span the range of expertise and experience to manage in detail such an array of activities. Most knowledge and experience in universities reside at the grassroots level, as do creativity and value added. Even when augmented by knowledgeable executives, the central administration really does not understand the details of much of the "business" of the university. Beyond the disciplinary expertise of academic leadership at the level of departments, schools, and colleges, other activities such as federally sponsored research, clinical programs, student services, information technology, investment management, and even intercollegiate athletics require highly specific, competent, and experienced management. Hence delegation of authority and decentralization of responsibility become essential.

Second, despite the university president's executive responsibilities for all these activities and purposes, the position itself has surprisingly little authority. The president reports to a governing board of lay citizens with very limited understanding of academic matters and must lead, persuade, or consult with numerous constituencies such as the faculty and students that tend to resist authority. Thus the university presidency requires an extremely delicate and subtle form of leadership, sometimes based more on style than substance, and usually more inclined to build consensus rather than take decisive action.

Third, universities are quite unusual social institutions in the priority they give to individual over institutional achievement. Their culture is a highly competitive meritocracy, in which students and faculty are encouraged—indeed, expected—to push to the limits of their ability. While the sum of these individual activities can have great impact, the university itself is simply not designed to optimize institutional agendas. Despite the fact that team efforts in teaching and research do occur, the reward structure continues to stress independence and individual achievement.

Finally, one of the great strengths of American higher education is its remarkable diversity both in the nature of its colleges and universities and how they perceive and pursue their missions. For example, community colleges and regional four-year public universities tend to be closely tied to the needs of their local communities. They are the most market-sensitive institutions in higher education, and they tend to respond very rapidly to changing needs. Liberal arts colleges tend to respond to change in somewhat different ways, ensuring that their core academic mission of providing a faculty-intensive, residential form of liberal education remains valued and largely intact, perhaps reflecting the need for greater unity and coherence in undergraduate education than in other areas. The research university, because of the complexity of its multiple missions, its size, and its array of constituencies, and its unusual degree of decentralization, tends to be most challenged by change. While some components of these institutions have undergone dramatic change in recent years, notably those professional schools tightly coupled to society such as medicine and business administration, other parts of the research university continue to function much as they have for decades, such as the core academic disciplines, their faculty cultures, and their reward structures.

Recognizing the importance of this great diversity in character and mission is essential to developing effective approaches to address the fragmentation that characterizes particular institutions. Efforts to tame the disciplinary fragmentation may have an obvious and appropriate strategy for institutions such as liberal arts colleges with relatively narrow agendas—that is, undergraduate education. However, for more complex institutions, such as the comprehensive public research university, coordinating diverse activities such as undergraduate, graduate, and professional education, basic and applied research and scholarship, and service activities in clinical care, technology transfer, and international development is more problematic. Here one must take great care that such initiatives, aimed at responding to the demands of the moment for public (and political) accountability and focus, do not trample upon the complex intellectual structures for learning, scholarship, and serving civilization that have taken centuries to evolve.

Traditional Integrating Methods

With this as background, let us turn briefly to a consideration of the traditional methods university presidents have used to rein in the centrifugal forces of fragmentation and lead their institutions toward important objectives. Usually at the top of the list is the control of resources and budgets to establish priorities among academic programs and activities. A skillful president can bias the university system for resource allocation such that new proposals tend to win out over those that aim to sustain or strengthen established programs. While this requires some intellectual good taste on the part of both president and provost, it is an extremely important device for navigating the university toward the future rather than drifting along on currents from the past. During good times with growing budgets, this amounts to picking winners. During hard times, when resources are declining, this can amount to lifeboat decisions about which units will survive and which may be discontinued. Although most universities find it important to put into place well-defined policies for academic program reduction and discontinuance, with ample mechanisms for consultation, in the end the president usually shoulders the blame for these decisions.

Unfortunately, such control is weakened considerably by an organizational structure along disciplinary lines that has been nurtured over the years by our incremental style of resource allocation, in which units and activities simply continued unless a very good case could be made for doing something else. Most experience suggests that while these units are capable of modest internal change, they generally feel threatened by and resist broader institutional agendas. They make strategic resource allocation very difficult, as evidenced by the cumbersome, frustrating nature of efforts to reduce or eliminate programs. Furthermore, since most universities have so little budget flexibility, there is usually not sufficient discretionary capacity to have major impact. Whether for department chair, dean, provost, or president, budget flexibility beyond a few percent is rare, particularly on the annual time scale of most budget decisions.

Perhaps a more effective tool involves the appointment of key academic leadership, particularly at the level of provosts and deans, a power that most successful university presidents control. While the provost, as chief academic officer (and at many institutions, also chief budget officer) is important, even more critical is the selection and culture of deans. Achieving an appropriate balance between competitiveness on behalf of one's academic unit and collegiality with other deans on institution-wide objectives is a challenge. In a sense, deans serve as brokers between the two cultures of the university: the faculty (collegial, center periphery, colleagues, peer respect) and the administration (hierarchical, top down, bosses, performance evaluations). Since deans must represent the views of the faculty and never be seen as losing, they can become quite conservative, seeking to minimize risk and maximize flexibility. Furthermore, it is sometimes difficult to recruit the best people unless you give them full control of the reins, particularly in deans-driven universities like Michigan.

What about "the vision thing"? To be sure, there have been many examples of university presidents able to capture the commitment of an institution to pursue a compelling vision. Yet the creative anarchy arising from a faculty culture that prizes individual freedom and consensual decision-making poses a challenge to visionary leadership. Most big ideas from top administrators are treated with either disdain or ridicule (this too shall pass . . .). The same attitude usually occurs for formal strategic planning efforts, unless, of course, they are attached to clearly perceived budget consequences or faculty rewards. The academic tradition of extensive consultation, debate, and consensus building before any substantive decision is made or action taken poses a particular challenge in this regard, since this process is frequently incapable of keeping pace with the profound changes swirling about higher education. Most visions are usually trapped within the framework of existing constraints and are rarely capable of grappling with major institutional transformation.

The reality is that major institutional change is seldom motivated by excitement about a future vision. Rather it occurs as a response to some perceived crisis or threat—for example, a sustained period of cuts in state appropriations or a shift in federal research and development funding priorities can provide clever academic leaders with an opportunity to trigger change. Of course, it is important not to scare people into their foxholes; they need some sense of security and confidence that they are well armed to defend themselves. However, as one of my colleagues put it, if you believe change is necessary and you do not have a convenient wolf at the front door, then you had better invent one.

Taking a Bolder Approach _____

At the University of Michigan, both because of the institution's size and its strong tradition of decentralization, we found that the traditional tools used to pull together and steer the fragmented university were feeble and inadequate, particularly during a time of significant change (e.g., social diversity, globalization, and knowledge-intensive economies). In developing new approaches to unifying the fragmented university, we accepted at the outset two important assumptions.

First, we believed that the decentralized organization of the institution was a positive and valuable characteristic capable of unleashing great creativity and achievement and should not be abandoned. As Susan Lohmann (in press) suggests, the structures of the Western university have evolved over a millennium "to do some very heavy lifting and they produce a public good of great value." They enable the specialized and creative inquiry of individuals; the collective vetting, pooling, and accumulation of research results; the posting of research results on a global information commons; the protection of the university from the outside world and the inhabitants of the university from each other; and the underpinning of the scientific process, allowing scientific progress. The structures that do all this hard and hidden work should not be given up lightly.

We saw our challenge as university leaders as harvesting the good that bubbles up from the grassroots activities of the faculty, students, and staff, not to corral or dictate their behavior from above.

Second, rather than adhere to the traditional missions of higher education such as teaching, research, and service, we sought instead to protect what we viewed as the unique role of the University of Michigan. In this sense, we attempted to define and sustain Michigan's institutional saga, a term that noted higher education scholar Burton Clark (1970) used to refer to those longstanding characteristics, values, traditions, and practices evolving over many generations to determine the distinctiveness of a university. Clark's view is that

> Universities develop over time an intentionality about institutional life, a saga, which then results in unifying the institution and shaping its purpose. While all colleges and universities have social roles, some have purposively reshaped these into compelling missions that over time achieve sufficient success and acclaim that they become an embracing saga. (p. 8)

This is an important point for those attempting to address challenges such as the fragmentation of the contemporary university. If such efforts are carefully aligned with the institutional saga of a university—for example, its particular style of pedagogy or its approach to social engagement (e.g., the land-grant mission)—then there is hope of success. However, actions taken in ignorance or disregard of an institution's saga are likely to bounce off without making a dent—or worse, cause considerable damage.

It was our sense that the University of Michigan's combination of quality, breadth, and capacity, coupled with the flexibility provided by its unique constitutional autonomy, had allowed the university to be unusually agile and innovative. We saw Michigan's institutional saga throughout history as one of a trailblazer, launching the experiments and taking the risks to define the future of the public university, from our first president Henry Tappan's efforts in 1850 to build in the Michigan frontier the first true research university in America (in the spirit of von Humboldt) to the building of the Internet in the 1980s and the more recent successful defense of the importance of social diversity to higher education in the landmark U.S. Supreme Court case of 2003.

Perhaps as a consequence of this pioneering spirit, we tended to look at chronic issues such as declining state funding, government interference, and marketplace competition less as immovable barriers and more as challenges that could be transformed into opportunities to pull together a fragmented academic community with a sense of common purpose in controlling its destiny and preserving its most important values and traditions.

Organizational Strategies

While specialization and academic departments tend to dominate the educational activities of the university, other missions can reach across disciplinary boundaries. For example, research grants flow to principal investigators or research groups rather than academic departments. Many funding agencies such as the National Science Foundation and the National Institutes of Health intentionally structure their grants to encourage the interdisciplinary work necessary to address many of the most significant scientific challenges. This cross-flow of sponsored research dollars counters to a degree the vertical flow of instructional dollars through the disciplines and creates a matrix organization. In many large research universities, the magnitude of research funding is comparable to instructional support (e.g., at Michigan, sponsored research activity is more than $800 million compared to $1.2 billion for instructional activities), creating powerful pressures that counter the centrifugal forces of the disciplines.

Our university has had a long tradition of interdisciplinary research centers and institutes that reach across disciplinary boundaries. However, we needed to go further than this, building alternative structures—physical, organizational, virtual—that drew together students, faculty, and staff. We invested heavily in new facilities aimed at integrating disciplinary learning and scholarship, for example, the $70 million Media Union, an integrative center drawing together students and faculty to explore the application of rapidly evolving technology in transforming learning and scholarship; the $350 million Life Sciences Institute integrating the biological, health, and nanosciences in creative disciplines; and an entire campus (the university's North Campus) colocating and integrating the creative disciplines (music, performing and visual arts, architecture, engineering, information sciences, and design). Similarly an effort was made to establish administrative "affinity clusters" at the level of the provost that drew together basic disciplines and key professional schools—for example, linking the social sciences more strongly with professional disciplines such as business, education, and social work; the humanities and classical studies with law; and the sciences more closely with applied science professions such as engineering and medicine.

Since the rapid evolution of information technology had undermined the traditional organization hierarchy by allowing point-to-point interaction (e.g., email, instant messaging, multicasting, podcasting), we sought a more strategic use of this technology to reorganize the university into more contemporary forms. The launch of major technology projects such as the university's management of the Internet backbone, the Sakai project to develop the open-source middleware platform for learning and scholarship, and most recently the Google project to digitize and distribute the complete holdings of our libraries (8 million volumes), were examples of strategic initiatives aimed at using this powerful and rapidly evolving technology to integrate the activities of the university and propagate its knowledge assets on a global scale.

We faced a quandary similar to other organizations in business and government: Should we centralize management to take advantage of economies of scale, standardization, and globalization? Or should we decentralize, seeking autonomy, empowerment, and flexibility at the level of unit execution, while encouraging diversity, localization, and customization? Our experience suggests both . . . and neither. There is no unique way to organize knowledge-based activities, although it is likely that most colleges and universities are currently far from an effective or optimal configuration. Furthermore, flexibility and adaptability are the watchwords for any such organization during a time of extraordinarily rapid technological change. The challenge is to orchestrate and coordinate the multiple activities and diverse talent on campus.

The key to achieving this is to build layered organization and management structures. At the highest, centralized level one should seek a clear institutional vision, driven by broadly accepted values, guided by common heuristics, and coordinated through standard protocols. Below this at the level of execution one should encourage diversity, flexibility, and innovation. In a sense, institutions should seek to centralize the guiding vision and strategy—that is, determining "where" the institution should head while decentralizing the decision process and activities that determine "how" to achieve these institutional goals. Put another way, universities should seek to synchronize rather than homogenize their activities. Rather than obliterating silos of activity, one should create porous walls between them through joint appointments, shared facilities (particularly laboratories and libraries), and common administrative support (Sawhney & Zabin, 2001).

Resource Strategies

The more constrained resource base facing higher education in recent years has already forced many institutions to abandon traditional approaches such as incremental budgeting. Moving from crisis to crisis or subjecting institutions to gradual starvation through across-the-board cuts simply is not an adequate long-term strategy. Instead universities must develop the capacity to set institution-wide priorities and allocate resources to these priorities. Since in the fragmented university most revenues are generated and costs incurred at the unit level, centralized resource management has become problematic. Yet moving to the other extreme of totally decentralized resource management—for example, "every tub on its own bottom"—loses the capacity to steer the ship, to address university-wide missions and priorities. Many universities, including Michigan, have moved instead to hybrid budgeting approaches such as Responsibility Center Management, which shares resource allocation decisions through a partnership between academic units, administrative units, and the central administration. In our case, we allowed units to keep the resources they generated, making them responsible for meeting the costs they incurred, and then levied a tax on all expenditures (usually 10% or less) along with the state appropriation to provide a central pool of resources necessary to support central operations (such as the university library) while enabling the university to address key institution-wide priorities and missions.

A somewhat more Machiavellian approach is to take advantage of market forces at the grassroots level by exploiting what one of my colleagues calls the "fish foodball theory" of faculty behavior. Normally faculty activities are randomly distributed, much like fish swimming in an aquarium. However, just as fish will suddenly align to go after a ball of food suspended in their tank, faculty members in the entrepreneurial university will quickly reprioritize their efforts to go after new resources, even if relatively modest in size. For example, to encourage faculty members to more aggressively seek sufficient indirect cost recovery on sponsored research grants, we simply provided them with a small account of purely discretionary funds proportionate to their indirect cost recovery (e.g., 5%). Even though indirect costs frequently came off the top of grants at the expense of research funding, these modest incentives (our "faculty foodball") rapidly increased indirect cost recovery and eventually stimulated sufficient grant activity to propel Michigan to national leadership in federal research funding.

Yet another example involved the university's effort to increase dramatically the presence of underrepresented minority faculty on our campus, a component of a far more ambitious effort to achieve social diversity on our campus known as the Michigan Mandate (Duderstadt, 2000). Traditionally, university faculties have been driven by a concern for academic specialization within their respective disciplines. Such priorities all too often lead to replacement searches rather than enhancement searches. To achieve the goals of the Michigan Mandate, the university had to free itself from the constraints of this traditional perspective. Therefore, the central administration sent out the following message to the academic units: Be vigorous and creative in identifying minority faculty candidates who can enrich the activities of your unit. Do not be limited by concerns relating to narrow specialization. Do not be concerned about the availability of a faculty hunting license within the academic unit. The principal criteria for the recruitment of a minority faculty member should be the absolute quality of a candidate and his or her potential contribution to the university itself. If so, both the base and startup funding necessary to recruit the candidate would be provided by the central administration.

There was another shoe to drop in this initiative. Since we did not have any sudden new wealth to support such hiring, we instead simply wrote IOUs to the successful programs as they hired new minority faculty. At the end of the year, we totaled up these commitments and then subtracted them from the top of the university budget for the next year. Through this mechanism those programs successful in recruiting new minority faculty would effectively be subsidized by those who sat on the sidelines. For example, it took several years before our large Department of Internal Medicine realized that its failure to recruit minority faculty resulted in them actually subsidizing the expansion of our Department of English Language and Literature into exciting new areas such as Caribbean literature.

A final example is provided by efforts to shift resources from ongoing disciplinary activities to new university-wide initiatives. In the 1980s, the university began to reallocate each year 1% of its base academic budget into a priority fund to support new initiatives. Although small as one-time funds, these were reallocations that effectively reduced the base support of ongoing programs to 99%, 98%, and 97%, shifting very significant resources from the status quo to new initiatives. This effort was expanded during the 1990s with additional funding from private gifts and directed toward funding initiatives addressing institution-wide priorities such as undergraduate education, diversity, interdisciplinary scholarship, and international programs. Usually the approach launched competitive grants programs in a particular area to stimulate activity at the grassroots faculty level. Many of these projects were sufficiently successful that they were later mainstreamed with base funding and additional external funding.

The lesson to be learned here is that academic leadership is most effective and powerful if it taps into the energy, interests, and creativity of the faculty at the grassroots level. Providing a fish foodball of resources to fund faculty initiatives aimed at broad university priorities such as undergraduate education or diversity creates market forces that align well with the highly entrepreneurial nature of the faculty culture.

A Shift in Management Culture

Most universities face a great challenge in getting faculty to commit to institutional goals that are not necessarily congruent with their professional and personal goals. Furthermore, perhaps because of the critical and deliberative nature of academic disciplines, universities have a hard time assigning decision-making responsibilities to the most appropriate level of the organization. The academic tradition of extensive consultation, debate, and consensus building before any substantive decision is made or action is taken is often incapable of keeping pace with the profound changes permeating higher education. In the private sector, change is usually measured in months, not years; at the university, change is sometimes even measured in decades. In the university, as the saying goes, change occurs one grave at a time.

Clearly universities need to develop greater capacity to move more rapidly. Yet imposing changes on the university management culture can be a most difficult and dangerous undertaking, particularly for a university president. For example, suppose a university administration becomes convinced that major reorganization of the institution is necessary. How should one go about it? One approach would be a simple top-down edict. For example, some institutions have simply announced a major restructuring in which the winners and losers are identified up front, and dissent is ignored or repressed. Yet this approach is problematic in the creative anarchy characterizing the contemporary university, since those disadvantaged by the decisions will attack the process rather than the outcome. Furthermore, it is usually difficult for the university leadership to have sufficient understanding of intellectual issues, particularly within the disciplines, to determine the best organization. Such top-down reorganization, while perhaps being an efficient way to respond to existing concerns, can result in new empires that will eventually dominate the institution and once again constrain change.

In particular, we need to challenge a deeply ingrained management culture in higher education in which academic leaders are expected to purchase the cooperation of subordinates by providing them with incentives to carry out decisions. For example, deans expect the provost to offer additional resources in order to gain their cooperation on various institution-wide efforts. This bribery culture is one of the major factors in driving cost escalation in higher education today. It is also quite incompatible with the trend toward increasing decentralization of resources. As the central administration relinquishes greater control of resource and cost accountability to the units, it will lose the pool of resources that in the past was used to provide incentives to deans, directors, and other leaders to cooperate and support university-wide goals.

Hence it is logical to expect that both the leadership and management of universities will need increasingly to rely on lines of true authority similar to those found in business or government. That is, presidents, executive officers, and deans will have to become comfortable with issuing clear orders or directives from time to time that override the anarchy of disciplinary units. Throughout the organization, subordinates will need to recognize that failure to execute these directives will likely have significant consequences, including possible removal from their positions. Here the intent is not to suggest that universities adopt a top-down corporate model inconsistent with faculty responsibility for academic programs and academic freedom. Collegiality should continue to be valued and honored. However, it is clear that the modern university simply must accept a more realistic balance between responsibility and authority.

Transformative Leadership

Leading the transformation of a highly decentralized organization is a quite different task than leading strategic efforts that align with long-accepted goals. Unlike traditional strategic activities, where methodical planning and incremental execution can be effective, transformational leadership must risk driving an organization into a state of instability in order to achieve dramatic change, whether responding to a time of crisis or unusual opportunity. Timing is everything, and the biggest mistake can be agonizing too long over difficult decisions, since the longer an institution remains in an unstable state, the higher the risks of a catastrophic result. It is important to minimize the duration of such instability, since the longer it lasts, the more likely the system will move off in an unintended direction or sustain permanent damage.

So how does one stimulate and lead the process of transformation in the fragmented university? Sometimes one can stimulate change simply by buying it with additional resources. More frequently transformational change involves first laboriously building a consensus across disparate units necessary for grassroots support. But there are also times when change requires a more Machiavellian approach, using finesse—perhaps even by stealth of night—to disguise as small wins actions that are in reality aimed at blockbuster goals. And there are times when, weary of the endless meetings with group after group to build consensus, including, at times, the institution's governing board, one is tempted instead to take the Nike approach and "just do it," that is, to move ahead with top-down decisions and rapid execution—although in these latter cases, the president usually bears the burden of blame and hence the responsibility for the necessary apologies.

Recognizing that sometimes a bold agenda will pull together a fragmented community to address a common purpose, we turned to a Michigan faculty member, C. K. Prahalad, for his concept of strategic intent (Hamel & Prahalad, 1996). The traditional approach to developing strategies focuses on the fit between existing resources and current opportunities. In contrast, a strategic intent is a stretch vision that intentionally creates an extreme misfit between current resources and future objectives that requires institutional transformation to build new capabilities. After considerable discussion across the university at various levels of faculty, students, staff, and our governing board, we finally adopted the strategic intent of providing the university with the capacity to reinvent itself as an institution more capable of serving a rapidly changing state, nation, and world (Duderstadt, 2000). Our earlier strategic efforts had required a careful optimization of the interrelated characteristics of institutional quality, size, and breadth. The strategic intent would require more: tapping the trailblazing spirit of the Michigan saga. It would emphasize risk-taking and innovation. It would demand the bold agenda of reinventing the university for a new era and a new world.

As the various elements of the transformation agenda came into place, our leadership philosophy also began to shift. We came to the conclusion that in a world of such rapid and profound change, as we faced a future of such uncertainty, the best way to achieve our strategic intent, to reinvent the university, was to explore possible futures of the university through experimentation and discovery. That is, rather than continue to contemplate possibilities for the future through study and debate, it seemed a more productive course to build several prototypes of future learning institutions as working experiments. In this way the university could actively explore possible paths to the future.

For example, we explored the possible future of becoming a privately supported but publicly committed university by completely restructuring our financing, raising more than $1.4 billion in a major campaign, increasing tuition levels, dramatically increasing sponsored research support to national leadership levels, and increasing our endowment tenfold. Ironically, the more state support declined as a component of our revenue base (dropping to less than 10% by the late 1990s), the higher our Wall Street credit rating rose, finally achieving the highest Aaa rating (the first for a public university).

Through a major strategic effort known as the Michigan Mandate, we altered very significantly the racial diversity of our students and faculty, doubling the population of underrepresented minority students and faculty over a decade and thereby providing a laboratory for exploring the themes of the "diverse university."

We established campuses in Europe, Asia, and Latin America, linking them with robust information technology, to understand better the implications of becoming a world university.

We played leadership roles first in the building and management of the Internet, then assisted in the creation of Internet2, and finally began efforts to develop the cyberinfrastructure necessary for a cyber-space university through efforts such as the Media Union, the Sakai middleware project, and the Google library digitization project to explore the implications of rapidly evolving technology on higher education.

Our approach as leaders of the institution was to encourage strongly a "let every flower bloom" philosophy, to respond to faculty and student proposals with "Wow! That sounds great! Let's see if we can work together to make it happen! And don't worry about the risk. If you don't fail from time to time, it is because you aren't aiming high enough!" We tried to ban the word *no* from our administrators.

Some of these experiments succeeded; others crashed in flames. Even in failure we learned much. Furthermore, while all these efforts were driven by the grassroots interests, abilities, and enthusiasm of faculty and students, they also were aimed at pulling together the university in a common cause. While such an exploratory approach was disconcerting to some and frustrating to others, fortunately there were many on our campus and beyond who viewed this phase as an exciting adventure. And these initiatives were important in understanding better the possible futures facing our university. All have influenced the evolution of our university.

Some Lessons Learned

There are many lessons, both good and bad, to be learned from our efforts at Michigan to lead the university toward common goals and a public purpose. Beyond the obvious challenges (build on institutional history; keep your eyes on the goals; be candid, demanding, and evidence-based in your appraisal of progress), there are other important aspects of any successful effort that relate more to the unique nature of academic communities.

First, it is important that since such efforts frequently involve institutional transformation, one should always begin with the basics by launching a careful reconsideration of the key roles and values that should be protected and preserved during a period of change. After all, the history of the university in America is that of a social institution, created and shaped by public needs, public policy, and public investment. It is the role of the president to stimulate this dialogue by raising the most fundamental issues involving institutional values.

Clearly the senior leadership of the university must buy in to the effort and fully support it. This includes not only the executive officers and deans, but also key faculty leaders. It is also essential that the governing board of the university be actively involved in the effort. This can require considerable consultation and persuasion. But everyone on the leadership team should be onboard when the transformation train leaves the station-or else be left behind.

It is important to provide mechanisms for active debate concerning the objectives and process by the campus community. At Michigan, we launched a series of presidential commissions on key issues such as the organization of the university, recruiting outstanding faculty and students, and streamlining administrative processes. Each of our schools and colleges was also encouraged to identify key issues of concern and interest. Effective communication throughout the campus community is absolutely critical for the success of institution-wide efforts. It is important to identify individuals at all levels, and in various units of the university, who will buy in to the agenda and become active agents on its behalf. In some cases, these will be the institution's most influential faculty and staff. In others, it will be a group of junior faculty or perhaps key administrators.

To be sure, significant resources are required to fuel such efforts, probably at the level of 5%–10% of the academic budget. During a period of limited new funding, it takes considerable creativity (and courage) to generate these resources. As noted earlier, since the only sources of funding at the levels required for such major initiatives are tuition, private support, and auxiliary activity revenues, reallocation becomes an important component of any strategy.

Large decentralized organizations such as universities will resist change. They will try to wear leaders down, or wait them out. Here one should heed the warning from Machiavelli (1532/1985):

> There is no more delicate matter to take in hand, nor more dangerous to conduct, nor more doubtful of success, than to step up as a leader in the introduction of change. For he who innovates will have for his enemies all those who are well off under the existing order of things, and only lukewarm support in those who might be better off under the new. (p. 27)

The resistance can be intense, and the political backlash threatening. Yet it is also clear that the task of leading the fragmented university toward institutional objectives cannot be delegated. Rather, the university president must play a critical role both as a leader and as an educator in such efforts to unify the campus community.

A Final Admonition _____

The decentralized structure of the university as a complex adaptive system has evolved over the centuries to solve extremely complex problems. Ironically, fragmentation sometimes serves a useful purpose, since within the confines of the institution it allows people to apply themselves to solve problems that are impossibly difficult for individuals or groups working in an institution-free environment. Again quoting Lohmann (in press),

> In its ideal form, the university will remain precariously poised between powerful academic, bureaucratic, political, and market forces, servant to none. On the one hand, the university must preserve a free space in which specialized and creative inquiry can flourish. On the other hand, it must be responsive to social and technological change.

What may appear to critics—particularly those from outside academe—as a badly flawed institutional structure is, in reality, one of the most valuable characteristics of the contemporary university. Comprehending the complex workings of this knowledge ecology is difficult for outsiders (and even those within academe). Over the centuries, powerful walls have sprung up (e.g., university autonomy, academic freedom, tenure) to prevent outsiders from tampering with the university's affairs.

While university leaders should seek to pull together the fragmented academic communities to address many of the public purposes of higher education, they should also bear in mind an important caveat: It could well be that the contemporary university is so resistant to efforts to fix its fragmentation not because remedies are insufficiently strategic and robust or leadership is inadequate, but rather because the contemporary university, evolving as it has over many centuries, has acquired the optimal configuration of a complex adaptive system as the natural and logical organization of a knowledge institution.

Hence, in seeking remedies for the fragmented university, it is important that university presidents always bear in mind the physician's warning, "First, do no harm!" Efforts to tamper with the longstanding intellectual structure of a university pose certain risks, particularly if inadequately informed by its values and traditions—that is, its institutional saga. Yet procrastination and inaction can also be a dangerous course, particularly during a time of great change. Timid, incremental approaches, while perhaps avoiding mistakes, can also miss opportunities. It is both the challenge and the responsibility of academic leadership to address this dilemma and achieve an appropriate balance between preserving those valuable attributes of the decentralized university while unifying the academic community in addressing its most fundamental purposes.

References

Clark, B. R. (1970). *The distinctive college: Antioch, Reed and Swarthmore.* Chicago, IL: Aldine.

Duderstadt, J. J. (2000). *A university for the 21st century.* Ann Arbor, MI: University of Michigan Press.

Duderstadt, J. J., & Womack, F. W. (2003). *The future of the public university in America: Beyond the crossroads.* Baltimore, MD: Johns Hopkins University Press.

Hamel, G., & Prahalad, C. K. (1996). *Competing for the future.* Boston, MA: Harvard Business School Press.

Lohmann, S. (in press). *How universities think: The hidden work of a complex institution.* Cambridge, England: Cambridge University Press.

Machiavelli, N. (1985). *The prince* (6th ed., D. Donno, Trans.). New York, NY: Bantam Classics. (Original work published 1532)

Sawhney, M., & Zabin, J. (2001). *The seven steps to nirvana: Strategic insights into eBusiness transformation.* New York, NY: McGraw Hill.

Wilson, E. O. (1998). *Consilience: The unity of knowledge.* New York, NY: Alfred A. Knopf.

4

Recreating the Faculty Role in University Governance

Roger Benjamin

It is not clear that the parts of the university add up to a greater whole. One of the problems is the fragmentation of faculty who are distributed in departments, schools, and colleges isolated one from the other. This fragmentation has led to the virtual collapse of governance in public universities, which causes a variety of serious problems. Aided by previous thinking, I will consider whether and how governance and faculty participation might be redefined in the public research university in a way that encourages more faculty participation (Benjamin, 2003; Benjamin & Carroll, 1997, 1998; Benjamin, Carroll, Jacobi, Krop, & Shires, 1993) The public research university seems ideal for this subject because it is where most graduate education takes place and thus develops the future professorate that teaches in other sectors of higher education (Steck, 2003).

If governance at the institutional level, now dormant in most public research universities, can be revived, albeit in a new form, perhaps the lessons can be applied elsewhere. Why is this issue an important question? Why not simply be content with the corporate model of university governance, which emphasizes efficiency in resource allocation and appears increasingly accepted? The answer is that the university does not produce private goods. It produces public goods. Attempts to limit decisions in universities to narrow market-like efficiency criteria are inappropriate in this setting. Public goods (in this case education, research, and services) cannot be reduced to simple exchanges between interested parties. Their production and consumption require many participants and much sharing in production and consumption to produce goods of high quality. Faculty involvement is needed to produce results of such quality.

I will attempt to show why this assertion has merit by distinguishing the roles of teaching and learning from research. In addition, I will introduce the role that general education and assessment might play in giving faculty members across the institution a common language they might use to reengage at the institutional level in public research universities. It should be clear at the outset that this chapter rests on a set of assumptions that lead to a possible scenario; it adopts the public choice approach (Benjamin, 1980; Harsanyi, 1969; Lindblom, 1990). Public choice adherents assume that institutional change is driven by the presence of mixes of incentives and sanctions that persuade individuals to respond. Conversely, they view cultural arguments as useful descriptions but not explanations of behavior. How do individuals and the institutions they inhabit change if they are not forced to make choices about the costs compared to the benefits of taking new action? Given these assumptions, public choice adherents (Hirschman, 1970; Hirschman & Rothschild, 1973) posit an ideal type, a synthesis gleaned from the "real" world that if realized would create the imperatives for change in individual and hence institutional behavior.

This chapter therefore proceeds in the following manner. After restating the problem of the decline of shared governance in universities, I develop a set of distinctions between research and undergraduate education. My argument here is that the research enterprise, especially sponsored research, has become too complex for consideration by the traditional structure of faculty senates. Apart from anything else, these bodies include the "have" and "have-not" professors when it comes to getting large research grants. Professors in the humanities, much of the social sciences, and several professional schools lack the opportunities for lucrative funded research. However, all faculty units do participate in undergraduate education, with the humanities and social sciences in featured roles. If faculty interest in undergraduate education can be raised from the department to the institutional level, it could revive a renewed interest by faculty senates in discussing and recommending university-wide policies on improving undergraduate learning, especially general education.

For this result to occur there must be strong incentives and/or the prospects of sanctions that entice or compel faculty to set their sights on improving teaching and learning at the institutional level. The positive incentives relate to the benefits accruing from raising the quality of undergraduate education—better retention and graduation rates and better incoming students over time. The potential negative sanctions in this case flow from the accountability movement in higher education that increasingly demands real evidence of student learning. I create an argument based on my understanding of the direction of this accountability movement and the probable or possible responses by the faculty in public research universities. It offers a plausible model—not a description—of the accountability and assessment literature in higher education. To be plausible, the model reflects my thinking about the intersections between accountability and assessment requirements. The utility of this chapter will depend on how much it encourages readers to think about the problem of spurring greater faculty participation in university-wide governance.

Governance

Elsewhere, I define governance as the decision-making units, policies and procedures, written and unwritten, that control resource allocation in universities and colleges (Benjamin et al., 1993). This characterization focuses on all the actors, both internal and external to the institution, who influence resource allocation. And resource allocation is not limited to financial resources but also includes the distribution of prestige, goal setting, and development and maintenance of the vision and mission of the institution.

Why Faculty Participation in University Governance Is Important

Faculty remain the critical lynchpin for the following:

- Deciding what curriculum is taught
- Choosing the pedagogy used
- Determining what departments and fields within them exist and their size and emphasis
- Deciding individually what research is stressed
- Defining and implementing the criteria and evaluation for determining the quality of faculty
- Defining functionally the standards of admissions and graduation for students

Because these factors define much of the activities of the university, without collective faculty support, explicit or at least tacit, deans, provosts, and presidents struggle or are ineffective. Another critical consideration is the public assumption by the collective faculty of the equality of all fields of knowledge within the university (Benjamin & Carroll, 1996). Though few individual professors believe all fields are equal, they are reluctant to argue publicly that any one field is less important than another. In part, professors want to avoid alienating colleagues in other departments. In addition, the salience of fields has often shifted. Physics was dominant in the early 20th century and microbiology grew in importance near the end of that century. Obscure fields in veterinary biology dealing with retroviruses became vital with the discovery of AIDS. Despite shifts in demands and importance of fields, professors are reluctant to recommend restructuring or cutbacks in other departments or colleges. The administration and trustees must therefore take the lead in reallocations as well as reductions because of the faculty's reluctance to cut publicly their colleagues' programs.

Despite this faculty reluctance, the administration cannot provide direction to public universities without persuading the faculty of the necessity for reductions and reallocation. The faculty need not participate in making cuts and shifts, but it must accept their necessity. A second point is that the board of trustees and the central administration formally set standards for admission and graduation. But the faculty implements and interprets the meaning of those standards. If there is not congruence between the definitions of those standards by the faculty and the administration, the goals of the administration and board of trustees are not achievable. In the end, the faculty implements the vision and mission statements of the institution they serve. If the faculty does not accept the vision and mission statements of the institution, they remain paper documents only. Finally, the developments in new and old fields of knowledge, as practiced by the faculty of a research university, create the sparks of innovation that produce paradigm shifts. Therefore, if the faculty is not involved in the governance of the university, the institution is diminished greatly because the administration is only a bureaucratic infrastructure dedicated to enabling teaching, research, and service. Any university becomes a hollow structure without the rich advice of its faculty about the university's goals based on their diverse knowledge from a range of fields.

The Challenge of the Changed Environment

There was a time, from before World War II until the early 1990s, when the increases in demands on colleges and universities roughly matched the growth in resources. In retrospect, growth in student enrollment and faculty positions seemed orderly and slow. Under these

conditions, each of the three major internal partners of university governance—trustees, administration, and faculty—played well-understood and mutually reinforcing roles. The three may have operated in
rough concert because of a general agreement about the nature and
goals of teaching and research—two of the central functions of the university (the other being service). The era before World War II preceded
the compact between the federal government and the university that
generated the extraordinary growth in large-scale research in the health
sciences, engineering, and a number of applied areas. It also predated
the focus of universities on externally funded research. Under these
conditions, professors across the university had an interest in seeing the
distribution of resources somewhat equitably across fields. In undergraduate education, a campus consensus at least tacitly existed, that students needed a common core of liberal education in order to graduate.
Faculty had an interest in participating in the senate that oversaw the
terms of engagement for undergraduate curriculum across the university.

Faculty played a strong role, through the faculty senate, along with
the administration and trustees and the trustees at the institutional
level. This process became known as shared governance (American
Association of University Professors, 1966). "As essential participants in
the governance process, each acts as a checks-and-balance mechanism
by which the power of the other is counterbalanced. Both better decisions and broader decision acceptance can be anticipated as a result"
(Del Favero, 2003, p. 906). Measures of success of the ideal arrangement include achievement of consensus and widespread acceptance
of decision-making (Benjamin & Carroll, 1998). Where did this ideal
occur? The answer is where memberships of faculty senates consisted of
distinguished faculty at the institution, and where administrations developed university policy in close collaboration with the faculty senate. The
assent of most top administrators from prominent roles in faculty senates exemplified this close cooperation.

In fact, a strong possibility of the breakdown of this ideal always
existed. The reason is that at least two of the participants—the faculty and
the administration—could and did claim the same piece of the governance pie: control of the allocation of resources in the broadest sense.
For example, administrators controlled the financial resources. Faculty
controlled the curriculum, who taught it and who should be recommended to teach it. Why did cooperation rather than conflict characterize the relationship between these two groups? There was a "traditional" environment in which supply and demand factors remained in
reasonable equilibrium, growing roughly the same rate until the 1990s.

But such stasis, if it ever really existed, has changed dramatically. Growth became exponential and diverse in demands for more research, both theoretical and applied. Student enrollment became more heterogeneous, especially in fields outside the traditional arts and sciences.

By comparison, the growth in the share of resources for public universities from state budgets has steadily declined. In the early years of the 21st century, acute budget cuts in many states have left public universities in the position of having to reduce funding for some programs. Moreover, the volatility of budgets and new demands for instruction and research make the classic shared governance model slow, inefficient, and inadequate to meet the demands of this competitive, dynamic world of public research universities. Under these conditions, state boards of higher education demand greater control (Carlin, 1999), the accountability movement grows, and apathy toward participation by professors in university governance increases (Lazerson, 1997). Shared governance appears, says Breneman (1995), poorly suited ". . . to the sorts of wrenching challenges that lie ahead" (p. 1). The question remains, what should replace it?[1]

During the 1950s and 1960s, the typical public research university grew substantially and the "multiversity" became the unquestioned organization (Kerr, 1995). With size comes economies of scale (so it is thought), greater efficiency, and greater effectiveness. Another term for this is *critical mass*. With great size comes a large faculty with differentiated skills and interests which, in turn, means that many more interests of students for instruction and potential clients for research can be accommodated. With great size also comes economies of scale regarding the development of one physical plant design team, say, for an entire state's higher education system, the facilities management group, the finance office, and so on. Moreover, the size and complexity of the faculty and ancillary enterprises grow dramatically as well (Benjamin et al., 1993). And, outside the institution, accrediting agencies, coordinating and system boards, the state legislature, and a variety of special interest and advocacy groups exert pressure, sometimes requiring the college to respond to demands ranging from the context and rigor of the curriculum to the number of books in the library.

Such size and complexity could only exist by ceding much of the academic governance to the academic departments. The concept, fully developed by the early 20th century, claimed that specialists in the fields of knowledge know best what to teach, who should teach what subjects, and what to do in research. Senior members of the departments know best what quality means in their fields and which professors deserve recommendations for promotion, tenure, and merit increases. Of course, deans and vice presidents had to agree, but they really held only the power to block, not initiate. And in any event, the department typically reports to a dean within a college, another separate unit in the university.

These colleges in research universities stand in isolation one from the other. Campus governance arrangements promote a departmental and not a university view of the critical issues of research focus and undergraduate education, especially that part accenting the liberal arts and sciences for all undergraduates. In most public research universities, the concept of a core curriculum as the venue for a liberal education has disappeared. Under such conditions, professors argue that their courses or their department major is the appropriate level of analysis for undergraduate education.

Incentives and rewards for professors are also department based in the research university. A primary reason is that research productivity determines the merit pay of faculty and their recommendations for promotion and tenure. And the senior members or chair of one's department determine the criteria to make judgments about the level of research productivity of individual professors. Multi- and interdisciplinary research centers increasingly join in this role of judging research. They are often formed to receive the external funding that drives many research programs and, in turn, the careers of scientists and engineers. Deans and provosts can confer on and deny promotion, tenure, or merit increases but departmental specialists who can best judge research results initiate the recommendation. Under these conditions of departmental or college dominance, the university becomes an abstract notion not of practical relevance to the day-to-day activities of professors. Departments, colleges, and multidisciplinary centers constitute the real world of recommendations and resources for professors.

The New Governance Challenges and Possibilities

Today, in a number of key areas, university leaders find themselves in uncharted territory. For example, priorities in research have shifted. Multidisciplinary research increasingly replaces single, department-based research at the frontiers of knowledge. The infrastructure for large-scale science has become so great that several entities have to fund these projects. Increasingly, those partnerships link universities and industry. The latter provides equipment, researchers, and funding, morphing such assets into virtual labs that allow both industrial and university scientists to work jointly on research programs. The leaders of such projects become successful scientific entrepreneurs who make their own arrangements and commitments with the central administration of universities and businesses and federal research agencies. Under these conditions, it is difficult if not impossible to figure out how to set research priorities for the faculty at the university level. However, undergraduate education—especially general education—may well be a different matter.

Undergraduate education in most public research universities has a bewildering number of majors and distribution requirements in general education. The concept of a core curriculum is typically absent. Under such conditions, faculty representatives on college- or university-wide curriculum committees engage in logrolling when voting on the new courses submitted for approval by other departments. They tend to vote yes in the hope and expectation that the other department representatives will reciprocate when their turn comes to submit proposed courses for approval. The result is a factionalized curriculum with no real incentive for faculty to focus on setting the institutional learning goals for undergraduates. Hence, faculty no longer focus on the quality of undergraduate education, and faculty senates no longer consider it a critical issue.

As noted earlier, the absence of comparative evaluation criteria for setting priorities for resource allocation constitutes a special challenge for university governance. In addition, a seemingly limitless number of internal and external actors have some claim, role, or influence on resource allocation. The net result is that the degrees of freedom for action in the university are reduced. The faculty role in governance becomes problematic because the institution no longer clearly governs itself in terms of the definition offered earlier. It is not surprising that distinguished professors do not participate in faculty senates, whose influence withers away. Indeed, fragmentation raises the question of whether it is even appropriate to speak of a university. The whole of the university is no longer clearly more than the sum of its parts.

The fall in state funding has not helped the unity of the university, since it encourages the production of self-generated income from research, tuition, and gifts at the college, school, and department levels. My prediction of the steady decline in the percentage of state budgets allocated to higher education has accelerated in the early years of the 21st century (Benjamin, 1998). All indications are that this trend will continue. Universities have attempted to make up the difference with tuition increases. These annual increases have been at or above 10% from 2002 to 2004 followed by stabilization of public university budgets in most states. There is increasing concern that upper limits exist to tuition growth, because they increase student debt and threaten access to postsecondary education by underrepresented groups. Faced with the prospect of continued financial erosion, all parties in public research universities have an incentive to maximize their claims on the university budget.

Higher Education as a Public Good

Higher education, particularly undergraduate education, is a public good. *Public good* means if the good is supplied to one individual it is supplied to all members of the community or class. Classic public goods are such items as national defense or K–12 education—if supplied to one American they are supplied to all. Similarly, the environment (good or bad), health, and education are thought of as public goods. In the real world of the 21st century, we know that the classic distinction formulated by Samuelson (1967) is not so clear. Public goods also produce private benefits. Private goods such as airlines produce public goods if a single airline serves a small community in a rural state.

Clearly, undergraduate education has been and should be treated as a public good served by a set of institutional arrangements called the university. We will explore the consequences of the erosion of this understanding of public goods. The obverse—private goods—are market based and the product of a simple transaction. Party A desires good B and party C supplies good B to party A at an agreed price. Both parties are presumably satisfied, otherwise they would not agree to the transaction. Public goods are not easily partitioned into sets of well-defined producers and consumers. That is why we call them public goods in the first place. We agree to tolerate ambiguity of production and consumption in public goods precisely because the good they bring is thought to be so critical to all members of society.

Differences of Faculty Research and Undergraduate Education

- The contribution of the individual to research can usually be ascertained, for example, by the quantity and quality of research papers, the size and number of research awards, and the number of citations.
- The contribution of the individual faculty member or even the individual department to the knowledge and skills acquired by graduates is not easy to ascertain. For example, grades vary from one faculty member to another, from department to department, and across colleges. General education skills in student learning are not generally assessed; courses and majors are, but these are difficult to compare.

University-wide research priorities can be established. However, based on the assumption of the equality of knowledge and department-based governance, it is understandably difficult for the faculty collectively through senates to contribute effectively to this process. Funding requirements to mount successful efforts in area A of science detract from the possibility of doing so in area B of science. Such conflicting interests may be why scientific entrepreneurs make their own arrangements with provosts and presidents. Although the public position of these officers claims the importance of undertaking research in all fields of knowledge, externally sponsored research gets most of the attention from the administration. The stability of funding of public as well as private research universities now increasingly depends on it. The administration may not resist research and scholarship in the social sciences, humanities, and some professional schools. But the provision of funding is where the assumption of the equality of knowledge stops for the central administration. Large-scale science projects, which generate significant external funding, dominate the decisions of presidents and provosts. Those decisions provide matching funds, commit faculty positions, and allocate money for laboratory equipment and space mainly for science, engineering, and medicine. In contrast, faculty senates, which represent the collective faculty, cannot realistically deal with research because it divides their constituency into haves and have-nots. As a result, faculty as a whole have a disincentive to participate in governance related to the research mission on a university-wide basis.

Undergratuate Education

Undergraduate education currently does not attract the attention of the university faculty. Little incentive exists for participation on a university-wide basis in deliberating on matters, such as the knowledge and skills graduates should possess and the means of assessing their achievement. But this neglect could change, for the following reasons.

Most university mission statements insist that their institution exists to improve critical thinking, analytic reasoning, and communication skills, or what may be called the skills of liberal or general education. These skills exhibit public good-like qualities. No one department course or major produces them and all graduates should have them. Professors may and do argue that since they do not teach these skills in their departments, they should not be evaluated for their achievement by students. Nor should assessment of student learning be focused on their acquisition. This position has carried the day until very recently. Now, employers, commentators, and observers of higher education increasingly argue that it is these public good-like skills that are precisely what undergraduate education should improve; that narrow content or specialization should not be the major focus of undergraduate education. Undergraduate education should teach students how to think and not just train them to be proficient in a specific academic field. From this perspective, the institution, not the department, becomes the focus of assessment because no one department produces or improves these skills. But such a shift would prove surprising given the history of the fragmenting university over the past 50 years.

The Case for the Whole

Departments are important. The majors they offer students are essential. But it may be time to also consider the institution as the key unit of academic analysis. Outsiders are certainly calling for it. Education is not only about specialized content, it is about teaching students how to think. All institutions commit to improving the critical thinking skills of their students. These sentiments are etched in most mission statements of colleges and universities. Employers increasingly call for improvements in the critical thinking, analytical reasoning, and communication skills of the graduates they hire. Surveys of the informed public indicate the same desire. It is the promise of the institution to improve these general education skills. In this sense, undergraduate education may be considered a candidate to be a public good again, if a way can be found to provide a discourse that faculty and administrators can use for communicating across departmental boundaries.

Undergraduate Education and University Governance

How can focusing on improving undergraduate education unite the faculty and renew university governance and faculty senates? First, we must view undergraduate education as a public good that produces improvements in the general education skills of critical thinking, analytical reasoning, and written communication. Next, to make faculty comfortable in focusing on improving undergraduate education, we must encourage the development of an assessment system that gives faculty the information needed to make effective changes in the curriculum, pedagogy, and other internal processes affecting undergraduate education.

It is admittedly a tall order to convince research university faculty to focus on improving undergraduate education and to create an appropriate assessment system to support that effort. How can we focus faculty attention on the quality of undergraduate education? And how can we promote the faculty senate as the venue for decision-making that fosters institutional improvements in undergraduate education? My approach is based on the public choice assumptions that incentives and sanctions (existing or the prospect of) drive individuals who make up collectives such as faculty to change their behavior. What follows is a sketch of an argument for focusing faculty thinking in a more systematic way on the quality of the general education component at the institutional level. I am not arguing this scenario will be played out tomorrow. We will see whether and when the argument gets played out in real time in public research universities.

Putting aside the questions of timing, I believe that undergraduate education will be gradually more differentiated from research, and that faculty will increasingly focus on the quality of undergraduate education at the institutional level.

This result may occur initially because of real and perceived accountability pressures but also because of the rewards associated with improving teaching and learning. I make the case for using an assessment approach to provide the discipline and common language necessary for the quality of undergraduate education to become a focal point of a strengthened role of faculty in university governance. This argument uses assessment as a method of reviving faculty governance.

The Argument

The "public" (taxpayers, legislators, and governors) wants to be assured that their college students are receiving a quality education. This interest in accountability is fueled by the same factors that have led to higher tuitions, namely shrinking state budgets and the increasing cost of higher education (Jones, 2003). In the past, institutions relied on accreditation reviews and various types of actuarial data, such as graduation and minority access rates, to demonstrate quality. That approach is no longer adequate for colleges, just as it no longer sufficient for K–12 education (as evidenced by No Child Left Behind legislation and the emphasis on statewide testing of students).

The public wants to know whether its education institutions are helping students acquire the knowledge, skills, and abilities they will need when they graduate (Immerwahr, 2000). In addition, policymakers increasingly want to know how much students actually have learned, not how much they believe that they have learned. Forty-four states have established accountability systems (Burke & Minassians, 2002) for higher education.[2] Seat time, course grades, and graduation rates are no longer sufficient. In short, the public is increasingly asking its colleges and universities to show that acceptable progress has been made in student learning.

To satisfy this demand for accountability, higher education institutions need to demonstrate that their students have acquired important skills and knowledge in addition to achieving other goals such as graduating, achieving necessary prerequisites for professional schools, and gaining employment. The only credible way to show such learning is to test them on what they are supposed to know and be able to do. Institutional ratings, student and faculty surveys, and other indirect proxies are just not sufficient. Instead, direct measures of outcomes are needed. Colleges and universities already assess students, but hardly ever for the purpose of demonstrating the value the institution adds to a student's knowledge and skills. At least until recently, their reasons for testing have had nothing to do with accountability. Instead, colleges and universities have tested incoming students to make sure they have the skills needed for coursework. Students with insufficient skills are generally placed in remedial programs. In addition, some colleges administer tests at the end of the sophomore year to make sure students are ready for their upper-division studies. These so-called rising junior exams, like the initial placement tests, focus on basic reading, writing, and math skills. They focus on the individual student without attempting to measure the contribution of the institution to student learning.

Some colleges are now expanding their testing programs to include assessing other abilities, such as critical thinking skills, that are central to the college's mission but cut across academic majors. College administrators see this as a way to demonstrate the beneficial effects of the educational experiences at their institutions to prospective students and their parents.[3] Nevertheless, most institutions continue to rely on their faculty—individually not collectively—to assess their students' content knowledge and skills.

This approach satisfies the faculty, who generally believe professors already provide sufficient and appropriate assessments of student learning. They use midterm and final exams, term papers, classroom participation, and other evidence to assign grades. And they feel these grades reflect how much students learn in their courses.[4]

Unfortunately, professor grades are idiosyncratic. Two courses with the same title may cover different content, even at the same college. There also are large differences in grading standards among professors across colleges. What constitutes B work at one school may correspond to A or C work at another institution. The same is true across professors within an institution.[5] There also has been substantial grade inflation over time.[6] Hence professor-assigned grades cannot be relied on to provide a valid measure of whether the students in one graduating class are more or less proficient than those in another class or at another college. Nor are value-added comparisons made of the contributions of institutions to growth in student learning from entry to exit. Some other metric is needed.

The search for another index has led some colleges to experiment with portfolios, grades in capstone courses, or other institution-specific indicators of learning (Banta, Lund, Black, & Oblander, 1996). However, all these measures have the same fundamental limitation as regular course grades, namely, the absence of a way to interpret reliably and validly scores outside the context of a particular course or school at a given point in time. To correct this problem, the measures have to be administered under the same standardized conditions to everyone and the scores obtained have to be adjusted for possible variation in average question difficulty, reader leniency, and other factors. Locally constructed measures, such as course grades or portfolios, do not have these essential features and therefore cannot be used for making valid comparisons within institutions over time or for comparisons among institutions at a single point in time.

Those limitations are not present with the measures that are used for statewide K–12 testing (such as the Stanford-9, Iowa Tests of Basic Skills, and the National Assessment of Educational Progress), college and graduate school admission decisions (such as the SAT, ACT, GRE, and LSAT), or licensing exams in the professions (such as accountancy, law, medicine, and teaching). Thus, when results really matter, such as for high-stakes decisions about individuals, procedures are used that help to eliminate the effects of extraneous factors, such as who drafted the questions or scored the answers.

The Role of the State

States have a legitimate and critical role in assuring accountability in their higher education institutions. Many states set objectives for educational levels to be achieved by entering students; participation rates by ethnic/racial groups; minimum passing scores for law, medicine, and other professional schools; and numbers of graduates in particular fields to be achieved such as teaching, nursing, and technology.[7]

The states also provide the instructional budgets for public undergraduate education and infrastructure support, including buildings, libraries, and scientific equipment. States clearly have a right and a responsibility to require accountability from the institutions they support. Why, then, are we not further ahead in developing assessment systems of student learning that work from the point of view of the institutions and the states?

The problem is that the assessment measures used at the institutional level differ from most of the accountability indicators favored by states. First, the concept of accountability must be specified. Most broadly, in the context of higher education, accountability can be defined as the extent to which public higher education institutions meet the goals set for them by the state. (In the best case these goals are mutually agreed to by both parties.) Just as faculty and institutions set assessment goals for a variety of purposes, states set accountability goals for different purposes. Most states desire accountability for prudent use of resources, or at the very least, absence of fraud. Some state leaders demand evidence of increased participation, retention, and graduation rates for underrepresented groups. Still others, an increasing number, want to be assured that students have gained knowledge and skills from their educational experiences. Approaches and measures of student learning favored by faculty differ from those preferred by state leaders. Here we focus on this last goal of state-based accountability, evidence of student learning outcomes (Naughton, Suen, & Shavelson, 2003).

Approaches to student learning outcomes by faculty have the following characteristics:

- Their goals are to improve curriculum and pedagogy as well as set targets for students.
- They focus on individual students, departments, or to a lesser extent institutions but not on inter-institutional comparisons.
- They are content rich, tailored to the context of the institution, and generated by faculty themselves and are often time intensive and costly.
- Because the emphasis is on content, they tend not to be replicable from one institution to the next.

In comparison, state-based approaches are:

- Focused on accountability objectives
- Aggregated at the regional or state level and ideally replicable and comparable across institutions
- Centered on indirect proxies of student learning outcomes such as the percentage of passing rates for teaching examinations
- Inclusive of teacher, nurses, and other professional school examinations; number and percentage of students that take the GRE; retention and graduation rates

- Poor in content or tailored to the context of the individual institutions and not developed by faculty
- Use cost-effective methods, making use of existing data

The result is a disconnect between the faculty and institutions on the one hand and the state on the other.

Assesment Principles

The assessment principles adhered to by institutions need to be comparative based in some manner and focused on general education skills in order to respond to the accountability requirements. Here is what that would entail.

Measures whose scores are interpretable across professors, colleges, and time allow relevant comparisons to be made within and between institutions. For example, the scores on such measures can be used along with grades on other tests (such as the SAT or ACT) to assess whether the students at a school are doing better or worse on an outcome measure than would be expected given their entry-level skills. Measures that are applicable across institutions also may serve as benchmarks for interpreting the results with similar but locally constructed instruments or course grades. Measures that are designed to permit comparisons across institutions thus provide a signal of academic performance (and therefore a motivator for change). Such signaling can indicate whether the faculty and administrators need to take a closer look at the resources, curriculum, pedagogy, and programmatic structure underlying undergraduate teaching and learning. In short, such measures may help colleges document the progress they are making in fostering student learning. The measures also may contribute to improving academic programs by providing institutions with baseline and outcome scores to help identify the effects on learning of programmatic and curricular changes.[8]

To accomplish these ends, cross-institutional measures must have certain essential characteristics. The scores must be reliable in the sense that they are not overly affected by chance factors. If the results are aggregated to the university level (such as to providing information about programs), then the degree of reliability required to identify effects is much less than would be needed for making decisions about individual students. The scores must be valid in the sense of providing information about student characteristics that are important to the institution's goals, such as improving their students' ability to communicate in writing and to think critically about issues. The tests themselves must be fair to all takers, that is, regardless of the students' demographic or other characteristics. Finally, results have to be reported to students and institutions promptly and in a way that is understandable to the recipients and facilitates decision-making.

The process of implementing such measures at the university level is fraught with land mines. For instance, any top-down effort to impose them on faculty and students is likely to run into trouble.[9] Instead, it will be essential for the academic community to see them as a valuable adjunct to its own measures or even embed them into capstone courses. Similarly, attempts to use the results to punish institutions for having less than stellar or even average improvement scores would stop the assessment effort in its tracks. Instead, the results need to be used to identify best practices that other institutions could try as well as to spot potential problem areas where additional support is needed. In addition, the measures themselves must be intrinsically interesting and engaging so that students will be motivated to participate in the assessment activities and to try their best to do well.

It is not feasible to measure all or even most of the knowledge, skills, and abilities that are central to college or university learning goals. Much of what is learned takes place outside the classroom. This situation leads to the concern that what is tested will be overly emphasized in the institution's instructional programs. In short, some will say that the only abilities that count are the ones that are measured. This position is akin to saying "You shouldn't measure anything unless you can measure everything." This concern can be addressed by varying the types of measures used over time and by augmenting the measures that are used across institutions with local program-specific instruments.

States are increasingly developing assessment systems that emphasize accountability. Resistance by faculty to accountability-oriented systems of assessment (ones focused on indirect, proxy measures of student learning) also continues and is unlikely to change. This reaction is unfortunate, even problematic if, as I believe, the state-level demand for accountability is only going to grow. We should reject the argument that the unit of analysis for accountability must be only the state (Callan, Doyle, & Finney, 2001; Callan & Finney, 2003; National Center for Public Policy in Higher Education, 2000) or the argument that the unit must only be the institution (Banta et al., 1996). How might we reconcile the implications of the two units of analysis? The prime focus of accountability should be on student learning. And it is the growing insistence on the part of the state that institutions be held accountable for the quality of their student learning that, I predict, will drive faculty to implement the principles of assessment noted above in the service of an increased focus on the quality of general education at their institution.

If the growing pressure convinces faculty to focus more attention on the quality of general education, representatives of the state and institutions will need to work out the equivalent of a legal agreement that both parties will implement. These rules of engagement must give both parties incentives to cooperate. What should the rules of engagement be? There must be agreement on the measures to be used. The measures must meet faculty objectives but the ability for inter-institutional comparison should be built in to satisfy the needs of the state. Although the two parties need to agree on common measures to be used, their goals are different. Since faculty are primarily interested in assessment for educational improvement while the state is primarily interested in assessment for external accountability, the two parties will need to reach agreement on what information from the assessments may be aggregated at the regional or state level.[10]

Relations between the institution and the state will improve immensely if there is agreement that the initiative should focus on increasing the value-added contribution of the institution to general education skills over time rather than on absolute levels achieved. Indeed, if there is agreement that the value-added approach is appropriate, there can be a time lag built in during which institutions identified as being below minimum levels of quality can be asked to show improvement over a several-year period. Since institutions, as well as the state, are interested in demonstrating that they are improving, this strategy should provide common ground between the two groups.

Bridging the Disconnect Between Assessment and Accountability

There is a disconnect in assessment and accountability goals focused on student learning between the institution and the state. Can it be overcome by the state exerting control through its levers of power—that is, the power of the purse or regulation? Probably not, or, to put it another way, the result would certainly be a pyrrhic victory with no winners on either side. Can the disconnect be bridged? The answer is yes. It appears that, increasingly, state leaders will be judged on how well they improve the skills of their workforce to make their states more competitive economically.[11] Faculty and administrators will come to recognize the right of state political leaders to be concerned about the quality of undergraduate education. As a result, they will accept the right of states to set goals for improvement in student learning outcomes at their public colleges and universities. Eventually, along with the growing recognition that the role of the state in setting goals is reasonable, should also flow state-based incentives, accepted by higher education leaders as appropriate, to encourage their public higher education institutions to meet those goals. This result will occur because of growing recognition, by all parties, that human capital is the most important asset possessed by a region, state, or nation (Krueger, 2003). However, in the case of higher education, reliance on the experts (the faculty) to define the most appropriate methods of assessment is, necessarily, a prerequisite to success. This recognition of the need to work together by faculty and administrators at the university on the one hand, and state leaders on the other, may well take some time and the road getting there will likely be bumpy. However, if human capital is as important as we believe, state and national leaders will ultimately be entrusted with the task of setting standards for improvement in student learning. If we reach a wider consensus on how to implement this principle, we will be able to develop policies and practices in assessment that benefit the institution and the state and, most importantly, the citizens they both serve.

A New Role for the Faculty Senate

If public universities start down this road, a number of important policy questions must be answered. And these questions, I believe, will call for substantial faculty input, again, on an institution-wide basis.

1) Assuming the assessment done uncovers the need for improvements, what, if any, assessment data should be made public to outside agencies and on what terms?

This question enters uncharted territory. State commissions and departments of higher education are calling for evidence of performance. To date, faculty have generally resisted their requests; or the data collected has been sufficiently far from the classroom that faculty can ignore the process of data collection and the results. Faculty might well react differently if data on direct measures of cognitive learning, as discussed earlier, are assembled. Faculty will probably wish to use the information for formative assessment purposes. State officials will want to use the information for summative, evaluative purposes.

The rules for what data should be reported publicly and to whom can be sorted out. But there must be a real bargaining process, with faculty involved in this negotiation. Where else would the faculty make their case than in a representative assembly such as the faculty senate?

2) Assuming the assessment results cover all the programs, departments, and colleges in the public research university, what role, if any, should they play in resource allocation?

For example:

- Should more funding go to units that have lower results from the assessment of student learning to improve them?
- Should units that do well on the same measures get more resources to reward them?
- Should instructor/student ratios be lowered in order to improve student learning outcomes?
- Should there be fundamental changes in the curriculum on a university-wide basis, for example, establishment of a core curriculum?
- Should there be changes in pedagogy?

These and related questions need the input of the faculty if the university is to respond to them properly. What other venue makes sense than the faculty senate? Since there are a variety of questions, there would be increased business for the senate education committee, the budget committee, and the committee on facilities and instructional equipment. Since the humanities and social sciences faculties, by definition, play an important role in the undergraduate curriculum, heightened attention to improving teaching and learning should raise the profile of these parts of the faculty.

If the movement to focus on general education skills in addition to courses and majors succeeds, institutional forums will again become the venue for deliberation and recommendations by faculty across the university. If the faculty senate is nonexistent or moribund, it will have to be recreated to provide such a venue. If this comes to pass, there will be a variety of side benefits that will reconnect the faculty and the administration in public research universities. And that will be a good thing.

A Not So Modest Proposal

The time has come to offer a proposal that could not only revive university-wide faculty governance in faculty senates but also the central importance of the arts and sciences faculty on campus. It could also breathe new and needed life into student learning assessment.

1) Faculty or university senates should once again take charge of the goals, courses, content, and outcomes of general education.

No single move could do more to fix the fragmented university at the undergraduate level, answer the complaints of external critics about learning outcomes of graduates, or restore the arts and sciences faculty to their appropriate role in university governance and undergraduate education. The proposal focuses on general education because that is the collective responsibility for the faculty—especially in the arts and sciences, while academic majors belong to the diverse departments.

> *2) Senates should appoint a blue-ribbon faculty commission of leading professors—largely from the arts and sciences—to propose the goals, content, and outcomes of general education.*

Such a step would end the common practice in public research universities of leaving general education requirements to the determination of colleges and schools for their own majors. These commissions should draw heavily on the excellent work in general education of the Association of American Colleges and Universities (AAC&U). This group notes that employers and academics already agree on the desirable outcomes of general education (AAC&U, 2005). It includes the intellectual and practical skills of written and oral communication; inquiry and critical and creative thinking; quantitative and information literacy; teamwork; and the integration of learning. The knowledge derived from general education should also involve an appreciation of the arts and humanities, the social sciences, and the sciences and mathematics.

> *3) That commission—with assistance of faculty and staff experts in evaluation and institutional research—should develop the multiple methods for assessing, systematically and periodically, the extent to which graduates actually acquire that knowledge and those skills, and propose how to use the results to improve institutional performance.*

Reliable information and evaluation techniques are the hallmarks of scholars. This proposal would ask leading scholars in the arts and sciences to bring the same tools they use in research to evaluating the knowledge and skills acquired by students during their college years.

Not Probable, But Possible and Desirable

Academic skeptics will sneer at both the possibility and the desirability of this proposal. Even campus realists, looking at the record, may well deny the possibility of this proposal, while perhaps accepting its desirability. Both will doubtless pose that fateful question: What will make faculty senates and the faculty in the arts and sciences tackle now what they have assiduously avoided for decades—addressing and assessing general education?

The answer is simple. Taking charge of general education and assessing its results is now in the self-interest of the arts and sciences faculty, especially those from the arts, humanities, social sciences, and the sciences with limited opportunities for funded research and less than burgeoning demands for undergraduate enrollments.

Four potent forces are coalescing to make the adoption of this proposal possible, if not probable: pressure, power, prestige, and payoff.

Pressure

The pressure, especially on public research universities, to both demonstrate and improve the knowledge and skills of undergraduates has never been stronger. State, business, civic, and now federal leaders are demanding it. Faculty leaders probably accept the skills and knowledge listed earlier as the goals of general education. But they have clashed over the methods or courses that best achieve those objectives and have resisted assessing learning outcomes, especially those that require or encourage institutional comparisons. Clearly, the faculty, especially in public research universities, does not want to assess student learning outcomes.

One prospect may well change the faculty's position. That is the growing probability that outsiders will impose the goals of undergraduate learning and the methods of assessing their achievement. Either the faculty will do it, or outsiders will do it for them. Faced with that choice, the faculty will decide to do it.

Power

The faculty in most of the arts, humanities, social sciences, and even some science disciplines cannot be happy with the way that the professional schools have hijacked general education, or dismissed its importance in the name of job training. (That unhappiness hides their own preference for specialized courses in their disciplines over their responsibility for general education.) How it must grate on professors in those areas to read on their university web sites that students should look at the listings of their colleges and schools to discover the course requirements of general education.

Taking charge of general education and its assessment is not only a self-defense against outside imposition, it is the way to power in faculty governance. The move to have faculty senates and arts and sciences faculty take charge of general education and assessment will win strong support from trustees, presidents, and provosts. Given the numbers of professors in the arts and sciences, they often have majorities in the faculty senates. The way to power is clear. Arts and sciences faculty have the numbers and the expertise. All they need is the will.

Prestige

Once, the prestige on campus went to the liberal arts and sciences for their special contribution to undergraduate education. Now the shift of prestige mostly to sponsored research has especially diminished the position of professors in the arts, humanities, and the social sciences, where large research grants are scarce.

The fragmentation of general education, along with the university, has ended that special position of the arts and sciences. It has prevented the arts and sciences faculty from getting the benefits from their natural accent on synthesis and connections across the disciplines, which should bring prestige when problems both theoretical and applied fall increasingly in the connections among the disciplines. Prestige in an age of collaboration, cooperation, and connection should go to the faculty in the arts and sciences. But first that group must ensure that the general education conveys those connections and that graduates can use them to solve complex problems.

Payoff

Even the most idealistic professors at this point might well say "Power and prestige are fine but what about the financial payoff?" There is money in taking charge of general education. Governors and legislators would reward well a public university that identified the knowledge and skills expected of its graduates and assessed the extent of their achievement. In turn trustees, presidents, and provosts would happily provide funding for a program that responded in an academically responsible way to those demands for accountability. Presidents and provosts know that only the faculty can and should develop such a program. Clearly, they would reward the effort.

Another possible result is that a new metric for faculty rewards other than research productivity may emerge. The way it might work is that financial incentives are offered to faculty participating in general education in response to their achieving demonstrated improvements as measured by value-added growth, answering the question of how much improvement in the growth in general education skills of students occurs. Thus the arts and sciences faculty could receive some part of their merit pay increases based on the contribution to general education.

Another funding benefit is not so obvious. Not all departments in the arts and sciences can attract large research grants or increasing student majors, which these days produce the lion's share of departmental funding. Tuition is a rising source of income in public research universities as they increase enrollment to close the gap in revenues from the fall in state funding. To encourage such self-generated income, many universities have adopted variations of Responsibility Center Management or budgeting that allow colleges and schools to keep most of their earned income. Some of these systems give most of the tuition income to the units that register the majors. The University of Michigan has taken a different tack that could increase the financial payoff to colleges, schools, and presumably departments in the arts and sciences enrolling general education students. It allocates 75% of the tuition income to course enrollments rather than major registrations (Michigan Engineering, 2004). Such a provision could prove a real boon to arts and sciences departments offering attractive courses that fulfill the general education requirements.

A Final Thought

Daniel Burnham, a Chicago architect at the end of the 19th century, challenged his colleagues "to make no small plans." Now is the time for public research universities to once again think big with the breadth, style, and verve that once characterized governance proposals from the faculty in the liberal arts and sciences. This not so modest proposal seeks to save general education from specialized training, silence the external critics on student learning, and revive academic senates as centers of university governance. Even in this age that glorifies multitasking, that is no small plan. But perhaps it is a proposal big enough to interest the arts and sciences faculty in public research universities.

Acknowledgments
The section of this chapter titled "The Argument" owes much to my colleague Stephen Klein.

Endnotes
1) See several chapters in Tierney (2004) that extend this point.
2) See Naughton, Suen, and Shavelson (2003), who recorded 227 indictors related, in some way, to student learning. See also *Measuring Up* (National Center for Public Policy and Higher Education, 2002), which gives student learning an incomplete for all the states. The

regional accrediting association now requires evidence of the quality of student learning. See the web discussion of this topic by the Western Association of Schools and Colleges (www.acswasc.org/about_crite ria.htm). See also the publications and activities devoted to this subject by the national accrediting body, Council for Higher Education Assessment.

3) The number of colleges developing general education programs is rising, led by national associations of higher education such as the Association of American Colleges and Universities (2002). And most colleges embed the goal of increasing these skills in their mission statement. See also Immerwahr (2000) for a discussion of the expectations of parents and students about higher education.

4) Moreover, although attendance at meetings on higher education assessment held by groups such as the Association of American Colleges and Universities has increased in recent years, we believe most faculty remain skeptical of the kind of assessment discussed here.

5) For example, Klein, Kuh, Chun, Hamilton, and Shavelson (2005) developed a method to deal with the problem of widely divergent grading patterns across institutions. They converted GPAs within a school to z-scores and then used a regression model (that included the mean SAT score at the student's college) to adjust the correlations with GPAs for possible differences in grading standards among colleges.

6) For example, Harvard University, where, until 2005, 90% of the undergraduate students were deemed honors students, is, like other institutions, attempting to cope with the problem of grade inflation. (Donadio, 2005).

7) See the master plans of state higher education coordinating commissions or governing boards of state higher education systems, for example, Texas and Nevada.

8) With at least two noteworthy exceptions—(the Cooperative Institutional Research Program and the National Survey of Student Engagement)—efforts at higher education assessment have focused on developing approaches and instruments that deal with individual courses or majors that are often diagnostic in nature. However, one needs assessment data that permits comparison in order to successfully conduct formative assessment within institutions. The variation in learning goals and teaching approaches is enormous across American higher education. How can one know how well an institution is faring unless one compares the performance of the institution with that of other institutions?

9) Norms ceding power to faculty on key issues remain strong. These norms were developed over time in the wake of the construction of the modern American university during the last quarter of the 19th century. Graduate research functions were married to the undergraduate mission. That move created the basis for the professional development of the doctorate as the final degree for faculty along with the recognition that only those who received the Ph.D. in their field should make decisions about the issues noted earlier. Central administrators and boards of trustees may decide the size of the undergraduate enrollment, the resources that go to each department or college. However, the faculty must rule on curriculum matters, including whether and how to assess its quality.

10) On the relationship between assessment focused on the formative (the institutional focus) versus the summative (the state focus), the literature on this subject with respect to K–12 assessment is instructive. See William and Black (1996) and Shepard (2003).

11) For example, see the publications devoted to aspects of this topic on the National Governors Association (NGA) web site (www.nga.org). The NGA is the official association for the 50 state governors.

References

American Association of University Professors. (1966). *Statement on government of colleges and universities.* Retrieved August 9, 2006, from www.aaup.org/statements/Redbook/Govern.htm

Association of American Colleges and Universities. (2002). *Greater expectations: A new vision for learning as a nation goes to college.* Washington, DC: Author.

Association of American Colleges and Universities. (2005). *Liberal education outcomes: A preliminary report on student achievement in college.* Washington, DC: Author.

Banta, T. W., Lund, J. P., Black, K. E., & Oblander, F. W. (1996). *Assessment in practice: Putting principles to work on college campuses.* San Francisco, CA: Jossey-Bass.

Benjamin, R. (1980). *The limits of politics: Collective goods and political change in postindustrial societies.* Chicago, IL: University of Chicago Press.

Benjamin, R. (1998, March/April). Looming deficits: Causes, consequences, and cures. *Change, 30*(2), 12–17.

Benjamin, R. (2003, January). The environment of higher education: A constellation of changes. *The Annals of the American Academy of Political and Social Science, 585*(1), 8–30.

Benjamin, R., & Carroll, S. (1996, December). Impediments and imperatives in restructuring higher education. *Educational Administration Quarterly, 32*, 705–719.

Benjamin, R., Carroll, S. (1997). *Breaking the social contract: The fiscal crisis in California higher education.* Santa Monica, CA: RAND.

Benjamin, R., & Carroll, S. (1998). The implications of the changed environment for governance in higher education. In W. G. Tierney (Ed.), *The responsive university: Restructuring for high performance* (pp. 92–119). Baltimore, MD: Johns Hopkins University Press.

Benjamin, R., Carroll, S., Jacobi, M., Krop, C., & Shires, M. (1993). *The redesign of governance in higher education.* Santa Monica, CA: RAND.

Breneman, D. (1995). *Higher education: On a collision course with new realities.* Washington, DC: Association of Governing Boards of Colleges and Universities.

Burke, J. C., & Minassians, H. (2002). *Performance reporting: The preferred "no cost" accountability program.* Albany, NY: The Rockefeller Institute of Government.

Callan, P. M., Doyle, W., & Finney, J. E. (2001, March/April). Evaluating state higher education performance. *Change, 33*(2), 10–19.

Callan, P. M., & Finney, J. E. (2003). *Multiple pathways and state policy: Toward education and training beyond high school.* San Jose, CA: National Center for Public Policy and Higher Education.

Carlin, J. F. (1999, November 5). Restoring sanity in an academic world gone mad. *The Chronicle of Higher Education*, p. A76.

Del Favero, M. (2003, March). Faculty-administrator relationships as integral to high-performing governance systems. *American Behavioral Scientist, 46*(7), 902–922.

Donadio, R. (2005, March 27). The tempest in the ivory tower [Review of the books *Harvard Rules* and *Privilege*]. *The New York Times*, p. 12.

Harsanyi, J. C. (1969). Rational-choice models of political behavior vs. functionalist and conformist theories. *World Politics, 21*(4), 513–538.

Hirschman, A. O. (1970). *Exit, voice, and loyalty: Responses to decline in firms, organizations, and states.* Cambridge, MA: Harvard University Press.

Hirschman, A. O., & Rothschild, M. (1973, November). The changing tolerance for economic inequality in the course of economic development. *Quarterly Journal of Economics, 87*(4), 544–566.

Immerwahr, J. (2000). *Great expectations: How the public and parents—white, African-American, and Hispanic—view higher education*. San Jose, CA: National Center for Public Policy and Higher Education.

Jones, D. (2003). *State shortfalls projected throughout the decade*. San Jose, CA: National Center for Public Policy and Higher Education.

Kerr, C. (1995). *The uses of the university* (5th ed.). Cambridge, MA: Harvard University Press.

Klein, S. P., Kuh, G., Chun, M., Hamilton, L., & Shavelson, R. (2005, May). An approach to measuring cognitive outcomes across higher education institutions. *Research in Higher Education, 46*(3), 251–276.

Krueger, A. B. (2003). *Education matters: A selection of essays on education*. London, England: Edward Elgar.

Lazerson, M. (1997, March/April). Who owns higher education? The changing face of governance. *Change, 29*(2), 10–15.

Lindblom, C. E. (1990). *Inquiry and change: The troubled attempt to understand and shape society*. New Haven, CT: Yale University Press.

Michigan Engineering, Division of Resource Planning and Management. (2004). *Understanding the UM budget model and CoE's operating budget*. Retrieved August 18, 2006, from the Michigan Engineering, Resources Planning and Management web site: www.engin.umich.edu/admin/rpm/fin/Understanding_the_UM_and_CoE_Budget_Models.ppt

National Center for Public Policy and Higher Education. (2000). *Measuring up 2000: The state-by-state report card for higher education*. San Jose, CA: Author.

National Center for Public Policy and Higher Education. (2002). *Measuring up 2002: The state-by-state report card for higher education*. San Jose, CA: Author.

Naughton, B. A., Suen, A. Y., & Shavelson, R. J. (2003). *Accountability for what? Understanding the learning objectives in state higher education accountability programs*. Paper presented at the Annual Meeting of the American Educational Research Association, Chicago, IL.

Samuelson, P. (1967, Fall). In determinacy of governmental role in public—good theory. *Papers on Non-Market Decision Making, 3,* 47.

Shepard, L. A. (2003). Reconsidering large-scale assessment to heighten its relevance to learning. In J. M. Atkin & J. E. Coffey (Eds.), *Everyday assessment in the science classroom* (pp. 41–59). Arlington, VA: National Science Teachers Association Press.

Steck, H. (2003, January). Corporatization of the university: Seeking conceptual clarity. *The Annals of the American Academy of Political and Social Science, 585*(1), 66–83.

Tierney, W. G. (Ed.). (2004). *Competing conceptions of academic governance: Negotiating the perfect storm.* Baltimore, MD: Johns Hopkins University Press.

William, D., & Black, P. (1996, December). Meanings and consequences: A basis for distinguishing formative and summative functions of assessment? *British Educational Research Journal, 22*(5), 537–548.

5

Strategic Direction and Decentralization in Public Research Universities

Daniel James Rowley, Herbert Sherman

Strategic planning is, ironically, a management process that is well known but not well understood, though it is certainly better understood in business than in higher education. Part of the reason for this condition is that strategic planning should be tailored specifically to a given industry, and then fitted for an individual organization. The point of strategic planning is to align better the organization with its most crucial environments and assure that it can produce a revenue surplus and support growth while pursuing the organization's mission. Strategic planning has the same purpose for businesses, nonprofit organizations, and public research universities, although their missions are quite different (Rowley, Sherman, & Armandi, 2006). However, different industries face different internal and external challenges. For strategic plans to be successful in any organization, planners need to recognize these differences as they develop their long-term premises, and then formulate their plans. This caution about difference is especially true for colleges and universities.

Colleges and universities are no strangers to strategic planning, and some might say they are the worse for it (Birnbaum, 2001). The reason is that universities often try to employ strategic planning processes that do not fit their internal social, technical, and structural systems (Lisensky, 1988). The Kellogg Commission's (1996) call for public universities to set priorities and to diminish institutional fragmentation accents the importance of strategic planning. The commission also championed making student learning and public engagement as important as faculty research. Given the challenge to align internal capabilities with external needs and to elevate the importance of student outcomes and public service, strategic planning becomes a natural tool to help institutions reach these goals. Strategic planning examines environmental shifts and institutional strengths to set institutional priorities and has the ability to align unit goals with stakeholder priorities.

The strategic planning process looks at external needs and internal capabilities. Planning can use these findings to accomplish the following objectives:

- Align institutional and academic unit priorities
- Provide an atmosphere of trust and mutual respect where the faculty and the administration have open communications with one another
- Allow participants to exercise their right and responsibility to share in the governance of the institution and have their opinions both respected and integrated into the formulation of the strategic plan
- Focus on the needs of their learners and society as driven by market forces and discipline capabilities

Strategic planning has not always been easy to institute, and its results have proven difficult to implement. We think the reason is that many institutions of higher education mistakenly use a generic business model—typically a top-down approach centered on a small number of strategic objectives, such as profits and growth. Higher education is structured much differently, and requires a level of cooperation and teamwork that marries top-level decision-makers and the institutional faculty in a way unheard of in business institutions.

Public research universities face their own set of complex environments, and unlike their private counterparts, they confront a complex set of internal and external constituencies. These complexities make their planning efforts unique. They include state funding agencies, politicians, and the general public demanding high-quality education at reasonable costs, as well as students and faculty expecting significant state support. Large public research universities face additional challenges in strategic management because of growing scrutiny by state governments and the public, as well as declining external funding. More and more, large public research universities—reacting to the continuous dwindling of state funds—are turning more frequently to private funds and capital campaigns to sponsor their teaching, research, and service agendas. Public universities are also finding themselves in increasing competition with private universities across the country for resources such as grants and contracts (Allison, 1994; Starling, 1993). They also face problems related to their internal complexity created by their large size, with a dozen or more colleges/schools, a hundred departments, and thousands of professors. (See Fazackerley, 2004, Henkel, 1999, and Watzman, 2004, for examples of government intervention with public research universities' operations and funding.)

While strategic planning does not guarantee success, without it colleges and universities face a bleak future with many unknowns and several wildcards that can lead to disaster. Hoff (1999) suggests that the leaders of today's higher education institutions must create and enhance their vision of how to meet the needs of the changing student population into the 21st century. He also argues that the leaders of colleges and universities must recognize and embrace change.

Strategic planning can help individual institutions define who they are and their markets as well as their missions, visions, strategies, goals, and objectives. It can also delineate how they can implement effective strategic plans, evaluate their successes and failures, and use this information as feedback for future planning. In summary, strategic planning sets the stage for organizational visioning, learning, change, and development by creating a nurturing environment that supports creativity and problem solving (Rowley et al., 2006). Creating an effective strategic plan can be problematic at best, but in developing it, campuses are faced with yet another challenge: how to create an effective plan while maintaining the integrity of the institution's decentralized structure.

Research Universities, Decentralization, and Strategic Planning

O'Brien (1998) notes that the development of public research universities in the 20th century led to two contrasting models of institutions of higher education in the United States: the faculty-controlled research university and the administration-led traditional college. In the beginning, American higher education was predominantly affiliated with denominational religious groups and the authority of the president and board went unquestioned. The advent of the research university over time shifted authority away from the president to the faculty, whose members' specialized skills gave them a new importance. In times of turmoil, the clash between the traditional college and the modern research university has given rise to questions such as "How will ambiguously governed institutions respond intelligently to the financial, technical, and cultural changes affecting higher education?" and "When it's crunch time, who will decide which departments should stay or be shut down?"

To bring clarity to these concerns, it is generally agreed that public research universities must create a comprehensive strategic plan that, while cognizant of the important external stakeholders, includes their large and diverse internal stakeholders as partners in the planning process. Without such an internal partnership, institutions cannot adequately devise an effective strategic plan that depends on these groups to provide the essential outputs of higher education: discovering, defining, and disseminating knowledge. The participation of internal stakeholders together with the complex goals of higher education make strategic planning in universities fundamentally different from business organizations as well as other professional organizations such as law firms and hospitals.

For a public research university, the strategic planning process begins with proponents *planning to plan*. With the objectives and parameters of planning in place, top administrators and top faculty leaders should select a multidisciplinary team to conduct the planning initiative. The first step of this team is to conduct a substantive examination of both the external environment (to gain an understanding of the needs of its service area and the demands that the state, taxpayers, and other important stakeholders are making) and the internal environment (its capabilities and limitations in responding to external opportunities and threats). Formulating a responsive academic agenda from planning requires data gathering and analysis to help planners understand external conditions as well as the institution's capabilities.

At this point, it is appropriate to revisit the university's mission and fine-tune it to represent accurately what the university *should* be doing in the future to align it better with its external environment. Based on this updated mission, the committee then defines the underpinnings of the institutional vision and values. They form the basis for developing strategies to begin incremental change that can move the campus toward a better environmental fit. This stage involves identifying specific strategic objectives and developing long-term and short-term goals that address specific outcomes that will define how the mission will be realized in the future. Generally at this point, the strategic planning committee has formulated its initial strategic plan. The governing board, faculty groups, staff groups, and campus administrators then review the plan and give critical feedback, so that the committee can then create a more polished plan for adoption with campus-wide support.

Next come the problematic issues of implementation. As we have written elsewhere (Rowley & Sherman, 2001), many plans die for lack of good implementation strategies. The budget constitutes one of the most important implementation tactics for institutionalizing the approved plan. The budget is perhaps the most powerful tool in implementing the plan by funding strategic priorities and not funding activities that do not support strategic goals.

So far, this presentation describes an event. However, strategic planning is a process that continues in the assignment of responsibilities to a standing committee or to the job responsibilities for administrative and academic personnel. Regardless of the form, strategic planning continues as those responsible examine results, compare actual against expected results, and intervene to reorient the plan to meet changes in the environment or in the institution's ability to fulfill its mission.

Everyone on or off campus must understand that strategic planning does not result simply in a single plan. An effective plan in higher education must be multilayered, with an institutional-level plan coordinating functional divisions (such as academics, student services, administration, and institutional services) as well as more academic plans for colleges, schools, departments, and programs. The coordination of the numerous stakeholders and functional plans in the planning process requires strong commitment on the part of the institution's top administrators, functional area top managers, and faculty leaders. To further complicate the process, all these steps must occur within the dictates of state, regional, and federal regulatory bodies (Barrow, 1996).

The Challenges and What to Do About Them_____

Strategic planning and strategic management are hard to accomplish and implement. Not only is the process of developing a good plan difficult, implementation requires a high level of organizational commitment on a continual basis. This commitment is challenging to achieve on any campus, and large, complex public research institutions find it particularly difficult. The real task represents not so much what a campus says it will do as what it actually does (Peters, 1984). On most university campuses, constituents see strategic planning as an arduous process, one that takes time away from normal activities. Moreover, once the plan is written, many participants believe they have done their part and need not be bothered further. As a result, many strategic plans in higher education are never properly implemented, if implemented at all (Rowley & Sherman, 2001).

As noted earlier, many universities err by adopting the traditional business strategic planning model, a top-down process. In higher education, however, with the expertise of the technology located in the faculty, simple top-down planning has not worked well. But experience has also shown that bottom-up planning fails for lack of support from campus administrators and from a reluctance to match institutional direction to external challenges. We believe that a cooperative model works best: It incorporates administrative priorities and goals along with the academic capabilities of the campus to devise an effective strategic planning model. In this mode, perhaps strategic planners can treat the planning process as a more comfortable scholarly exercise. After developing a greater understanding of both external conditions and internal capabilities, the process then uses the best expertise available on campus to analyze data and develop solutions based on an uncertain environment and future realities.

Unfortunately, given the historic divisions between central administrations and the faculty, such an alliance is often neither normal nor particularly comfortable. Large research institutions especially find it difficult to align all the various constituencies into a coherent program and to find common principles and language that help them understand what the others are saying.

Though departmentalization leads to greater flexibility in reacting to segmented markets, it also restrains internal coordination. The university often gives units autonomy to pursue their own mission, goals, and objectives without particular consideration for the operation of other units or the organization as a whole. In a for-profit organization, this may seem appropriate, since the underlying objective of every business operating unit is to maximize the firm's profitability, even if the unit must operate in a manner somewhat contradictory to the overall organization's mission. Procter & Gamble has become quite successful with this structure by having its products compete with one another in the marketplace. This internal rivalry has driven out many competitors' products and resulted in a larger market share. However, public research universities that operate in this mode—using specific units to drive their research, teaching, and service—will have institutional agendas that are random rather than deliberate (Mintzberg, 1987). These academic centers are driven by market and faculty demand for research, instruction, and service rather than the public, state, or university demand for specific knowledge and services. The university's strategy then becomes a composite of the units' agendas and not a unified plan with coordinating mechanisms that would integrate these actions. The university's decentralized structure encourages this fragmented approach.

Professors

Professors are trained to be specialists, not generalists, and consequently are not necessarily schooled to engage in macro-level planning. They may also not be inclined to participate in the planning process, since this effort represents time not spent on research, grant writing, instruction, consulting, or professional and community service. One of the authors distinctly remembers one senior faculty member publicly exclaiming at a campus-wide planning session that engaging in strategic planning at the university "was nearly as painful as going to the dentist, and far less useful." Planners need to expect and prepare for faculty resistance to engaging in the planning process, since this initiative may be perceived by some professors as meddling on the part of the administration.

Interestingly, the faculty's fear of interference by administration through the strategic planning process appears unwarranted. Schmidtlein and Taylor (1996) found that none of the 150 administrators at 35 research universities they interviewed used their strategic planning processes as the immediate vehicle for identifying programs or departments for major reductions or elimination. Further, Heveron (1987) discovered that strategic planning and strong leadership boosted the reputations of academic departments. Apparently, faculty members are not necessarily opposed to strategic planning itself. They simply may be protecting their turf and can view strategic planning as a threat to the status quo. Further, it is a mistake to view the faculty as a solid block— every faculty member is different from a colleague, and certainly those outside their department, college, or school. Some faculty will be more amenable to working for change, others more reticent. Finding those professors who want to work for the overall good of the institution and have the leadership to influence their colleagues becomes a central tenet of the planning process. Entrepreneurial professors working with entrepreneurial administrators can combine their efforts to develop a strong and innovative strategic plan.

Administrators

Administrators, on the other hand, live more in the day-to-day world operating a university by managing internal challenges and dealing with external demands. They are bombarded with budget realities and external concerns as they seek to sustain and extend the academic vitality of the campus while buffering the faculty and students from these impingements (Thompson, 1967). Administrators are also generalists, and while many are excellent managers with a wider range of appreciation for the activity of others, they tend to have a broader view of the institution and often have little patience for faculty opinions that come from a narrower, more parochial viewpoint. Finding common ground with the faculty on the strategic plan, especially professors dedicated to narrow fields of research and teaching, can be a challenge. The potential for conflict rises when it becomes clear that the academic core of the university does not adequately address the needs of external stakeholders. Falling enrollments in particular disciplines, decreases in research funding, and diminished productivity at the doctoral level constitute strong signs of a need for change, yet this is a hard message for administrators to deliver to professors from declining fields. But administrators and professors from areas with increasing demands for enrollment, research, and service increasingly want it told. Fortunately, more areas are growing, or stable and growing, than are declining.

Strategic planning remains the best option for balancing the institutional priorities to meet societal needs with the continued development of academic requirements. Strategic planning provides a way to integrate both without sacrificing academic quality. Current trends in funding for public research universities increase the importance of strategic planning. As states continue to reduce funding in higher education, self-generated income from research grants and student tuition becomes more important, but creates more competition for those funds as well. These realities force more substantive environmental scans in a strategic plan to identify specifically external demands for instructional programs and research projects, as well as an internal assessment to determine the institution's strengths and weaknesses. The planning process should also identify and analyze competitive advantages the university has or may need to develop.

Prinvale (1989) documented in his study of a major western U.S. research university that to determine the success of a strategic plan one must consider the extent to which the administrators' goals are accomplished when the plan is applied to their institution. However, the use of a typical top-down strategic planning process yields poor results. The final plan should reflect the institution's needs, not the administration's or the faculty's desires. Two troublesome factors at this university were the lack of a planning culture and the limited participation of those who would be directly affected by the planning. Prinvale claims that ignoring these two features is a fundamental reason why—after more than five years—major disagreements revolve around the plan and the strategies designed to bring the university's education programs to a place of excellence.

Planning to Plan

We believe that one of the most important components in effective strategic planning is a comprehensive preplanning preparation.

Strategic planning requires that administrators and faculty come to an understanding of their various positions as well as their individual contributions to the process. Administrators should recognize that academic units are responsible for the content of their offerings and resent any interference in their own academic planning from outside sources, including other departments, the administration, or other stakeholders.

Preplanning involves three important topics:

- How to include top administrative and academic leadership in the process.
- How to gain campus-wide understanding and support.
- How to assign leadership to the process that can unite the strategic planning committee while developing the necessary respect for the process from a decentralized community. Preplanning is where those pushing for the planning initiative can identify the potential for divisiveness and mistrust between administrators, professors, and staff members. At this stage important campus leaders can be identified, recruited, and educated on the need for planning and on the process itself. Preplanning also permits discussion of appropriate leadership for the process that can reassure constituents of their inclusion and allay their concerns.

Dealing With the Conundrum: Strategic Planning and Conflict Resolution

The importance of decentralization constitutes a critical consideration in the preplanning or planning-to-plan stage. Decentralization at the academic unit level is necessary to support quality research, teaching, and service. Professors, as experts, require autonomy to pursue the practice of their disciplines and the authority to enforce their judgment on academic matters in their fields. Nonetheless, this independence comes at a price of the potential lack of coordination and of understanding the needs of the institution as a whole. The institution and the state must bridge the demands of society and the capability of the academic units to meet those demands. Yet it's fair to ask how this can be accomplished without destroying decentralization.

We believe that the university can develop strategic planning in such a manner that the values of decentralization can be preserved, and perhaps even extended. In a public research university, one that requires a cross-functional, interdisciplinary team approach, the plan can engender a willingness to share power in decision-making between faculty units and administrators. This may require that the strategic plan create unique organizational structures to increase the information flow within the university, especially between administrators and professors. The purpose of these new structures is to help faculty members invest their time and energy in the institution along with their research, and to have them realize their stake in both the process and the outcome of strategic planning. In those settings, where an interdisciplinary, cross-functional, team-oriented approach is not endemic in the culture, the planning process itself may well need to begin at this point—using the plan-to-plan session to devise a planning system that supports and rewards an all-inclusive approach.

Planners need to be patient in educating participants and the campus population on the need for strategic planning and the benefits to the university. Cooperation cannot be commanded; its benefits must be demonstrated and its steps must be learned. When this issue is addressed up front and the integrity of the decentralized process is assured, resistance and suspicion should be appreciably reduced. Once the campus constituencies believe this message and become more supportive of the approach, the next phase of planning can proceed on a much smoother path.

Achieving cooperation and developing a cooperative environment is the preferred model for engaging the faculty actively in the strategic planning process. But what happens if the faculty members still refuse to cooperate? Resistance, as stated earlier, can and should be expected since professors often see strategic planning as at best a waste of time and effort and at worst a bothersome distraction from their research.

As an alternative, more overt co-optation might work. In this approach, planning leaders work to win support of opponents by finding ways of aligning their interests with those of the organization. Forming a university-wide planning committee with academic, research, and administrative representation to identify the need for change offers an example. Co-optation, though, requires sharing information and sharing power and therefore leads to a loss of secrecy and a loss of insular control. In order for the institution to employ this change technique, administrators must trust the members of their faculty. This may require a shift in leadership philosophy and organizational culture, a very difficult change in and of itself for institutions that do not subscribe to shared governance.

We believe that the most effective method to overcome potential faculty resistance to planning is to create a shared vision and a shared culture; to seek not only cooperation but also commitment from the faculty. We accept the notion that this is a difficult goal to achieve.

However, given the increased external pressures on public research universities to reduce their dependence on state appropriations, institutions will have little choice but to turn inward and seek the assistance of their faculty in devising new ways of surviving and prospering. The faculty should not feel that the process is a threat and administrators should not see it as an opportunity to extend their influence beyond their own decision-making responsibilities. Trust is vital from both sides, and must be encouraged from the outset.

If everyone understood that strategic planning is meant to be practiced as a long-term process, the problem of faculty commitment would diminish. As each new round of planning begins, it is important for planners to communicate that the plan will be implemented in such a way that it will become long-term policy, fully supported by the governing board, and will represent continuous improvement for the campus, its faculty and support staff, and its external constituencies. The process does this to change the campus culture.

An important advantage in moving toward a longer-term planning culture is that it will allow the university and its programs to perceive better emerging trends and challenges. Ansoff (1984) suggests that one of the hallmarks of an effective strategically managed organization is its ability to search for and recognize emerging signals from the environment. The long-term focus has clear implications for research institutions and specialty researchers. Such a long-term, externally oriented culture can hopefully detect crucial trends, such as the decline of a discipline. Such a culture can protect the campus against unwelcome surprises. And where the trends are negative, early options—such as attrition—can make the transition process nearly painless.

Strategic Planning in a Decentralized Environment ___

The process of maximizing strategic planning in a decentralized environment requires that the university ensure that all participants have a shared understanding of the need for strategic planning. They should understand that a centralized strategic plan does not necessarily usurp control of resources that are needed to support programs and research. Rather, the process needs to reaffirm the importance of the institution as a whole as well as the importance of its academic programs, and how critical it is to better align resources to support excellence and build an environment of continuous improvement. Academic excellence is achieved in the units, where decentralization of resource control is a positive contribution to effective operations.

We believe that decentralization supports academic freedom, creativity, and innovation. Strategic planning also allows the institution to state, set, and pursue its priorities and direction through defining overall strategic goals that serve both the institution and its academic programs. Collaboration and cooperation—pivotal to effective planning—allow all segments of the campus to identify their needs, but also encourage a strategic direction based on what is best overall for the institution. Strategic planning does not seek to minimize any of these tenets of a viable university. Campus constituents should understand strategic planning as an institution-wide process that aids units in identifying external needs and threats and then informs the units as to how they can reorient or maximize their operations to improve continually their performance over the foreseeable future and contribute to university-wide priorities. Collegiality is a worthwhile objective of the strategic planning process and will help to allay suspicions and misunderstandings and support the benefits of centralized administration and decentralized units working together for the benefit of the whole. All of this must be addressed in the beginning plan-to-plan to avoid surprises along the way.

The Role of Faculty Senates

The most obvious division that has permeated the public research university system is the difference in orientation between academics and administrators. The faculty senate can serve as a potentially effective coordinating mechanism between the entire faculty and the institution's administrators. Colleges and universities rely on faculty senates and similar governing units to build consensus and solve problems on campus creatively (Miller & Pope, 2001). Monsma (2001) suggests that in order to facilitate campus-wide strategic planning, faculty senate representatives can be brought into the campus strategic planning process early on to help improve communications as the process matures and to underscore the importance of the faculty.

However, as Burgan (2001) has pointed out, a faculty senate cannot be effective as a participant in strategic planning without reform of its two main failures: lack of clear direction and the inefficient management of participatory time. Some senates have been so ineffective that, for example, the trustees at George Mason University criticized the faculty senate for its skill in the art of delay and questioned whether the senate really represented the faculty (Magner, 1999). The faculty senate at Francis Marion University (FMU) was dissolved by the university's board of trustees following a report by an accreditation team that implied the system tended to create an adversarial relationship between the faculty and administration and between the faculty and the board of trustees (Magner, 1997). The American Association of University Professors voted in June 1997 to place FMU on its list of institutions sanctioned for infringement of governance standards and was later removed in 2000 (Molotsky, 2000).

Where faculty senates are strong and functional, they need to be a significant part of the strategic planning process. They represent an important interdepartmental body that already addresses academic planning issues. As a strategic planning initiative begins, the faculty senate can become a partner in providing strategic leadership that represents the academic programs involved in research and instruction. If the initiative can gain senate support, this can aid the institution in bridging any gap that may exist between administrators and faculty. In order to institute such a relationship between the planners and senate, the chair of the senate should most likely be involved in the plan-to-plan to provide the leadership necessary to bring together administrators and faculty in a collegial manner.

Changing the Culture

Planners must also deal with actual or potential conflict related to the locus of control between the faculty and the administration. In the plan-to-plan, there should be some language that identifies the roles of administrators, staff members, and faculty members as equal members of the committee, a central tenet to the planning process. It will be necessary to identify the importance of administrators' drive for efficiency, effectiveness, and quality results for the institution, while at the same time recognizing the importance of the faculty's drive for quality information and protection of their disciplines. It need not be institutional efficiency versus academic unit quality. Both can coexist with the right pattern of communication and cooperation. A balance, agreeable to both sides, must be reached between these maxims in order to meet both of these stakeholders' goals.

Cultural change is not a simple task. Considering that culture is made up of relatively stable and permanent characteristics, it is by nature resistant to change. It clearly follows that the stronger the culture, the greater the resistance. Public research universities tend to have what can be called differentiated or fragmented cultures (Ott, 1989). They are characterized by the presence of subcultures that are broken down into either dominant and minority coalitions, or multiple somewhat equitable coalitions. These cultures are inconsistent, and have ambiguity, which forces the university to react inconsistently to change. While some subcultures will embrace it, other parts will resist it, based on the source and nature of the change.

According to Graham and Shuldiner (2001), historically, cultural change takes place when

- A dramatic crisis creates a shock that undermines the status quo and calls into question the relevance of the existing culture
- Top leadership changes and brings with it a new set of key values
- The organization is young and small, having a less entrenched culture
- The culture itself is weak, where members do not agree on key values

For the public research university, because of its fragmentation, the institutional culture may indeed be weak. Fragmentation itself offers an opportunity for the strategic planners to use the process to create cultural change by demonstrating respect for shared values as well as high regard for the success of both the administrative and academic segments of the campus.

Leaders and Planning Committee Members as Change Agents

As the plan-to-plan phase comes to an end with, hopefully, a much more solid understanding of how the planning process should proceed, who should be involved, and the potential problems it may face, the full strategic planning committee should be identified and should begin its work. During the planning process, leaders and other planning committee members will find themselves tested along the way by administrators and professors who believe that their programs may be at serious risk of reduction or even elimination. At times, planning leaders may be involved in resolving conflict as they create new organizational structures and social systems; find ways of empowering administrators, faculty members, and staff members; and seek to build a better university and change the culture while preserving decentralization. Discovering how to do all of this within each university is time consuming and cumbersome. Nonetheless, the strategic planning committee must consider itself a group of change agents. All members should offer themselves as resources to the rest of the campus and work to support change that will begin a process of continuous improvement at all levels in the community. Instituting and solidifying this objective is one of the major considerations in deciding who provides leadership to the strategic planning committee.

Leadership and Committee Membership

Leadership on the strategic planning committee is a paramount issue and (unfortunately) poses its own set of tribulations since the leader of the committee must have both transformational and transactional skills (Hughes, Ginnett, & Curphy, 2002). Both skills are necessary for creating a shared vision of the institution and empowering administrators and professors to work as a team to achieve it. Who makes the best leader is, however, not a straightforward or easy issue to address. In most of the models we have seen, the president or chancellor or provost chairs the strategic planning committee (though in large public research universities, where the president or chancellor focuses more on fundraising and state relations, the provost will likely lead the strategic planning initiative). This approach to leadership has pros and cons. Committee leadership involves factors of personality, motivations, agendas, and political standing that will help make or break the initiative, especially with the president or chancellor in charge.

First and foremost, it is dangerous for any president or chancellor to dominate the proceedings, especially when trying to build and support a process based on collegiality. For those campuses where the institutional head is concerned about being perceived as too dominant, the provost is often chosen as the leader of the process instead. In this model, the institutional head is still involved but more as a guide on the side. He or she can concentrate on facilitating the operation of the committee while being in a position to reject a strategic plan that goes off track. The role of the president or chancellor must be thoroughly thought out to ensure that their support for the process is evident, yet their personal agenda for the outcome does not become the driving force. Members of the faculty and staff must believe that their opinions also count and that the strategic plan that emerges represents the greater good of the campus as a whole. If participants across the campus (let alone the planning committee members) believe that the strategic plan has been predetermined but concealed, they will see the planning process as at best disingenuous and at worst manipulative.

We are not arguing against the president or chancellor being involved, or even chairing the strategic planning committee. An even greater danger to the success of the process than presidential dominance is lack of top-level support. If the top administrator of the university does not participate, the legitimacy of the entire process could be severely compromised. Rather, we believe that the position of leadership must be carefully considered and that actual leadership of the committee be seen as a collaborative alliance between top administrators, faculty leaders, and other campus stakeholders. This issue of leadership could be addressed in a planning-to-plan activity that precedes the formation of the strategic planning committee.

In the event that the chair is not the president or provost, the leader must have enough power and clout to run a successful strategic planning event. However, we believe that choosing the best person to run the strategic planning committee is a decision not based on a particular position or title but on the needs of the university and the availability of support. Leaders from each university need to understand the dynamics of the relationship of their own particular faculty and administrative core to

- Determine which individuals are respected by both the faculty and the administration
- Identify those who have no obvious personal agendas and are willing to share responsibility and authority
- Be sensitive to institutional constituent needs
- Have a demonstrated sense of understanding external needs
- Be able to lead an effective data collection process to gather and analyze internal strengths and weaknesses as well as external opportunities and threats
- Inspire a sense of participation and trust

If the wrong leader heads the process, it is likely that one or more areas of the campus will not support the process or recommendations developed by the committee.

Perhaps an additional alternative is that the leadership role can be filled by more than one person. It might be a joint chair with a representative from both the faculty and the administration. Alternatively, a committee with a central coordinator or coordinating committee could be formed with topical leaders leading subcommittees focused on specific areas of study. If finding a chair of the committee is difficult or problematic, the institution might employ an outside facilitator to guide the institution through an effective change process. This alternative avoids the possible pitfalls associated with having insiders chair the process and allows for an outsider's perspective on both the external and internal operating environments. However, this choice is not the best solution because while outsiders bring expertise and objectivity, they find it hard to gain important campus-wide trust or to be seen as credible since they typically leave after the initiative ends.

Yet another issue relates to the committee composition, since each member contributes to successful strategic planning. We believe that both top administrators and top academic leaders should work together to choose members of the committee, perhaps on the recommendations of those who are involved with the plan-to-plan. Committee members should do more than represent administrative or academic areas. Each should demonstrate broad respect on campus and a commitment to tying institutional performance to external needs and to increasing the quality and quantity of required results. The committee should include senior professors who understand the need for strategic change along with senior administrators who believe in the process, have demonstrated their ability to work with faculty and administration, and have experience and expertise that can contribute to the planning process. Most important, committee members should have the respect of their colleagues in program or operational areas and be able to represent the interests of the institution to their constituents and those of the units to the committee—the latter as information, not demands.

The Environment, Crisis, and Strategic Planning _____

The issue of timing in relation to the environment represents a critical ingredient to successful strategic planning. The environment can impact the planning process positively or negatively. Strategic planning combines the demands of the marketplace and the capabilities of the university to determine how the campus should respond to external demands and changes. However, regardless of the state of the environment, strategic planning can help provide direction and responsiveness. Where strategic management becomes institutionalized and ongoing, the institution will be able to respond more quickly and efficiently than on campuses that do not have effective processes.

Crises also impact the timing of strategic planning. We have found that strategic planning in higher education often works best when there are well-understood challenges to the campus, but before these challenges become catastrophes. The varying intensity of crises can dramatically alter the strategic planning process (whether internally or externally driven) by increasing the speed of planning and identifying available solutions. Crises often diminish the quality of data collection and coalition building, and reduce the ability of the institution to come up with the right solutions. A catastrophe might not be adequately addressed by strategic planning because the university may simply be out of time.

Yet severe challenges and crises occur at an ever-increasing pace, and more campuses turn to strategic planning as a short-term event that has the promise of changing the situation for the better. Regardless of the misunderstanding of strategic planning as an event and not a long-term process, a benefit of crisis is a shared understanding of a severe threat and the need to move quickly ahead to seek a new status of equilibrium. Consensus and unity are often easier to build in a crisis. However, unless the participants understand the full implications of strategic planning on structural change, it may not be successful. As a result, regardless of the time constraints, every strategic planning initiative should be considered long term with the continual improvement of the campus as its focus.

On the other hand, good times can be a negative motivator for strategic planning. Producing change in academic organizations requires a strong internal sense of necessity. Without a severe challenge or a crisis, the need for cooperation is harder to demonstrate (if it isn't broken, why are we fixing it?). If no need for change is seen, academic units may not support the planning process and this perception may well lead to a greater rift between administration and academic units. Recognition of the necessity of change becomes especially critical when planning can lead to the loss of priority and resources to some academic programs. When implementing change, some units lose. Some also gain, but more fear loss than anticipate gain. This fear of possible loss again underscores the need to address the issue of why the campus must engage in strategic planning in the plan-to-plan and why strategic planners need to educate the entire campus as to its purpose, methods, and long-term nature.

Perhaps the best strategic planning period for colleges and universities is during a time of challenge that is not yet catastrophic, as stated earlier. Everyone on campus sees the challenges ahead and may even be feeling them, yet panic has not set in. Across-campus participation is most promising at this juncture, since it is a good time for the administrative and academic leadership to appeal to the common good of all by denoting shared problems. As a result, leadership must act as ongoing environmental scanners, seeing important changes in the state and national environments, and begin to share this knowledge with the campus through the strategic management process. This scanning and communicating should consider internal as well as external changes.

Though not necessarily a crisis, a strategic planning initiative occurs when a campus has problems or has changed top leadership. It is not unusual for the incoming president or chancellor to call for a new strategic planning initiative. While it is always a good idea to be in an effective strategic planning mode, there can be dangers when institutional leadership is new and unproven. Since leadership is critical to an effective process, it should be solidified before a major campus-wide initiative is undertaken. This solidification can happen quickly when the problems are severe or the new leader is especially charismatic, but could also be an arduous process as the new president or chancellor learns how the politics of the campus operate and finds ways of working within the system to get it to move.

Recommendations

We believe there are several actions all colleges and universities, especially large public research institutions, can take to develop a comprehensive and effective strategic plan while preserving the benefits of a decentralized operational structure.

Planning-to-Plan

One of the main keys to success, planning-to-plan allows many of the crucial questions and issues to surface. It also permits strategic planning protagonists to address major issues up front, allowing a smoother planning process.

Ensuring Adequate Faculty Participation

Overcoming the fear of an administrative initiative that has the potential of altering the academic program and research agenda is best addressed by having strong faculty representation. This participation cannot be window dressing—it must be substantive and must add value to the planning process and the resulting strategic plan.

Creating a Collaborative Planning Culture

Planners need to address mutual mistrust and suspicion on those campuses where it exists. It is important to teach the importance of thinking strategically and building a plan that will lead to continuous improvement that will change the culture.

Choosing the Right Leaders

Presidents and chancellors should be involved, but do not necessarily need to chair the planning process. Leadership should focus on a team-centered approach where leaders from the university's top administration, academic programs, and other major campus constituencies work together to lead both downward and upward.

Involving the Right People

The committee should have a carefully chosen core of generalists and specialists. It should include academics from fields in strategic planning or organizational theory.

Determining How to Structure the Committee

The committee must be a combination of top administrative and academic minds, so top academic and administrative leaders should select members of the strategic planning committee. This plan-to-plan should address this issue.

Formalizing Strategic Planning

The good news is that strategic planning can permanently improve the university. The bad news is that strategic planning is a process, not an event. Whether it is an ongoing institutional committee or an assignment to specific administrators and faculty leaders, each university needs to devise a way of keeping strategic planning at the forefront of administrative and academic thinking for the long term.

Budgeting Bolsters Strategic Planning

Along with changes to a university's structure and culture, the best way of assuring strategic changes is to use the budget to support priorities and objectives identified in strategic planning.

Selecting the Best Implementation Methods

Given the timing allowed for planning and the state of the environments, strategic planners should choose an appropriate implementation method. (See Rowley & Sherman, 2001, for more options based on varying states of the environment.)

Ensuring a Continuous Planning Process

An ongoing planning process requires indicating the duration of each strategic plan so that a time for review and revision is established.

Tan (1995) suggests several planning premises that support these recommendations. They include a defined planning process, a permanent planning committee, a link between planning and budget, a proactive approach, and the understanding that planning is a process instead of an event. Though written for a business strategic plan, Tan's recommendations also apply to higher education and can help to assure an effective strategic planning process in these turbulent times.

Final Thoughts

The university is one institution, but the diversity of activities that occur in campus administration and academics makes it easy to see divisiveness rather than diversity. Strategic planning needs to celebrate diversity in the makeup of the university and confirm the values of decentralization as it develops the strategies, goals and objectives, and policies that will guide the institution over the long term. It should also add institutional direction to that diversity and decentralization.

Strategic planning can help guard against catastrophic events that can threaten the viability of the campus and its vital academic processes. In order to accomplish this task, an enlightened leadership must identify both internal and external challenges to the university, manage structured conflict and resistance to change, create a strategic management process that includes key stakeholders, and empower the faculty and staff to engage actively in planning by creating an integrated culture that expects commitment to both institutional and disciplinary goals. The strategic planning process need not be the same for every institution. However, the commonalities of purpose (serving students, the disciplines, the taxpayers, and society) should create an environment of trust and collegiality—without which any strategic plan, even with the best intentions, will fail.

References

Allison, G. T. (1994). Public and private management: Are they fundamentally alike in all unimportant respects? In F. S. Lane (Ed.), *Current issues in public administration* (5th ed., pp. 16–32). New York, NY: St. Martin's Press.

Ansoff, H. I. (1984). *Implanting strategic management.* Englewood Cliffs, NJ: Prentice Hall.

Barrow, C. W. (1996, June). The strategy of selective excellence: Redesigning higher education for global competition in a postindustrial society. *Higher Education, 31*(4), 447–469.

Birnbaum, R. (2001). *Management fads in higher education: Where they come from, what they do, why they fail.* San Francisco, CA: Jossey-Bass.

Burgan, M. A. (2001, May/June). Governance: A practical guide. *Academe, 87*(3), 80.

Fazackerley, A. (2004, November 12). Fury over treasury research meddling. *Times Higher Education Supplement,* pp. 1, 5.

Graham, M. B. W., & Shuldiner, A. T. (2001). *Corning and the craft of innovation.* New York, NY: Oxford University Press.

Henkel, M. (1999). The modernisation of research evaluation: The case of the UK. *Higher Education, 38*(1), 105–122.

Heveron, E. D. (1987, Winter). Boosting academic reputations: A study of university departments. *Review of Higher Education, 11*(2), 177–197.

Hoff, K. S. (1999, October). Leaders and managers: Essential skills required within higher education. *Higher Education, 38*(3), 311–331.

Hughes, R. L., Ginnett, R. C., & Curphy, G. J. (2002). *Leadership: Enhancing the lessons of experience* (4th ed.). New York, NY: McGraw-Hill/Irwin.

Kellogg Commission on the Future of State and Land-Grant Universities. (1996). *Taking charge of change.* Washington, DC: National Association of State Universities and Land-Grant Colleges.

Lisensky, R. P. (1988). Integrating the control systems. In D. W. Steeples (Ed.), *Successful strategic planning: Case studies* (pp. 15–22). San Francisco, CA: Jossey-Bass.

Magner, D. K. (1997, May 2). Trustees of Francis Marion U. dissolve the faculty senate. *The Chronicle of Higher Education,* p. A11.

Magner, D. K. (1999, June 18). Battle over academic control pits faculty against governing board at George Mason U. *The Chronicle of Higher Education,* p. A14.

Miller, M. T., & Pope, M. L. (2001). *Faculty senate presidential skills: Identifying needs for training and professional development.* George Washington University: Graduate School of Education and Human Development. (ERIC Document Reproduction Service No. ED456699)

Mintzberg, H. (1987, June). Strategy concept 1: Five Ps for strategy. *California Management Review, 30*(1), 11–24.

Monsma, G. N., Jr. (2001, January/February). Faith and faculty autonomy at Calvin College. *Academe, 87*(1), 43–47.

Molotsky, I. F. (2000). *Francis Marion University: A governance success story.* Retrieved August 19, 2006, from www.aaup.org/publications/foot notes/FN00/FN00FM.HTM

O'Brien, G. D. (1998). *All the essential half-truths about higher education.* Chicago, IL: University of Chicago Press.

Ott, S. J. (1989). *The organizational cultural perspective.* Chicago, IL: Dorsey Press.

Peters, T. (1984, Spring). Strategy follows structure: Developing distinctive skills. *California Management Review, 26*(3), 111–125.

Prinvale, J. M. (1989, November). *Achieving distinction in an uncertain future.* Paper presented at the fifth annual meeting of the Association for the Study of Higher Education, Atlanta, GA.

Rowley, D. J., & Sherman, H. (2001). *From strategy to change: Implementing the plan in higher education.* San Francisco, CA: Jossey-Bass.

Rowley, D. J., Sherman, H., & Armandi, B. (2006). *Strategic management: An organizational change approach.* Lanham, MD: University Press of America.

Schmidtlein, F. A., & Taylor, A. L. (1996, May). *How graduate/research universities deal with strategic issues.* Paper presented at the 36th annual forum of the Association for Institutional Research, Albuquerque, NM.

Starling, G. (1993). *Managing the public sector* (4th ed.). Belmont, CA: Wadsworth.

Tan, D. L. (1995, Summer). The state of strategic planning: A survey of selected research universities. *College and University, 71*(1), 24–32.

Thompson, J. D. (1967). *Organizations in action.* New York, NY: McGraw-Hill.

Watzman, H. (2004, April 2). Israeli council plans to assert more control over universities. *The Chronicle of Higher Education*, p. A45.

6

Using the Budget
to Fight Fragmentation
and Improve Quality

William F. Massy

Universities exist to create value through education, research, and public service. Because budgets enable activities and activities create value, budgets can be said to mediate value creation. Hence budget development should be viewed as a key tool for steering the institution, not just as another administrative process. No area in public research universities is more in need of steering than the quality of undergraduate education, the second topic to be covered in this chapter. The lack of robust value-added metrics limits the market's ability to distinguish between student intake quality (talented freshmen remain talented at graduation) and the quality of the education itself. Thus the institution must take full responsibility for quality. When supplemented with an appropriate performance evaluation methodology, the budget can be a prime tool for discharging this responsibility. Academic audit, discussed in this chapter's last section, provides just such a methodology.

Budget-making begins with institutional governance, and then continues as a management process. I believe the academic rather than the financial side should drive institutional budgets. Furthermore, the process of budget development and the budget itself should be transparent because effectiveness in mediating value creation depends on broad understanding and acceptance throughout the university.

Budget decisions should be guided by the university's strategic plan. To accomplish this, the plan should call out initiatives for consideration in the budget process and describe the performance indicators that, if the initiatives are funded, will be used to gauge success. Moreover, each year's budget process should require the chief academic officer, deans, and other university leaders to review performance against the plan and consider what new actions are needed. Taken together, strategic plans and the budgets that implement them are key tools for fighting fragmentation in both public and private universities.

Budgeting Principles

Budget terminology is far from standardized, so it will be helpful to explain the definitions used in this chapter. First, the budget is a combination of revenue targets and spending authorizations. For example, an organizational unit may be expected to generate a certain level of tuition revenue and/or be authorized to spend a certain sum. Because budget balance requires revenues to equal expenditures, achievement of revenue commitments is just as important as adherence to spending limits.

This discussion will mainly focus on the university's *current-funds budget*—unrestricted funds plus grants and contracts, restricted gifts, and endowment spending to support current operations. Auxiliary enterprises and funds restricted or designated for facilities construction (plant funds) are excluded. Budgeting goals can be more readily achieved using this broad definition than by budgeting only the institution's unrestricted funds (sometimes called the *operating budget*). The base budget represents funding for ongoing activities (*base activities*), as opposed to *non-base* or *one-time* activities.

Budget-making can be viewed as having seven major goals. It is helpful to keep all seven in mind as one designs and uses a budgeting system of any type.

1) To steer the institution by investing in new programs or activities and/or disinvesting from current ones. New academic investments shape the institution over the long term, especially if less desirable current programs can be eliminated at the same time (*growth by substitution*).
2) To sustain the purchasing power of current budget-base activities absent explicit decisions to resize them. This goal requires quantifying and funding salary increments and other kinds of cost-rise explicitly.
3) To stimulate growth of operating revenue—for example, by the creation of new academic programs. Such top-line growth often is cited as a reason for devolving revenue responsibility to deans or departments.
4) To provide support and incentives for short-term projects to accomplish particular purposes and to seed activities that may eventually

qualify for long-term institutional investment or outside funding. Teaching improvement and research development funds fall into this category.

5) To give after-the-fact rewards for activities that enhance current or future performance. Such activities may implement priorities in the strategic plan or reflect individuals' or departments' self-directed efforts to improve their performance.

6) To supplement traditional sources of financial and physical capital. Examples include transfers from the current-funds budget to quasi-endowment and/or plant accounts (e.g., to fund depreciation).

7) To quantify and mitigate financial risk. Methods include identifying and estimating the variance of risky financial quantities, managing the timing of expenditures, and optimizing contingency reserves.

Resource limitations require *tradeoffs* within and among the goal categories. For example, provision of seed and incentive funds means less money will be available for sustaining the institution's current portfolio of ongoing programs and investing in new ones. Deciding what candidates to add to the portfolio and which existing activities to remove also requires tough tradeoffs. While inevitably controversial, the tradeoffs should be made explicitly, according to well thought-out criteria, and informed by evidence.

Budgeting should be viewed in a *multiyear context*. This means that budget analyses should encompass more than one year, and that the process should have memory of prior years' decisions and the considerations on which they were based.

Accountability enters through the budget process's institutional memory. Each prior-year tradeoff depended on a combination of evidence and someone's commitment to perform in a certain way. Current decision-making should take the track record of meeting expectations into account. The development of a track record requires agreement on performance metrics and the development of appropriate data collection processes.

In summary, budget-making is a method—some would say *the* method—for steering the institution. While obvious, this principle is too often forgotten as beleaguered administrators try to make ends meet for yet another year. Budgeting always should be viewed in a strategic context, in bad years as well as good. It should steer in the direction of doing the right things and doing them right. The steering objective remains salient even when financial stringency prevents investing in new activities. It is no less important, and perhaps even more important, to perform current activities effectively and efficiently when times are tough. Improved performance need not require large investments, but it does require the proper incentives, rewards, and metrics. Most importantly for the purposes of this chapter, budget-making is a prime tool for fighting fragmentation.

Steering the University

The purpose of budgeting is to steer the university in ways that maximize its ability to create "value." Steering is done directly through the central administration's budget decisions in centralized systems. The process is more complex in decentralized systems but effective steering still is possible. It is obvious that steering represents the antithesis of fragmentation.

Budgeting begins with governance, which determines how value is defined. Governance is inherently messy, but the budget process can call forth alternative proposals and provide venues for debating their merits. How governance should work and who should be involved is beyond the scope of this chapter, but there is no doubt that participation should be wide. Faculty in particular need to feel their views have been taken into account, since they may assert "property rights" to programs and in general the implementation of academic initiatives is largely their decision.

It is the role of the budget to call forth activities to create that value. But value is not the only consideration. Markets enter the picture too, as do questions of productivity (how effective a given set of activities is at creating value) and the long-term requirement that expenditures not exceed revenue. How do presidents, provosts, and chief financial officers balance all these considerations when developing a budget?

This question has two kinds of answers: one at the level of high principle and one at the level of practical administration. The principle is that leaders steer the university by determining how much each school and program contributes to, or is subsidized by, the central pool of resources—that is, they determine the institution's pattern of cross-subsidies. (The same principle applies to deans' resource allocations to departments.) Far from being dirty little secrets, cross-subsidies are the central feature of not-for-profit organizations (Hopkins & Massy, 1981; Massy, 1996, 2003). They reflect the mission centered part of being market smart and mission centered (Zemsky, Wegner, & Massy, 2005a, 2005b). Do away with cross-subsidies, and one has a for-profit business. For-profits are driven by market forces and only market forces, whereas not-for-profits seek to balance values and market forces. The balancing of values and market forces is what it means to steer the university and/or its constituent parts.

For purposes of this chapter, I will assume that university and college leaders have performed the governance steps needed to inform and legitimize their decisions about value tradeoffs. The problem now is to translate these inputs into practical budget decisions—ones that steer the institution in desired directions without stifling individual initiative or impinging on academic freedom.

To be effective, the administrative processes that produce a budget need to be evidence based and transparent. Whatever the style of budgeting, cognizant decision-makers should insist that claims made in spending proposals be supported by evidence to the extent possible. The evidence need not be quantitative, but it should be probative. Furthermore, all proposals should include performance indicators for gauging progress (assuming, of course, that the proposal is funded). Once again, one should not slavishly pursue quantification. The real question is, "How will you (and we) know whether the activity is in fact creating value?" One should be wary of proposals for which there is no way to answer this question.

Transparency furthers several purposes: to continuously improve the budget process, to sustain its legitimacy, and to send signals about what the institution values and what it does not. Secretive processes deprive deans and others of information they need to align themselves with institutional objectives and improve their use of evidence. Secrecy also leaves participants with the feeling that someone else got a better deal, probably by nefarious means. Transparency requires not only that the results of the budget process be known, but also that the process itself be reasonably open. One way to achieve openness is to include deans as full participants in sessions where the merits of alternative budget proposals are being debated. Not only does this practice boost communication, but no one is better at critiquing the proposal of a fellow dean than a "friendly competitor" for the same resource pool. Given that budget-making is a management process, however, decisions should be made by the chief academic officer rather than by vote.

Centralization or Decentralization?

Colleges and universities use a variety of budgeting systems. Line-item systems, where all revenues are retained centrally and most expenditure authorizations are for specific purposes, can work well in small institutions. Larger schools generally decentralize the expenditure authorization process, but they differ on the degree to which revenues are devolved. Responsibility Center Management (RCM) systems devolve both revenue and spending authority to colleges and schools, whereas block or one-line systems devolve spending authority alone (Massy, 1996; Whalen, 1991).

The choice of budgeting systems requires tradeoffs among the seven goals. Line-item systems fight fragmentation by making expenditure decisions centrally. However, they limit incentives for entrepreneurship and thus fall short on the goal of achieving top-line growth. In large institutions, moreover, the organizational distance from the center to where activities are actually performed is so great that it is hard to make well-informed decisions. Block grant systems solve the organizational distance problem by decentralizing decisions about spending but, because most revenue is retained centrally, they do little to encourage entrepreneurship. Systems that devolve revenue must retain sufficient funds under central control to provide project-oriented incentives and after-the-fact rewards for pursuing institution-wide priorities.

Many research universities have adopted some form of RCM, either as a set of formulas or a way of informing block grant allocations. Formulaic systems allocate unrestricted revenues to schools on the basis of enrollments and other performance indicators. (Restricted revenues flow automatically to the schools or departments where the restrictions apply.) Then they tax back the funds needed for cross-subsidies and charge overhead on schools' expenditures to fund central services. RCM has proven effective in achieving top-line growth. Unfortunately, however, the approach does little to reduce fragmentation and may actually increase it. This effect is particularly true if RCM's subvention system is allowed to ossify. Jon Strauss and John Curry (2002), an originator and an early adopter of RCM, put it this way:

> If they [subventions] become entitlements through lack of frequent refreshing and renewing of their rationales, then the president and the provost can lose their abilities to affect the direction of the whole. Which is to say, the whole defaults to the sum of the parts. (p. 33)

Nor does RCM give great priority to what should be a sine qua non for all universities, public or private: educational quality, especially for undergraduates. Demand and thus enrollment depend on student choices, but students often lack good information about the quality and/or the background needed to use such information effectively. In other words, the market may be unable to police the true quality of education except in extreme cases. The problem is especially severe for undergraduate education. Master's and nondegree programs are likely to be better policed.

The key to decentralizing a budget system is to devolve revenues in areas where the market can discipline quality and where the potential for fragmentation is small, but to retain central control elsewhere. In other words, the best system for a particular institution usually is a hybrid of the block allocation and RCM styles. The stronger the market discipline for a particular revenue stream, the stronger the case for devolving that stream, other things being equal. Conversely, the case for devolvement becomes weaker as the danger of fragmentation rises. The following discussion suggests how the tradeoffs should be evaluated in specific cases.

Undergraduate Tuition Revenue

Application and yield rates depend more on prestige and convenience than the delivered quality of education (Massy, 2003), but market discipline may more strongly influence how matriculated students choose among majors. Because the effect of market forces is mixed—weak external discipline favors centralized budget allocations coupled with strong quality assurance while internal market forces favor decentralization—the choice often rides on the question of fragmentation.

The consequences of fragmentation depend on whether the institution has a single mission for undergraduate education or whether the missions have been devolved to the schools. Take business studies, for example. Institutions that consider business as one among many majors in what is fundamentally a generalist undergraduate curriculum would centralize this revenue stream whereas those that consider business as an independent professional program would devolve it. The degree of devolvement is not simply an artifact of budgeting, it is fundamental to governance—for example, it determines the influence of core as opposed to discipline-specific curricular goals. It is no wonder there is a lack of consensus among institutions on whether undergraduate tuition revenue should be retained centrally or devolved to schools.

Master's and Professional Tuition Revenue

Applicants for these programs tend to be savvier consumers than are undergraduates—they are more mature and often get advice from college faculty or on-the-job associates. Most master's and professional programs are more specialized and job-related than their undergraduate counterparts, which makes them easier to evaluate. In terms of fragmentation, such programs tend to further a school's mission rather than that of the central university. They provide fertile ground for faculty entrepreneurship and many have positive contribution margins. Hence the criteria tend to point in the same direction: toward revenue decentralization.

Government Appropriations

Two cases can be distinguished: The appropriation depends formulaically on degrees or enrollments, or it does not. The formulaic case is similar to the one for tuition revenue because there is a direct linkage between marketplace performance and funding. No such linkage exists in the second case, which means the effect of market forces is weak or nonexistent. Thus the tendency in the second case is toward retaining the revenue centrally.

Gifts and Spending From Endowment

Colleges and schools cannot do much to affect university-level unrestricted gifts and endowment, so these revenues are best retained centrally. Restricted gifts go automatically to the colleges, schools, or departments where the restrictions apply. Endowed chairs present a special policy issue. Budget-makers may withdraw general funds from units that get endowed chairs without violating the gift covenant, but withdrawing funds equal to the payout destroys much of the incentive for deans and chairs to help raise the money. Enlightened institutions "gain-share." While perhaps withdrawing some general funds, they leave a substantial part of the gain with the college, school, or department.

Overhead Recovery on Grants and Contracts

Though gain-sharing on overheads is often a bone of contention, it has become more the rule rather than the exception in public research universities. Contention arises because much of the money recovered is, at least in principle, to reimburse the institution for central administrative, support, and infrastructure expenditures. By this principle, the recoveries should go where the money was expended in the first place, which is primarily by the central administration. But this placement ignores two facts. First, the linkage between expenditure levels and overhead rates has become so blurred in recent years as to be almost unrecognizable. This observation applies especially to institutions whose cognizant agency is the Department of Health, Education, and Welfare, which seems to regard overhead rates as prices to be negotiated rather than mechanisms for cost recovery as described by OMB Circular A-21. Second, many public institutions have already been funded for most overhead expenditures—in which case the recoveries represent something of a windfall. What remains is the strong incentive value in providing schools, departments, and even individual principal investigators with substantial shares of recovered overhead.

Revenues From Other School and Departmental Activities

These range from running conferences, to cooperative teaching and research programs with industry, to the exploitation of intellectual property. Such revenues depend strongly on entrepreneurship and market forces, and the activities tend to be fragmented by nature. Hence a strong case exists for devolvement.

The Strategic Budget Tableau

Because budgets are complicated, effective thinking and communication are aided by having a well thought-out financial planning paradigm. The so-called Strategic Budget Tableau presented in Figure 6.1 can be used at the central administration level and also by colleges, schools, and other operating units. While the line-item definitions will vary to some extent, the basic structure is the same everywhere. The tableau specifically addresses all the budgeting goals except Goal 3, top-line growth, which depends on the university's style of budgeting. However, the tableau can reflect any degree of decentralization.

Figure 6.1
Strategic Budget Tableau (Top Level)

Sources of Funds
- Allocations directly from government (for public institutions) or higher-level units in the organizational hierarchy
- Student fee revenue: gross, and net of financial aid
- Other operating revenue (e.g., overhead recoveries on grants and contracts, revenue from entrepreneurial activities)
- Other current income (e.g., gifts for current expenditure)
- Spending from endowment

Uses of Funds
- Prior year's base budget (last year's program at last year's prices)
- Cost-rise on base budget (incremental amount needed to fund last year's budget at this year's prices, Goal 2)
- Real budget change (net investment/disinvestment in base activities at this year's prices, Goal 1)
- Provision for incentive and project funding (Goals 4 and 5)
- Transfers to or from capital funds (plant and quasi-endowment, Goal 6)
- Discretionary transfers to/from reserves (risk mitigation, Goal 7)

Budget Surplus or Deficit (sources minus uses: the bottom line, represents a mandatory transfer to or from an operating reserve)

While space limitations require that only the tableau's top-level items be presented, forecasting and decision-making take place mainly at the sub-item level. Overhead recoveries will be forecasted separately from entrepreneurial income, for example, and the different kinds of governmental allocations, student fee revenues, and gifts generally will be treated separately. Presently, I am developing a software package for managing the full tableau in a centralized or decentralized multiyear budget environment.

The tableau should present data for more than one year. If one were working in FY 2006 to budget for FY 2007, for example, the tableau would include:

- Two or three years of financial history: 2003, 2004, and 2005. The data would cover actual revenues and expenses for these years, and longer histories should be available for those who wish to drill down.
- The current year (the launching point for the forecasts that follow): 2006. Data would include the 2006 budget and any adjustments needed to provide a valid base for forecasting.
- The planning period: 2007-2009. Puts next year's budget in the context of a rolling three-year financial plan. (Some institutions use five years.)
- The "steady state": 2010 and beyond. Consideration of a steady state forces planners to think about long-run trends beyond the point where they can anticipate particular events.

The steady state idea stems from the concept of Long Run Financial Equilibrium, or LRFE for short (Hopkins & Massy 1981; Massy & Zemsky, 1995). A university meets the conditions for LRFE when its budget is balanced, it has no hidden liabilities, and its structural growth rates for revenue and expense are approximately equal. Absent good reasons to the contrary, an institution should aim to achieve equilibrium at the end of the planning period. While unforeseen events will repeatedly bounce one away from the path toward equilibrium, each new tableau will project the path anew. An added benefit is that estimating structural growth rates helps focus attention on long-term issues instead of firefighting.

The first three lines in the tableau's "Uses of Funds" section separate cost-rise from real budget change. The approach highlights price increases in the university's input markets (e.g., for salaries, library acquisitions, and energy) and then focuses attention on real increases or decreases in activity levels. Positive real program change means the university can invest base funds in new programs. Negative values mean that some activities must be diminished or eliminated.

Preparation of each year's budget should be a two-stage process. The first stage sets budget guidelines (sometimes called parameters). The tableau provides a format for presenting the guidelines. The second stage makes detailed decisions within the envelopes called out by the guidelines—for example, which programs will be expanded or contracted. It is at the guideline-setting stage that the tradeoffs among the seven budgeting goals are mostly made. Hence setting guidelines is of crucial importance for fighting fragmentation.

Top-Line Growth

A theme of this book is that the locus of funding for many public universities is shifting away from core state appropriations and toward institutionally generated revenue—for example, to tuition, sponsored research, gifts, and entrepreneurship. Institutions like the University of Michigan have been pursuing such revenue growth for decades. Michigan's experience can be described as follows.

> In the 1980s the university identified ways to encourage its schools and institutes, as well as individual faculty members, to develop new markets to offset the declining value of state appropriations. As Michigan gained mastery of the market, those at the university came to talk openly about "The University of Michigan, Inc." What that mastery provided was both institutional confidence and added funds. In the 1970s Michigan and UC-Berkeley received roughly the same levels of core revenue. Three decades later, however, Michigan's core revenues exceeded those of Berkeley by more than $400 million per year. (Zemsky et al., 2005b, p. 8)

Spurring revenue growth requires at least some degree of revenue devolvement. Effective fundraising, for example, depends on strong involvement of deans (and to some extent individual faculty members) with potential donors. Yet deans usually are unwilling to spend the time without gaining a commensurate reward-gain-sharing on endowed chairs, for instance. Another example is the retention of surpluses from profitable master's and nondegree programs. Faculty have few incentives to mount such programs if all tuition revenue flows to the central administration and only the direct costs are fed back to the department. Even centralized institutions are beginning to see the value in devolving such revenues to the initiating unit, subject perhaps to overhead charges and/or a modest tax on the surpluses generated.

Performance Measures_____

Experts on quality improvement say that you can't manage something you can't measure. That is, effective management depends on feedback about performance, which allows one to build on success or diagnose and correct problems. The same applies to budgeting. Budget-making without performance measures amounts to flying blind without a compass—a recipe for trouble.

There are two kinds of performance measures. I describe them as quantitative performance indicators (PIs) and qualitative performance evaluations (PEs). PIs generally focus on measurable attributes and events: enrollment trends, publications in alpha journals, surveys of student satisfaction or engagement, the achievement of project milestones, and so on. Such data can be powerful and should be sought vigorously, but one also should recognize that not everything that is important can be measured quantitatively. Education quality, for example, has more dimensions than enrollment counts and student satisfaction. While comprehensive PIs have not been developed and may never be, broadly-effective PEs are entirely feasible. Educational performance evaluation will be discussed in the last section of this chapter.

PIs can enter the budget process in one of two ways: to drive formulas that determine how funds are allocated or to inform judgments about the allocations. The choice depends on whether the indicators capture most or all of what an institution really cares about—that is, whether they are "sufficient" indicators of value. (The sufficiency criterion is similar to the idea of a sufficient statistic, which captures all the relevant information contained in a data series.) The closer the sufficiency criterion is to being met, the more feasible a formulaic approach becomes. On the other hand, basing a formula on insufficient PIs risks steering the institution in the wrong direction. Indicators that tap only part of what's important can provide decision-makers with useful inputs, but the information must be filtered judgmentally. Qualitative performance evaluations also can be used to inform judgment. Sometimes their results can be quantified as indices and used in formulas, but the criterion of sufficiency applies with even more force in this case—just because something can be quantified does not mean it should be.

What kinds of information should inform budget-base allocation decisions? The intrinsic importance of a subject area, its alignment with the university's strategic plan, and its potential for excellence are important. But universities also should consider the area's effectiveness in delivering on its potential. Investments in areas with good track records are likely to produce more value than investments in those with poor records, other things being equal. Moreover, knowledge that good performance can pay off in the budget process provides a powerful incentive to become more effective—a virtuous circle that also helps align local goals with those of the university's strategic plan. Conversely, a belief that good performance in a particular area will not pay off, either because administrators do not believe such performance is important or because they cannot or will not measure it, exerts a chilling effect on improvement. Regular performance evaluations can create the desired virtuous circles.

Responsibility Center Management provides the best-known instance of formulaic budgeting. It relies on PIs (especially enrollments) to allocate revenues and thus the authority to make academic investments. Block budgeting relies heavily on PEs, though PIs can inform judgment when they're available. Advocates of RCM argue implicitly that enrollment and similar PIs are sufficient indicators of value and thus are appropriate for formulaic steering, whereas skeptics say they are not. I've already noted that while RCM stimulates top-line growth, such strong decentralization also generates fragmentation as each center pursues its own agenda—perhaps with little if any regard for the central university's value system.

The fragmentation can in theory be mitigated by taxing revenue and redistributing it as subventions-cross-subsidies for which decisions are informed by PEs. But taxes and subventions are controversial and difficult to administer. Furthermore, they generally reflect an area's intrinsic importance to the institution instead of its performance. The virtuous circles just discussed are harder to build into RCM systems than block grant systems and, as noted earlier, market forces often provide insufficient feedback on education quality.

Incentive and Project Funds

Mechanisms do exist for steering in a decentralized budget environment, but their design and implementation require much careful thought. Specifically, the central administration can "top slice" income to create funding pools for projects, rewards, and incentives. Simply making it known that funds are available to support projects of a certain type boosts activity in the targeted area. Calls for proposals can occur at any time during the budget year, and the funds can be carried over until the project is completed or canceled. A good system requires that proposals include evaluation metrics, provide follow-up to see what has been accomplished and what has been learned, and disseminate the results widely within the institution.

It is also possible to boost incentives by promising after-the-fact rewards for exemplary performance. Teaching awards fall under this rubric, as do the performance funding awards offered by some state oversight bodies. One needs to clearly identify the criteria for judging effectiveness, provide multiple venues for conversations about the criteria and their importance, and field a systematic evaluation process. I designed such a scheme for Hong Kong's University Grants Committee (UGC). The scheme focused attention on alignment of university activities with the region's objectives for its universities, collaborative work among the institutions and with industry, and the improvement of undergraduate education quality. UGC members and heads of institutions felt the exercise was worthwhile because it focused attention and marshaled evidence on a small number of issues that were truly important.

Reward and incentive (R&I) systems have little in common with RCM's subventions. Subventions compensate for market forces whereas R&I funds are targeted toward institutional renewal. Subventions reflect the institution's core values, not particular behavior to be encouraged or tasks to be accomplished. And even when subventions are reviewed frequently, they provide base funding—money a school can build its programs on. A unit's R&I money, on the other hand, is expected to vary from year to year depending on performance.

As with other aspects of the budgeting process, transparency and insistence on evidence in the distribution of R&I funding are essential. In addition to boosting credibility, they make it easier for deans and others to predict the kinds of proposals that will receive serious consideration. Such predictability minimizes wasted effort and adds credibility to the exercise. Transparency and use of evidence also boost organizational learning, which amplifies the effects of incentive schemes. Nowhere is this more important than in the improvement of education quality.

Education Quality Work

One of the biggest pitfalls in budgeting is the belief, widely accepted in academe, that quality is proportional to spending. While there is no doubt that more spending creates opportunities to improve quality, "proportionality" assumes that university activities already are maximally effective. This assumption is manifestly false. There always is room for improvement—in absolute terms and in better alignment of local activities with the university's core objectives. Purging the budget process of the proportionality misconception should be a high-priority institutional goal.

One way to do this is to link funding to demonstrated success in delivering education quality. Budgets that consider only the intrinsic importance of programs while failing to address the quality of teaching and learning will not allocate resources optimally. That budgeting can and should spur education quality improvement is one of this chapter's key tenets. Doing so without spending more is especially important when funds are scarce.

Improving education quality without incremental spending requires organized effort—effort I have come to call education quality work (EQW). Such work can be defined as follows:

> Education quality work consists of *organized process-es dedicated to improving and assuring educational quality*. Such processes systematize a university's approach to quality instead of leaving it mainly to unmonitored individual initiative. They provide what higher education quality pioneers David Dill and Frans van Vught call ". . . a framework for qual-ity management in higher education . . . drawn from insights in [W. Edwards] Deming's approach, but grounded in the context of academic operations" (van Vught, 1994; Dill, 1992). (Massy, 2003, p. 159)

Education quality work should not be confused with teaching and learning itself. Course development is not the same as teaching, for example. One might say that EQW plans and governs the delivery and evaluation of teaching and learning. Departments whose quality work has reached a high level of maturity will deliver better teaching and learning, other things being equal, than those where EQW is haphazard or nonexistent.

Education quality work covers five focal areas of activity. The areas are listed in Figure 6.2 along with questions that illustrate the kinds of issues that are likely to arise in each area (Massy, 2005). Few departments cover all five areas systematically. They generally start with curriculum development based on the academic discipline, not carefully thought-out learning objectives that apply to their actual student body as opposed to an idealized one. Moreover, curricular decisions too often represent the endpoint of a department's collective EQW. Teaching and learning meth-ods, student learning assessment, and education quality assurance more often are seen as issues for individual faculty members than as depart-ment-wide responsibilities (Massy, Wilger, & Colbeck, 1994).

Good EQW is a necessary condition for sustained excellence in undergraduate education. Some institutions, liberal arts colleges, for example, seem to sustain EQW as an integral part of their academic culture. But this is less true for large universities and ones that aspire to research prowess. While there are synergies between teaching and research, powerful research incentives can squeeze out the time available for EQW. The best way to mitigate this problem and its long-term deleterious effects on undergraduate education is through the budget process. EQW activities and support services should be called out as key results areas, and appropriate incentives and rewards should be provided. Above all, the quality of EQW should be monitored explicitly and the results of such monitoring used to inform departmental, school, and college funding.

Figure 6.2
Education Quality Work Focal Areas

1) Learning Objectives
What knowledge, skills, and values should students acquire from their educational experience? How will this experience pay off in employment, societal contributions, and quality of life? Are the objectives based on the needs of actual or potential students rather than some ideal student?

2) Curriculum and Cocurriculum
How does the curriculum relate to the program's learning objectives? What is being taught, in what order, and from what perspective? Does the curriculum build cumulatively on students' prior knowledge and capacity? To what extent does the cocurriculum support the curriculum and the program's learning objectives generally?

3) Teaching and Learning Methods
What teaching methods are used—for example, for first exposure to materials, for interpreting materials and answering questions, for stimulating student involvement, and for providing feedback on student work? Is learning active? Is it collaborative? Is technology being used, and if so is it exploited effectively?

4) Student Learning Assessment
What measures are used to assess student learning? Are they constructively aligned with your learning objectives? Do they compare beginning and ending performance to ascertain value added? Who is responsible for student learning assessment? Are the assessment results trending upward or downward? Do they inform quality improvement efforts and if so, how?

5) Quality Assurance
How do departmental leaders assure themselves and others that the designs for curricula, teaching and learning methods, and student assessments are being implemented as intended? How do they assure themselves that other priorities don't push the education quality to the sidelines?

Academic Audit_____

Interventions for evaluating and improving departmental teaching and learning quality have a long and vexed history. Program review is the method of choice at many U.S. universities. As practiced at most institutions, however, program review focuses more on a department's research and its *capacity to* teach well than on the delivered quality of education or the maturity of EQW. Many states have required public universities to develop programs for student learning assessment but, here too, the outcomes have fallen short of expectations. Charles Cook, longtime director of New England's regional accreditation agency, summed the record up this way: "Millions have been spent by thousands going to hundreds of assessment workshops, . . . and you need a microscope to find the stuff" (McMurtrie, 2000, p. A31). So what, then, does one have to do to make educational quality job one (Zemsky et al., 2005b)?

Frustration with efforts to assess and improve student learning has produced a worldwide search for more effective methods. Most approaches involve reviews by extra-departmental faculty, either from inside or outside the institution. There are two basic approaches: ask the reviewers to evaluate the delivered quality of education or ask them to audit the department's own quality assurance and improvement processes—in other words, its EQW. I will refer to the first approach by the name coined in the United Kingdom: subject-level evaluation. The second approach usually is called academic audit.

The difference is profound. Subject-level reviewers make their own quality evaluations whereas academic auditors review the department's evaluations and the actions that flow from them. The attractiveness of subject-level evaluations lies in its objectivity, but the advantage is illusory in my opinion. The problem is that because the delivered quality of education is so difficult to judge during a short visit, subject-level evaluators have great difficulty in making a valid assessment. Furthermore, such reviews pit the department against the evaluators: Local faculty members present their work in the best possible light and the evaluators try to break through the façade.

Audit places the responsibility for quality evaluation squarely on the department. Then it asks how well the responsibility is being discharged, whether the results can be relied on, and whether there is a continuous cycle of improvement. The following discussion describes the audit process I developed for use in Hong Kong (Massy & French, 2001). The same process is being used currently by the University of Missouri System and the Tennessee Board of Regents (Massy, Graham, & Short, in press), and similar methods have been developed in the

United Kingdom, Sweden, Denmark, Australia, and New Zealand. Academic audit is important in its own right. It also illustrates a systematic approach to qualitative performance evaluation.

The essence of audit is to engage faculty in structured conversations about education quality and how they perform their EQW. The conversations are preceded by reflection and preparation of a self-study document, just as in program review, but the questions asked in academic audit are different. First, the exercise postulates no increase in resource levels. "What could be done with an additional faculty line" is simply not on the table, for instance. Second, audit covers all five focal areas. The conversations between auditors and faculty flow freely but, because the team ensures that no area is omitted, potentially difficult subjects like learning assessment and quality assurance get their due. Finally, the department and the audit team address questions of process. How things get done is of critical importance, and the devil is in the details.

The seven quality principles listed in Figure 6.3 inform many of the questions posed in academic audit (Massy, 2005). Originally distilled from the quality improvement experience of business, government, and health care by researchers at the National Center for Postsecondary Improvement using resources at the American Productivity and Quality Center (Massy, 2003), the principles continue to evolve. They provide faculty with a provocative basis for reflection and self-study preparation and the auditors a framework for guiding conversation during the site visit. The principles direct everyone's attention to areas that need fixing and to how improvement can be achieved. In effect, they provide standards for effective EQW and thus a blueprint for the improvement of teaching and learning. Criteria for the effective use of evidence provide additional standards (Massy, 2005; Western Association of Schools and Colleges, 2002).

The availability of standards makes it possible for auditors to assess the maturity of a department's EQW. Maturity levels range from indifference, to firefighting (dealing with problems only when they become acute), to experimentation with the quality principles, to organized effort, to a full-blown culture of quality. Fully mature departments can demonstrate exemplary performance almost without effort, but immature ones struggle. Auditors have no difficulty distinguishing the good, the bad, and the ugly when it comes to EQW maturity. When a department is audited for the first time, it invariably is found to be relatively immature. Fortunately the increased focus on EQW provided by audit can, when coupled with follow up by deans and provosts, raise maturity levels in a relatively few years.

Figure 6.3
Quality Principles

Define Quality in Terms of Outcomes

Learning outcomes should pertain to what is or will become important for the department's students. Exemplary departments carefully determine their students' needs and then work to meet those needs. They know that student learning, not teaching per se, is what ultimately matters.

Focus on How Things Get Done

Departments should carefully analyze how teachers teach, how students learn, and how they all approach learning assessment. Departments should consult their discipline's pedagogical literature and collect data on what works well and what doesn't. They should stress active learning, exploit information technology, and not hesitate to experiment with new teaching and learning methods. Faculty should be quick to adopt their colleagues' successful innovations, which should become part of the department's modus operandi and form the baseline for future experimentation and improvement.

Work Collaboratively

Professors should demonstrate collegiality in education-related work, just as they do in research. For example, working in teams brings an array of talent to bear on difficult problems, disseminates insight, and allows members to hold each other accountable for team assignments. This makes the department a learning organization not only for disciplinary content but also for education quality processes.

Base Decisions on Evidence

Departments should monitor outcomes systematically—for example, by collecting data from students, graduates, and employers. Data on student preparation and learning styles can be helpful as well. The data should be analyzed carefully in light of disciplinary standards and the faculty's professional experience, and findings should be incorporated in the design of curricula, learning processes, and assessment methods.

Strive for Coherence

Departments should view learning through the lens of the student's entire educational experience. Courses should build on one another to provide the desired depth and breadth. Student portfolios of educational experiences also should reflect coherence. For example, a mix of large lectures and small seminars may produce better learning than a succession of medium-size classes that consume the same amount of faculty time.

Learn From Best Practices

Faculty should identify and analyze good practices in comparable departments and institutions, and then adapt the best to their own circumstances. They should compare good versus average or poor-performing practices within their own departments, assess the causes of the differences, and seek ways to improve the lesser performers.

Make Continuous Improvement a Priority

Departments should strive to improve teaching and learning on a regular basis. While many professors will continue to place strong emphasis on research, they should spend enough discretionary time on education quality processes to maintain an impetus for improvement. Personnel committees should consider the results of such work, along with research and teaching performance, as significant evidence for promotion and tenure.

Experience with academic audit belies the conventional wisdom that formative and summative reviews cannot be combined (Massy, 2003). Audit is formative in that the reflection, self-study, and conversations with auditors are designed to help departments improve their education quality. Yet it is simultaneously summative in that auditors form opinions about EQW maturity. The opinions do not depend on the willingness of the unit audited to disclose its shortcomings. Mature departments will present compelling evidence of exemplary performance. Departments that lack mature EQW will not be able to present such evidence. It is the lack of evidence that downgrades their maturity rating, and the shortfall cannot be papered over. In other words, audit aligns the goals of units (to be able to demonstrate compelling evidence about EQW) and auditors (to be able to see such evidence). Hence audit results are well suited for informing a university's budget-making process.

Conclusion

This chapter has described how the process of budget-making can be used to steer an institution. Steering addresses the macro issues of academic investment (what programs will be expanded or contracted) and top-line growth. However, it also needs to address the micro issues: for example, how the quality of undergraduate education can be sustained and improved. Too many budget processes concentrate on the macro and ignore the micro—ignoring, in effect, the impact of budget-making on rewards, incentives, and quality.

The suggestions contained herein provide guidance for those who wish to remedy this oversight and at the same time find an appropriate position on the centralization-decentralization spectrum. For example:

• Consider budgeting as the primary method for steering the institution, not as just another administrative process. Use the budget process to provide venues for communicating institutional goals and planning objectives and to elicit proposals about how schools and departments can further these goals and objectives.

- Use the strategic budget tableau as a way to analyze and communicate budget data. Make the budget process and the values and evidence that support it as transparent as possible.
- Separate price from quantity in projecting budget variables. Calculate the amount needed to fund last year's programs at this year's prices (cost-rise) and then the amount available for real additions or reductions.
- Review the institution's position on the centralization-decentralization spectrum, for both revenues and expenditures. Balance the need for top-line growth with the need to fight fragmentation.
- Develop explicit mechanisms to support short-term projects as well as budget-base activities, and to provide rewards and incentives for desired activities (including quality improvement). These mechanisms are especially important in decentralized budget systems.
- Link the budget process to strategic planning for capital needs and the mitigation of financial risk.
- Develop metrics for gauging the importance of programs and activities and use them explicitly in the budget process. The metrics should include both quantitative performance indicators (PIs) and qualitative performance evaluations (PEs).
- Recognize education quality work (EQW) as a necessary activity and be sure it's adequately funded and rewarded. Consider adopting academic audit as the performance evaluation metric for EQW.

Performance measurement and feedback, reward, and incentive are critical in any type of budgeting system. In most cases the virtuous circle hinges on systematic qualitative performance evaluation of the kind illustrated by academic audit.

In closing, let me comment on who should participate in budget-making and how. Colleges and universities should be mission centered and market smart. The mission embodies an institution's values, which are determined and elaborated by its governance processes. Just who should participate in governance is beyond my scope, but the general consensus is that participation should be broad and should include the faculty in an important way. Public institutions differ from private ones, of course, in that value determination must take into account state mandates. This adds additional stakeholders and a new layer of complication, but it does not change the process in any fundamental way.

Once values are determined, it is up to management to devise the ways and means by which they can be maximized subject to market, productivity, and financial constraints. Included in this task is the development of performance indicators and evaluations (PIs and PEs) that, taken together, are sufficiently reflective of the institution's values. These PIs and PEs should be embedded in the budget process, and the combination should be recalibrated regularly with stakeholders to ensure continued alignment with values.

In my view, the key management figures for budget-making are the president, the chief academic officer, the chief financial officer, and the deans of schools. At Stanford University, the provost is responsible for developing the budget and presenting it to the president and the board of trustees. My job as vice president for business and finance was to support and facilitate the process, but not to lead it—let alone determine its outcomes. This division of labor reflects the provost's responsibility for the academic judgments that drive the budget. The trustees held me accountable for the financial judgments that underpinned the tableau—for example, the sum shown as available for new program allocations. Then they would grill the provost on the allocations themselves. Deans carry a similar responsibility in any budget environment, including both RCM and block budgeting, that decentralizes expenditure decisions.

Other schemes are of course possible, but the fundamental principle is that financial considerations, while critical, should not dominate budgeting. To repeat the proposition with which I began this chapter:

> Universities exist to create value through education, research, and public service. Because budgets enable activities and activities create value, budgets can be said to mediate value creation. Hence budget development should be viewed as a key tool for steering the institution, not just as another administrative process.

References

Hopkins, D. S. P., & Massy, W. F. (1981). *Planning models for colleges and universities.* Stanford, CA: Stanford University Press.

Massy, W. F. (Ed.). (1996). *Resource allocation in higher education.* Ann Arbor, MI: University of Michigan Press.

Massy, W. F. (2003). *Honoring the trust: Quality and cost containment in higher education.* Bolton, MA: Anker.

Massy, W. F. (2005). Academic audit for accountability and improvement. In J. C. Burke & Associates, *Achieving accountability in higher education: Balancing public, academic, and market demands* (pp. 173–197). San Francisco, CA: Jossey-Bass.

Massy, W. F., & French, N. J. (2001, April). Teaching and learning quality process review: What the program has achieved in Hong Kong. *Quality in Higher Education, 7*(1), 33–45.

Massy, W. F., Graham, S., & Short, P. (in press). *Academic quality work: A handbook for improvement.* Bolton, MA: Anker,.

Massy, W. F., Wilger, A. K., & Colbeck, C. (1994, July/August). Overcoming "hollowed" collegiality. *Change, 26*(4), 10–20.

Massy, W. F., & Zemsky, R. (1995). *Using information technology to enhance academic productivity.* Washington, DC: Educom.

McMurtrie, B. (2000, July 7). Accreditors revamp policies to assess student learning. *The Chronicle of Higher Education*, p. A29.

Strauss, J. C., & Curry, J. R. (2002). *Responsibility center management: Lessons from 25 years of decentralized management.* Washington, DC: National Association of College and University Business Officers.

Western Association of Schools and Colleges. (2002). *Evidence guide: A guide to using evidence in the accreditation process: A resource to support institutions and evaluation teams.* Alameda, CA: Accrediting Commission for Senior Colleges and Universities, Western Association of Schools and Colleges.

Whalen, E. L. (1991). *Responsibility center budgeting: An approach to decentralized management for institutions of higher education.* Bloomington, IA: Indiana University Press.

Zemsky, R., Wegner, G. R., & Massy, W. F. (2005a, July 15). Today's colleges must be market smart and mission centered. *The Chronicle of Higher Education*, p. B6.

Zemsky, R., Wegner, G. R., & Massy, W. F. (2005b). *Remaking the American university: Market-smart and mission-centered.* New Brunswick, NJ: Rutgers University Press.

7

Assessing Institutional Effectiveness and Connecting the Pieces of a Fragmented University

J. Fredericks Volkwein

Based on a model of institutional effectiveness, this chapter examines the modern fragmented research university and makes three recommendations. At the institutional level, universities should adopt "Management By Objectives" planning to reduce university fragmentation by ensuring that unit goals are congruent with institutional goals and that responsibility for action and goal attainment is pinpointed. At the program level, undergraduate general education programs should be reshaped and accredited based on their alignment with the student outcomes identified by the recent national initiatives of the Association of American Colleges and Universities. Such accreditation should follow the program review model, and student liberal education outcomes should form the central evidence for the self-study, review, and accreditation. At the individual level, faculty should begin to build the assessment of student liberal education outcomes into appropriate courses.

Figure 7.1 proposes a model for assessing institutional effectiveness. The five parts of the model summarize the steps for assessing institutions, programs, faculty, and students. The first step in the model distinguishes the dual purposes of institutional effectiveness: the inspirational, which is oriented toward internal improvement, and the pragmatic, which is oriented toward external accountability.

The second step poses five assessment and evaluation questions. I suggest that effective universities and programs are those that can ask and answer these questions about themselves: Are you meeting your goals? Are you getting better at it? Do you meet professional standards? How do you compare to others? Are your efforts cost effective? These questions in Step 2—goal attainment, improvement, meeting standards, benchmarking, and productivity—drive the other steps and provide foundations, especially for research design, data collection, and analysis in Steps 3 and 4.

Step 3 is the research design. The appropriate assessment measures and methods vary for each of three evaluation levels—institutional, program, and individual. Within each of these, assessment strategies will vary depending on whether they are designed for demonstrating academic effectiveness on the one hand, or administrative effectiveness on the other. However, the design is easier when institutional, program, and individual goals are aligned.

Step 4 requires the execution of the research design by collecting, cleaning, and analyzing data. Step 5 contains the actions that our regional and specialized accrediting bodies constantly challenge us to do more of—but alas, most institutions are much better at collecting data than at communicating and acting on it.

Figure 7.1
Building Institutional Effectiveness

A Model for Assessing Institutional Effectiveness

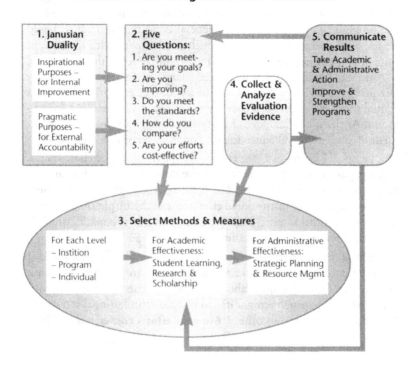

The ancient Roman god Janus is the god of doors and gateways. Like the two sides of a door, Janus has two faces: one looking outward and one looking inward. While Janus encourages us to consider the external as well as the internal aspects of our endeavors, Janusian thinking also reminds us that passing through a door means simultaneously entering and leaving. This insight of one action viewed in opposite ways recognizes the dual nature of almost everything we do. Commencement is both an ending and a beginning. For every action in the physical (and political) world, there is a reaction. When we strengthen the student experience inside the university, we simultaneously make the institution appear more attractive externally.

Universities face many Janusian dualities. In particular, assessing institutional effectiveness requires us to serve twin masters: the need for internal assessment for purposes of improvement, and the need for external performance reporting for purposes of accountability. Resolving the tension between the internal and the external uses of assessment and performance presents a classic Janusian challenge. In public and private institutions alike, we must do both. Facing internally, we need to improve ourselves and become better teachers, learners, scholar/researchers, and administrators. Facing externally, we need to demonstrate our effectiveness and be accountable to key external stakeholders: taxpayers and legislators, tuition payers and trustees.

To resolve this tension, I describe these opposite forces as the inspirational versus the pragmatic—doing something because you want to versus doing something because you have to (Volkwein, 1999).

The inspirational foundation for evaluation and assessment is doing it for self-improvement, especially for the enhancement of student learning and growth. We in higher education are at our best when we carry out educational change, assessment, and evaluation not to please outsiders, but to satisfy ourselves—to achieve an organizational climate of ongoing development and continuing improvement.

The pragmatic foundation for evaluation and assessment recognizes the external need to demonstrate our accountability to stakeholders: legislators and trustees, taxpayers and tuition payers. Moreover, assessing institutional effectiveness enables universities to compete successfully for enrollments and resources and gain a strategic advantage over others. In an atmosphere of scarcity, those campuses that can measure their effectiveness and reshape themselves will compete better for enrollments, resources, and professors. On campus, academic departments and programs that provide presidents and provosts with evidence about their students will compete more successfully for campus resources.

Thus the simultaneous and competing needs for both internal improvement and external accountability provide the first foundation for demonstrating institutional and program effectiveness. The regional accrediting associations also are helping to resolve this dichotomy by requiring each campus to present evidence of student learning and growth as a key component in demonstrating the institution's effectiveness. This is especially visible in the publications and written standards of the Middle States Commission on Higher Education, North Central Association, and the Western Association of Schools and Colleges.

Five Assessment and Evaluation Questions _____

The second foundation for institutional effectiveness arises from the frequent lack of clarity of assessment goals. Evaluation and assessment force professionals to engage in evidence-based thinking, but the nature of the evidence gathered depends on the questions asked at the beginning of the process. As suggested in Figure 7.1, institutional effectiveness generally seeks answers to one or more of these generic evaluation questions: Does the institution or program meet or exceed certain standards? How does the institution or program compare to others? Does the institution or program achieve its desired goals? How can the institution or program be improved? Is the institution or program cost effective? As drivers for assessment activity, each of these questions—standards, comparisons, goal attainment, improvement, and cost effectiveness—has a relevant contribution to make to the overall effectiveness wardrobe (Volkwein, 2004b).

1) Is the institution or program meeting goals?

Internal-referenced, goal-driven assessment is important and relevant at every level—individual students and faculty, classroom, program, department, and institution. What should our students be learning? What are the goals and purposes of this program? What is the university's particular mission? Answers require clear, measurable goals and objectives. This formative assessment concentrates on narrowing the gap between goals and actual performance, and thus requires measures or judgments of congruence and incongruence.

2) Is the institution or program improving?

This improvement-driven evaluation compares institutions, programs, and individuals against themselves over time. Formative self-comparison requires consistent, longitudinal data, or at least Time 1 and Time 2 data; recognizes that all institutions and programs are at different starting points; and assumes that every student, faculty member, and program can improve.

3) Does the institution or program meet standards?

Summative, criterion-referenced evaluation is the traditional accreditation approach, and requires assessing institutions, programs, and individuals against criteria established by an external authority. Consequently, this criterion-based form of assessment overrides local control and autonomy and places a high priority on ensuring minimum levels of competence or performance. It also requires agreement and clarity about the standards and performance measurement. Whether applied at the institution, program, or individual level, such assessment usually leads to summative decisions about continuance and discontinuance.

4) How does the institution or program compare?

Answering this question requires comparison against external norms and benchmarking against peer institutions and programs. Although administrative benchmarking for internal management is now well established, comparison assessment recognizes that institutions and programs are competing, and that many in society like to "keep score" and identify who's on top. Using regional and national comparisons has legitimacy with some stakeholders, especially the parents of traditional college students. This belief explains the interest in *U.S. News & World Report* ratings and rankings, and assumes that competition for faculty and students will drive each institution either to improve or to see its market position deteriorate. Even though most campus officials dislike the guidebook ratings game, they eagerly follow the performance indicators related to research and scholarly productivity. Whether based on perceived reputation or objective statistics, comparison assessment requires no consensus about performance levels or standards—it merely shows how your college or program stacks up against the competition. As a means of assessment, comparison measurement requires the selection of appropriate reference groups and common information about them.

5) Is the institution or program cost effective?

This is the harsh productivity question that compares costs with benefits, expenditures and resources with results. Such evaluation usually involves a high degree of professional judgment to go along with the measurement of costs and benefits. The costs of higher education constitute an enormous national investment, and universities are pressured to demonstrate that teaching, research, and service programs are conducted economically. These external accountability concerns stimulate current legislative and trustee interest in class size, faculty workload, administrative salaries, time to degree, loan default, economic impact, and research productivity, among other measures. Internally, some universities use indicators of productivity and performance to assess various administrative and academic support services.

Balancing Efficiency and Effectiveness _____

Universities are fascinating because they house several strong cultures within a single organization. One of the strongest is the administrative culture—the bureaucracy—that bases authority and responsibility on position in the hierarchy. Another strong culture, of course, is the faculty's academic or professional culture, where authority rests not so much on one's position as on one's knowledge or expertise, and decision-making becomes less hierarchical and more collegial (Birnbaum, 1988; Etzioni, 1964/2000).

The major goal activities (transmission of knowledge or teaching, discovery of knowledge or research and scholarship, and application of knowledge or service and outreach) are carried out by the academic side of the organization, so its needs and value system generally dominate. This academic mission is why university-appointed presidents and provosts generally need to have faculty experience and Ph.D.s in order to be selected. The "loose-coupled" faculty culture needs autonomy and freedom from the operational concerns of the university, and places high value on maintaining educational quality and effectiveness, on protecting standards, and on participatory decision-making. On the other hand, the administrative bureaucracy supplies the support services that make faculty goal activities possible. The administrative culture is much more tightly coupled and hierarchical, more cost conscious, and values control and efficiency (Volkwein, 1999). The academic side pushes for decentralization, the administrative side for direction.

These two university cultures have learned to live and work together, one giving a higher priority to efficiency and productivity, the other to educational and scholarly effectiveness. Both cultures have external and internal faces. The administrative culture's external face looks toward strategy planning, resource acquisition, and accountability. Its internal face provides direction, support, and structure. The academic culture adheres to external peer standards for research and scholarship and values loyalty to the discipline with its outerface. Internally, the academic culture provides instruction and university service. The arrangement reflects a modern balance between the almost universal need for managerial direction and cost control on the one hand, and a commitment to maintaining high standards in research and teaching on the other. Indeed, the separate administrative and academic structure of colleges and universities reflect these competing needs. Within the same academic year, outside supporters may ask a university simultaneously to reduce spending and improve educational outcomes. The university administration addresses one problem while the academic professionals address the other.

Designing Effectiveness Studies in American Higher Education

One problem in higher education is that we think we know how to measure efficiency and cost, but cannot agree on what constitutes effectiveness. The editor of this book and his scholarly colleagues have described three competing models or philosophies about what constitutes excellence in higher education (Burke & Minassians, 2002; Burke & Serban, 1998; Volkwein & Grunig, 2005).

First, the academic community traditionally embraces the *resource/reputation model* derived from the work of Astin (1985), who described but strongly disapproved of it. This model emphasizes the importance of financial resources, faculty credentials, student test scores, external funding, and reputation ratings and rankings by peers. Under this model, faculty, sometimes joined by accreditation bodies, argue for more resources to support educational effectiveness. This drives up costs and attends to inputs rather than outcomes.

Second, many parents, students, and student affairs professionals cling to a *client-centered model*. This market-oriented model derived from the literature on quality management emphasizes all possible student services, faculty availability and attentiveness, student and alumni satisfaction and feedback, low tuition, and high aid. Seymour (1992) articulates this model in his book *On Q: Causing Quality in Higher Education*. Under this model, the first priority of a college or university is to fulfill the needs of students, parents, employers, and other "customers" of higher education. Institutions that best meet the needs of their constituents are considered the most effective. Therefore, an organization's customers, rather than the views of experts, define quality. Good customer service is very labor intensive and emphasizes the student experience over student outcomes.

Third, the civic and government community generally believes in the *strategic investment model* (Ewell, 1994; Volkwein & Grunig, 2005). This model emphasizes the importance of return on investment, cost-benefit, results-oriented and productivity measures such as admissions yield, graduation rates, time to degree, and expenditures per student. Under this model, government officials and even trustees evaluate each new initiative in light of its perceived payoff. This model represents the only one with potential to dampen costs.

Different higher education stakeholders interpret educational excellence differently. Hence the potential for misunderstanding, if not outright conflict, exists, catching presidents frequently in the middle between faculty and accreditors, students and parents, government officials and trustees. Addressing all five questions of institutional effectiveness becomes a wise and productive investment that enables multiple responses to multiple audiences.

Driven by a diverse economy and society, higher education has become a complex industry of public and private educational providers, and an array of quality assurance, funding, and accreditation. The evolving certification mechanisms reflect this complexity. The literature reflects four major areas of higher education quality assurance.

- The classroom/course/student level—assessing the performance, certification, and learning outcomes of individual students
- The individual faculty member—assessing faculty performance in teaching, scholarship, research, and service
- The department and program level—reviewing, evaluating, and accrediting academic and administrative programs and services
- The university or institution level—regional accreditation, performance reporting, governance control

Table 7.1 separates these evaluative foci into concerns about efficiency and cost on the one hand, versus effectiveness and quality on the other, and indicates who the major actors are with primary, though not exclusive, responsibility at each level.

The focus on efficiency and cost occupies the attention of many stakeholders inside and outside the university. As shown in the middle column of Table 7.1, the responsible actors at each level generally include those who supply the funding to the institution and its faculty and students, or those who administer and control those funds after their receipt.

However, the remaining pages of this chapter examine the influences at work in the right-hand column of Table 7.1. What are the mechanisms that assess and promote quality and effectiveness at each level of evaluation?

Table 7.1
Levels of Evaluation and Quality Assurance in the United States

Levels of Evaluation	Dominant Focus of Evaluation and Primary Responsibility for Quality Assurance	
	Efficiency/Cost	Effectiveness/Quality
Institution/Campus	• State and local government • Governing boards and trustees	• Presidents and chancellors • Regional and national accreditation bodies • State higher education agencies, trustees and governing boards
Discipline/Program/ Department	• Campus administration, especially financial officers	• 100 academic and vocational accrediting bodies and societies • State higher education agencies • Campus provosts/deans
Individual Faculty Member/Researcher/ Instructor	• Federal and foundation grant providers	• Federal and foundation review boards • Campus provosts/deans
Classroom or Individual Student/Graduate	• Campus financial and enrollment management officers • Federal and state financial aid authorities	• The faculty • State and professional licensure such as for teachers, lawyers, nurses, physicians, accountants, social workers, engineers, architects

Institutional Effectiveness

At the institutional or campus level, presidents or chancellors and trustees are the obvious first line of quality assurance followed by the various national and regional accrediting bodies (see Chapter 8). In addition, the use of externally mandated performance indicators for publicly supported institutions is now well established. States have largely abandoned their early initiatives to mandate testing in favor of less expensive and more practical institutional performance indicators (Ewell, 2005). Borden and Banta (1994) summarized 250 performance indicators in 22 categories of input, process, and output. Burke and Serban (1998) examined the indicators used for performance funding in 11 states, finding that only 18% could be classified as indicators of quality among four-year schools.

Internally, campus leaders have imported an array of management tools to monitor and improve institutional performance. These include the Baldrige Seven Quality Criteria, Six Sigma, and Dashboard

Performance Indicators. A growing number of institutions such as Pennsylvania State University, Ohio State University, Miami University, Tufts University, and Illinois State University have developed elaborate scorecards or performance "dashboards" to annually track and monitor their progress and effectiveness compared to a group of peers. In their study of performance dashboards, Terkla, Wiseman, and Cohen (2005) report 11 broad categories of indicators with one to five subgroups containing 6 to 100 different indicators in each subgroup.

The largest numbers of these dashboard indicators reflect measures of admissions, enrollments, faculty and student profiles, and finances, including tuition, employee compensation, financial aid and fellowships, endowment, alumni giving, and Moody's ratings of financial health. Institutions are struggling to add indicators of academic and student outcomes performance, but few have gotten beyond retention and graduation rates, degrees awarded, class size, student/faculty ratios, honors and study abroad participation, student/faculty/alumni satisfaction, research funding/expenditures/patents, employment/graduate school attendance by graduates, library rankings, and reputational ratings. Of course, many of these are indicators that the public associates with quality, but we know from the meta-analysis by Pascarella and Terenzini (2005) that they reflect only indirectly on the actual educational experiences and learning outcomes of students.

In Chapter 8 of this book, Ralph Wolff discusses the regional accrediting groups more thoroughly. They constitute the oldest and best-known vehicles providing external accountability and quality assurance and follow processes designed collaboratively by the member institutions.

The accreditation process has undergone dramatic changes in the past 20 years (Ewell, 2005; Wolff, 2005). As noted earlier, one clear trend places student outcomes assessment at the center of the accreditation review. Accreditation bodies, not only at the regional level, but also in many disciplines (such as engineering and business), have shifted their policies and processes away from meeting rigid quantitative standards for inputs and resources, and toward judging educational effectiveness from measurable outcomes. This paradigm shift was led by several of the regional accreditors (most prominently the Middle States Commission on Higher Education, North Central Association, and the Western Association of Schools and Colleges), who revised their manuals and review processes to give greater attention to student learning outcomes and program goal attainment as the institution's demonstration of its educational effectiveness. A second related trend in accreditation is the greater emphasis on improvement. Outcomes assessment evidence is now the centerpiece of educational effectiveness, and using that evidence to improve is a hallmark of healthy institutions and programs. Regional and program accreditors alike are prodding all in higher education to build "cultures of evidence" that feed into continuous improvement systems that are the hallmarks of a self-renewing, learning organization.

Ewell (2005) describes the sad history of accreditation and state policy attempts to establish institution-centered assessment in higher education. Unfortunately, these attempts have received variable levels of institutional cooperation; faculty generally treat assessment as a compliance exercise; and no acceptable tests or other measures of student learning have been designed that are capable of judging both individual student and institutional performance. A few model institutions including the University at Albany and the University of California–Davis have conducted institution-level assessments and posted the findings for all to see as recommended by Ewell (2005). However, institutions increasingly post their accreditation self-studies on their web sites as recommended by Volkwein (2004b).

Department and Program Effectiveness

At the program level, the picture is less complicated. There are two major types of program evaluation—program review internally, and program accreditation externally. Both contribute to institutional effectiveness, especially when the planning process aligns program and institutional goals.

Specialized academic and vocational accrediting bodies and professional societies scrutinize and accredit officially recognized programs in an array of specialties. Institutions are eager to meet the standards set by these professional organizations because accredited programs attract the best students and faculty, as well as federal, foundation, and state funding.

Several scholars (e.g., Banta, Lund, Black, & Oblander, 1996; Barak & Mets, 1995) maintain that campus-based program review represents the most effective form of institutional assessment. Accreditation bodies have reinforced this conclusion during the past decade by calling on institutions and programs to create a culture of evidence that promotes academic self-renewal.

As a person involved in these quality assurance processes at the program, campus, and accreditation team levels over the past 35 years,

I have reached a different conclusion. These discipline-specific accreditation and department program reviews generally tend to reinforce institutional fragmentation. Program reviews and disciplinary reaccreditation all too often view the department and program in isolation. Such reviews reflect a faculty-driven process based on the resource/reputation model, focusing on faculty credentials, student selectivity, and resource acquisition. Even when these processes call for evidence of student outcomes, they tend to center on student attainment in the major or the graduate degree program, giving little or no attention to student general education or liberal learning, nor to alignment with institutional goals.

Some hopeful signs of healthy change do exist among some of the professional accrediting bodies. For most of its history, the Accreditation Board for Engineering and Technology (ABET) enforced accreditation criteria that dictated all major elements of an accredited engineering program, including program curricula, faculty, and facilities. In the mid-1990s, following intense dialogue within the engineering community, ABET crafted new accreditation criteria for engineering programs called *Engineering Criteria 2000* (EC2000). EC2000 shifted the basis for accreditation from inputs (what is taught) to outputs (what is learned).

The new criteria specify 11 learning outcomes and require programs to assess and demonstrate their students' achievement in each of these areas. EC2000 retains earlier accreditation standards on the development of students' mathematical, scientific, and technical knowledge, but it also emphasizes other professional and general education skills, such as behaving ethically, communicating effectively, working in teams, understanding contemporary issues, and engaging in lifelong learning. ABET commissioned the Center for the Study of Higher Education at Pennsylvania State University to conduct a national study of the impact of these new accreditation criteria (Prados, Peterson, & Lattuca, 2005; Volkwein, Lattuca, Terenzini, Strauss, & Sukhbaatar, 2004). The Penn State study has found rather consistent improvements in engineering programs, student experiences, and student learning outcomes resulting from the new standards (Lattuca, Terenzini, & Volkwein, 2006).

Even in the absence of external accreditors, most campuses have their own provost-led and faculty-endorsed program review processes. Program reviews under ideal conditions are integrated into the fabric of academic affairs and constitute a constructive process of self-examination and continuous improvement. At times, a university-wide council that examines publicly all institutional reviews helps integrate these processes. The State University of New York at Albany (now called the University at Albany) pioneered such a model review process in the 1970s and 1980s, and The University of California–Santa Barbara and Florida International University appear to have one now. Additionally, in many parts of the nation, state-mandated, periodic reviews of academic programs exist, especially at the graduate level. At most universities, it seems there is an unending stream of self-study documents and site visit teams from regional, state, and discipline based bodies. At least these groups focus mostly on educational effectiveness, rather than on the latest guidebook ratings and expenditures per student.

The Review Process

In general, the procedures for both institutional and program-level review, whether conducted locally or by different accrediting associations, have many similar features. The process typically includes three components.

1) *A self-study prepared by the unit reviewed that responds to the evaluation criteria established by the institution or accreditation body.* The heart of the self-study usually contains an assessment of program and faculty strengths, weaknesses, outcomes, and actions from the previous review, along with recommendations. Increasingly, campus guidelines and accrediting bodies alike require units to go further than they have in the past to articulate educational goals and to develop measures of student learning. When these program and learning goals are aligned with institutional goals, the self-study and review can reduce fragmentation and contribute to effectiveness.

2) *Visit by a team of peer external evaluators.* In the case of locally sponsored reviews, the team may frequently contain a mix of faculty from other departments at the institution and one from another higher education institution. These evaluators review the assembled evidence and submit a report.

3) *Action based on the self-study, the site visit report, and the department or institution response.* If accreditation sponsored, the accreditation body decides to accredit, accredit with conditions, or not to accredit the institution or program under review. If locally sponsored, the president or provost usually decides what priority to give the program for personnel and other resources, and program chairs and faculty are responsible for making any needed adjustments in curricula, instruction, admissions, or other program requirements and policies.

The old evaluation and accreditation philosophy, most dominant before the 1980s, encouraged institutions to maximize the quality of the *inputs* in order to guarantee the quality of the outputs. While the external pressure for maximizing input quality has diminished, growing external attention to performance outputs and outcomes (such as academic achievement and graduation rates and faculty publications) has forced us as researchers to start at the end and look backward at the conditions that produce favorable performance. Universities supposedly educate, research, serve, and develop students, but every institutional researcher knows that the empirical connections between high inputs and high outputs remain very strong, and lie behind Astin's (1985) notion of comparing actual versus predicted graduation rates, based on the profile of entering students. More selective student bodies tend to have higher graduation rates. More heavily credentialed faculty in the aggregate win more research grants and produce more publications. In any case, institutions everywhere are finding that it is in their self-interest to devote continuing attention to the quality of their faculty and student credentials on entry because GIGO (good-in, good-out) is at work (Volkwein, 1999).

The new accreditation philosophy, growing in strength since 1990, encourages institutions and their stakeholders to measure the *outcomes*, to judge the results of our educational programs. Although most of us are more comfortable with this approach, it runs the danger of providing information too late in the process to render anything but a summative, acceptable versus unacceptable judgment. Consequently, an overemphasis on outcomes may not provide the information needed for internal development and educational enhancement (Volkwein, 1999).

Renewed interest now centers on *process* measures on the theory that good outcomes will not result from flawed educational processes. In Chapter 10 of this book, George Kuh describes the advantages of the process approach. Measurement at critical process points enables institutions to determine which student experiences have the greatest (and least) impact, and to make corrective intervention. Moreover, the research evidence indicates that outcomes such as student growth and satisfaction are most heavily influenced by those campus experiences that produce student academic and social integration, which in turn produce favorable student outcomes (Strauss & Volkwein, 2002).

Effective program review processes are time consuming and expensive and constitute the ideal higher education jobs bill:

• The need to measure and improve inputs because of their strong empirical connection to important performance outcomes like academic achievement and graduation rates

- The need to measure critical processes both because of their role in student integration and growth, and because such measurement facilitates corrective intervention
- The need to measure a variety of outputs and outcomes because results matter the most

Faculty Effectiveness

At the individual level, faculty research and scholarly performance has for decades been peer reviewed by federal grant agencies, by foundation and industry sponsors, and by journal editors and book publishers, among others. At the campus level, annual reports of faculty activity have been a long tradition, and they increasingly focus on instructional, research, and scholarly productivity, rather than mere activity. Additionally, most institutions use annual reviews of faculty productivity in order to make merit pay decisions.

Assessing faculty effectiveness has changed dramatically since the publication of Boyer's (1990) perspectives on the four domains of scholarship: discovery, application, integration, and teaching. Boyer has reshaped our thinking about these dimensions of scholarship and the connections among them. Braxton (2006) and his colleagues summarize what we have learned about the impact of Boyer's four domains, finding that the majority of doctoral, master's, and baccalaureate institutions have developed a more complex, nuanced view of scholarship that incorporates many aspects of teaching, service, and integration of knowledge. Moreover, many campuses have reshaped the faculty evaluation and academic rewards structure in ways that align not only with Boyer's domains, but also with differential institutional mission (e.g., see Braxton, Luckey, & Helland, 2006; Colbeck & Michael, 2006; McKinney, 2006; O'Meara, 2006). Boyer's thinking has reduced university fragmentation and promoted integration.

In addition to Boyer's influence, an array of national bodies and higher education scholars have expressed concerns about the state of undergraduate education in research universities. Led by Chickering and Gamson (1987), the American Association for Higher Education (AAHE) published seven principles of good educational practice aimed at influencing faculty instructional behavior. The National Center for Higher Education Management Systems added its 12 characteristics of effective instruction (Ewell & Jones, 1996).

Responding to these national concerns, some research universities such as Penn State adopted policies calling not only for student evaluations of instruction in every course each semester, but also for periodic post-tenure evaluations of faculty performance that document accomplishments in teaching, research and creative work, professional activity, and university or public service. Many research universities have developed rather elaborate systems of faculty evaluation. For example, the University of California System links faculty assessment to decisions about merit pay and steps within rank, and takes place every two to three years for each ladder faculty member, including post-tenure professors. Students at the end of each course evaluate faculty teaching performance. Individual instructors and individual depart-ments can vary the survey items and teaching dimensions assessed, but most reviews include the overall rating of the instructor and the course. Faculty evaluations of teaching include classroom observations by col-leagues at the point of preparation for promotion and merit review. These processes at UC Santa Barbara and UC Davis seem especially well conducted. While research achievement gets priority over teach-ing, the great majority of the administrators, faculty committee chairs, and deans do stress teaching in personnel decisions. These healthy changes seem especially effective because they include participation by faculty governance.

Assessing Students

At the student and classroom levels, the picture is more complicated. Students and the areas of their learning vary widely among institutions and degree programs. Students are diverse and the dimensions of the learning processes in American higher education are extremely com-plex. Likewise, assessing student performance is complex and hence difficult to summarize for institutional performance.

Most American higher education scholars think of assessment as ". . . the systematic gathering, interpretation, and use of information about student learning for purposes of improvement" (Marchese, 1997, p. 87). Assessment tends to be locally designed and executed evaluation research intended to determine the effects of the institution on student learning to improve teaching and learning (AAHE, 1996). Student outcomes assessment assembles and analyzes both qualitative and quantitative teaching and learning outcomes evidence to examine their congruence with an institution's stated purposes and educational objec-tives (Middle States Commission on Higher Education, 1996). Each of these three approaches suggests that student outcomes assessment is goal driven, empirically based, and improvement oriented.

Traditionally, student performance and learning are evaluated where learning primarily takes place, where faculty and students interact—in the classroom. However, the 20th-century testing movement made it possible to ensure minimum standards by requiring particular levels of performance on standardized examinations. These performance standards now range from college entrance tests (such as the SAT and ACT exams), to tests of student basic skills (like *College BASE*, or a foreign language proficiency test), general education skills (such as the ACT Collegiate Assessment of Academic Proficiency and the ETS Measure of Academic Proficiency and Progress), and attainment in the major (such as the ETS Major Field Exams). Upon graduation, individual students may face not only graduate school entrance tests, but also assessments of their qualifications to become a practicing professional in many fields including accounting, law, engineering, medicine, and teaching.

In *Liberal Education Outcomes*, prepared as part of the Liberal Education and America's Promise (LEAP) initiative, the Association of American Colleges and Universities (AAC&U) expresses caution about the role of standardized testing in assessment (AAC&U, 2005). Recognizing that "biologists use quite different inquiry methods than historians; engineers use different forms of teamwork and communication than teachers," the LEAP report suggests that ". . . standardized testing can play a useful supplementary role in the assessment of student learning," but that the best evidence comes from assessing ". . . students' authentic and complex performances in the context of their most advanced studies: research projects, community service projects, portfolios of student work, supervised internships, etc." (AAC&U, 2005, p. 10).

Since standardized tests may or may not fit the goals, curricula, or needs of particular institutions and programs, the field has developed an array of other assessment strategies for measuring student learning outcomes (Tebo-Messina & Prus, 1995; Volkwein, 2004a). The following are some of the most common assessment tools, and each has its advantages.

• Locally developed comprehensive exams (including essays)
• Appraisals of student performances, exhibits, and simulations
• Surveys of student attitudes, values, and experiences
• Student self-evaluations of abilities, skills, and gains
• Senior theses or research projects
• Capstone courses
• Interviews
• External examiners
• Archival records and analysis of courses and student experiences
• Portfolios

- Behavioral observations (including internships)
- Classroom research and course-embedded assessments
- Alumni studies and placement data

Although these assessment strategies may be quite useful for assessing one type of student learning or another, they all share the *disadvantage* of being not very useful reflections of educational effectiveness for undergraduate education as a whole. Even standardized tests have limited usefulness. While they may be appropriate for particular areas of knowledge in the major, such tests are not regarded as good ways to measure complex thinking, communication skills, teamwork, or ethical reasoning. Hence it is very difficult to aggregate the results of student learning assessment up to the institution level. This measurement challenge provides a practical obstacle to using student outcomes assessment for institutional effectiveness.

To overcome this obstacle, some universities have divided their assessment activities into decentralized efforts that focus on assessing outcomes for individual students versus centralized efforts that assess the outcomes of large populations of undergraduates. This latter more centralized approach relies heavily on the collection of self-reported student experiences, involvement, skills, and gains in knowledge. The use of self-reported measures to describe and assess the relative differences among large groups of students and alumni is now widespread (Kuh, 2005). Under the right conditions, student self-reports are both valid and reliable, especially for measuring the outcomes for groups of students, rather than individuals. A growing body of research over the past 30 years has examined the adequacy of self-reported measures of learning and skill development as proxies for objective measures of the same traits or skills. Although results vary depending on the traits and instruments examined, these studies report correlations of 0.50 to 0.90 between self-reports and actual student grades, SAT scores, the ACT Comprehensive Test, the College Basic Academic Subjects Examination, and the Graduate Record Examination (Lattuca et al., 2006). Such research has spawned the use of a large number of instruments and scales for measuring student outcomes. These include the ACT-COMP, ACT Student Opinion Survey, ETS-CAPS, College Student Experiences Questionnaire, National Survey of Student Engagement, HERI College Student Survey, and an array of institution-specific and discipline-specific instruments.

The Assessment Matrix in Table 7.2 summarizes the dimensions of assessment at a single campus in the 1980s and 1990s (Volkwein, 1992). Following a year of study by a campus task force, the University at Albany identified four categories of student learning assessment: basic skills, general education, personal growth, and attainment in the major (Jacobi, Astin, & Ayala, 1987; Terenzini, 1989). The various data collection and assessment activities then were divided into those measuring the performance of groups and those measuring the performance of individuals. This assessment matrix shows the range of assessment activities resulting from this simple exercise at one university. It includes testing student basic skills for proficiency and curricular tracking, collecting self-reported estimates of student growth, examining grades in general education and courses in the major field, surveying alumni to assess their experiences, administering senior comprehensive exams, and other capstone experiences. The survey instruments administered to groups of students and alumni contained many items and scales aligned with institutional and general education goals.

Table 7.2
Assessment Matrix

Assessment Categories	Centralized Studies Measuring the Performance of Groups	Decentralized Studies Measuring the Performance of Individuals
Basic Skills (for both proficiency and curricular placement)	• Entering student surveys (using self-reported measures)	• Foreign languages • Mathematics/calculus • Reading (EOP students) • Science (EOP students) • Writing (all students)
General Education Skills	• Undergraduate and alumni surveys (using self-reported measures) • National instruments	• Student grades in general education courses • Course embedded assessments
Personal/Social Growth Maturity and Satisfaction	• Freshman-senior cohort studies • Alumni surveys • Student surveys	• Interviews • Observations • Focus groups
Attainment in the Academic Major	• Freshman-senior cohort studies and alumni surveys with analysis by major	Discipline-Specific Strategies • Comprehensive exam (11 depts.) • Capstone and interview (11 depts.) • Essay and interview (16 depts.) • Thesis/research project (6 depts.) • Performance/exhibit (3 depts.) • Internship/fieldwork (2 depts.) • Portfolio (2 depts.) • Alumni satisfaction data (16 depts.) • Multi-method (20 depts.) • Student grades in courses in the major (all depts.)

Several especially good readings exist for assisting institutions with their outcomes assessment programs. Terenzini's (1989) article "Assessment with Open Eyes" represents perhaps the best 20 pages ever written on outcomes assessment. Banta and Associates (2002) and Banta et al. (1996) are helpful resources for campus assessment efforts. Linda Suskie's (2004) book, *Assessing Student Learning: A Common Sense Guide,* is indeed a practical guide. Additionally, there have been several constructive national attempts to develop guidelines and standards for good assessment practices. The most significant of these are AAHE's (1996) *Nine Principles of Good Practice for Assessing Student Learning* and the eight recommendations of the AAC&U (2004a).

Thus we have a complicated collage of evaluation and assessment challenges for institutions, programs, professors, and students. Professors mostly assess individual students by assigning them grades in individual courses. They rarely evaluate students holistically. Provosts, deans, and chairs mostly evaluate faculty ad seriatum and most thoroughly at the points of promotion and tenure. Federal and foundation sponsors, as well as publishers and editors, also focus on particular manuscripts and particular research proposals. Rarely is a faculty member's contribution to institutional and program goal attainment a matter of documented review. Program reviews are widespread but narrow, including both formative internal reviews and summative external reviews by specialized accreditors. The variety, complexity, and typical focus of these program, faculty, and student assessments are enormous, hence contributing to university fragmentation.

Assessing General Education Outcomes and Institutional Effectiveness

Robert Hutchins and Clark Kerr would probably agree that a university is a collection of schools and departments held together only by a central heating system, a common grievance over parking, and a coherent general education program. Good general education programs do not happen by decentralizing their responsibility to colleges, schools, departments, and individuals. They require direction from the institution.

Becoming educated is more than paying tuition and accumulating grades in a collection of courses. Public concern about high tuition cost magnifies concern about quality. Most customers are willing to pay more for higher quality and better service, but it is not clear that our higher prices translate into higher quality. In fact, there is ample evidence from employers and researchers alike that many college graduates are not as well educated, nor as employable, as they were in the past, and as they need to be in the future. Undergraduate general education, especially in research universities, has received harsh criticism, The Boyer Commission (1998) says boldly,

> The first-year experience at most research universities was in the past governed by the perceived need to give every student a common base of knowledge. The "general education" requirements are now near extinction at many research universities; what has survived is often more influenced by internal university politics than educational philosophies. The freshman experience needs to be an intellectually integrated one, so that the student will not learn to think of the academic program as a set of disparate and unconnected requirements. (p. 19)

Persuading faculty is one challenge; persuading students may be another. More than 70% of the freshman class of fall 2004 rated job training and making more money as important reasons for going to college ("Attitudes and Characteristics of Freshmen," 2005). In their quests for financially rewarding careers, college students currently demand undergraduate vocational curricula and focus on their majors.

One might assume that businesses and corporations are delighted that universities produce a cadre of vocationally prepared workers. However, employers generally disagree, because globalization and advancing technology require workers that are adaptable, creative, and multicultural. The rapid advances in technology mean that highly specialized workers may find their skills becoming quickly obsolete. Moreover, companies increasingly have international customers. They want employees not only with tolerance and with respect for diversity, but also with language and communications skills and knowledge of different cultures, races, ethnicities, and lifestyles. According to David Kerns, former CEO of Xerox Corporation, "The only education that prepares us for change is a liberal education. In periods of change, narrow specialization condemns us to inflexibility—precisely what we do not need" (qtd. in AAC&U, 2005, p. 6).

Businesses want employees with a broad general education that allows them not only to succeed in their first job, but also to adapt to this constantly changing world and to solve its problems. These desired qualities from business are the same outcomes desired by civic leaders, professional accreditors, and college educators. In several of its studies, the AAC&U has documented this disconnect between student views of important college outcomes and what employers, educators, and accrediting bodies believe are desirable (Humphreys & Davenport, 2005).

Our review of the literature leaves several clear impressions. First, most general education (GE) programs currently consist of a menu of courses in broad areas of knowledge, which students and faculty alike seem to prefer because it maximizes flexibility and choice. It generates needed FTE (full-time equivalent) enrollments for many departments and allows professors to teach the specialized courses they prefer. Although organizing GE courses into theme clusters can strengthen this cafeteria approach, it often falls short of the coherence needed.

Second, many institutions have a cadre of professors who enjoy teaching GE courses, are good at it, and mostly want to do it for the right reasons (namely enhancing the intellectual depth and breadth of undergraduates, rather than merely generating FTE). Unfortunately, such devotion usually earns intrinsic rewards. While faculty generally recognize the value of a GE program that provides a coherent educational experience for students, they frequently feel forced to choose between supporting student specialization in the major and curricular breadth. It takes years to galvanize faculty agreement about a coherent GE structure. Indeed, many professors believe that students obtain satisfactory GE skills (such as writing and critical thinking) from courses in their major. Moreover, many faculty leaders and chairs fear that anticipated resources will not support a more elaborate general education model.

Third, certain aspects of the GE program have been strengthened on some campuses by bringing greater clarity and organization to the diversity and writing requirements, by using data warehouses to identify students with common interests and clustering them into theme courses, and by providing an enriched GE experience for honors students and other selected undergraduates. In particular, writing across the curriculum appears widespread now and responds to faculty, employer, and alumni concerns about inadequate writing skills of today's graduates.

The most recent phenomenon involves undergraduates in research. The Boyer Commission (1998) put a magnifying glass to the inadequacies of undergraduate education in research universities and recommended 10 ways to improve it, including an inquiry-based first year, research-based learning, communications skills, information technology, and greater interdisciplinarity. Although most undergraduates, especially freshmen, lack the necessary expertise to participate fully in research, those who favor it argue that early exposure to systematic, evidence-based inquiry is the best way to promote student cognitive development and to teach practical research skills. Some universities, such as UC Davis, have adopted undergraduate research involvement as a prominent part of their undergraduate GE program.

Research experience is perhaps desirable, but hardly a substitute for trying conscientiously to achieve undergraduate liberal education goals, particularly those of 1) understanding the various areas of knowledge, 2) active engagement with the world beyond the academy, and 3) a commitment to lifelong learning and ethics. General education suggests the need for institutional direction, rather than decentralization. If left to academic departments, general education would lose its institution-wide approach. Moreover, to assess student learning requires a clear sense of student learning goals, and the goals for student research involvement at most institutions are weakly articulated. With one of the better models, University of California–Berkeley conceives of a three-level student research education: exposure, experience, and capstone experience. But most universities define research very loosely and allow students to fulfill the requirement not only by involvement in a faculty research project, but also by enrolling in courses that require a research paper, by independent study, and also by working off campus or by attending a research conference. Few if any institutions have enough professors to staff freshman research seminars and spend time involving the full range of undergraduates in their research.

In 1994, the AAC&U published *Strong Foundations: Twelve Principles for Effective General Education Programs.* In the intervening years, the AAC&U has revisited and refined these principles. In 2002, the AAC&U released *Greater Expectations: A New Vision for Learning as a Nation Goes to College*, a report on improving student general education outcomes in American higher education. The Greater Expectations national panel recommended the skill sets that all students need to succeed in the 21st century by defining what the "intentional learner" should know and be able to do. More recently, the AAC&U joined with major accrediting bodies to form the Project on Accreditation and Assessment (PAA) and published *Taking Responsibility for the Quality of the Baccalaureate Degree* (2004b). The PAA group forged a consensus among regional and specialized accreditors, and its report describes the components of good practices in curriculum and instruction and assessment. An effective general education curriculum is purposeful, coherent, engaging, rigorous, extends through all four years, has good leadership from the faculty and the administration, is the collective responsibility of the faculty, and enjoys sufficient resources to achieve its purposes. Most of all, it produces intentional learners who integrate their learning in general education and in the major (AAC&U, 2005). The work of the AAC&U is particularly important because each of the major accrediting bodies has had its own definition of general education.

Three Recommendations/Proposals for Connecting the Fragmented University

Connecting the fragmented pieces of the university requires action at each organizational level: institutional, program, and individual.

1) At the institutional level, put teeth in strategic planning.

Burke and Associates (2005) indicate that universities should be tight on goals, loose on means. The evidence suggests that research universities have been tight on neither when it comes to undergraduate education (Boyer Commission, 1998).

In the 1970s, the State University of New York at Albany was one of the first universities in the nation to establish a strategic planning and program evaluation process, linked to campus mission and involving every office and department on the campus (Shirley & Volkwein, 1978; State University of New York at Albany, 1977, 1980; Volkwein, 1984). Although some elements of this process began earlier, President Vincent O'Leary completed the creation of an elaborate mission-driven annual process with unit-level goals and objectives that was linked to performance programs and budget decisions; it was also tied to periodic academic and administrative program evaluations, progress reports during the year, and accountability meetings at the end of each year. If this planning, budgeting, and evaluation process had taken place in a corporation, it would have been called Management By Objectives, or MBO, but O'Leary never permitted anyone on his staff to use the term.

This MBO-like process had several distinctive, if not unique, features in American higher education at the time. First, a series of multi-year rolling plans were created and revised annually within the context of an overarching mission statement that chartered new directions for Albany and took advantage of its location in the largest state capital in the nation. Second, every school and college, academic department, and administrative support service on the campus developed its mission-aligned long-range goals, medium-range objectives, and short-range action steps that were evaluated and revised annually by the president, vice presidents, deans, and faculty senate committees. Third, the planning process and the budget process proceeded together with checks for alignment at several key points during the year. Fourth, the process was so open that key faculty senate committees (with student members) participated in the planning, budgeting, and evaluation cycles and made recommendations directly to the university president. Finally, the Albany administrative team built the entire process on a foundation of institutional research activity that included both external environmental scanning and internal performance indicators, both academic program reviews and evaluations of administrative services, both student outcomes research and faculty instructional and research productivity information.

In the intervening years since the 1970s, strategic planning has swept higher education. My recent Google search on "university mission-driven planning" produced 7.5 million hits. Whether the process is called Vision Ohio (as at Ohio University), Academic Plan (as at Ohio State University), Plan-Do-Check (as at University of Wisconsin System), Agenda for Excellence (as at Penn State), or Compact Planning (as at North Carolina State University), or 20/20 Vision (as at UC Davis), or Bridges to the Next Horizon (as at University of Iowa), it seems that every president and provost, even some deans, are thinking strategically and aligning the university internally in order to compete for students and resources externally.

Although strategic thinking and planning have penetrated most institutions of higher education, few of today's planning processes contain all the elements present in the O'Leary-designed Albany model with its pinpointed action steps for every department and office, annual accountability, formal links to the budget process, and participation by faculty governance. However, the most MBO-like of the current mission-driven planning processes are those called "Planning Compacts" or "Compact Planning" now under way at University at Albany, North Carolina State University, and Utah State University.

A compact is an annual, written management agreement between the university management team and each academic department or administrative office. A compact is jointly developed and

> delineates directions and actions, respective responsibilities, investments, outcomes, and mutual performance expectations in the context of unit and university long-range goals. The compact represents a pledge by both parties to pursue and support the initiatives summarized in the compact document. (University at Albany, 2005, p. 1)

Writing the compact is an iterative process. Compacts are developed both by interactions among faculty and staff within each unit and by interactions among the unit head and the deans, vice presidents, and other university administrators in order to align university and unit goals and directions. Through a series of two or three meetings with formal written feedback, each proposed compact is refined until the final document reaches a mutually agreed-upon form. The Albany process is particularly inclusive. "To support the university's faculty bylaws and commitment to the principle of faculty governance, the compact planning process contains provisions to ensure that initiatives receive faculty governance consultation and/or approval . . ." (University at Albany, 2005, p. 2). Although designed on an annual cycle, the alignment of unit and university goals, and the desirable link to performance metrics and the budget process, may take several years to complete. Additionally, compact plans, because they reflect shared and agreed-upon understanding of unit and university goals and priorities, are used to shape various other planning and decision-making processes, such as annual budget requests, long-range capital improvements, university master plans, enrollment management and marketing plans, priorities for a major capital campaign, and performance evaluations of vice presidents, deans, department chairs, and directors.

Such MBO-like planning has the potential to reduce university "looseness" and fragmentation by ensuring that unit goals are congruent with institutional goals and by pinpointing responsibility for action. Since general education cuts across unit boundaries, it needs its own planning compact if it is to be effective.

2) At the program level, restore/repair/accredit general education and liberal learning.

"Every institution needs to rethink both what every future citizen, regardless of specialty or interests, needs to know in order to receive a degree and at what point that knowledge is best acquired" (Boyer Commission, 1998, pp. 19-20). Apparently, institutions are not conveying the purpose and the importance of a liberal education to today's students. Many students believe that a general education is something acquired in high school, while others even believe that a liberal education is "one that is politically skewed to the left" (Schneider & Humphreys, 2005, p. B20). Higher education must do a better job of conveying the purpose and importance of a liberal education, especially in this student-as-customer era. If institutions want students to achieve their goals, then universities and colleges must do a better job of conveying the views of business and civic leaders to them.

The AAC&U Greater Expectations, LEAP, and PAA projects have already identified a set of college student outcomes that are needed by today's citizens. Even earlier, the 1988 report *Strengthening the Ties that Bind* identified the student outcomes that higher education should promote in order to integrate professional education and the liberal arts (Stark & Lowther, 1988). Table 7.3 shows the recommended liberal education outcomes according to the combined judgments of an array of national stakeholders in 1988 and 2004. The AAC&U initiatives (2004a, 2004b) echo those discovered by Stark and Lowther (1988).

Table 7.3
Higher Education/Industry Consensus
Liberal Education Outcomes

Knowledge of Human Culture and the Natural World	
Stark and Lowther, 1988	AAC&U, 2004a, 2004b
• Professional identity • Aesthetic sensibility	Understanding and experience with the inquiry practices of disciplines that explore the natural, social, and cultural realms—natural sciences, social sciences, arts, and humanities
Intellectual and Practical Skills	
Stark and Lowther, 1988	AAC&U, 2004a, 2004b
• Communication competence • Adaptive competence • Scholarly concern for improvement • Critical thinking • Leadership capacity	• Written and verbal communication skills • Quantitative and analytical skills • Information literacy • Teamwork and problem solving • Integrative thinking and the ability to transfer skills and knowledge from one setting to another
Individual and Social Responsibility	
Stark and Lowther, 1988	AAC&U, 2004a, 2004b
• Contextual competence • Professional ethics • Motivation for continued learning	• Intercultural knowledge and collaborative skills • Proactive sense of responsibility for civic, individual, and social choices

The AAC&U efforts also have discovered congruence between the regional and specialized accrediting agencies. The specialized accrediting agencies that participated in the PAA were unanimous in their belief that a strong liberal education was essential to success in each of their professions. For example, 7 of the 11 EC2000 learning outcomes for engineering and technology graduates (Accreditation Board for Engineering and Technology, 2002) might be visible in the list of desired general education outcomes at most leading institutions and several are visible in Table 7.3:

- Ability to analyze and interpret data
- Ability to function on multidisciplinary teams
- Ability to understand professional and ethical responsibility
- Ability to communicate effectively
- Ability to understand the impact of engineering solutions in a global and societal context
- Ability to recognize the need for, and an ability to engage in, lifelong learning
- Knowledge of contemporary issues

When accrediting bodies and universities decide to change their behavior, the evidence suggests that the impact on students is measurable. For example, in the first large national study of the impact of a change in accreditation standards, Lattuca et al. (2006) have shown that the change in ABET accreditation criteria had a consistent and significant impact on engineering programs, curricula, student experiences, and outcomes. As another example, the Boyer Commission (1998) and other national reports on undergraduate education emphasize the value of discovery/inquiry/research in undergraduate general education. Despite the lack of undergraduate expertise, involving undergraduates in research is something that faculty can embrace, and apparently, they have. In a 2005 analysis of student-reported College Student Experiences Questionnaire data, Hu, Kuh, and Gayles present compelling evidence that faculty mentorship of undergraduate student research experiences has increased at all types of institutions since the Boyer Commission report.

I believe there is a clear need for coordinated and concerted action by faculty, by campus academic leaders, and by accrediting agencies. If there is a growing national consensus about the gaps between what students need, what they want, and what institutions and their faculty provide, then the AAC&U research results need more urgent discussion by university faculty and accrediting agencies alike. Moreover, strengthening general education requires the leadership of an appropriate campus spokesperson to lead an examination of general education alternatives.

Now that the AAC&U projects have forged a national consensus about the knowledge, skills, and values needed by today's citizens, and now that we have a set of college student outcomes highly prized by accreditors, universities, business employers, and government leaders alike, it is time for coordinated action. I recommend the accreditation model. We need a national system for accrediting general education programs according to their alignment with the student outcomes identified by the AAC&U Greater Expectations, LEAP, and PAA initiatives. Such an accreditation model would rest on the program review that includes an institutional self-study, an external review, and final seal of approval if warranted. Liberal education outcomes should form the central evidence for the self-study, review, and accreditation decision. Through the accreditation process, universities should publicize to students the purpose and value of acquiring those liberal education outcomes that all students, regardless of major or academic background, should achieve during their undergraduate study. If the importance of these liberal education outcomes has the backing of corporate leaders, and the evidence suggests it does, today's parents and job-conscious teenagers will be quick to see the value of attending universities with accredited GE programs.

3) At the individual level, faculty need to build the assessment of student liberal education outcomes into appropriate courses.

Perhaps the greatest obstacle to faculty support for assessment is the extra workload and the feeling that "I already assess student performance in my courses." Most faculty members devote a great deal of effort to evaluating student learning in their courses and assigning grades, and they groan when they hear the word assessment.

The trouble is that professors assign grades using inconsistent standards. We aggregate course grades each semester and over the student's career to produce a grade point average. The infamous GPA has grown to support a variety of uses from academic probation to academic honors, from making retention decisions to graduate school recommendations, from financial aid eligibility to employee hiring. But student learning is multidimensional and the grade in most cases is but a crude reflection of actual student performance. More importantly, professors use a mishmash of criteria and standards to assign grades. Under these conditions, it is impossible to use cumulative grades as reflections of student learning.

Not only are grading practices inconsistent, but also professors currently have little means to indicate how the course and student's performance in it contribute to the educated person. The bigger assessment problem is how does this course and what the student learned contribute to knowledge and skills required for a well-rounded undergraduate education. Forty great courses do not necessarily sum to an excellent undergraduate education. Ideally, general education encourages the acquisition of the knowledge and skills that all students should have in addition to the knowledge and skills in their specialized majors.

Therefore, since we appear to have a national consensus among business, government, and accreditation leaders about the liberal education outcomes that all undergraduates should possess, I recommend that all university faculty engaged in undergraduate instruction consider the ways that these outcomes can be built into each appropriate course. Ideally, we should get all professors to grade students on what they actually know rather than other factors like improvement, effort, or comparison. In the meantime, however, enhanced general education assessment within each course would provide students with better information and make them more introspective about their own learning and would encourage faculty to be more self-reflective and precise about their feedback to students. Professors not only need to state the student group intended for the course, but also need to describe what is to be learned and whether it contributes to the students' specialized or general knowledge. Course-level assessment of liberal education outcomes places the ownership of student learning assessment back in the hands of the faculty, where it belongs. Moreover, such an assessment system may be much more cost effective than the current disjointed assessment efforts that faculty feel so far removed from.

Conclusion

Institutional goals and objectives provide the foundation for sound planning, and continuous self-study is an essential ingredient to test the adequacy of the resulting plans and budgets. Under ideal conditions, the mission statement clarifies institutional purposes, goals, and objectives. The campus planning and resource allocation processes translate these ideals, through faculty and staff, into specific instructional and cocurricular programs that affect student learning and development.

Student outcomes assessment ideally provides a lever for increasing both effectiveness and efficiency. Student learning outcomes are central to the purpose of educational organizations. The greater the evidence of congruence between organizational outcomes and the statements of mission, goals, and objectives a university achieves, the more it demonstrates institutional effectiveness. Though institutional effectiveness may be demonstrated in a variety of ways, surely student outcomes assessment supplies some of the most important documentation. It represents the inspirational face of Janus.

The pragmatic face of Janus recognizes that assessment of student learning, evaluation of faculty, and reviews of academic programs are highly decentralized, unit-centered, and fragmenting activities that rarely produce evidence that can be aggregated up to the institutional level for accountability purposes. Moreover, universities are using variable metrics even for their aggregate measures of student growth. Universities are rather more successful at describing the student outcomes that reflect the goals and objectives of particular degree programs than they are at producing outcomes evidence reflecting the *institution's* educational goals. Instead, we develop indicators of institutional performance that reflect only indirectly on student learning.

Excessive fragmentation is both inefficient and ineffective, but research universities have already proved that they can combat it. They have moved from dividing into smaller and smaller departments to building multidisciplinary linkages among units (Clark, 1998). General education programs need a similar approach. Just as most good research is no longer department bound, promoting student liberal learning requires cross-disciplinary collaboration as well.

By introducing principles of good management to campus strategic planning, by reinvigorating and accrediting the general education curriculum to bring it into alignment with the growing national consensus, and by motivating faculty to do their part at the course level to assess liberal education outcomes, research universities may yet put the *uni* back in *university*. In order to fix the fragmented university, we face the Janusian challenge of strengthening the liberal learning outcomes of undergraduate education and proving to the business and government communities that we are doing so. To fail in this task is to produce a generation of narrow-minded "ugly Americans" incapable of adapting to the challenges of a global society and unable to earn the respect of the rest of the world: not politically, not economically, not educationally.

Acknowledgements

The author gratefully acknowledges the research support for this chapter supplied by Alex Yin, a research assistant in the Center for the Study of Higher Education at Pennsylvania State University.

References

Accreditation Board for Engineering and Technology. (2002). *Criteria for accrediting engineering programs: Effective for evaluations during the 2003–2004 accreditation cycle.* Baltimore, MD: Author.

American Association for Higher Education. (1996). *Nine principles of good practice for assessing student learning.* Washington, DC: Author.

Association of American Colleges and Universities. (1994). *Strong founda-tions: Twelve principles for effective general education programs.* Washington, DC: Author.

Association of American Colleges and Universities. (2002). *Greater expec-tations: A new vision for learning as a nation goes to college.* Washington, DC: Author.

Association of American Colleges and Universities. (2004a). *Our students' best work: A framework for accountability worthy of our mission.* Washington, DC: Author.

Association of American Colleges and Universities. (2004b). *Taking responsibility for the quality of the baccalaureate degree.* Washington, DC: Author.

Association of American Colleges and Universities. (2005). *Liberal education outcomes: A preliminary report on student achievement in college.* Washington, DC: Author.

Astin, A. W. (1985). *Achieving educational excellence: A critical assessment of priorities and practices in higher education.* San Francisco, CA: Jossey-Bass.

Attitudes and characteristics of freshmen at 4-year colleges, fall 2004. (2005). *The Chronicle of Higher Education 2005–6 Almanac.* Retrieved August 21, 2006, from http://chronicle.com/weekly/almanac/2005/nation/0101801.htm

Banta, T. W., & Associates. (2002). *Building a scholarship of assessment.* San Francisco, CA: Jossey-Bass.

Banta, T. W., Lund, J. P., Black, K. E., & Oblander, F. W. (1996). *Assessment in practice: Putting principles to work on college campuses.* San Francisco, CA: Jossey-Bass.

Barak, R. J., & Mets, L. A. (Eds.). (1995). *New directions for institutional research: No. 86. Using academic program review.* San Francisco, CA: Jossey-Bass.

Birnbaum, R. (1988). *How colleges work: The cybernetics of academic organ-ization and leadership.* San Francisco, CA: Jossey-Bass.

Borden, V. M., & Banta, T. W. (Eds.). (1994). *New directions for institu-tional research: No. 82. Using performance indicators to guide strategic decision-making.* San Francisco, CA: Jossey-Bass.

Boyer Commission on Educating Undergraduates in the Research University. (1998). *Reinventing undergraduate education: A blueprint for America's research universities.* Retrieved August 20, 2006, from the Stony Brook University web site: http://naples.cc.sunysb.edu/Pres/boyer.nsf/673918d46fbf653e852565ec0056ff3e/d955b61ffddd590a852565ec005717ae/$FILE/boyer.pdf

Boyer, E. L. (1990). *Scholarship reconsidered: Priorities of the professorate.* Princeton NJ: Carnegie Foundation for the Advancement of Teaching.

Braxton, J. M. (Ed.). (2006). *New directions for institutional research: No. 129. Analyzing faculty work and rewards: Using Boyer's four domains of scholarship.* San Francisco, CA: Jossey-Bass.

Braxton, J. M., Luckey, W. T., Jr., & Helland, P. A. (2006). Ideal and actual value patterns toward domains of scholarship in three types of colleges and universities. In J. M. Braxton (Ed.), *New directions for institutional research: No. 129. Analyzing faculty work and rewards: Using Boyer's four domains of scholarship* (pp. 67–76). San Francisco, CA: Jossey-Bass.

Burke, J. C., & Associates. (2005). *Achieving accountability in higher education: Balancing public, academic, and market demands.* San Francisco, CA: Jossey-Bass.

Burke, J.C., & Minassians, H. (2002). *Performance reporting: The preferred "no cost" accountability program.* Albany, NY: The Rockefeller Institute of Government.

Burke, J. C., & Serban, A. M. (Eds.). (1998). *New directions for institutional research: No. 97. Performance funding for higher education: Fad or trend?* San Francisco, CA: Jossey Bass.

Chickering, A. W., & Gamson, Z. F. (1987, June). Seven principles for good practice in undergraduate education. *AAHE Bulletin, 39*(7), 3–7.

Clark, B. R. (1998). *Creating entrepreneurial universities: Organizational pathways of transformation.* Oxford, England: Elsevier Science.

Colbeck, C. L., & Michael, P. W. (2006). The public scholarship: Reintegrating Boyer's four domains. In J. M. Braxton (Ed.), *New directions for institutional research: No. 129. Analyzing faculty work and rewards: Using Boyer's four domains of scholarship* (pp. 7–19). San Francisco, CA: Jossey-Bass.

Etzioni, A. (2000). Administrative and professional authority. In M. C. Brown (Ed.), *Organization and governance in higher education* (5th ed., pp. 111–118). Boston, MA: Pearson. (Original work published 1964)

Ewell, P. T. (1994). Developing statewide performance indicators for higher education: Policy themes and variations. In S. S. Rupert (Ed.), *Charting higher education accountability: A sourcebook on state-level performance indicators* (pp. 157–176). Denver, CO: Education Commission of the States.

Ewell, P. T. (2005). Can assessment serve accountability? It depends on the question. In J. C. Burke & Associates, *Achieving accountability in higher education: Balancing public, academic, and market demands* (pp. 104–124). San Francisco, CA: Jossey-Bass.

Ewell, P. T., & Jones, D. P. (1996). *Indicators of "good practice" in under-graduate education: A handbook for development and implementation.* Boulder, CO: National Center for Higher Education Management Systems.

Hu, S., Kuh, G. D., & Gayles, J. G. (2005, April). *Undergraduate research experiences: Are students at research universities advantaged?* Paper presented at the annual meeting of the American Educational Research Association, Montreal, Canada.

Humphreys, D., & Davenport, A. (2005, Summer/Fall). What really matters in college: How students view and value liberal education. *Liberal Education, 91*(3), 36–43.

Jacobi, M., Astin, A. W., & Ayala, F., Jr. (1987). *College student outcomes assessment: A talent development perspective.* San Francisco, CA: Jossey-Bass.

Kuh, G. D. (2005). Imagine asking the client: Using student and alumni surveys for accountability in higher education. In J. C. Burke & Associates, *Achieving accountability in higher education: Balancing public, academic, and market demands* (pp. 148–172). San Francisco, CA: Jossey-Bass.

Lattuca, L. R., Terenzini, P. T., & Volkwein, J. F. (2006). *Engineering change: A study of the impact of EC2000, executive summary.* Baltimore, MD: Accreditation Board for Engineering and Technology.

Marchese, T. J. (1997). The new conversations about learning: Insights from neuroscience and anthropology, cognitive science and work-place studies. In *Assessing impact: Evidence and action* (pp. 79–95). Washington, DC: American Association for Higher Education.

McKinney, K. (2006). Attitudinal and structural factors contributing to challenges in the work of the scholarship of teaching and learning. In J. M. Braxton (Ed.), *New directions for institutional research: No. 129. Analyzing faculty work and rewards: Using Boyer's four domains of scholarship* (pp. 37–50). San Francisco, CA: Jossey-Bass.

Middle States Commission on Higher Education. (1996). *Framework for outcomes assessment.* Philadelphia, PA: Commission on Higher Education, Middle States Association of Colleges and Schools.

O'Meara, K. (2006). Encouraging multiple forms of scholarship in faculty reward systems: Have academic cultures really changed? In J. M. Braxton (Ed.), *New directions for institutional research: No. 129. Analyzing faculty work and rewards: Using Boyer's four domains of scholarship* (pp. 77–95). San Francisco, CA: Jossey-Bass.

Pascarella, E. T., & Terenzini, P. T. (2005). *How college affects students: A third decade of research* (Vol. 2). San Francisco, CA: Jossey-Bass.

Prados, J. W., Peterson, G. D., & Lattuca, L. R. (2005, January). Quality assurance of engineering education through accreditation: The impact of engineering criteria 2000 and its global influence. *Journal of Engineering Education, 94*(1), 165–184.

Schneider, C. G., & Humphreys, D. (2005, September 23). Putting liberal education on the radar screen. *The Chronicle of Higher Education,* p. B20.

Seymour, D. T. (1992). *On Q: Causing quality in higher education.* Phoenix, AZ: American Council on Education/Oryx Press.

Shirley, R. C., & Volkwein, J. F. (1978, September/October). Establishing academic program priorities. *Journal of Higher Education, 49*(5), 472–488.

Stark, J. S., & Lowther, M. A. (1988). *Strengthening the ties that bind: Integrating undergraduate liberal and professional study.* Ann Arbor, MI: University of Michigan, Professional Preparation Network.

State University of New York at Albany. (1977). *Missions, programs, and priorities for action.* Albany, NY: Author.

State University of New York at Albany. (1980). *Self study for reaccreditation.* Albany, NY: Author.

Strauss, L. C., & Volkwein, J. F. (2002, April). Comparing student performance and growth in two-year and four-year institutions. *Research in Higher Education, 43*(2), 133–161.

Suskie, L. (2004). *Assessing student learning: A common sense guide.* Bolton, MA: Anker.

Tebo-Messina, M., & Prus, J. (1995, June). *Assessing general education: An overview of methods.* Paper presented at the 10th annual assessment and quality conference of the American Association for Higher Education, Boston, MA.

Terenzini, P. T. (1989, November/December). Assessment with open eyes: Pitfalls in studying student outcomes. *Journal of Higher Education, 60*(6), 644–664.

Terkla, D. G., Wiseman, M., & Cohen, M. (2005, August). *Institutional dashboards: Navigational tool for colleges and universities.* Paper presented at the 27th annual EAIR Forum, Riga, Latvia.

University at Albany. (2005). *Compact planning handbook.* Retrieved August 20, 2006, from the University of Albany, Office of Academic Affairs web site: www.albany.edu/academic_affairs/cp/UAlb_cp_instructions_FINAL.pdf

Volkwein, J. F. (1984, May/June). Responding to financial retrenchment: Lessons from the Albany experience. *The Journal of Higher Education, 55*(3), 389–401.

Volkwein, J. F. (1992). Outcomes assessment at Albany: A summary of what we have learned since 1978 (Institutional Research Report No. 12). Albany, NY: University at Albany, Office of Institutional Research.

Volkwein, J. F. (1999). The four faces of institutional research. In J. F. Volkwein (Ed.), *New directions for institutional research: No. 104. What is institutional research all about? A critical and comprehensive assessment of the profession* (pp. 9–19). San Francisco, CA: Jossey-Bass.

Volkwein, J. F. (2004a). Assessing student learning in the major: What's the question? In B. Keith (Ed.), *Contexts for learning: Institutional strategies for managing curricular change through assessment* (pp. 145–172). Stillwater, OK: New Forums Press.

Volkwein, J. F. (2004b). *Meeting minimum standards, attaining goals, and improving: A working paper on accreditation in American higher education.* Retrieved August 20, 2006, from the Pennsylvania State University, Center for the Study of Higher Education web site: www.ed.psu.edu/cshe/pdfs/Volk_Accreditat_Paper.pdf

Volkwein, J. F., & Grunig, S. D. (2005). Resources and reputation in higher education: Double, double, toil and trouble. In J. C. Burke & Associates, *Achieving accountability in higher education: Balancing public, academic, and market demands* (pp. 246–274). San Francisco, CA: Jossey-Bass.

Volkwein, J. F., Lattuca, L. R., Terenzini, P. T., Strauss, L. C., & Sukhbaatar, J. (2004). Engineering change: A study of the impact of EC2000. *International Journal of Engineering Education, 20*(3), 318–328.

Wolff, R. A. (2005). Accountability and accreditation: Can reforms match increasing demands? In J. C. Burke & Associates, *Achieving accountability in higher education: Balancing public, academic, and market demands* (pp. 78–103). San Francisco, CA: Jossey-Bass.

8

Accrediting the Public University: Part of the Problem or Part of the Solution?

Ralph A. Wolff

Regional accrediting agencies are the only organizations that evaluate all public and private colleges and universities, within and across systems, states, and regions. They have the potential to provide vital information on the priorities and performance of public universities. Through their standards, reviews, and reports, they should influence how both universities and their publics define quality in higher education. How well does accreditation perform these functions? This chapter suggests that the greater the prestige of the university, the smaller the impact on performance. Recent and significant reforms have improved accrediting processes, but much more needs to be done to make it more effective at public research universities. This chapter makes recommendations for accrediting agencies and universities to make the accreditation process more meaningful and effective for institutions and the public.

While accreditation was not specifically addressed by the Kellogg Commission, regional accreditation can play a role in addressing the three challenges identified by the commission, by 1) using the accreditation self-study and review process to identify and set a clearer institutional direction, 2) focusing the institution more on student and learning outcomes, and 3) encouraging public universities to become more engaged with states and society.

Regional accreditation evaluates the priorities and performance of the total institution, while specialized accreditation may spur fragmentation by focusing on individual academic programs as separate entities. While accreditation historically focused mostly on the resource inputs of students, faculty, and finances, there has been a significant shift within the practices of regional accreditation to emphasize that colleges and universities assess institutional results, especially of student learning outcomes. As a result, accreditation has a significant role to play in improving institutional performance. As this chapter suggests, accreditation has focused mainly on evaluating and recommending improvements at the institutional level, whereas the public agenda is increasingly to address common, system-wide issues of performance and alignment of public institutions with public priorities. More can be done by accreditation to address these public concerns, and to make the accreditation process more effective at public institutions, especially at public research universities.

This chapter explores the following questions: To what extent has regional accreditation assured institutional direction by examining university missions and goals and their implementation in colleges, schools, and departments? To what extent has its reviews encouraged attention to undergraduate education, and especially identifying student learning goals and assessing their achievement? Finally, to what extent have regional agencies reviewed and stimulated the public engagement mission of state universities? Though recent reforms in institutional accreditation have shifted the emphasis from assessing resource inputs to evaluating performance results, the evidence suggests that more can be done to align the accreditation process to be more responsive to the three challenges of the Kellogg Commission.[1]

Some History

Accreditation constitutes one of the primary agents of quality assurance for all of higher education. Created more than 100 years ago to evaluate high schools to assure the qualifications of their graduates for college in the New England and North Central regions, it soon spread to assessing colleges themselves through the activities of seven regional commissions in six regions.[2] Accreditation was originally a uniquely American creation, but countries all over the world have in recent years adopted it. Unlike many such agencies abroad, U.S. accreditation organizations remain nongovernmental and voluntary with colleges and universities as members. This voluntary character helps protect colleges and universities from government intrusion, but the fact that agencies are membership organizations, and that the accrediting commissions are composed largely of presidents, chancellors, and other employees of higher education, have led some to argue that the associations are captive to campus interests (Dickeson, 2006). While I disagree with this view, the nature of accreditation and its composition lead to a focus inward on institutional issues, but not necessarily on those issues some public policymakers would like to see higher education address.

Three types of accreditation agencies exist: regional, specialized (or professional), and national. Regional and specialized agencies accredit nonprofit public and private colleges and universities, while national agencies principally serve proprietary and nondegree institutions. Historically, accreditation agencies had dual purposes: to assure that institutions meet *minimum standards* and to recommend areas for *institutional improvement*. They assumed a larger and more significant role with the passage of the National Defense Education Act after World War II, a law that linked eligibility for federal financial aid to institutional accreditation. In return, the secretary of education, through a National Advisory Committee on Institutional Quality and Integrity, reviews and "recognizes" accrediting agencies under an increasingly broad array of standards and regulations. Despite an occasional reference to specialized agencies, this chapter focuses on regional accreditation.

Longstanding common practice and the U.S. Department of Education recognition system have shaped an accreditation process that includes an institutional self-study, a team visit and written report, action by the accrediting commission, and follow-up reviews when needed. Institutions have a maximum of 10 years between reviews for regional accreditation. As demands for accountability in higher education have increased, so too have the prescriptions of Congress and the Department of Education for accrediting agencies. They include adding areas for accrediting standards and additional regulations requiring greater accountability of accrediting agencies for their own initial and re-recognition processes. For example, in the 1980s Secretary of Education William Bennett first challenged accrediting agencies to examine student academic achievement. That started a persistent and increasing trend. The 1992 Reauthorization Act mandated that accrediting agencies develop standards for examining student learning. In 1998, that standard leaped from the last of nine standards to the first, reflecting increased priority given to student academic achievement by the Department of Education and, in turn, by accrediting agencies.

Although Congress supposedly reviews the Higher Education Act every five years, it is often postponed. Reauthorization of this act has increasingly become the place where higher education policy gets debated and later established. Part H of the act deals with accreditation, and for the past several years the Reauthorization Act, and especially

Part H, have been a forum for debates on new mandates for accountability. In the current drafts of the Reauthorization Act, still not adopted at the time of this writing, proposals are circulating for changes to key issues such as transfer of credit, disclosure of accreditation actions, due process, monitoring of distance education, and increasing the contents of "institutional profiles" made public on institutional web sites.

In addressing the role of accreditation at public universities, this chapter first takes a critical look at the accrediting process and accrediting organizations to assess their capacity to evaluate the quality of public universities. After reviewing accrediting agencies from several dimensions, it then examines how public research universities engage the accrediting process and the challenges they face. This chapter concludes with recommendations for both accrediting agencies and institutions that will improve the effectiveness of regional accreditation, and in turn, of public universities.

Does Regional Accreditation Work Well in Public Universities?

Accreditation serves a *gatekeeping* function to assure that new colleges and universities meet minimum standards. This function is most important for the many new institutions that emerged in the past 20 years and for special purpose institutions, such as freestanding schools of psychology and online colleges and universities. New public colleges and universities have completed this process, as did California State University–Monterey Bay several years ago, and as the University of California–Merced and California State University–Channel Islands are now doing. Well-established public universities, especially research universities, do not find minimum accreditation standards relevant to them, thus demonstrating compliance is considered a pro forma administrative task. Renewal of their accreditation can be presumed, and the data support this assumption. No public four-year institution has ever lost its accreditation, though accrediting agencies occasionally give warnings to public universities to address specific issues.

For most public, and especially research, universities, the only relevant function of accreditation becomes *improvement*, not *minimum standards*. For accreditors, this reality represents both a strength and a challenge. The strength stems from the support university administrations provide to addressing a selected issue or issues that are chosen for attention and improvement. For example, the University of Wisconsin–Madison successfully used this approach to devote their self-study to strategic planning in its last review by the Higher Learning

Commission of the North Central Association. Though such focused reviews respond to institutional interests, they do not necessarily demonstrate accountability for addressing the full range of issues considered of the greatest importance to policymakers or the public, such as retention and graduation rates, or student learning outcomes.

Accrediting agencies have typically defined *minimum standards* in terms of resources, structures, and processes. Even with constrained state support, public institutions usually have sufficient resources, structures, and processes to meet minimum standards. Applying the traditional dual-purpose model of accreditation—while giving more emphasis to student learning outcomes—presents a significant dilemma for accrediting agencies. Should student learning outcomes be treated as a *minimum requirement* or as an area for *improvement*? Should—or, more realistically, would—a major public university lose its accreditation for failing to identify student learning goals, assess the extent of their achievement, and demonstrate an acceptable level of performance? To date, especially with research universities, accrediting agencies have not used "the stick" of the threat of the loss of accreditation, since there are many other indicators of quality evident at such institutions. Such a threat is viewed as being counterproductive in promoting only surface compliance, when deeper engagement and culture change is what is needed. Accrediting agencies have tried to resolve this tension by treating issues such as assessment of student learning or retention and graduation rates as both minimum expectations and areas for institutional improvement. This approach has led to many institutions being asked to file follow-up reports or to have special visits. Both the Middle States Association and the Higher Learning Commission of the North Central Association, for example, report that more than 40% of comprehensive reviews result in such follow-up requirements, with most addressing assessment of student learning as one focus. Even with such follow-up activities, the traditional framing of the dual function of accreditation has not generated the required sustained attention of major public universities to these critical undergraduate issues or significantly affected the work of the faculty.

In contrast to campus reactions, many external policymakers at the state and federal levels increasingly see regional accreditation as an agent for institutional accountability—not just for minimum standards but also for institutional responsibility for addressing key areas of performance. At the same time, serious questions remain about whether accreditation can effectively address accountability issues at prestigious universities, including public research universities, which should show higher standards of accountability than their private counterparts.

As the calls for accountability increase, the purpose of accreditation will need to shift toward a greater *accountability* model, where accrediting agencies operate not just as enforcers of minimum standards for new and struggling institutions, or "agents of selective improvement" for well-established colleges and universities. Instead, accrediting agencies must work with institutions to develop agreement on key areas of accountability for higher education that then become more central to the accrediting process. Retention and graduation rates and demonstration of student learning constitute such critical areas.

In addition to revising the stated purpose of accreditation toward a more focused accountability model, agencies must direct more attention to making the *review process* more effective with large public research universities. The vast majority of today's college students enroll in public colleges and universities. Using fall 2000 statistics, 77% of students were in public institutions, 40% in four-year institutions. The 15 largest campuses are all public, and 34 public universities enroll more than 30,000 students. Accreditation was formed well before such large-scale institutions emerged. The accrediting model developed when universities were much smaller and more homogeneous. How can a team of 7–12 people spending four days on a site visit—two days of which are devoted to interviews with groups on campus—ever come to understand or penetrate a complex university with 30,000 or more students, 12 or more colleges and schools, more than 100 programs at every level, and an astonishing array of faculty research and service activities? It would be impossible for any process to review every program and school in such institutions. Instead, accrediting teams focus increasingly on key systems of quality assurance, engage in sampling techniques, and allow institutions to select special issues or topics for review. Until recently, however, the review process changed very little, and remained mostly the same for small colleges and large universities.

Several accrediting regions attempt to provide consistency by having every institution address each of the agency's standards. Leaders at research universities see such comprehensive reviews as make-work that adds little value to institutional performance. Conversely, these accrediting agencies regard such reviews as assuring public accountability that minimum standards are being met. They can state publicly that the process has successfully reviewed the institution under agency standards and made recommendations for improvement. However, my experience suggests that these reviews tend to lead to forced engagement and show little staying power once the process has been completed. Moreover, such a comprehensive minimum-standards approach has not led to fundamental changes within large public research universities.

In response to such concerns, several regional agencies have developed new approaches that adapt the review process to serve large institutions more effectively, and to encourage deeper engagement of their faculties. Several agencies allow large well-established or premier institutions to engage in a "special themes" approach. Most research universities have selected this option when given the opportunity. It has proved successful from the institution's standpoint, since it allows the university to focus on a limited number of issues that its leaders and its faculty consider important. Conversely, this approach provides no assurance that the issues selected are the most critical for public accountability, or that the process will lead to desirable changes in institutional performance. Though the special themes approach continues, three accrediting agencies have devised new models for their reviews that hold great promise for leading to deeper change within institutions, especially large public research universities.

In 1999, the Higher Learning Commission of the North Central Association developed its Academic Quality Improvement Program (AQIP). This model adapts to accreditation the quality system of the Malcolm Baldrige process, used primarily in industry. It involves choosing critical areas for improvement, an extensive program of institutional engagement with related issues, and submission of annual reports of progress that external experts review off site for evidence of institutional progress. More than 100 institutions have chosen this optional and innovative process. Most of the participating members are community colleges, along with several comprehensive universities, such as Kent State University and Southern Illinois University–Edwardsville. However, not one of the members of the Association of American Universities or other public research universities has yet selected this promising approach to accreditation. This lack of interest is especially disappointing, since AQIP links high expectations, significant improvement, and institutional interest—three critical ingredients essential to success in accreditation, as well as for accountability.

The Senior College Commission of the Western Association of Schools and Colleges (WASC) adopted in 2001 a three-stage model of review that makes the accrediting review more learning centered. It stimulates institutional learning through multiple stages of review, while focusing the process more on student learning outcomes and results. This new model benefited from five years of research on quality assurance models worldwide, active consultation with institutional leaders, and extensive experimentation before its adoption. Leaders of research universities, public and private, actively participated in its development and played a leading role in generating several of its key features.

Each institution must file, two years prior to the site visits, a proposal identifying outcomes for the accrediting review. The goal is to engage the institution in key areas for improvement, including giving significant attention to improving institutional systems and faculty involvement in the assessment of student learning. The proposal is peer reviewed by a committee of representatives from a wide range of institutions, including research universities. This model allows the university to adapt the accrediting process to its own context, stage of development, and key concerns, while requiring it to address critical areas of educational effectiveness (including the assessment of student learning outcomes). Once the proposal is accepted, two site reviews occur. The first focuses on institutional capacity, including resources, structures, and processes to address student leaning outcomes assessment and the effectiveness of the institution's data gathering and analysis systems. Eighteen months later, an educational effectiveness review occurs. Using the key areas of learning assessment identified by the institution in its proposal, the review evaluates the institution's quality assurance systems, learning outcomes and results, graduation rates, and organizational learning systems.

Unlike the optional AQIP approach, this model requires all institutions, including research universities, to go through this process. It has been applied successfully to several major research universities, including the University of California–Berkeley and the University of California–Santa Cruz, and to a number of large comprehensive public universities, such as San Diego State University.

The Southern Association of Colleges and Schools (SACS) recently developed its own version of a two-stage review process for all its colleges and universities. Implementation of this model also came after pilot reviews and with the involvement of several research universities within the Southern region. Each institution files a compliance report addressing the SACS standards of accreditation, which a compliance review committee evaluates off site. That committee issues a compliance finding that identifies areas requiring further attention, which a site review committee uses in its examination a semester later. That site review focuses primarily on each institution's Quality Enhancement Plan (QEP). While the details of the QEP are being developed, the intent is to engender a systematic engagement of the institution, and each of its programs and units, in assessing performance and setting targets for improvement.

These three agencies designed the new models to engage large institutions more effectively, focus more on quality systems than the traditional emphasis on inputs and resources, and allow institutions to concentrate on quality improvements adapted to each institution's context. Although early signs suggest that each represents improvements to the traditional model of accreditation, they are not yet well understood nationally, and their promise for identifying and improving institutional results, which are considerable, has not been fully recognized. For example, Charles Miller, chair of the Department of Education's Commission on the Future of Higher Education, has stated,

> Historically, accreditation has been the nationally mandated mechanism to improve institutional quality and assure a basic level of accountability in higher education. Accreditation and related issues of articulation are in need of serious reform in the view of many, especially the need for more outcomes-based approaches. Also in need of substantial improvement are the regional variability in standards, the independence of accreditation, its usefulness for consumers, and its response to new forms of delivery such as internet-based distance learning. (Miller, 2006)

While I would question these conclusions in light of recent efforts by regional agencies to address many of these issues, they reflect all too common views of the process. Since nearly all public universities, and especially research institutions, are on a maximum 10-year review cycle, not all institutions have gone through the review process with the new emphasis on learning outcomes. Thus there is a need for greater communication to the public of the current emphases of accrediting agencies and better demonstration that the promises of these changes are being realized.

Another of the greatest challenges facing accreditation is making its processes, even with these significant reforms under way, better understood and embraced by public research universities, which serve a significant proportion of undergraduate baccalaureate students. College and university leaders externally champion accreditation as a *process* of accountability, but within institutions at the college, school, and department level, the understanding and support for institutional accreditation, as opposed to professional or program accreditation, is much more mixed. Within research universities, the emerging role of institutional accreditation as a form of accountability is even less understood or welcomed (Wolff, 2005).

For accreditation to play a larger role in influencing change within public universities, accreditors must more clearly define its purpose as moving beyond minimum standards to a shared view of accountability for performance and results. As the report of the National Commission on Accountability in Higher Education (2005) declares, "Accountability for better results is different from accountability for minimum standards" (p. 11). The new definition must move beyond the process of self-review to the demonstration of performance in key areas. As the Business–Higher Education Forum (2004) states,

> For accountability to occur, evidence about perform-
> ance must be defined in the context of institutional
> and social goals that reflect a public agenda. In addi-
> tion, that evidence must be communicated in a way
> that is broadly accessible, rather than in the language
> of education insiders. (p. 9)

Among the areas or priorities accreditation might address more clearly in working with public universities are access for underrepresented groups, retention and graduation rates, and evidence of effective student learning and the contributions of the university to workforce preparation and the quality of life for states and society.

Regional accreditors must also further redefine the accrediting process to make it demonstrably more effective at public universities. The reforms described earlier reflect serious attention to these issues. Evidence suggests that a number of public universities, including research universities, are beginning to show more concern with student learning as a result of these new changes in accreditation. But much more must be done to achieve the full promise of these reforms. The next section discusses the issues that impede improvement of the process, especially in public universities.

How Do Accreditors Evaluate the Special Mission of Public Universities?

Accreditation has historically asked each institution to state clearly its mission and demonstrate its achievement. To what extent, then, does accreditation focus on the mandated mission of public institutions? Given the comprehensive scope of such missions, accrediting agencies do not address all dimensions of the university's mission. Moreover, in selecting those dimensions of the mission to emphasize, accreditation may not be seen as addressing the same issues considered important by policymakers.

The missions of public universities usually state the importance of serving state and regional needs as a public mandate, and not just a voluntary role as found in private institutions. The mission statements of public universities typically talk of assisting K–12 education, developing the state or regional workforce, and serving their communities and states through the public service and engagement of professors, students, and staff members. The public mission mandates teaching, research, and service to the community, the state, and the nation as well as to the academy and its disciplines.

The real challenge is closing the gap between the stated and the operational missions of state universities. Though these institutions do undertake a number of activities to fulfill these functions, what drives both their faculty and their administrators is all too often improving their national reputations by increasing student selectivity and sponsored research and slighting their attention to undergraduate education and public service. For example, at one institution recently reviewed by WASC, the evaluation team commended the institution for exceptional service to its region, its commitment to students, and the progress being made in assessing student learning throughout the institution. At the same time, the institution began a process to revise its mission statement to give more emphasis to research. Although the accreditation team urged the university to make certain the revision did not diminish its commitment to student learning and public service, the added accent on research could have that effect. Unfortunately, the drive to increase research productivity and national reputation is unrelenting at most public universities, especially those emphasizing research, which affects their undergraduate teaching and service missions.

Regional accrediting agencies are not well equipped to evaluate all aspects of the public mission of public universities and do not make a special focus of the *public* character of the institution. What indices should they use for assessing the success of the service missions of state universities? For example, how would an accrediting team assess and critique the level of service to state and regional goals, given the breadth of these goals and the significant range of possibilities for university activities? Who would define success—the university and its trustees, the local mayor, the governor, or legislative and civic leaders? Many institutions have begun to generate data on the economic impact of their activities, including the additional earnings generated by students with degrees and the impact of institutions on the local and regional economy through their payrolls, grants, research, startup businesses, and so forth. Accreditation reviews typically do not analyze such surveys and studies in any significant way, though they acknowledge the university's effort to link its activities to its public purpose.

More typically, accrediting teams ask each institution to identify its goals and to indicate the extent of their achievement. Responses on public mission, if presented at all, usually list the extensive range of service activities rather than submitting evidence of success in these endeavors. Accrediting reviews give primary attention to the performance of educational programs, especially at the undergraduate level. Time limitations mean the evaluation team must limit the areas examined. Given the national concerns over the quality of undergraduate education, accrediting agencies arguably give correct attention to the most critical parts of the missions of state universities. Despite the need to focus on educational issues, review teams should support and not disparage the public service mission, especially of state universities.

In its new accrediting standards, the Higher Learning Commission of the North Central Association emphasizes the public purpose of higher education by including as one of its criteria "Engagement and Service." Criterion Five states, "As called for by its mission, the organization identifies its constituencies and serves them in ways both value" (Higher Learning Commission, 2003, p. 40). A subcomponent speaks of the need to evaluate the effectiveness of this service to the community and beyond: "Internal and external constituencies value the services the organization provides" (p. 40). This important step creates a platform through accrediting standards of promoting and evaluating public service as a clear part of the mission of all institutions, public and private.

An additional step that accrediting agencies could take is reviewing the support and rewards given for those professors and staff members actively involved in public engagement. Such a review could test whether service is a reality on campus and not just rhetoric in self-study reports. Typically, work in these areas of "service" ranks well below research and scholarship, and even teaching effectiveness, for promotion and rewards. Evaluation teams could also review how the governing board assesses performance of the public mission. For example, has the board insisted that the university define the criteria and develop indicators to assess the success of its mission for public engagement?

Does Mission Distinctiveness Still Matter?

Despite all the rhetoric, mission differentiation is important in regional accreditation. Accrediting reviews have traditionally focused on institutional mission and its achievement. Accreditors do expect institutions to identify their distinctive characteristics, and every college or university has devoted countless hours to drafting and periodically revising its mission statement to ensure that it reflects its distinctive institutional character. In practice, however, the distinctiveness of public universities may not be as great as their mission statements suggest.

To be sure, some do show significant differences. Size makes a difference in institutional culture, although all public research universities tend to be large. Some of them stress their regional or urban character by their type and range of teaching, research, and service programs. Still public research universities exhibit more similar than distinctive characteristics. Campuses may have a different "feel" or culture, which often reflects campus design, architecture, and cocurricular activities more than teaching, research, and service programs.

Pressures from within and without public research universities have undermined the traditional notion of mission distinctiveness. For example, regardless of the institutional type, professors face increasing pressures from their departments, schools, and institutions to emphasize research and scholarship, which consistently ranks first in the evaluation for merit, promotion, and tenure at most public universities. In public research universities, research always comes first, teaching a very distant second, and public engagement usually an even more distant third.

Specialized accrediting agencies, through their prescription of required courses or areas of coverage, often have a flattening effect on program distinctiveness. Licensing requirements in many fields have the same effect. Nursing programs, for example, must cover a similar, often the same, curriculum regardless of the institutional mission. Serving the needs of a region also leads to the development of a common array of majors so that students do not have to travel to other parts of the state to get a basic and comprehensive array of programs.

From a student standpoint as well, and especially at the undergraduate level, it is not clear that the actual courses and programs students take are markedly different among public institutions regardless of the varying institutional types and mission statements, or between public and private institutions. As public universities grew in size, they became ever more comprehensive in scope, offering a common array of undergraduate and graduate programs in the arts and sciences, and often all the professional fields. While variation of course offerings exist in all disciplines at the margins, all usually offer a similar range of core courses. The same is true of the general education program at most universities. Indeed, despite the desire for distinctiveness, studies have shown that the basic goals and outcomes of undergraduate education are common across all institutions, regardless of their type (Association of American Colleges and Universities, 2004, 2005).

Given these pressures to "homogenize" the undergraduate experience, it will be increasingly important for institutions, especially public research universities, to become clearer about what distinguishes them from their counterparts. How will accreditors assess whether the student experience matches the announced distinctiveness in undergraduate education? Research universities typically cite their research culture as a total hallmark for undergraduates as well as graduates. However, to what extent does the research culture of the faculty at top public universities actually affect the experience and learning of its undergraduates?

A recent accreditation review of the University of California–Berkeley examined this question. The self-study committee at Berkeley found a wide variety of views regarding what type of research undergraduates should undertake, little agreement on the learning outcomes of the research experiences, and fragmented data on the types of research activities that undergraduates actually undertook. As part of this review, Berkeley attempted to articulate more clearly what an "undergraduate research experience" meant at their institution. In addition to the improvement of data collection, the self-study for educational effectiveness (the second of a two-part review process) articulated a framework for discussion with the university community:

> System-wide and campus efforts to quantify under-graduate research activity have underscored the need for clear definitions of what is meant by undergraduate research. Such a conceptual framework enables:
>
> • Undergraduates to set personal goals at the outset of their academic careers and plan ahead to take advantage of research opportunities;
>
> • Faculty and departments to become more explicit about their research-based student learning objectives, to develop specific ways to evaluate intended learning outcomes, and to partner with academic support units to promote the development of research competencies in their students;
>
> • The administration to make informed decisions about allocating available resources to support these educational goals and objectives on both a unit- and campus-wide level; and

> • The campus and University as a whole to bring greater visibility to the place of undergraduate research in the educational experience, to assess how well we are meeting our objectives for undergraduate participation in research, and to communicate goals and successes to various stakeholders. (University of California–Berkeley, 2003, p. 5)

The self-study went on to articulate three stages of research competency and several dimensions for evaluating research competency. They suggested that students needed exposure (stage 1), experience (stage 2), and a capstone research experience (stage 3) to develop effective research competence (University of California–Berkeley, 2003). They also suggested several dimensions for evaluating the research experience of students:

> • The extent to which answers to research/creative problems that students engage are known or unknown;
> • The extent to which the research/creative process is directed by the faculty mentor or self-directed;
> • The extent to which the research/creative product has a potential audience beyond the instructor and classroom. (University of California–Berkeley, 2003, p. 6)

The data collection, analysis, and recommendation of learning outcomes and criteria for reviewing achievement of these outcomes by UC Berkeley serves as a powerful case study of taking one distinctive characteristic and beginning the process of developing thoughtful outcomes. All institutions should be challenged to develop clarity about their expected educational outcomes—general and distinctive—and move beyond the rhetoric of mission statements and broad statements of generic competencies and skills. All too often we have found that there is little agreement among the faculty of public research universities on what should be distinctive about the education provided at their institution, what such distinctions should mean in terms of specific learning outcomes and characteristics, and what evidence exists that the university is achieving these objectives.

As good as the Berkeley example may be, it reflects but the first part of a long journey of moving outcomes through an institution. It would take a very sustained and committed effort to drive a conversation about learning outcomes for research within each of the schools and departments, building agreement on how such a statement would be applied within the school or department, and then collecting and analyzing data to determine the extent to which students are achieving such an outcome. Beyond research, such a process will need to be used for other outcomes as well. Thus it remains undetermined whether such self-study efforts actually will lead to improved performance at both the department and the university level in large comprehensive universities, and especially at research universities. The development of learning outcomes is also needed for other elements of undergraduate education, particularly the outcomes of the general education experience that is intended to be shared by all students.

How Can Universities Balance Mission Distinctiveness and Improve Transfer?

National and statewide efforts to improve student transfer create competing demands on institutions—to balance institutional distinctiveness with common curricula in general education and with accommodating transfers from community colleges and other four-year institutions. Accrediting agencies have historically urged not only mission clarity but program distinctiveness, asking, "What distinguishes your program from others?" This reflects the underlying assumption that each institution's programs should be distinctive and aligned with the institution's distinctive mission and character.

Policymakers, on the other hand, citing data that a majority of undergraduates will attend more than one institution, challenge institutions to reduce barriers to transfer. They express concern that barriers to transfer—including distinctive core courses for general education—are causing enormous personal and economic burdens on transfer students, such as increased tuition costs, time to completion, financial aid, and in many cases, unnecessary attrition.

At one research university, for example, the faculty spent several years designing and gaining approval for a truly distinctive general education program. At the same time, this innovative program posed significant challenges for community college students wishing to transfer to that institution without having taken these distinctive courses. That general education program often forced transfers to take several additional courses. It took several years to develop articulation agreements, supported by the adoption of statewide policies mandating acceptance of community college courses. The solutions to this dilemma are not simple, for no one wishes to see a homogenized curriculum across statewide systems, but policymakers naturally want ease and efficiency of transferring among institutions.

Given the "swirl" of students between institutions during their undergraduate careers and the increasing pressure on institutions to take responsibility for student learning at the time of graduation, both institutions and accrediting agencies must do much more to address these issues. Institutions must devote more attention to transfer requirements for general education. They must also identify prerequisite courses in their majors, since they too can become a major barrier to seamless transitions from one institution to another. To improve communication and articulation, institutions need to collect better data that go beyond the number of transfer students in order to determine the extent of acceptance of transfer credits and the reasons for nonacceptance. In working with several institutions addressing this issue in their accrediting process, we have found much more folklore about transfer issues than useful data.

Accrediting commissions also need to make the issue of both institutional distinctiveness and transfer transparency more of a priority in the accrediting process. For example, in asking what makes a program distinctive, a common response is "our research emphasis" or "our emphasis on community engagement." Public research universities especially must match those intentions with hard evidence that they have incorporated them into their courses, programs, and student activities and that they are producing the intended results, especially in student learning. The accrediting process must also devote much more attention to addressing these transfer problems, since transfer students comprise a significant percentage of upper-division students. It should require institutions—especially public research universities—to review their transfer data, and ask the question "Is it good enough?" and publicly set goals for improvement.

In addition, there is a need to disaggregate data by student group, to determine authentic retention and graduation data. All too often institutions rely on aggregate data, only to discover that if a more thorough analysis is conducted, graduation rates for some groups, especially underrepresented students, are significantly lower. Retention and graduation rates vary significantly by department as well, which can raise questions about whether there is a true commitment throughout the institution to see *all* students succeed.

Balancing Mission Centrality With the Call for Publicly Reported Outcomes_____

Most of us within higher education would agree that the diversity of institutional missions represented by the 3,000 regionally accredited institutions offering degrees in the United States constitutes one of the most important and successful characteristics of American higher education, making it truly distinctive in the world. Differing curricular emphases often reflect, or are presumed to reflect, mission diversity. A baccalaureate degree would differ supposedly when offered by a small church-related college, a large public research university, a medium-size comprehensive public university, or a selective liberal arts college. As a result, most leaders within higher education respond to calls for greater accountability through the lens of institutional diversity or uniqueness. To insiders, diversity and uniqueness make providing comparable data impossible and inappropriate.

Institutional missions, the students enrolled, and other distinguishing characteristics of the rich variety of institutions in the U.S. deny the credibility of comparisons demanded by government, business, and civic leaders. In short, for the higher education community, mission centrality is the cornerstone for addressing accountability, which means that each college or university wants to define accountability on its own terms.

Regional accreditation focuses on institutions individually and uses the institutional mission of the institution as the centerpiece of its review. Working with individual institutions separately means that there is little aggregation of results or generation of generic issues from the reviews of all institutions within a system or a state, or over the course of a period of time. In a few instances, state system reviews are coordinated or combined, but accreditation largely centers on individual institutions, which encourages the notion of institutional uniqueness.

At the same time, state and national policymakers want aggregated and comparative data to assess the effectiveness of groups, systems, or institutions. They find such comparable data seldom available, though crucial for good policymaking. They counter the contention of campus leaders that uniqueness makes comparisons impossible with the comment, "How can you claim the impossibility of comparing colleges and universities when they award common degrees?"

The National Center for Public Policy and Higher Education launched a major effort to provide aggregated and comparative data to assist state policymakers. Every two years it publishes *Measuring Up*, which provides statewide "report cards" for higher education on five indicator categories—preparation, participation, completion, affordability, and benefits. The center provides comprehensive overviews of state performance and state-by-state grades. It attempted to apply a sixth indicator—learning—but until 2004 gave every state an incomplete because of the lack of common data for comparison among states and institutions on undergraduate learning. In *Measuring Up 2004*, five states participated in a pilot program that has led, for the first time, to a public effort to evaluate the level of student learning and achievement against a number of publicly reported and compared indicators (National Center for Public Policy and Higher Education, 2004). That report aggregated the data by each of the five states without making a distinction between institutional type and mission. Though the data suggested broad areas with lagging student performance, many educational experts find such data difficult to use, precisely because it does not reveal differences among institutions or retention and graduation rates related to the academic preparation of students on entry. Another missing link in the report cards is the ability to measure down to the institutional level to identify the sources of successes and shortcomings in statewide performance (Burke & Minassians, 2002).

Measuring Up has increased the call for more public data on the performance of graduates. The accountability for student learning study by the Business–Higher Education Forum (BHEF) distinguished between performance measures used *within* institutions to foster improvement, and measures publicly reported between institutions to demonstrate accountability and stimulate policy awareness. The BHEF (2004) report states,

> Generally speaking, the growing interest in student learning outcomes has been focused on ways to connect learning assessment with institutional improvements, not with broad public goals for higher education. The internal focus has been motivated by the conviction that improvement in performance should, after all, be the primary purpose of any system for public accountability, because accountability is about results and performance. But the inward focus means that there may be weaknesses in an institution's public communication about performance, as well as in the tools that root out performance problems occurring *between* rather than inside institutions. (p. 22)

While acknowledging that a single set of metrics will not work for all institutions given the diversity and decentralization of higher education in the Unites States, the report recommends more public disclosure and analysis of data that moves outside the single institution to common issues within institutional types. It concludes, "Much of the information is not translated to the public, and lacks context from comparative data about other institutions or from national measures of expected outcomes. Public accountability cannot be achieved when the learning assessment system is so self-referential" (BHEF, 2004, p. 28).

In a similar vein, *Our Students' Best Work*, published by the Association of American Colleges and Universities (2004), calls for departments and institutions to set clear performance standards and benchmark these against outside institutions to obtain an external reference on quality and a broader perspective on how the institution's or department's performance compares to peers.

The gap between the insider's view of accountability—mission centered and context focused—and the outsider's view—data driven, public, and comparative—seems to be widening. Whether through *Measuring Up* or the secretary of education's Commission on the Future of Higher Education, increasing discussion is occurring on the use of standardized assessments such as the Collegiate Learning Assessment to provide comparative performance data on student learning. Closing the gap in a responsible way will require much more work. As one higher education official reportedly said about the ability of college leaders to communicate with the public on higher education and accountability, "they might as well be talking backwards, in Russian" (Jaschik, 2005).

It remains unclear whether accrediting agencies can—and perhaps should—address this gap. On the one hand, accreditation has been historically tied to each institution's mission and evidence of its achievement. Yet accreditation's role in ensuring accountability becomes increasingly important precisely because it evaluates periodically every major institution in the United States. Initial drafts of the Reauthorization Act in 2005 would have required institutions to make public more information about student learning outcomes and performance, but later drafts deleted these provisions.

Much more could be done by both institutions and accrediting agencies to address the need for both internal assessment and external reporting of data on performance results. Indiana University–Purdue University Indianapolis (IUPUI) provides one example of public reporting of performance. The IUPUI web site provides a performance report using indicators and color coding to give a quick overview of how the university is doing in key performance areas (IUPUI, 2005).

As institutions increasingly use their web sites to present portfolios for accreditation reviews, several are beginning to extend these portfolios to the public and to invite greater external interest in performance data. Portland State University has recently joined IUPUI in providing this information. Both move their portfolio from an archive for accreditation to a dynamic resource for presenting, analyzing, and discussing performance results, including areas for needed improvement.

Accrediting agencies should be stimulating these efforts, and especially with public universities, should be promoting far greater development and dissemination of information about institutional performance. Student learning and assessing performance constitute the area in most need of development. Institutions should design accreditation self-study processes to include external reference points that not only build on peers, but also challenge universities to benchmark against the best institutions in problem areas that require improvement. Accrediting agencies should also move beyond the nearly exclusive internal focus of institutional assessments, especially of learning and performance, and require that external references be used to establish targets for improvement.

Moving Beyond "Input Excellence" to Quality Results

All too often, institutions highlight their quest for excellence by citing improvements in the input characteristics of students, faculty, and finances. Despite protestations about the methodology of the rankings in *U.S. News & World Report*, universities work hard to improve those ratings by increasing incoming student SAT scores and building up endowment income. Institutions also cite the number of National Merit Scholars they have recruited, or valedictorians, and so on. On the output end, institutions will similarly cite the performance of the best students who get into premier medical and law schools or Ph.D. programs. This "excellence" mode of thinking allows institutions to believe that because some students are highly performing, the institution itself is performing well.

Such thinking also influences the attitudes of administrators and professors about quality assurance within the institution. For example, if 12 out of 55 departments have a capstone or thesis requirement, institutional leaders often believe they have sufficiently addressed the need for an integrative experience. In my view, a significant difference exists between "excellence input" thinking and "quality systems" thinking. Quality systems thinking focuses not just on the best, but on consistency of performance across all student types, the range of variation in performance, the breadth and comprehensiveness of quality assurance across the institution, and the extent of motivation to seek and adopt the best practices for improvement.

WASC accrediting teams have applied the principles and process developed by William Massy (2005) in Hong Kong for the academic audit. They review the range of variation in quality and effectiveness of program reviews and conduct test samples of such reviews at each of the schools and colleges. This approach goes far beyond showcase reviews of a few model programs to a more authentic representation of performance levels in a range of different departments selected by the team for review, rather than the institution. Teams are trained to go beyond the existence of several capstone courses to probe across the institution the assessment of student ability to integrate the knowledge and skills acquired in their undergraduate education. Equally important is the general attitude of administrators, professors, and staff members toward improving student learning across the board. "Trying" to address a problem differs dramatically from the internal passion to "be the best" in serving students, by actively discovering and implementing relevant best practices used by leading universities and colleges. Moreover, there are often good practices already in place within large comprehensive universities, but these are seldom shared with other schools and departments. In a quality-centered system, there is widespread sharing of practices—including successes and failures—within the institution to promote organizational learning.

Accreditation has historically focused on quality systems, but without the depth of understanding exhibited by quality systems and the continuous improvement developed in business and industry and adapted for higher education. These systems become especially important in public colleges and universities with their stated purposes of providing access to underserved populations, producing an educated workforce, and reducing failure rates. Accrediting agencies can encourage pursuit of these goals by holding high expectations of institutional performance that require a shift to "quality thinking" across the institution.

Improving Results Despite Apparent High Satisfaction

Adopting this demanding approach to external accountability and quality improvement poses a challenge to regional accreditors and institutions alike, because it comes at a time of rising reputations and resources of public research universities. These institutions enjoy increasing student applications, high satisfaction in student and alumni surveys, and successful capital campaigns to increase nonstate resources. Most of their professional schools and programs have gained specialized accreditation as marks of quality and distinction, and can point to civic, business, and professional leaders as their graduates. So why should presidents, provosts, and trustees risk their institution's reputation by adopting high standards that demand improved performance results rather than depend on resources and inputs to drive attitudes about quality and effectiveness?

The answer is that government, business, and civic leaders are now demanding not just an accounting of inputs, but also evidence of performance results, especially of the knowledge and skills acquired by graduates. These external leaders want to know whether the education received by graduates meets the needs of careers and life in a knowledge economy.

Graduation rates and learning results have increasingly become the real test of performance, especially of public universities. These two goals become critical for such institutions. They must provide access to a range of citizens of the state and prepare the majority of the next generation of leaders in all fields. Government, business, and civic leaders now contend that, despite the rising reputation and resources of universities, public universities are falling short on their most critical goal of graduating students with high levels of knowledge and skills.

The record of public universities is especially questionable in achieving these goals with the most disadvantaged in our society. The high school graduation and college attendance rates for African Americans and Latinos are significantly lower than for whites. Both institutions and accrediting agencies need to engage in far more focused reviews of how to improve on these essential goals. Fewer than 55% of students will graduate in six years, especially at public universities, and graduation rates for African Americans and Latinos are more than 20% lower than for whites. Raising graduation rates, especially for underrepresented groups, warrants far greater institutional attention. In this area, a "quality mindset" coupled with the motivation to seek out best practices could lead to major improvements. That some institutions are achieving high graduation rates means it can be done. Accrediting teams should expect and promote best practices through their review processes, and ensure that data on retention and graduation rates become central to their institutional assessment.

Data on student learning results warrant institutional attention, even from research universities with selective enrollments. Raising the bar at admission must also mean raising the performance bar at graduation. Despite internal assessment data that students are completing learning requirements, external national data tell a different story. The National Assessment of Adult Literacy, conducted every 10 years, found that while the performance of college graduates (including those with graduate degrees) was greater than the population as a whole, performance had declined significantly in the past decade for proficiency in prose and document reading and applications. A similar test given to college seniors also discovered serious deficiencies in prose and mathematical literacy. Test results did not differ significantly among public institutions, regardless of their missions or types. Students at selective public research universities did not fare significantly better than their peers from other types of institutions. While students from families with the greatest incomes scored the highest in general, given the priority of public institutions to provide access to underrepresented and economically diverse students, much more is needed to improve the graduation rates and level of proficiency of those students whom public institutions are intended to serve. These test results suggest that "good in" is producing less than "good out." What these results suggest is a wake-up call for many public and research universities.

Too often, leaders of these institutions argue that the assessments of literacy do not assess what is taught in college. But employers consistently find that college graduates are not meeting their expectations of performance. The claim that colleges and universities do not teach what literacy tests score and what employers want is telling, for these are the knowledge and skills supposedly engendered in general or liberal education, which all college graduates should acquire, whatever their major. Instead of seeing assessment as peripheral, and accreditation as something to get out of the way, institutions will need to use processes to improve learning results, especially in general education, as the core business of the institution. Public universities must raise the motivation on campus to address these issues or outsiders will move in to raise it for them. Derek Bok (2006) concedes,

> . . . neither faculties nor their deans and presidents feel
> especially pressed to search continuously for new and
> better ways of educating their students, nor do they
> feel compelled to offer the very best education possible
> in order to avoid losing large numbers of applicants or
> suffering other consequences that matter. (p. 34)

While all accrediting agencies now give greater emphasis to assessment, they must also move from evaluating the activity of assessment to the standards of performance applied by the institution to itself and its students, and those of its faculty in assessing student learning. What is good enough? How does the institution know that standard is achieved? To what extent is that learning standard consistent across all departments and major fields of study? To what extent is data disaggregated to assess learning levels for different types of students? Much room still exists for improving the sophistication and level of the review conducted by accrediting agencies and assessment of its institutional implementation. Accreditation and assessment must become a continuous process, not a 10-year event.

Disclosure and Dissemination of Results: Levers for Change?

College and university leaders fear most the extension of the philosophy of the No Child Left Behind legislation to higher education. Underlying No Child Left Behind is a pervading belief that public disclosure of standardized testing results will promote, or better still compel, improvement. That education change comes not just from testing, but also from publishing the results. At the time this chapter was written, the Commission on the Future of Higher Education initially pushed hard for some form of national testing of college graduates and/or students. After opposition from higher education leaders and commission members, the final report dropped the mandate for standardized testing. Despite this, many in higher education fear that the thinking of No Child Left Behind is moving into higher education. That movement certainly shows the increasing desire for greater information on student learning and the growing frustration of government, business, and civic leaders about the reluctance of colleges and universities to supply or even collect such information.

Discussions also occurred in proposed revisions to the Reauthorization Act on greater disclosure of accrediting actions. Despite some initial calls for full disclosure of all accrediting team reports and actions, draft legislation in the House of Representatives would provide for a summary of findings accompanying each action. Accrediting agencies strongly resist full disclosure of team reports. They contend such publication could imperil the candor of institutional self-studies, of team assessments of performance, and identification of the areas for improvement. Private colleges and universities especially oppose such publications.

At most public institutions, accrediting team reports are "publicly available." Thus for public institutions the issue is not really disclosure but effective *dissemination*. At too many institutions, especially large public and research universities, reports filed with accrediting agencies and those from accrediting teams are placed on the web but are difficult to locate and thereby ineffective for disclosing publicly performance results. Rarely does an accreditation report lead to widespread discussion and engagement of critical performance issues even on campus, much less in the community beyond. A handful of administrators and professors are aware of the presence of these documents, but they soon become artifacts of a process rather than levers for change.

So too is the fate of information on learning results. Data abounds in most universities, but rarely does it lead to strategic discussions among administrators, professors, staff members, and students about how to improve performance results. All too often, for example, highlights of results from the National Survey of Student Engagement are reported, but not discussed in detail and coordinated with other data, especially data on learning results. At far too many research universities as well, little dissemination occurs about accrediting results following reviews about best practices in the assessment of learning.

Institutions will need to be more strategic in disseminating accreditation findings and recommendations, and assigning discussions and responses to different groups within the institution to ensure that there is genuine consideration and follow-up to these reports and actions. Given the magnitude of the changes needed in faculty awareness, training, and motivation to make the assessment and analysis of student learning a greater priority within faculty work, decennial reviews may only perpetuate the mindset that accreditation requires a volcanic eruption of effort immediately prior to the visit, only to return to business as usual in the intervening years. The calls for a "culture of evidence" suggest that much more work needs to be done between accrediting visits to gather and analyze qualitative and quantitative data, to engage faculty with such data, and to develop a plan of action for improving student learning.

The Vital Role of Leadership

None of the desired changes will occur without committed, clear, and sustained leadership at all levels. In a 2005 editorial in *The Chronicle of Higher Education*, Derek Bok wrote about the responsibilities of different groups. Faculty need to be engaged in ongoing systematic efforts to discover what students are and are not learning and to adjust their pedagogy to address student learning needs. Professors are not trained for this task, though many undertake it instinctively or because of their concern for their students' welfare and learning. More attention in the last decade has been given to training faculty on the use of technology than to research about student learning and the powerful pedagogies discovered to address different disciplines and student learning needs.

The deep commitment to serve students, to improve access and graduation rates, and to ensure that the institution will meet the needs of students has to come from the senior leadership, especially presidents, provosts and, no less important, deans and department chairs. That leadership demands more than rhetorical statements. Support and understanding of the interconnectedness of multiple efforts and the value of consistent and comprehensive quality systems are all part of this commitment. As Bok (2005) states, "Presidents are the natural source of initiative to see that problems of student learning are identified and reforms are developed. In practice, however, few presidents have made serious, sustained efforts to push those initiatives" (p. B12).

Presidential leadership becomes all the more important in committing public institutions to concentrate on assessing and improving undergraduate learning, followed by public disclosure and dissemination of reports on performance results.

Ultimately, however, commitment means matching goals with resources. Trustees, presidents, and provosts must make sure that faculty training, student assessment, and data collection receive adequate funding. In too many institutions, these things are the last funded in good budget years and the first cut when funding falls.

Accrediting agencies will also have to provide a new and different kind of leadership. Accrediting agency leaders and staff will need to achieve a new level of sophistication in addressing in a more substantive way issues of accountability, transparency, and educational effectiveness. Accrediting results will need to be made more public, even if in a periodic and aggregated way. For public institutions, accrediting agencies should play a more visible role in identifying key parameters of accountability and in ensuring they become the central elements of the review process.

Conclusion

The calls for accountability have become increasingly more frequent and sophisticated. They are directed most often at public universities, since they receive the bulk of state funds, though states now support a diminishing portion of their budgets. The gap between the insiders' view of higher education and the outside expectations of policymakers has widened into a chasm. The past five to seven years have brought significant changes in accreditation, which has developed a more visible leadership role in promoting attention to student learning outcomes and quality issues.

Regional accrediting agencies must highlight more the special position of public institutions, especially research universities, in the review process so that there is far clearer articulation of the public purposes and goals of the institution and greater evidence of their achievement. Accreditation will need to move beyond minimum standards to defining key areas of priority for review, and become a more visible and proactive part of the accountability dialogue now occurring.

The times also demand a greater partnership between institutions and accrediting agencies to guarantee meaningful dissemination and campus engagement with accreditation. Underlying it all is the need for a fundamental commitment not always present—a sustained, comprehensive commitment to serve *all* students enrolled at the institution, and to fulfill, together, the purposes of the public university as a vehicle for addressing public priorities and preparing the next generation of leadership.

Though both accrediting agencies and institutions are now well poised for this challenge, much mutual work lies ahead. Regional accreditation has stopped being part of the problem, and has started becoming part of the solution.

Some concluding recommendations:

For Accrediting Agencies

- Identify more clearly the chief accountability priorities and foci of the accreditation process.
- Become more specific in requiring public institutions to document the alignment and integration of their stated purposes—such as civic engagement, public service, and even research—into the learning outcomes of the institution, the institution's assessment efforts, and the reported learning results of students.
- Devote a greater part of accreditation reviews to those issues relating to transfer students—articulation, transfer student support, and completion rates.
- Focus more on the institution's learning results and the institution's assessment of "Is it good enough?" by reviewing the standards of performance relied on by the institution.
- Communicate more publicly, even in an aggregated manner, annual results of its reviews, especially with such important issues as retention, graduation rates, and student learning outcomes and results.

- Develop a more active relationship with public universities, especially research universities, to engage faculty in the process of moving beyond individual course grades to program and school assessment of student learning outcomes.

For Institutions

- For leadership at all levels—presidents, provosts, deans, department chairs, and faculty leadership—articulate and embrace a commitment to the success of all students and to the evaluation and dissemination of student learning results.
- More clearly articulate the public mission of the institution, and assess the extent to which that mission is reflected in the actual activities, programs, and learning outcomes of students.
- Move into a "quality mindset" that considers consistency of outcomes across the institution; engage in active sharing of best practices from within and outside the institution.
- Provide necessary resources to support faculty and staff commitment to assessing student learning beyond course grades, and to developing new pedagogies that promote more effective learning.
- Carry on a comprehensive institutional dialogue about retention and graduation rates, focusing on disaggregated data by different student groups and majors.
- Legitimate and reward the scholarship of learning to make studies of how learning in various disciplines can be more effectively evaluated and improved—a serious part of institutional and faculty research.
- Publicly disseminate learning and performance results within and outside the institution to promote effective dialogue about what is working and what needs improvement, set targets for improvement, and report periodically on whether such improvements have succeeded.

Endnotes

1) A consultant for the Commission on the Future of Higher Education saw accreditation as a part of the problem rather than a method for improving the quality of American higher education (Dickeson, 2006). But the final report from the Commission on the Future of Higher Education softened its initial draft's criticism of accreditation (U.S. Department of Education, 2006b). Secretary Spellings is calling for a conference and dialogue with accreditors (U.S. Department of Education, 2006a).

2) The six regions are the New England Association, the Middle States Association, the Southern Association, the Higher Learning Commission of the North Central Association, the Western Association, and the Northwest Commission on Colleges and Universities. The Western Association is divided into a community and senior college commission.

References

Association of American Colleges and Universities. (2004). *Our students' best work: A framework for accountability worthy of our mission.* Washington, DC: Author.

Association of American Colleges and Universities. (2005). *Liberal education outcomes: A preliminary report on student achievement in college.* Washington, DC: Author.

Bok, D. C. (2005, December 16). The critical role of trustees in enhancing student learning. *The Chronicle of Higher Education,* p. B12.

Bok, D. C. (2006). *Our underachieving colleges: A candid look at how much students learn and why they should be learning more.* Princeton, NJ: Princeton University Press.

Burke, J. C., & Minassians, H. P. (2002). *New directions in institutional research: No. 116. Reporting higher education results: Missing links in the performance chain.* San Francisco, CA: Jossey-Bass.

Business–Higher Education Forum. (2004). *Public accountability for student learning in higher education: Issues and options.* Washington, DC: Author.

Dickeson, R. C. (2006). *The need for accreditation reform.* Retrieved August 21, 2006, from www.ed.gov/about/bdscomm/list/hiedfuture/reports/dickeson.pdf

Higher Learning Commission. (2003). *Handbook of accreditation* (3rd ed.). Chicago, IL: Author.

Indiana University–Purdue University Indianapolis. (2005). *IUPUI portfolio: Performance indicators.* Retrieved August 20, 2006, from the Indiana University–Purdue University Indianapolis, IUPUI Portfolio web site: www.iport.iupui.edu/performance/

Jaschik, S. (2005). *Crisis of confidence.* Retrieved August 21, 2006, from http://insidehighered.com/news/2006/02/13/ace

Massy, W. F. (2005). Academic audit for accountability and improvement. In J. C. Burke & Associates, *Achieving accountability in higher education: Balancing public, academic, and market demands* (pp. 173–197). San Francisco, CA: Jossey-Bass.

Miller, C. (2006). *Memo from the chairman.* Retrieved August 21, 2006, from www.insidehighered.com/views/2006/01/24/miller

National Center for Public Policy and Higher Education. (2004). *Measuring up 2004: The state-by-state report card for higher education.* San Jose, CA: Author.

National Commission on Accountability in Higher Education. (2005). *Accountability for better results: A national imperative for higher education.* Boulder, CO: State Higher Education Executive Officers.

University of California–Berkeley. (2003). *Educational effectiveness report.* Retrieved August 21, 2006, from the University of California–Berkeley, Accreditation web site: http://education.berkeley .edu/accreditation/pdf/Educational_Effectiveness.pdf

U.S. Department of Education. (2006a). *Secretary Spellings announces plans for more affordable, accessible, accountable and consumer-friendly U.S. higher education system.* Retrieved September 29, 2006, from www.ed.gov/news/pressreleases/2006/09/09262006.html

U.S. Department of Education. (2006b). *A test of leadership: Charting the future of U.S. higher education.* Washington, DC: Author.

Wolff, R. A. (2005). Accountability and accreditation: Can reforms match increasing demands? In J. C. Burke & Associates, *Achieving accountability in higher education: Balancing public, academic, and market demands* (pp. 78–103). San Francisco, CA: Jossey-Bass.

9

Performance Reporting: Putting Academic Departments in the Performance Loop

Joseph C. Burke

The Departmental Disconnect_____

Performance reporting has swept the country. *Measuring Up* grades the 50 states on their higher education results (National Center for Public Policy and Higher Education, 2000; 2002; 2004). Forty-six states have some form of accountability reporting, and most college or university systems and public institutions publish their own reports (Burke & Associates, 2005; Burke & Minassians, 2002). Despite all this reporting, doubts remain about the performance of higher education and its colleges or universities. In 2002, Pat Callan, the president of the center issuing *Measuring Up*, described the "national picture of higher education" as "one of unevenness and even mediocrity" (National Center, 2002, p. 16). Two years later, he declared, " . . . our findings are not encouraging. They constitute . . . a 'wake-up call' for the country . . . " (National Center, 2004, p. 8).

One reason for this poor performance is that reporting programs require states, systems, and institutions to measure up on meeting societal needs, but few colleges and universities measure down to assess the contribution of their academic departments to institutional and public priorities. A survey of institutional research directors in six states suggests that performance reporting becomes increasingly invisible on campus below the vice president level. Forty-five percent of the directors from two- and four-year public colleges and universities claim their academic deans had little or no familiarity with accountability reporting in their states; 70% claim this about their department chairs (Burke &

Minassians, 2002). No planning process can promote external accountability nor improve institutional performance when it leaves the units most responsible for academic results out of the loop.

Leaving academic departments out of the performance loop is especially prevalent in large public research universities. Their size and complexity make decentralization a necessity, not just a tradition. Without direction, this decentralization fosters a disabling disconnect between societal concerns, institutional priorities, and departmental performance, the three connections essential to public accountability. State accountability programs hold presidents, vice presidents, even trustees responsible for meeting state needs but they do not teach students, do research, or provide services. Professors, mostly organized in academic departments, perform these tasks. Due to the information disconnect between the institution and its academic units, departments remain largely unaware of state needs or market demands directed at their universities, and all too aware of outside demands pressed directly on them, mostly for applied research. The disconnect between campus priorities and departmental performance often turns presidential pledges, especially on academic results, into problematic promises.

The Kellogg Commission on the Future of State and Land-Grant Universities flagged this problem (see Chapter 1). "The university has become an institutionally fragmented aggregation of departments" (Kellogg Commission, 2000, p. 10.). Despite these complaints, the commission noted that "the departmental organization of academic life has been strangely absent from the reform conversation" (p. 31). It cited an article by the chief academic officer of the University of Nebraska–Lincoln that analyzed a survey of colleagues in 68 public universities. The responses from only 37 academic officers suggest less than enthusiastic interest in engaging departments in university reforms. Still, more than 80% of those responding called "significant changes in academic departments" "highly important." Yet their narrative comments suggest that "change at the departmental level is occurring very slowly and very timidly, if at all" (Edwards, 1999, p. 22). The author concluded,

> The current reform agenda envisioned change at the
> institutional and individual levels but leaves depart-
> ments out of the process. . . . Moreover, by leaving
> departments out of the process, by default it makes
> them the natural centers of opposition to institution-
> al change. (Edwards, 1999, p. 27)

The Kellogg Commission hoped to fix the fragmented university by aligning institutional and departmental priorities to fit societal and student needs. Meeting those needs meant elevating the university mission in undergraduate education and public engagement to the same exalted status as faculty research (see Chapter 1). Each of these goals remains a mission impossible without a mechanism for making departments part of a performance loop.

State, Institutional, and Departmental Performance Reports

The prevalence of performance reporting offers a means for assuring and testing the alignment of priorities at the state, university, and departmental levels. This chapter examines performance reports at all three levels to assess the alignment of their priorities. It explores three questions: Are the priorities of public research universities aligned with state and societal needs? Are the goals of colleges, schools, and especially departments aligned with university priorities? And finally, how can campus leaders ensure the alignment of state needs, institutional priorities, and departmental goals?

Methodology

A search of the web sites of higher education coordinating or governing boards in 17 states[1] and those for 28 of their public research universities[2] identified the number and the content of performance reports at the state, institutional, and departmental levels.[3] A comparison of their performance indicators determined the extent of their alignment at all three levels. The search consciously selected the states and most of the universities represented by the participants of the Kellogg Commission, which advocated the alignment of institutional and departmental priorities in the service of public needs. Michigan, Minnesota, and Pennsylvania at the time of this search did not have coordinating boards and state performance reports on higher education.[4] Iowa does not publish a state performance report but proposes performance indicators for its public institutions. The remaining 13 states and each of the 28 universities have some form of performance reporting. Departmental reporting was noticeable mostly by its absence.

State and Institutional Reports

Governors and legislators often call public universities unresponsive to state needs, and business leaders say the same about market demands.

Champions of colleges and universities counter that state needs are seldom well defined and often change with election and market cycles. A recent work recommends that representative groups of civic, business, political, and education leaders develop a public agenda, not of what everyone wants, but of what each state needs most from its higher education system (Burke & Associates, 2005).

Though bows to state differences are always in order, the knowledge and information era means that societal needs from higher education increasingly know no boundaries. Several national organizations compile lists of top priorities for higher education. Recent lists reveal general agreement on the following priorities for higher education, especially public colleges and universities (American Association of State Colleges and Universities, 2005; Association of Governing Boards of Universities and Colleges, 2005; State Higher Education Executive Officers, 2006):

1) Access, affordability, diversity
2) College/school collaboration
3) Degree completion
4) Economic and workforce development
5) Research competitiveness
6) Student learning

These policy issues follow the Kellogg Commission in stressing undergraduate education, though less so for public engagement except in areas of economic development. They also echo the six categories of the *Measuring Up* reports—preparation, affordability, participation, completion, benefits (mostly degrees awarded), and student learning (National Center, 2000, 2002, 2004). The policy issues and *Measuring Up* differ only in the latter's neglect of faculty research as a category.

Unfortunately, the plethora of performance indicators in both state and institutional reports obscures a sense of public and university priorities. The reports suggest coverage and compliance more than purpose and performance. Despite consolidating many distinct but similar indicators into generic measures to facilitate comparisons, the state reports average 29 generic measures with a high of 48 and a low of 12. An earlier study of 29 state reports showed a much higher average of 40 generic indicators, with a high of 87 and a low of 5 (Burke & Minassians, 2002). More state reports have reduced their indicators, some of them to align with *Measuring Up* categories (National Commission on Accountability in Higher Education, 2005).

The state reports and those from the universities generally follow four of the six priorities identified by the national associations: access, affordability, and diversity; degree completion; workforce and economic development; and research competitiveness. The striking exceptions come from college/school collaboration and student learning. These issues attract only scant and scattered attention in the indicators of the state or university reports. Table 9.1 tracks the top 20 indicators found in a previous study of 29 state performance reports for higher education (Burke & Minassians, 2002). The following discussion also includes some percentages of indicators in state and university reports that fail to make the top 20.

As expected, indicators reflecting *Access* rank the highest. Conversely, those representing *Diversity* of both students and faculty receives strong support, which is both welcome and somewhat surprising, especially in the state reports. *Enrollment (level, race, gender)* appears in all reports at both levels. The priority of degree completion with its indicators of *Degrees Awarded* and *Graduation Rates* also places highly in both reports, with state percentages only slightly above those for the universities. Differences emerge on affordability. Almost all the state reports include indicators on *Tuition and Fees* (92.3%), but those from the universities give it a more measured response (75%). Obviously, university leaders prefer less statewide attention to student charges and more campus control. A larger and more surprising difference appears on the *Financial Aid* measure, with the states' 75% usage, 25 points higher than the universities'.

Though the above differences are interesting, the most telling divergence comes on measures related to admissions selectivity. More than 82% of the university reports use *SAT/ACT Scores*, nearly 36% higher than the states' average. The same holds true for another selectivity measure—*Freshman, High School GPA/Rank*—with the university average (60.7%) also far above the state reports (38.5%). Clearly, student selectivity constitutes a fault line between state and university leaders.

Both states and universities push the priority of research competitiveness. *Sponsored Research* appears in more than two-thirds of both reports. The economic development interest of the states is also clear in their use of *Patents, Licenses, and Disclosures* (61.5%), considerably higher than the university reports (42.9%). Surprisingly, universities give little support to other scholarship measures. Only three of the institutional reports and just one from the states has an indicator on *Publications and Citations*.

The university reports favor *Private Fundraising* (50%) more than those from the states (38.5%). Not surprisingly, state reports focus

Table 9.1
Top Performance Indicators

State	%	University	%
Enrollment (level, race, gender)	100	Enrollment (level, race, gender)	100
Tuition and Fees	92.3	Enrollment, Residency	85.7
Graduation Rates, 6 Years	84.6	SAT/ACT scores	82.1
Faculty (race, gender)	84.6	Degrees Awarded (level, race, gender)	78.6
Degrees Awarded (level, race, gender)	84.6	Graduation Rates, 6 Years	78.6
Financial Aid	76.9	Retention Rate	78.6
State operating funding	76.9	Tuition and Fees	75.0
Faculty Compensation	76.9	Faculty (race, gender)	71.4
Sponsored Research	69.2	Sponsored research	67.9
Enrollment, Residency	61.5	Acceptance/ enrollment rates	53.6
Enrollment, transfers	61.5	Library holdings/ expenditures	53.6
Retention Rate	61.5	Student credit hours by level	53.6
Patents, Licenses, and Disclosures	61.5	Faculty Compensation	53.6
College participation rate	53.8	Financial Aid	50.0
Expenditures per student	53.8	Private fundraising	50.0
Acceptance/ enrollment rates	46.2	Patents, Licenses, and Disclosures	42.9
Graduation/retention, race	46.2	Faculty tenure	42.9
Licensure exam pass rates	46.2	Faculty, full-/part-time	39.3
Time to degree/credit hours for graduation	46.2	Student/faculty ratio	35.7
Enrollment, fields	38.5	Annual student costs	35.7

Note. Common indicators in bold.

much more attention on cost items, such as *Expenditures per Student* (53.8%), than institutions (10.7%). Both university and state reports stress *Faculty Compensation*—76.9% for the state as opposed to 53.6% for the university. University reports tend to include an indicator on tenure (42.9%), but those from the states usually omit this item. State reports use the *Job Placement* indicator rather more sparingly than expected (38.5%), while the institutions predictably are even more skeptical of this measure (10.7%).

Unfortunately, neither report pays much attention to assessing program quality and student learning. Assessment appears in only two state reports and one for universities. In addition, both give scant attention to quality indicators such as *Student, Alumni,* and *Employer Satisfaction*. State reports do emphasize *Licensure Exam Pass Rates* (46.2%) to universities' meager 7.1%. University reports are slightly more favorable to *Program Accreditation* (21.4%) than those from the state (15.4%).

Neither the state reports (15.4%) nor the university reports (13.7%) give the expected endorsement to the indicator *K–16 Collaboration*, which the national and state policy organizations call critical for success in college and national competitiveness. Though *Teacher Training* has a few random indicators in both reports, it too receives surprisingly little attention. For example, only one of the 28 universities includes *Pass Rates on Teacher Exam, Race*. Though higher, the state average of 23.1% fell far short of an endorsement of either quality teacher training or minority teacher preparation.

The Kellogg Commission's push for public and community service also finds small support in the university indicators. Only 14.3% of the institutional reports include an indicator on *Public Service*, while the state reports more than double that percentage. The same usages appear on *Student Internships*. The Kellogg Commission had advocated *Student Involvement in Faculty Research* as part of its emphasis on undergraduate education. Unfortunately, only 14.3% of the university reports incorporate this indicator, while the state percentage is 9 points higher.

The state and university performance reports show mixed support for public priorities. The university indicators favor the enrollment side of the access equation, but with the caveat of increasing selectivity and concern about affordability measures. Such a caveat and concern may cause trouble with the states and the public, which view expanding participation and continuing affordability as two of the primary purposes of public universities. Diversity wins welcome backing from both the states and the universities. Both also sanction degree completion, with the university approval only slightly behind that of the state support. Research competitiveness also garners endorsement, though limited to indicators on sponsored activities and neglecting publications. The comparatively low rating on *Patents, Licenses, and Disclosures* perhaps reflects the reluctance of faculty in the arts and humanities to accept a measure that is outside their purpose. The scant use of *Publications and Citations*, the favorite research measure in many academic disciplines, confirms the contention that departments give little or no attention to performance reports.

The most disturbing failures are the lack of support for measures on 1) student learning and 2) school improvement. The first represents a major purpose of public universities and the second constitutes the most pressing problem in the United States. Finally, one wonders whether the university reports are meant more for external compliance than institutional improvement. The large number of indicators suggests external compliance. The lack of departmental reports suggests little or no impact on institutional improvement in academic areas.

Trends and Targets

Assessing performance requires trends to review data over time rather than for a single year. Performance indicators should also include performance targets that set periodic goals for results. Of the states with performance reports, all 13 provide trends over time. Of the 28 universities, 24 do the same. Performance targets are much less widespread. Less than half the states and just 6 of the 28 universities set such goals.

Departmental Reports

A search of the web sites of the 28 universities shows that only 12 universities report at all on departmental indicators. The reports include 38 generic indicators, but 45% of that total appears only in the departmental reports from the University of Illinois at Urbana-Champaign. Only three other institutions—Clemson University, Texas A&M University, and University of Oregon—report on at least 6 indicators. The Urbana-Champaign web site allows searchers to access 10 years of data on departmental indicators. Unfortunately, most of those measures compile routine data on faculty/staff, enrollment, course, section, and cost analysis. That university does report on degrees awarded, student teaching evaluations, sponsored research, and time to degree, but does not record graduation rates, job placements, or any of the measures of program quality and student learning. Clearly, the University of Illinois at Champaign-Urbana has the most extensive report on departmental results, but even it falls short of the range of performance indicators found in most of the university and state reports. The search confirms that in performance reporting, academic departments have clearly been left out of the loop.

Creating Integrated Performance Reporting

Creating integrated performance reporting begins with development of institutional priorities and performance indicators. State needs and market demands, even when adopted in public agendas, do not—and should not—dictate all of a university's priorities or performance indicators. Dictation is rarely found and always fought on campus. Of course, institutional mission and type influence institutional priorities and performance indicators. Internal aspirations at the institutional and unit levels also affect them. At times, those aspirations are more felt than affirmed. Aspirations become effective when vision and values statements express what a university hopes to become and what its community holds dear, with some degree of specificity in priorities and performance measures. Institutional sagas can inspire campus commitment, but improving performance requires institutional priorities. Setting institutional priorities and picking performance indicators can support sagas while bringing dreams down to earth.

Sadly, priorities and indicators announced by universities have a repetitive ring. They mimic traditional notions of quality in higher education based on resources and reputations, making the "imitative" rather than the "distinctive university" the ideal. The true ideal for a public university is to set priorities that direct institutional strengths toward societal and student needs. Performance indicators test the progress in reaching those priorities. Indicators perform two purposes: directing priorities and assessing performance. The first phase of the performance chain for universities demands realistic and distinctive priorities and the second requires restricted and relevant performance indicators. Priorities and performance indicators should not come as dictates from above, but they should communicate institutional directions.

Too often, the university reports with their priorities and indicators seem designed more for external consumption than internal use (Burke & Minassians, 2002). Presidents proclaim them at the institutional level and direct them at outside audiences, often because state governments or higher education coordinating or system boards mandate them. On the other hand, presidents and provosts rarely communicate these priorities or indicators to deans and chairs of colleges, schools, or departments as directions that should shape teaching, research, and services programs and measure their performance. One gets the sense that the reports are more for show than use.

Burke and Minassians (2002) note that nearly half the institutional researchers from two-year colleges said that state performance reports had improved policymaking on their campuses at least to a moderate extent. But nearly two-thirds of the institutional researchers from four-year public institutions claimed little or no effect. The new accountability in higher education moves from compliance with prescribed regulations to producing desired results. Reports with little or no effect that merely mark compliance or are done for show do not fit the demands of the new accountability. Performance reports should shape as well as record results.

A Participative but Directed Process

Evidence-based decision-making demands performance reporting at the university, college/school, and departmental level on a limited list of common measures. Successful reporting programs require broad participation in identifying priorities and developing indicators. These tasks call for a process that is at once participative in involving professors, administrators, and students, yet directive in insisting on priorities and indicators that embody state needs and institutional strengths.

Presidents, supported by the institutional trustees and central administrators, must make the case that academic units cannot flourish in attaining funding and quality if the university flounders in meeting state needs and market demands. They must convince the campus community that an integrated system of performance reporting is the way to achieve both goals, by preserving unit decentralization while providing institutional direction. Presidents must pledge up front an open process and the full participation of deans, chairs, and faculty leaders.

The best consultative process will reflect campus cultures and internal relations. Though both the process and the product will differ on every campus, they should heed the following principles:

- The debate on priorities and indicators should be about which not whether.
- Every group should have a say, but no group should have a veto.
- Participation is always critical, but consensus is seldom achievable.
- Deadlines stimulate rather than stifle serious discussion.
- The quality of decisions is not necessarily related to the length of discussion.
- In decision-making, timeliness is important and perfection impossible.

• The best improvements invariably come with practice.
• Not every piece of performance data has an unalienable right to be reported.
• Too many indicators mean no priorities.

Determining priorities and indicators is a community project, not a top-down process (Rowley, Lujan, & Dolence, 1997; Rowley & Sherman, 2001). One of the unintended but most damaging consequence of leaving departments out of the reporting loop is that it reinforces the mistaken belief that the administration owns the institution and the faculty owns the departments, with deans pummeled by both sides.

Though the paths for developing an integrated performance report will differ, the following describes an approach that achieves the goal and avoids at least some of the pitfalls. The university planning committee used for strategic planning is an ideal body to oversee the process of identifying institutional priorities and performance indicators. Its members should know state needs and market demands through external scans, and institutional strengths and weaknesses through studies of internal capabilities. Choosing the provost to chair that committee sends the message that the purpose of the project is academic, not bureaucratic, and also underscores its importance. Its membership should include respected deans and professors, representative of the university colleges, schools, and interdisciplinary centers. Professionals from institutional research, who know the possibilities and problems of performance indicators, should staff the campus committee and support the process at the university, college/school, and departmental levels.

The planning committee should ask itself and the university community: How can our university best meet critical state and student needs based on our strengths, and what performance indicators can best measure our progress on those priorities? It should consult broadly with the faculty, especially the faculty senates or councils and with student and staff groups. The process should be iterative. It should begin with lists of the best indicators drawn from the literature and outside performance reports, followed by soliciting reactions to a series of ever more refined and hopefully more limited lists of measures, tailored to the university strengths and suited for use at the institutional, college/school, and departmental levels. Public hearings at the university and unit levels encourage open discussion, and private soundings with deans and faculty leaders are essential to assess group attitudes.

Planning committees in colleges or schools, chaired by deans and including department chairs, should propose a tentative list of common indicators for review and recommendations by the departments.

After reviewing reactions from departments, the college or school committees should send a revised list for a second review and final recommendations by the departments. After a review of the second round of recommendations from the departments, the dean should send the college or school choices for common indicators to the university planning committee for its review. In addition to the common indicators, each college/school and department should be encouraged to propose several additional indicators that stress their special missions and strengths.

The university planning committee should examine carefully the common indicators suggested by the college/school committees. Based on those submissions and the need to align unit and university priorities, the university planning committee should send a tentative list of indicators to the unit committees for review and recommendations. After this second iteration, the university planning committee should recommend the combined set of university and unit indicators to the president. The president should convene a campus meeting where the provost and members of the university planning committee should explain their recommendation of indicators for the institution and departments. Finally, the president should bring the institutional and departmental indicators to the university trustees for approval. Of course, the president should have kept the board informed of campus deliberations from the beginning of the process.

Performance Loops

Developing institutional priorities and common indicators for academic units does not explain how performance reporting should operate in practice. Every university should develop a performance model of how it transforms priorities through its internal processes into desired results.

The Throughput Model

Alexander Astin (1991) diagrams a simple production process in colleges and universities as I-E-O, with student *Inputs* transformed by the campus *Environment* into learning *Outputs* (see Figure 9.1). The production model suggests the importance of the internal environment but does not explain the critical contributions of academic units, particularly departments, in shaping this environment. Many large public universities have multiple environments reflecting the differences in their colleges, schools, and departments.

The environment contains especially academic processes—such as the curricular requirements and teaching techniques—that pursue the goals and objectives of a particular university. The programs and courses

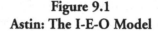

Figure 9.1
Astin: The I-E-O Model

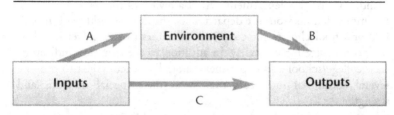

offered by departments in specialized studies and general education encourage the development of graduates who embody the academic goals of that institution. Unfortunately, the academic portion of the campus environment is seldom in practice tied closely to institutional priorities, especially in large, complex universities. Given the fragmented university, the academic portion of the environment—especially general education—often lacks coherence.

Information and Knowledge Loops

Institutional performance should represent more than a one-way process of acquiring student inputs, putting them through the institutional environment, then graduating them with the knowledge and skills conducive for meaningful lives and successful careers. Performance reporting through institutional priorities and performance indicators seeks to ensure the production of the desired results. On the other hand, performance reporting should not run as an elevator sending institutional directions down and bringing up unit results. It should function as a series of performance loops that allow academic units at every level not only to respond to priorities but also to revise them as part of the process of producing results.

The design of information and knowledge loops offers an alternative model capable of aligning public purposes, institutional priorities, and unit performance (see Figure 9.2). It proposes a more complex planning and performance model, with academic departments as the critical part of the process. The model links state needs and market forces to institutional priorities and connects them to college/school and departmental aspirations and accomplishments that in turn contribute to campus performance and priorities.

These feedback loops ensure both direction and decentralization. Institutional goals and objectives and a limited number of common indicators provide direction that encourages departments to pursue campus aims. At the same time, the design encourages decentralization by allowing academic units to add their own aspirations in ways that not only contribute to institutional results but also reshape campus priorities by providing feedback to institutional planning. Each link on the loops is both an *effect* and a *cause* in the performance chain, receiving others' *inputs* and recording its own *outputs* to the process. For example, the priorities and indicators of institutions and of colleges/schools affect the activities and aims of academic departments, but departments, and especially their results, in turn affect the results of colleges/schools and the institution and can lead to revised campus goals. The feedback loops represent virtuous circles composed of "respond and revise" rather than vicious cycles consisting of "accept and submit" or the more common "receive and ignore."

Institutional Information Loop

The planning diagram begins with the **Institutional Information Loop** (see Figure 9.2) conveying information about *State Needs* and *Market Demands* to universities that shape their *Priorities* and *Indicators (PIs)*. These *Institutional Priorities* and a limited list of common PIs are shared with all *Colleges/Schools* and *Departments*. Each of these units adds its unique *Priorities* and *Indicators*. Information on Departmental Results on both shared and unique Indicators are then aggregated into *Colleges/Schools Results* that connect with *Institutional Performance Reports*. After conveying institutional information to *Policymakers, Clients*, and the *Public*, the *Performance Reports* complete the **Institutional Information Loop** by feeding back into *Institutional Priorities* and *Indicators*.

Despite the importance of responsiveness to external needs and demands, this first stage in the performance chain often becomes in practice the first of many disconnects. Unfortunately, the many links in the public higher education performance chain that stretches from states to institutions to colleges/schools and finally to departments often resemble an old string of Christmas tree bulbs. When one link breaks down, all the lights go out. Unfortunately, the performance chain in practice at many universities reveals more breaks than connections, especially at the college/school and departmental levels.

Colleges/Schools and *Departments* should add their own unique *Priorities* and *Indicators* to those shared with the Institution. The process asks how each academic unit can contribute to *Institutional*

Figure 9.2
Information and Knowledge Loops

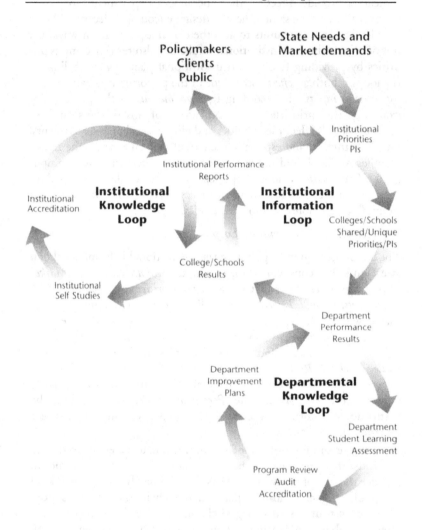

Priorities and what unique aims each would add, given its special expertise and interests. This participatory process should achieve the best and avoid the worst of both top-down and bottom-up planning. In the feedback loops presented in Figure 9.2, each college, school, and department not only receives direction and information from the preceding unit on the loop but also adds its own direction and information to the feedback process.

Knowledge Loops: Turning Information Into Knowledge

The **Information Loop** is important but insufficient, since information is not knowledge. Universities must do more than acquire and disseminate information; they must create knowledge about producing results as part of their planning, performing, and assessing processes. Information, unlike data, reveals relationships, but it does not import meaning and significance. Knowledge consists of information assessed, considered, and judged. Knowledge alone can generate the belief and commitment required for the reflective decisions and actions demanded to improve organizational results (Argyris & Schon, 1996; Senge, 1994; Serban & Luan, 2002;). Decision-makers receive information, but knowledge requires reflection.

Documents and reports formalize and codify *explicit knowledge*. *Tacit knowledge* is more elusive and collaborative. It involves the perceptions and insights that arise without being formally recorded. Their discovery often comes during dialogue among professors and professionals as they reflect on performance and results. The planning process must consider explicit knowledge but also create tacit knowledge (Serban & Luan, 2002).

Departmental Knowledge Loop

The process of turning information into knowledge begins with the **Departmental Knowledge Loop** (see Figure 9.2). It starts with *Departmental Performance Results*, which include at this stage only *information* about results. The internal dialogue among department members about *Departmental Student Learning Assessment* can convert this information on performance results into knowledge that contributes to *Departmental Improvement Plans*. *Program Reviews, Academic Audits, or Program Accreditations*, aided by the insights from external peers, also contribute to knowledge development as department members reflect on their collective performance and on Shared and *Unique Priorities and Indicators*. These insights, perceptions, and judgments from discussions on internal assessment and external reviews inform the *Departmental Improvement Plans* that feed back into *Departmental Performance Results*, which should convey fresh insights on performance connections among inputs, processes, outputs, and outcomes.

At many universities, multidisciplinary centers and institutes now offer instruction at all levels in addition to research programs and public and contract services. In such cases, the design would insert several new links and another loop. *Center/Institute Results* would be added to the **Institutional Information Loop** after *Colleges/Schools Results*. This link would lead to a **Center Knowledge Loop** similar to the one for departments, with links such as *Center/Institute Internal Assessment, Center/Institute Program Review,* and *Center/Institute Performance Plan,* which would reconnect with the *Center/Institute Results* on the **Institutional Information Loop.**

Institutional Knowledge Loop

The **Institutional Knowledge Loop** continues the conversion of information into institution-wide knowledge. It begins with *Colleges/Schools Results,* adds the perceptions and insights gathered from the dialogue among administrators and professors in preparing *Institutional Self-Studies* for regional accreditation and from reflections on the external reviews in *Institutional Accreditation Reports.* The knowledge derived feeds into the *Institutional Performance Reports,* which also receive the information previously processed on the **Institutional Information Loop.** The result is that the *Institutional Performance Reports* and *Institutional Priorities* and *Indicators* benefit not only from the information received about past performance but also from the knowledge derived from reflection on the inputs and processes that produced those results.

Critics will undoubtedly complain that the proposed process is complex and burdensome. It is complex, but hardly more burdensome than existing planning processes and program assessments. Nearly all the elements on the feedback loops are usually found in the planning and assessment processes at most universities. The information is collected but all too often remains unconnected, unassessed, and unused. The big difference is that the performance loops ensure connections in a continuous process capable of producing institutional assessment and improved results. The current system carries the most obvious burden— the cost of collecting much of the same information and preparing reports without the compensating value of using it to align priorities and improve performance.

Difficult but Doable

Most universities fall far short of having such a continuous process that conveys information on priorities and creates knowledge about performance results. Florida International University (FIU) demonstrates that it can be done (see Chapter 14). This research-extensive university— enrolling 34,000 students in 16 colleges and schools and offering 180 bachelor's, master's, and doctoral programs—has adopted a performance plan that is remarkably similar to that proposed in the performance loops.

The leaders of FIU asked the critical question for any public university:

> How can we institutionalize a performance assessment system that enhances the University's performance in three areas: first, meeting the needs, wants, and expectations of our students and other stakeholders; second, documenting our performance for stakeholder accountability; third, obtaining the performance feedback required to identify the opportunities for improvement needed to remain competitive in an increasingly competitive higher education environment? (FIU, 2003, p. 34)

A strategic plan, using external and internal environmental scans and wide participation of the university community, identified institutional goals and objectives. To ensure pursuit of those ends, the planning process at FIU produced a common set of performance indicators for all departments reflecting campus goals and objectives for use in assessing their performance results. In addition, departments also added unique measures that match unit strengths to university purposes in instruction, research, and service.

The shared performance indicators include student enrollment, degree attainment, and retention and graduation rates for first-time and transfer students by race and gender. They also cover the percentage of undergraduate credit hours taught by regular faculty, sponsored research, faculty publications, and percent of faculty effort devoted to public service and to public schools. (The shared indicators include items for master's and doctoral as well as bachelor's programs.) Most of the common measures have an intended outcome of meeting or exceeding a three-year average for the department. The university web site includes full information on departmental results on most of these indicators for the last three years, organized by colleges and schools. The FIU performance process resembles the **Institutional Information Loop** in Figure 9.2. It widely disseminates information on goals, objectives, indicators, and results at the institutional and departmental levels.[5]

Though discerning knowledge creation is much more difficult than detecting information dissemination, the FIU process develops knowledge about performance that should stimulate knowledge creation about departmental and institutional improvement. The departmental *assessment* of outcomes tracks unit performance on instruction, research, and service against established benchmarks. In addition, the examination of the responses from student, alumni, and employer surveys must contribute to faculty dialogue about departmental and institutional performance. A *program review* process, led by a representative campus council, feeds all the performance information from departments—including results on the common departmental indicators and other measures including graduation rates for majors—into a periodic evaluation using outside consultants. Those reviews consider information garnered from program accreditation. The process also is public with a university-wide forum where a department presents its review results along with improvement plans. FIU's department assessment and program review track the stages in the **Departmental Knowledge Loop**. The public and collaborative approach of FIU to self-studies for undergraduate, graduate, and research activities and for institutional accreditation also suggests a process that incorporates many elements in the **Institutional Knowledge Loop**.

Developing Departmental Indicators

Developing departmental indicators that reflect the common responsibility for meeting institutional priorities and state needs, along with winning campus acceptance, constitutes the most difficult step in performance planning. The good news is—as noted earlier—that state needs show growing similarities, which means that the institutional focus should be on producing the particular indicators that stress their special strengths. What follows are some suggestions for priorities and common indicators at the university, college/school, and departmental levels.

Most of the categories and many of the indicators intentionally resemble those in *Measuring Up* to provide the final link in a performance chain that reaches down to departments for internal, not external, review (National Center, 200, 2002, 2004). They also stress undergraduate education and public engagement, as the Kellogg Commission recommended. The following indicators for internal reporting should also show trends over time and, where relevant, race and gender. In addition they should include performance targets negotiated between department chairs and deans.

Funding/Staffing

• *Funding per FTE student.* Funding and results are not synonymous as some academics say, neither are they as unconnected as some outsiders contend.

• *Percent of undergraduate FTEs generated by tenure-track faculty.* This indicator reinforces the recommendation of the Kellogg Commission to raise the emphasis on undergraduate education in public research universities.

Participation

- *College/school collaboration contribution.* The most serious challenge to college participation in the United States and to our national competitiveness is the need to improve education from the nursery school through high school. Every university, college/school, and department should develop an indicator reflecting their particular contribution to school improvement.
- *Enrollment by major and FTE.* The major stresses specialized education, the FTE highlights the department's contribution to general learning.
- *Two- to four-year transfers.* Deans and department chairs in research universities often prefer first-time to transfer students, but full participation requires increased access to baccalaureate degrees for community college students.

Completion

- *Degree completion rates by major.* Access is just a promise; completion is the achievement. Institutional completion rates are really composites of very different completion rates by majors.

Societal Benefits

- *Degrees awarded.* Degrees granted at the undergraduate, graduate, and professional levels contribute to the human capital so essential to economic and civic success in a knowledge and information era.
- *Job placements/advanced education.* The first records the human capital developed, and the second develops it further.
- *Publications, performances, and exhibits.* This indicator records the scholarly and artistic contributions of the faculty.
- *Dollar volume of sponsored research per full-time faculty.* All colleges/ schools and departments should have an indicator on sponsored research. Those connected to science and engineering and biomedical fields may also add special indicators on licenses, patents, and startup companies.

Student Learning

- *Student learning assessment.* The measure should follow an institutional plan that tracks not just assessment processes but also student learning outcomes.
- *Results from program accreditation, program review, or academic audit.* External reviewers evaluate program quality in each of these processes.

Using the departmental indicators for internal institutional use allows the more qualitative assessment methods listed above.

Unique Departmental Indicators

• *Department-selected mission indicators.* Each department should select several indicators based on its special strengths that support institutional priorities.

Many deans and chairs will argue for more than 12 common indicators to include measures that show their units in the best light. University leaders should remind them of the principle that too many indicators mean no priorities.

The good news is that the information for most of the proposed indicators is already available in nearly all colleges and universities. The bad news is that presidents, vice presidents, deans, and chairs rarely use it to reinforce priorities and raise performance.

Conclusion

Adopting the proposed approach to performance reporting, institutional priorities, and common indicators for colleges, schools, and departments can achieve the following:

• Close the gap in the accountability chain by linking departments, schools, and colleges and institutional priorities and performance
• Stress priority results, not compliance coverage
• Combine departmental decentralization with institutional direction
• Attain the advantages and avoid the defects of both top-down and bottom-up planning
• Reconcile external accountability and internal improvement
• Move outcomes assessment from the fringe to the center of campus priorities by linking department, school, and institutional results
• Connect all the quality assurance approaches, such as institutional and program accreditation, outcomes assessment, academic audits, and program reviews
• Combine planning, assessing, and reporting

Universities are unique institutions, but as organizations and social systems, they must find ways to link the productivity of their parts to purposes of the whole. The **Information** and **Knowledge Loops** incorporate concepts from strategic planning, systems theory, and knowledge management. These are not alien notions to higher education, for academics developed every one of them and advocated their use for outside organizations. Surely the calls for additional accountability and improved performance suggest that it is time to bring these theories home to university planning.

Author Note

This chapter draws heavily from my 2005 article "Closing the Accountability Gap for Public Campuses: Putting Academic Departments in the Performance Loop," *Planning in Higher Education, 34*(1), 19–28.

Endnotes

1) Arizona, California, Florida, Illinois, Iowa, Maine, Michigan, Minnesota, Nebraska, New Jersey, Ohio, Oregon, South Carolina, Texas, Washington, and Wisconsin.

2) Arizona University and Arizona State University; Clemson University and University of South Carolina; Florida State University and University of Florida; Iowa State University and University of Iowa; Michigan State University and University of Michigan; Oregon State University and University of Oregon; University of Illinois at Chicago and Urbana-Champaign; University of Nebraska–Lincoln; Rutgers, the State University of New Jersey; Pennsylvania State University; Ohio State University and University of Cincinnati; Texas A&M University and University of Texas–Austin; University of California–Berkeley and Los Angeles; University of Maine–Orono; University of Minnesota; University of Washington and Washington State University; University of Wisconsin–Madison.

3) Special thanks go to Jiri Stocek, a graduate research assistant, for the web site search and analysis.

4) Minnesota later created a Commission on Higher Education.

5) See the FIU Planning and Effectiveness web site: www.fiu.edu/oir/

References

American Association of State Colleges and Universities. (2005). *Public policy agenda 2005*. Washington, DC: Author.

Argyris, C., & Schön, D. A. (1996). *Organizational learning II: Theory, method, and practice*. Reading, MD: Addison-Wesley.

Association of Governing Boards of Universities and Colleges. (2005). Ten public policy issues for higher education in 2005–2006 (Public Policy Paper Series No. 05–01). Washington, DC: Author.

Astin, A. W. (1991). *Assessment for excellence: The philosophy and practice of assessment and evaluation in higher education*. New York, NY: American Council on Education/Macmillan.

Burke, J. C., & Associates. (2005). *Achieving accountability in higher education: Balancing public, academic, and market demands.* San Francisco, CA: Jossey-Bass.

Burke, J. C., & Minassians, H. P. (2002a). *New directions in institutional research: No. 116. Reporting higher education results: Missing links in the performance chain.* San Francisco, CA: Jossey-Bass.

Edwards, R. (1999, September/October). The academic department: How does it fit into the university reform agenda? *Change, 31*(5), 17–27.

Florida International University. (2003). *Millennium strategic planning.* Retrieved August 25, 2006, from the Florida International University, Planning and Institutional Effectiveness web site: www.fiu.edu/~pie/docs/msp052802/mspdocwhole010603.PDF

Kellogg Commission on the Future of State and Land-Grant Universities. (2000). *Returning to our roots: Toward a coherent campus culture.* Washington, DC: National Association of State Universities and Land-Grant Colleges.

National Center for Public Policy and Higher Education. (2000). *Measuring up 2000: The state-by-state report card for higher education.* San Jose, CA: Author.

National Center for Public Policy and Higher Education. (2002). *Measuring up 2002: The state-by-state report card for higher education.* San Jose, CA: Author.

National Center for Public Policy and Higher Education. (2004). *Measuring up 2004: The state-by-state report card for higher education.* San Jose, CA: Author.

National Commission on Accountability in Higher Education. (2005). *Accountability for better results: A national imperative for higher education.* Boulder, CO: State Higher Education Executive Officers.

Rowley, D. J., Lujan, H. D., & Dolence, M. G. (1997). *Strategic change in colleges and universities: Planning to survive and prosper.* San Francisco, CA: Jossey-Bass.

Rowley, D. J., & Sherman, H. (2001). *From strategy to change: Implementing the plan in higher education.* San Francisco, CA: Jossey-Bass.

Senge, P. M. (1994). *The fifth discipline: The art and practice of the learning organization.* New York, NY: Doubleday.

Serban, A. M., & Luan, J. (Eds.). (2002). *New directions for institutional research: No. 113. Knowledge management: Building a competitive advantage in higher education.* San Francisco, CA: Jossey-Bass.

State Higher Education Executive Officers. (2006). *Higher education issues.* Retrieved August 25, 2006, from www.sheeo.org/issues.htm

10

Making Students Matter

George D. Kuh

Learning remains the reason we exist. . . . If public universities are to prosper in the future, they must become great student universities as well as great centers of research . . .

—Kellogg Commission, *Returning to Our Roots: Toward a Coherent Campus Culture*

The Challenges

It is one thing to assert that public universities should be student centered. It is quite another to do it. The challenges are substantial.

First, many public universities enroll tens of thousands of students. The numbers of part-time, temporary instructors are at an all-time high, in part to make up for the 10% decline since the mid-1980s in full-time faculty (Johnstone, 2005). As a result, students at large institutions can be essentially anonymous, unknown by their teachers and their peers. Also, public universities usually have multiple missions in order to respond to the variety of educational, social, and economic interests of the taxpayers who support them. To ensure access to higher education by historically underserved groups, many of these institutions admit students with a wide range of abilities; a nontrivial number come from educationally disadvantaged backgrounds. In part, this focus on access is why public universities are represented disproportionately among four-year institutions with the lowest graduation rates (Carey, 2004). Finally, public universities typically are expected to be engines of economic productivity, which makes it tough to appropriately balance undergraduate education, graduate training, research, and service to the state, region, and nation.

Taken together, these factors and others make it difficult to create learning environments where students feel supported and encouraged and to put in place other features long associated with student learning, such as small classes and frequent interactions with faculty members (Astin, 1993; Pascarella & Terenzini, 2005).

Is the Kellogg Commission's vision achievable? That is, can public universities be centers of research and student-friendly? Some institutions have been able to beat the odds, so to speak, and create conditions for teaching and learning that enable more of their students to survive and thrive in college than might have otherwise. Who are they? What did they do? And what steps might other institutions take to become more student-friendly and learning centered? This chapter offers some answers, drawing on findings from the National Survey of Student Engagement (NSSE) and the Documenting Effective Educational Practices study, otherwise known as Project DEEP.

To set the stage, I first summarize selected findings about student engagement in general and those that distinguish public and private colleges and universities. Student engagement in effective educational practices is empirically linked to desired outcomes of college and is an earmark of a student-centered university. Then I briefly describe the conditions common to the 11 high-performing public institutions in the DEEP project. Finally, I offer recommendations for enhancing student learning and improving educational effectiveness.

Student Engagement: A Key Component to Student Success

After synthesizing the results of thousands of research studies related to student development, Pascarella and Terenzini (2005) unequivocally conclude:

> If, as it appears, individual effort or engagement is the critical determinant of the impact of college, then it is important to focus on the ways in which an institution can shape its academic, interpersonal, and extracurricular offerings to encourage *student engagement.* (p. 602)

Student engagement represents two components. The first is the amount of time and effort students put into their studies, and into other activities that lead to the experiences and outcomes that constitute student success. The second is the ways the institution allocates and organizes its resources, learning opportunities, and services to induce students to participate in and benefit from such activities.

Certain institutional practices are linked with high levels of student engagement (Astin, 1991; Chickering & Reisser, 1993; Kuh, Schuh, Whitt, & Associates, 1991; Pascarella, 2001; Pascarella & Terenzini, 1991). Perhaps the best-known set of indicators is the Seven Principles for Good Practice in Undergraduate Education (Chickering & Gamson, 1987). If faculty and administrators more consistently used these and other promising practices—inclusive, supportive, and affirming institutional environments—students would ostensibly put forth more effort. That is, they would write more papers, read more books, meet more frequently with faculty and peers, and use information technology appropriately, all of which would increase the chances for such desired outcomes as student satisfaction, persistence, and gains in critical thinking, problem solving, effective communication, and responsible citizenship.

The National Survey of Student Engagement was developed to assess systematically the degree to which students participate in educational effective practices (Kuh, 2001, 2003; NSSE, 2000; 2004). Established with a grant from the Pew Charitable Trusts, user fees have supported NSSE since 2003, with more than 500 four-year colleges and universities participating annually.

To make student engagement concepts and results accessible to faculty, staff, governing board members, policymakers, and others, an early strategic decision divided the student behaviors and institutional conditions represented on the survey into five clusters of effective educational practices (see Appendix A). This division provides a common language and framework for understanding what matters to student learning and success. Commonly referred to as benchmarks, the five clusters are:

1) Academic challenge
2) Active and collaborative learning
3) Student-faculty interaction
4) Enriching educational experiences
5) Supportive campus environments

With responses from almost 900,000 first-year and senior students from close to 1,000 different institutions, we can make three definitive statements about the character and impact of student engagement on student success.

First, as Figure 10.1 shows, students at public colleges and universities are generally less engaged in effective educational practices than their counterparts at private institutions (Kuh, 2003; NSSE, 2004).

Figure 10.1
First-Year and Senior Scores on Clusters of Effective
Educational Practices by Public and Private Institutions

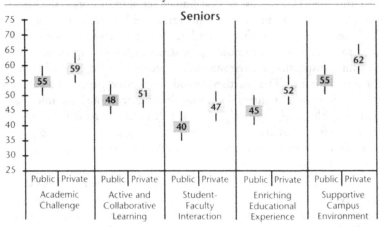

In part, private institutions are advantaged because of their generally smaller size and residential focus. As a result, classes are smaller and students interact more frequently with professors and peers and typically become more involved in the life of the institution. However, although smaller is generally better in terms of student engagement, the highest-scoring public universities are as engaging as many small private colleges (Kuh, 2003; Kuh & Hu, 2001; NSSE, 2001). This result, too, can be seen from Figure 10.1 by looking at the upper end of the public institution distributions, which generally equal or exceed the average performance of privates.

Second, student engagement varies more *within* than *between* institutions, institutional types, or sectors (Kuh, 2003). To illustrate, Figure 10.2 depicts the academic challenge benchmark scores of seniors at 15 different public universities, ranging from the lowest-scoring school on this benchmark to the highest scoring. The figure shows only the middle 80% of students at each institution so that outliers do not skew the display. The difference in mean scores between the lowest- and highest-scoring schools is only about 10 points, or 10% of the 100-point scale. However, the variation in student engagement within each institution is much greater. The pattern represented here is similar for all five NSSE benchmarks and across all institutional types.

Figure 10.3 provides another instructive view of this phenomenon, comparing the academic challenge benchmark scores for first-year students for two institutions expressed in percentiles. The average institu-

Figure 10.2
Level of Academic Challenge

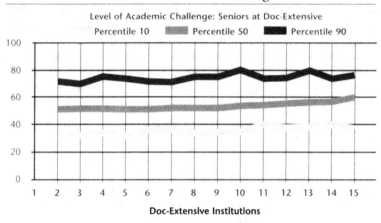

Level of Academic Challenge: Seniors at Doc-Extensive

Percentile 10 ▓ Percentile 50 █ Percentile 90

tional scores are essentially the same. But School B has an attenuated range of student scores compared with School A. So, while some students at School A are more engaged, a comparable number appear not to be very engaged at all. At School B, more students cluster close to the average. At which university, then, are the odds better that a given student will have a reasonably engaging college experience?

Figure 10.3
Academic Challenge Distributions at Two Public Universities

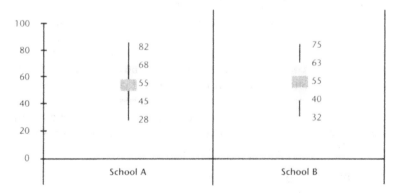

These displays indicate that every institution has a sizeable proportion of students who devote relatively little effort to their studies and other important aspects of undergraduate education, such as participating in cocurricular activities, volunteerism, and meaningful interactions with faculty and peers. Disproportionately represented among underengaged students are men, part-time students, commuters, and students who work 15 or more hours per week off campus (Kuh, 2003). More efforts are needed to identify early in their college experience students within these broad categories and others whose past behaviors and expectations for college indicate that they are likely to fit into this group.

Are low levels of academic effort by large numbers of students inevitable? Conversely, can public universities fashion policies, programs, and practices that encourage students to participate more frequently in educationally purposeful activities so they can more fully realize their potential? Can campuses shape their cultures to encourage a critical mass of faculty and staff to work toward student success as an institutional value and priority? The findings from Project DEEP offer some hope and glimpses of how to do so.

Lessons From High-Performing Colleges and Universities

The Documenting Effective Educational Practices (DEEP) project sought to discover and describe what strong-performing four-year colleges and universities do to foster student success, broadly defined to encompass reasonable levels of student engagement, satisfaction, and educational attainment. The two primary criteria for selecting the 20 schools in the study were higher-than-predicted scores on NSSE and higher-than-predicted six-year graduation rates determined by regression models accounting for relevant student and institutional characteristics. A 24-member research team reviewed countless documents, interviewed more than 2,700 people on these campuses, and observed many classes, studios, and labs in action. The findings are reported in detail in *Student Success in College: Creating Conditions That Matter* (Kuh, Kinzie, Schuh, Whitt, & Associates, 2005).

Conditions Common to Institutions in Project DEEP

This section briefly describes the six factors and conditions more or less common to the DEEP institutions and illustrates with examples from the 11 public colleges and universities of the 20 in the study. The six conditions are:

- "Living" mission and "lived" educational philosophy
- Unshakable focus on student learning
- Environments adapted for educational enrichment
- Clearly marked pathways to student success
- Improvement-oriented ethos
- Shared responsibility for educational quality and student success

Although I discuss the six conditions separately, they are not mutually exclusive. In practice, they overlap and link in complementary ways to promote student success.

"Living" Mission and "Lived" Educational Philosophy

A college's mission is a public declaration of its educational purposes and values, intended to guide all aspects of institutional life, including the policies and practices that foster student success. Large public universities usually have broad, expansive mission statements that promise something to almost everyone, as is expected by the taxpayers who support them.

Every institution has two missions. One is its *espoused* or written mission. The second—its *enacted* mission or what the school does in terms of programs and practices—matters much more to student success because it reflects what students actually experience. A university might, for example, claim a commitment to "educating the whole student" but in fact provide little encouragement or support for student involvement in intellectual or social activities outside the classroom. At strong-performing universities, the enacted mission overlaps significantly with the espoused mission. As a result, students, professors, and staff members have a fairly clear idea of what they are trying to accomplish. For example, the missions of California State University–Monterey Bay, Winston-Salem State University, and the University of Texas–El Paso emphasize that every person has the potential to learn. These institutions along with most of the other DEEP schools are dedicated to expanding educational opportunity for students who by traditional measures are not expected to succeed in higher education. These universities value diversity and high-quality undergraduate teaching. They promote social responsibility by encouraging students to give back to their communities. Moreover, their missions are "living" in that they are enacted by open admissions, an emphasis on undergraduate teaching, first-year transition and orientation courses that help students acquire study skills and self-confidence, and rewards for meaningful student-faculty interaction.

Over time, a college develops a "way of doing business"—those tacit understandings about what is important about students and their education. Ideally, this operating philosophy is a values-oriented compass, keeping the institution on track as it makes decisions about resources, curriculum, and educational opportunities. Although they differ in many respects, Miami University and Fayetteville State University both emphasize status distinctions. Fayetteville State teaches students early on to revere faculty members as aspirational figures and role models because of their achievements. The sought-after social and academic distance between faculty members and students works with other features of the campus culture to spur students to greater academic efforts. This approach contrasts starkly with the egalitarian ethic that pervades The Evergreen State College and the University of Maine–Farmington. Despite these very different orientations, all these institutions have been able to create engaging learning conditions for their students.

Unshakable Focus on Student Learning

DEEP schools stitch carefully into policies and practices an emphasis on holistic student development. They select faculty and staff members for their commitment to student success and effective educational practices. These institutions exhibit a "cool passion" (Chickering, 1981) for talent development and make time for students. Engaging pedagogies are mainstream, not relegated to the periphery. As with other aspects of high-performing institutions, these characteristics are carefully cultivated and much energy goes into preserving them.

For example, the provost at the University of Kansas made a persuasive case for why good teaching matters at his research-extensive university. Over time, his message became a widely recognized mantra echoed by other campus officials, students, and professors alike. The sea change that occurred at Kansas to emphasize undergraduate instruction included assigning experienced, highly skilled teachers to lower-division and introductory courses whenever possible, and reinforced this emphasis by multiple awards made annually to recognize outstanding teaching. Professors in each academic unit serve as faculty ambassadors to advocate the faculty needs and concerns to the Center for Teaching Excellence and lead discussions on instructional issues with their colleagues. In addition, the University of Kansas keeps course enrollments low in a high percentage of undergraduate courses;

80% of undergraduate classes have 30 or fewer students, and 93% have 50 or fewer students.

The dean of arts and sciences at the University of Michigan championed new learning initiatives with help from a special commission and several reports over a six-year period. The university invested $3 million to develop new interdisciplinary courses and the provost used a $10 million discretionary fund to support innovative initiatives directed toward improving undergraduate education.

Environments Adapted for Educational Enrichment

Despite being located in vastly different settings, students, professors, and administrators at all 20 DEEP schools believe their location and campus setting are advantages for student learning. Indeed, the students we talked with across all the institutions were enthusiastic about their school, routinely volunteering that their college was "special," that "there is no other place like it." For example, students at the University of Maine–Farmington thought that their rural Maine campus offered opportunities for learning and cocurricular leadership that did not exist anyplace else, as did students at Alverno College in Milwaukee, Wisconsin.

To a large extent, DEEP schools make themselves "special" because they are "place conscious" (Gruenwald, 2003). The physical—such as Jayhawk Boulevard at Kansas and the coherent brick architecture at Miami University in Ohio and Winston-Salem State University, landscaping, and campus design—mixes with memories of activities and events to build loyalty and connection among students, professors, and staff members. As a result, physical properties and emotion become inextricably intertwined to form an almost palpable sense of place, one that has profound, if not always clearly understood meanings.

The four-story George W. Johnson Center at George Mason University is figuratively and literally the heart of the campus. Designed to promote learning and integrate curricular and extracurricular pursuits of diverse groups, students, faculty, and staff pass through its doors throughout the day and into the evening to use services ranging from the Student Technology Assistance and Resource Center, the coffee and jazz café, retail outlets, the Center for Teaching Excellence, and facilities (including lockers) for commuter students. The feeling is energetic, cosmopolitan, and communal, an international bazaar with bright flags hanging from pillars, and students in native dress—North American to North African—eating, studying, or just "hanging" together.

The University of Texas–El Paso (UTEP) campus is distinctive in part by its Bhutanese architecture, which signals its aspiration to bring the world into its classrooms and playing fields. Equally important, by supporting six community health clinics, UTEP demonstrates its commitment to serving populations in the El Paso community that have been denied access to education by working closely with its neighbors. Its "Mothers and Daughters" and "Fathers and Sons" programs are part of a longstanding relationship between its College of Education and area public school districts, involving sixth-graders in activities designed to inspire them to seek college degrees.

Clearly Marked Pathways to Student Success

Many students do not have a clear, coherent image in their mind of what they need to do to succeed in college. It is as if they are completing a puzzle without the picture on the box top to guide them. This is particularly true for students who are the first in their families to attend college. To address this issue, DEEP schools do two things very well. First, they teach students what the institution values, what successful students do in their context, and how to take advantage of institutional resources for their learning. Second, they make available what students need *when* they need it, and have responsive early warning systems and safety nets in place to support teaching, learning, and student success.

Fayetteville State, UTEP, University of Maine–Farmington, and Winston-Salem State attract large numbers of students who—because of inadequate academic preparation and lack of knowledge about college—need explicit directions to use institutional resources and support services profitably. These institutions *require* students to take part in certain programs and activities, such as summer advising, orientation, and fall welcome week, and follow up with advising and other events that mark student progress over the course of the first year.

Some DEEP schools use a tag-team approach to challenge and support students, offering academic and other services in an integrated package to reduce the possibility that a student will fall through the cracks. Fayetteville State brought advising and learning assistance programs together. The University of Michigan expanded the number of living-learning programs to touch more students in meaningful ways with integrated student support and academic initiatives, such as the Community Scholars program and its WISE (Women in Science and Engineering) residential program. Winston-Salem State's First Year College houses under one roof most academic support offices and programs. All new students and transfer students with fewer than 30 credit hours must enroll in one of three new-student adjustment courses, with certain sections designated for students interested in specific majors. Faculty members teaching these sections also serve as students' academic advisors and mentors for the first academic year.

Miami University's Choice Matters initiative is a comprehensive, campus-wide effort to channel students' behavior toward desirable activities and reflect systematically on what they learn from their experiences, inside and outside the classroom. A variety of linked programs make up the initiative—first-year seminars, community living options that emphasize leadership and service, cultural, intellectual and arts events, and integrated core courses taught by full-time faculty.

Improvement-Oriented Ethos

DEEP schools seem to be in a perpetual learning mode—monitoring where they are, what they are doing, where they want to go, and how to maintain momentum toward positive change. Supporting this orientation toward improvement is a can-do ethic, making them emblematic of the learning organizations described by Peter Senge (Senge et al., 1999) and the firms studied by Jim Collins (2001) that went from good to great.

The University of Michigan launched a series of major studies of undergraduate experiences in the mid-1980s. The efforts produced some better-integrated undergraduate education programs, including the First-Year Seminar Program, the Undergraduate Research Opportunity Program, and the Sweetland Writing Center. These reports, the most recent of which was in 2002, are candid appraisals of the state of undergraduate education at the university and include innovative and responsive recommendations for improving undergraduate education (President's Commisions on the Undergraduate Experience, 2002).

Fayetteville State's commitment to student access and success went to a new level under the leadership of former Chancellor Willis McLeod between 1995 and 2003. Concerned about first- to second-year retention rates well below peer institutions', McLeod's 2003 position paper "Linking Retention and Academic Performance: The Freshman Year Initiative" challenged Fayetteville faculty and staff to develop a complementary set of effective policies and practices. They include the Bronco Cohort made up of students from educationally disadvantaged backgrounds, who are tutored by strong-performing upper-division students called Chancellor's Scholars. This Creating Higher Expectations for Educational Readiness (CHEER) program, which helps students acquire the academic skills and social confidence they need to succeed in college, and the campus-wide Early Alert System represent only two of many programs that make the campus special.

Shared Responsibility for Educational Quality and Student Success

Educators are everywhere on DEEP campuses—in the residence halls, food service, and playing fields as well as in classrooms, laboratories, and studios. Moreover, professors, staff members, and students at DEEP institutions enjoy mutual respect and share an affinity for their school's mission and culture. Collectively, they hold one another accountable and expect students to take responsibility for their academic work and social life and that of their peers. Indeed, students themselves went out of their way to get other students involved in their productive activities. Equally important, every day individuals make thousands of small gestures that create and sustain a caring community for students.

Miami's First-Year Experience and aforementioned Choice Matters initiatives are the product of what one administrator described as "an amazing collaboration" between the academic and student affairs divisions and their leaders. One faculty member observed, "It demonstrates a fundamental commitment to undergraduates, and an appreciation for the broad spectrum of their learning experiences." Miami also benefits by its staff members in student life who understand that their best work complements the academic mission of the university. As a result, collaboration with academic affairs is a high priority and a guiding operating principle.

Longwood University President Patti Cormier introduced the institution's "Citizen Leader for the Common Good" that now permeates the Farmville, Virginia, campus. A cornerstone of the initiative was a sustained change agenda to ensure that classroom experiences "challenge the theoretical against the practical." One result was that academic and student affairs redoubled their collaborative efforts. Several structural links bridge the usual organizational boundaries between academics and student affairs. For example, the vice president of student affairs reports directly to the provost and serves on the tenure committee, ensuring that out-of-class experiences of students are represented by student affairs during meetings of the academic deans. This connection, in turn, has resulted in a higher degree of faculty involvement in student affairs programs.

Shared governance is a point of pride at Kansas, one reason that collaboration and cooperation flourish there. For example, a faculty member is always the president of the 50-member University Council; the vice president—always a student—runs meetings when the faculty chair is absent. About three-fifths of the Writing Center tutors are undergrads and the credit-bearing "Tutoring and Teaching Writing" course has legitimized peer tutoring as a vehicle for sharing responsibility for student learning.

Recommendations and Implications

The findings from Project DEEP suggest that public universities can heed the Kellogg Commission's clarion call and "put student learning first." This section offers a series of recommendations that flow from the DEEP results. These and other ideas are discussed more fully in *Student Success in College: Creating Conditions That Matter* (Kuh, Kinzie, et al., 2005) and in a series of policy and practice briefs that are targeted to various groups—campus leaders, governing board members, department chairs, and the like (NSSE, 2005).

No one of these recommendations by itself will likely make a substantial difference in terms of student learning and success. To have a demonstrable impact on the nature and quality of student learning, it is necessary to do many different things better and more frequently so that one or more initiatives touch substantial numbers of students in meaningful ways. This approach works much better than investing vast amounts of resources, time, and energy in one large, complicated initiative (Collins, 2001; Kuh et al., 1991; Pascarella & Terenzini, 2005).

In addition, two meta principles must guide improvement efforts: alignment and sustainability. First, institutions must *align* their policies, programs, and practices with student academic preparation and needs as well as with institutional resources and personnel in ways that complement the institution's mission, values, and culture. Second, enough resources and energy must be available to *sustain* improvement efforts beyond a first or second cycle. This will require difficult choices between continuing to support productive activities and discontinuing those that are less effective or no longer viable so that new ideas can be weighed and implemented in a timely fashion. Thus some persons or groups regularly monitor the efficacy of current initiatives and review proposed new efforts to determine their complementarity and potential for enhancing student success.

Feature Student Success in the Institution's Living Mission

One of my favorite cartoons shows a herd of bison all headed in the same direction with the caption, "As if we all know where we're going . . ." The message is plain to faculty and staff: Improvement efforts often stumble because little attention is given to whether everyone is on the same page on how proposed activities complement the institution's mission and values and students' academic preparation, ability, and interests. Common language is essential so that people with different mental maps can more readily understand how their individual actions contribute to the big picture of institutional effectiveness. With this in mind, what can campus leaders do?

Senior leaders must publicly and repeatedly champion undergraduate education. DEEP presidents made it a point to remind people frequently of their institution's aspirations and high expectations for students. Provosts vigorously advocated on behalf of the undergraduate program. In multiple settings—annual state-of-the campus reports, governing board meetings, convocations, faculty meetings, and so on—presidents and provosts underscored the institution's commitment to high-quality undergraduate education and its centrality to the institution's mission.

Balance the institution's multiple missions. Senior academic leaders at DEEP universities such as Kansas, Michigan, George Mason, and UTEP effectively explained why balancing the research and teaching missions of the institution was crucial to maintaining high-quality undergraduate programs and support services while also illustrating how the research mission enriches the undergraduate experience. They understand that striking an appropriate balance between teaching and scholarship is a perennial challenge, never completely resolved.

Emphasize Talent Development in the Institution's Operating Philosophy

A steady, unwavering focus on students and their learning must permeate the entire institution—from senior administrators to faculty, professional staff, and support personnel.

Know your students. Institutional researchers and assessment personnel frequently examine students' needs and interests and typically share the results widely with people who can use the information to make a difference. Who are today's students? Where do they come from? What are their preferred learning styles and their talents? When and where are they likely to need help? Needs assessments do not guarantee learning and student success, but it is hard to improve without collecting assessment data.

Balance academic challenge with adequate support. When talking about the institution's vision and values, presidents, academic deans, and senior faculty members remind everyone that academic excellence is not a form of educational Darwinism. They tirelessly advocate on behalf of responsive, learner-centered support services, such as peer tutoring, special labs for writing and mathematics, and-if necessary and appropriate given the audiences—intrusive academic advising. High-performing institutions also provide lots of feedback to students along with redundant early warning systems, safety nets, and other forms of assistance.

Use pedagogical approaches that complement students' learning styles. Just as not all faculty members excel at everything, neither do all students. But nearly all students have the capacity to learn almost anything a college teaches. Many more students would thrive if colleges and universities used different combinations of teaching approaches and learning conditions. For example, there is some evidence that students who are concrete learners benefit more from active and collaborative learning approaches (Schroeder, 1993; Tagg, 2003). Students who score relatively low on standardized tests appear to benefit more in terms of learning outcomes from high-quality personal relationships, a supportive campus environment, and experiences with diversity, whereas students who score especially high on these tests may benefit less from active and collaborative learning (Carini, Kuh, & Klein, 2006).

Cultivate an Ethic of Positive Restlessness

To improve, organizations must create and nurture agreement on what is worth achieving and set in motion the internal processes by which people progressively learn how to do what they need to do in order to achieve what is worthwhile (Elmore, 2000, cited in Fullan, 2001). This is true of DEEP institutions, which are characteristically never quite satisfied with their performance. Rather, they constantly look for ways to improve the student experience and to encourage innovation by faculty and staff. Such examinations are sometimes formal, such as program reviews and accreditation self-studies. Because of their large scale and structural complexity, public universities would benefit from the following in order to encourage and support improvement efforts.

Focus on a real problem. Getting people to act is more likely if the target of the effort is an issue that many believe is important. Most colleges and universities have no shortage of areas where they can improve: persistence rates, underengaged students, a lackluster first-year experience, fragmented general education offerings, outdated pedagogical practices, incoherent sequencing of major field courses, insufficient opportunities for students to connect their learning to real-world issues and challenges, and capstone experiences, to name a few.

Use plain language to rally support. It is a noisy world. Everyone on campus—students, professors, and staff members—is bombarded daily with jargon-laded messages from a variety of sources about what they should attend to. A key to mobilizing interest and commitment for improvement is explaining why a particular "problem" needs to be addressed in language that everybody can understand and then consistently repeating this message in different forums over months and even years. Senior administrators at UTEP adopted the mantra "talent is everywhere, opportunity is not" to remind people—professors, staff members, and students alike—of the institution's commitment to helping all students succeed.

Use data to inform decision-making. What is measured gets attention. High-performing colleges and universities publicly report on their performance and build feedback loops into the curriculum and other educational policies and programs. Typically, DEEP schools pointed to a combination of external and internal conditions to draw attention to the need to do things differently. Fayetteville State, UTEP, and Winston-Salem State responded to changing demographics and state mandates to graduate more students. Michigan responded to calls by national reports in the 1980s to improve undergraduate education. California State University–Monterey Bay used an accreditation visit as a mobilizing event. At George Mason University, University of Michigan, and University of Kansas, retention and assessment committees brought together staff, faculty, and students from various units into working groups to ensure that policies developed were sound.

Put someone in charge. There is an old adage that when everyone is responsible for something, no one is accountable for it. Some individual or group must coordinate and monitor the status and impact of institutional student success initiatives and see that the change efforts bleed down into academic departments and front-line student support programs and services. This could be faculty or staff members with a reputation for getting things done, as was the case with the vice president for student affairs at Longwood University and the provost at the University of Kansas. Sometimes newcomers can be asked to lead the way—a new academic dean or student life officer with fresh ideas for better integrating students' in-class and out-of-class experiences. Those put in charge are not necessarily expected to bring about the changes themselves, but to monitor, prod, and support others who also are working on the issues. Other key resources can be teaching and learning center staff and members of campus policy bodies. Think about using a campaign strategy to drive data, planning, and action to the unit level in order to focus faculty and staff energy on activities that would promote student success (Hirschhorn & May, 2000).

Put Money Where It Will Make a Difference in Student Engagement

It's often said that to discover what an organization values, follow the money. At the same time, the evidence from DEEP schools suggests that *how* financial resources, faculty and staff time, and facilities are combined to create powerful, affirming learning environments matters more than the amount of resources (Gansemer-Topf, Saunders, Schuh, & Shelley, 2004; National Center for Higher Education Management Systems, 2004).

Invest in activities that contribute to student success. DEEP presidents and provosts generally made it a priority to fund promising initiatives, often with small, token amounts of money. Sometimes it was seed money to jump-start learning communities; in another instance it was a base budget allocation to augment the number of undergraduate research opportunities with faculty members. Michigan devoted millions of dollars over a decade to various activities, building them into the base budget. Miami committed significant resources to enhance the intellectual vitality on campus through funding summer research fellowships for students and creating a minority opportunity center. Discretionary dollars are in short supply at the University of Maine–Farmington, where most students are from modest means and are the first in their family to go to college. Many need to work to afford to stay in school. To encourage working on campus (which is correlated with persistence), the president created the Student Employment Initiative. Now more than half of students work on campus, performing many vital services, and the persistence rate is increasing.

Invest in teaching and learning centers. These units symbolize DEEP schools' commitment to instructional excellence. Moreover, with strong leadership and a modicum of financial support, many are hotbeds of pedagogical innovation and coordinate awards for excellent teaching and mini-grants for improving teaching and learning. Instructional support staff members also consult with professors about alternative approaches to assessing student learning and help to boost faculty morale by supporting, among other things, faculty learning communities, such as those at Miami University.

Consider a budgeting model that privileges student learning processes and outcomes. Consider adopting a process that allocates resources and rewards units that demonstrably contribute to student learning, persistence, and graduation. This may stimulate a college or university to audit annually and align the budget to determine whether resources are being used wisely to attain the institution's mission and educational purposes in ways consistent with its values and students' needs.

Feature Diversity, Inside and Outside the Classroom

Students who report more frequent experiences with diversity also participate more in other effective educational practices and benefit more in desired ways from college (Hurtado, Dey, Gurin, & Gurin, 2003; Kuh & Umbach, 2005)

Use a multifaceted, aggressive approach to diversify the student body, faculty, and staff. Institutions become more diverse in two ways. The most common is when demographics in the surrounding area change. The second is by determining what diversity means in the institutional context and intentionally recruiting and supporting students, faculty, and staff from historically underrepresented populations to address diversity goals. Rather than allowing admissions and hiring pools to emerge naturally, DEEP institutions engage in proactive activities to diversify their members. Targeted goals for recruitment have been common. These colleges and universities aggressively pursued qualified candidates from institutions known to produce scholars of color. Provosts were especially active in recruiting new faculty and staff from historically underrepresented groups by working with faculty on setting annual hiring goals and contacting key Ph.D.-producing institutions.

Ensure that diverse perspectives are represented in the curriculum. DEEP schools illustrate that developmentally powerful experiences with diversity transcend institutional type. Structural diversity, or the percentage of students from historically underserved populations present in the student body, may not be as important to desired outcomes as exposure to different ways of thinking, either in the curriculum or through interactions with students from different backgrounds (Hurtado et al., 2003; Kuh & Umbach, 2005).

Seek Out, Socialize, and Reward Competent People

As with other aspects of institutional performance, student success is ultimately about the right people doing the right things.

Align the reward system with the institutional mission, values, and priorities. Institutions have multiple ways to reward people, ranging from annual performance reviews and salary adjustments to public ceremonies that recognize excellence in teaching, research, and service. Because rewards and recognitions reinforce what is important at the institution, the reward system should be as transparent as is practical and operate in a manner consistent with what the institution through its leaders espouses to be important and valued.

Recruit faculty and staff who are committed to student learning. DEEP provosts and academic deans played a pivotal role, making certain the right people were in the hiring pool. They unapologetically and enthusiastically emphasized the importance of high-quality undergraduate education while probing the commitment of potential faculty members to this cause. Some DEEP schools, such as the University of Maine–Farmington, feature an extended campus visit (three days) so that both the potential hire and the institution can learn about each other in a variety of social and professional situations.

Emphasize student-centeredness in faculty and staff orientation. New faculty members are formed into scholars during graduate school, where they are socialized to do some things and not others and to value certain ideas and views about the professoriate—teaching and learning, for example (Shulman, 2004). Newcomers need to be taught what the institution values and, in some instances, must be countersocialized. Such efforts must be ongoing, not relegated to only an hour during new faculty orientation. Newcomers at Kansas hear plainly from senior faculty that they will occasionally be asked to set aside personal priorities for the good of the campus, such as when general education requirements were revised.

Encourage Collaboration Across Functional Lines and Between the Campus and Community

High-performing organizations are marked by partnerships, cross-functional collaborations, and responsive units—what some authors call "loose-tight" organizational properties (Birnbaum, 1988; Peters & Waterman, 2004; Senge et al., 1999).

Encourage and reward cross-functional activities focused on student success. Faculty collaboration was a key ingredient at DEEP schools, especially with regard to curriculum revision. Innovations typically crossed the traditional organization boundaries, such as the collaborations between academic and student affairs on learning communities at UTEP, early-alert programs at FSU, and first-year initiatives at Miami. Moreover, they often spread horizontally to different areas, which further increased the chances that many students would be touched by the effort. Achieving this level of "spread," the degree to which a good idea is adopted by different elements of an organization (Coburn, 2003), is essential to sustainability. For example, efforts aimed at enhancing undergraduate education at the University of Michigan involved administrative leaders in the president's and provost's office, and was championed by the board of regents, the division of student affairs, faculty members, and students. Moreover, the commitment to improving undergraduate programs became embedded in strategic planning activities and, subsequently, policy decisions.

Validate and link like-minded efforts. Most campuses have one or more initiatives under way that can be strengthened by weaving into them more frequent use of the effective educational practices represented on NSSE. Consider sharing student engagement data and the research undergirding effective educational practices with colleagues involved in programs such as the following:

- AASCU American Democracy Project
- AAC&U Greater Expectations activities
- General education reform task force
- Carnegie Campus Clusters/SOTL/CASTL
- Service-learning/Campus Compact programs
- Accreditation and reaffirmation steering committees
- Internationalization and diversity efforts
- Projects undertaken as part of Building Engagement and Attainment of Minority Students (BEAMS)

Tighten the philosophical and operational linkages between academic and student affairs. At DEEP schools, the fundamental mission of student affairs is to support the institution's academic mission. Unlike at many colleges and universities, there was no debate or confusion about this. A holistic philosophy of talent development permeated the campus, similar to the student development philosophy championed by student affairs professional associations. Student affairs professionals recognize their primary obligation is to support the institution's academic mission and view themselves as full partners in the enterprise, team-teaching with faculty members, participating in campus governance, and managing enriching educational opportunities for students such as peer tutoring and mentoring, first-year seminars, and learning communities. This philosophical commitment enables student and academic affairs to work together in such key areas as advising and career services as well as some curricular innovations.

Harness the expertise of other resources. Many librarians know a good deal about how students spend their time, what they think and talk about, and how they feel, yet they are an underused educational resource. Librarians at some DEEP schools contribute to first-year seminars and orientation to college courses, academic advising, student-faculty research activities, and capstone seminars. Information technology personnel play similar roles. High-performing institutions recognize and put to good use the talents of these and other members of the campus community.

Partner with the local community. DEEP colleges are well connected with their local communities. Advisory boards guide the development of internship opportunities, fundraising projects, reciprocal library programs, and community service and volunteer efforts by students, staff, and occasionally presidents and provosts. Among the longstanding, formal campus-community partnerships are the Century Club at George Mason and similar initiatives at Kansas. External affairs staff can help identify and coordinate such opportunities and point to community needs that campus resources can meet in mutually beneficial ways.

Lay Out Paths to Student Success

Students will be better prepared to manage successfully the many challenges that college presents if beforehand they have an idea of what to expect and when and how to deal with these issues. It is advisable to provide some of this information to students even before they start classes and then provide additional information, advice, and guidance at key points after they enroll, especially during the first weeks and months of college.

Draw a map for student success. What does being a successful student look like on your campus? Among the exemplars in this regard are Miami's Choice Matters initiative, Fayetteville State's University College, and California State University–Monterey Bay's Individualized Learning Plan that students develop in the transition course, update at various points in their studies, and review formally in a major-specific ProSeminar during their junior year. Michigan used to provide incoming students with a compact disc that described to students how they could get involved with faculty on research projects and implored them to take the initiative in order to see faculty members outside of class.

Front-load resources to smooth the transition. DEEP schools recognized that newcomers need considerable structure and support to establish themselves academically and socially and to learn how to take advantage of the institution's resources for learning. For this reason, academic advising was a high priority. Preceptors, peer mentoring, and tutoring programs were common, with student affairs generally providing the space and infrastructure for such services and faculty members selecting and supervising peer mentors.

Teach newcomers about the campus culture. DEEP colleges recognize that beginning college students need affirmation, encouragement, and support as well as information about what to do to succeed. They make special efforts during summer orientation and registration, fall welcome week, and events throughout the early weeks of college to teach newcomers about campus traditions and rituals and provide other information about "how we do things here and what things really mean." A key aspect of this preparation is becoming familiar with the institution's distinctive vocabulary, or "terms of endearment" (Kuh et al., 1991) sometimes expressed as slang, abbreviations, and other shorthand forms. At many schools, this information and other socialization activities are often introduced during a college transition course tailored to meet the unique needs of the students on campus.

If an activity or experience is important to student success, consider requiring it. Strong-performing institutions typically have in place many high-quality programs and practices. Moreover, they make certain that one or more initiatives touch substantial numbers of students in meaningful ways, especially those students known to be at risk of leaving school prematurely. In some instances, when an activity is empirically demonstrated to have desired effects, it is required in some form for all or large numbers of students. New students at Winston-Salem must take an adjustment to college course emphasizing self-evaluation of their abilities and study skills. All undergraduates at Miami complete a capstone seminar. These are examples of the kinds of educationally effective activities that high-performing colleges and universities intentionally thread into the undergraduate experience in order to reach large numbers of their students.

Develop interventions for underengaged students. Focusing on students who are already engaged at relatively high levels—for example, those who are in the upper third of the engagement distribution—will probably produce only marginal differences in overall institutional performance. This is not to say such students should be ignored or that they would not reap some benefit. With limited time and resources, it may make sense for many schools to target interventions toward students who are in the lower third of the engagement distribution (Kuh, 2003; NSSE, 2003). This selection cannot simply be done by student category (younger and older, full-time, and part-time), because this assumes that students in these groups are more alike than they actually are (Kuh, 2003). Both the Beginning College Student Survey of Student Engagement and College Student Expectations Questionnaire are designed to measure what students expect to do during college. These tools can be used in combination with NSSE to determine whether students' expectations are reasonable, given the institution's mission and aspirations for student learning. They can also identify areas that the institution might address to raise or otherwise modify student expectations and experiences in educationally purposeful ways (Kuh, Gonyea, & Williams, 2005; Miller, Kuh, Paine, & Associates, 2006).

Focus on Culture Sooner Rather Than Later

Efforts to enhance student success often falter because too little attention is given to understanding the properties of the institution's culture that reinforce the status quo and perpetuate everyday actions (Kuh & Whitt, 1988). In many ways, all the suggestions mentioned to this point bear on culture and areas where norms, traditions, and beliefs need to be taken into account. Although it is not possible within the scope of this chapter to explicate the complexities involved, two first steps are essential.

Identify cultural properties that are obstacles to student success. Students at DEEP schools were advantaged because over time their school had created a culture where the norm is shared responsibility for student learning, governance, and a variety of other complementary processes. Cultivating such cultures demands focused leadership over an extended period of time and periodic systematic review of policies and practices; this would test prevailing assumptions about students' aspirations, motivations, and preferred learning styles, and the teaching approaches and institutional practices that contribute to desired outcomes. We have developed a self-guided template for this purpose, the *Inventory for Student Engagement and Success* (Kuh, Kinzie, et al., 2005).

Increase and enlist the participation of cultural practitioners in the change effort. Most people who work at a college or university sooner or later become culturally competent. That is, they learn how to get along, what words mean when used in different contexts, what's valued and what isn't, what acceptable behavior is, and so forth. But relatively few people become astute cultural practitioners, able to analyze the influence of norms, tacit beliefs, and other cultural properties to determine what needs to be addressed to effect change. To cultivate an ethic of positive restlessness that values student success, it is essential to address aspects of institutional culture including whether reward systems and the criteria for distributing resources will encourage or discourage people to work toward desired ends. In other words, do these and other institutional policies and practices acknowledge student engagement, achievement, and success in a meaningful way?

A Final Word

In *Good to Great*, Jim Collins (2001) concludes that "the good-to-great transformations never happened in one fell swoop. There was no single defining action, no grand program, no one killer innovation, no solitary lucky break, no miracle moment" (p.186). So public universities will need to recultured to become student centered.

The challenges are formidable. Changing collegiate cultures is hard work. Good ideas are important, but persistence, effort, and a willingness to stay the course are needed to bring them to fruition. More than ever, we need institutional leaders who champion and reward proven teaching approaches and support experiments to enhance the learning environment in ways consistent with their school's mission, values, and aspirations. Key actors must work on one or more initiatives for an extended period of time in order to establish them, demonstrate their efficacy, and weave them into daily practice and belief systems. At the same time, professors, staff members, and even students everywhere say they are overextended. Many people at DEEP institutions were teetering on the brink of overload much of the time. At one institution, faculty described their teaching load as "crushing." Thus one of the most important questions organizationally complex public universities must answer to improve student learning is not what are we going to do next, but what should we *stop doing* now so there is time and energy to invest in promising new initiatives.

Further complicating the task are the mixed messages that policymakers and others send institutions about the relative value of research and undergraduate teaching alongside other activities such as intercollegiate athletics. The inability of states to fund higher education at previous levels suggests the most promising option to deliver on the Kellogg Commission's petition for public universities to become "great student universities" is to pursue an improvement strategy that combines clearer mission differentiation and program elimination augmented by more consistent use of effective educational practices across the board.

Among the two-score DEEP schools were several large public universities. If these extraordinary institutions can beat the odds and blend strong teaching with research productivity, others can, too. Aspiring to anything less is a recipe for mediocrity.

Author Note

This chapter is based on the book *Student Success in College: Creating Conditions That Matter* (Kuh, Kinzie, Schuh, Whitt, & Associates, 2005), especially Chapters 2–7 and 14.

References

Astin, A. W. (1991). *Assessment for excellence: The philosophy and practice of assessment and evaluation in higher education.* New York, NY: American Council on Education/Macmillan.

Astin, A. W. (1993). *What matters in college? Four critical years revisited.* San Francisco, CA: Jossey-Bass.

Birnbaum, R. (1988). *How colleges work: The cybernetics of academic organization and leadership.* San Francisco, CA: Jossey-Bass.

Carey, K. (2004). *A matter of degrees: Improving graduation rates in four-year colleges and universities.* Washington, DC: The Education Trust.

Carini, R. M., Kuh, G. D., & Klein, S. P. (2006, February). Student engagement and student learning: Testing the linkages. *Research in Higher Education, 47*(1), 1–32.

Chickering, A. W. (1981). *The modern American college: Responding to the new realities of diverse students and a changing society.* San Francisco, CA: Jossey-Bass.

Chickering, A. W., & Gamson, Z. F. (1987, June). Seven principles for good practice in undergraduate education. *AAHE Bulletin, 39*(7), 3–7.

Chickering, A. W., & Reisser, L. (1993). *Education and identity* (2nd ed.). San Francisco, CA: Jossey-Bass.

Coburn, C. E. (2003, August/September). Rethinking scale: Moving beyond numbers to deep and lasting change. *Educational Researcher, 32*(6), 3–12.

Collins, J. C. (2001). *Good to great: Why some companies make the leap . . . and others don't.* New York, NY: HarperCollins.

Fullan, M. (2001). *Leading in a culture of change.* San Francisco, CA: Jossey Bass.

Gansemer-Topf, A., Saunders, K., Schuh, J. H., & Shelley, M. (2004). *A study of resource expenditures and allocation at DEEP colleges and universities: Is spending related to student engagement?* Ames, IA: Iowa State University, Educational Leadership and Policy Studies.

Gruenwald, D. A. (2003, Fall). Foundations of place: A multidisciplinary framework for place-conscious education. *American Educational Research Journal, 40*(3), 619–654.

Hirschhorn, L., & May, L. (2000, May/June). The campaign approach to change: Targeting the university's scarcest resources. *Change, 32*(3), 30–37.

Hurtado, S., Dey, E. L., Gurin, P. Y., & Gurin, G. (2003). College environments, diversity, and student learning. In J. C. Smart (Ed.), *Higher education: Handbook of theory and research* (Vol. XVIII, pp. 145–189). Dordrecht, Netherlands: Kluwer.

Johnstone, D. B. (2005). Financing higher education: Who should pay? In P. G. Altbach, R. O. Berdahl, & P. J. Gumport (Eds.), *American higher education in the twenty-first century: Social, political, and economic challenges* (2nd ed., pp. 369–392). Baltimore, MD: Johns Hopkins University Press.

Kellogg Commission on the Future of State and Land-Grant Universities. (2000). *Returning to our roots: Toward a coherent campus culture.* Washington, DC: National Association of State Universities and Land-Grant Colleges.

Kuh, G. D. (2001). College students today: Why we can't leave serendipity to chance. In P. G. Altbach, P. J. Gumport, & D. B. Johnstone (Eds.), *In defense of American higher education* (pp. 277–302). Baltimore, MD: Johns Hopkins University Press.

Kuh, G. D. (2003, March/April). What we're learning about student engagement from NSSE. *Change, 35*(2), 24–32.

Kuh, G. D., Gonyea, R. M., & Williams, J. M. (2005). What students expect from college and what they get. In T. E. Miller, B. E. Bender, J. H. Schuh, & Associates, *Promoting reasonable expectations: Aligning student and institutional views of the college experience* (pp. 34–64). San Francisco, CA: Jossey-Bass.

Kuh, G. D., & Hu, S. (2001). Learning productivity at research universities. *Journal of Higher Education, 72*(1), 1–28.

Kuh, G. D., Kinzie, J., Schuh, J. H., & Whitt, E. J. (2005). *Assessing conditions to enhance educational effectiveness: The inventory for student engagement and success.* San Francisco, CA: Jossey-Bass.

Kuh, G. D., Kinzie, J., Schuh, J. H., Whitt, E. J., & Associates. (2005). *Student success in college: Creating conditions that matter.* San Francisco, CA: Jossey-Bass.

Kuh, G. D., Schuh, J. H., Whitt, E. J., & Associates. (1991). *Involving colleges: Successful approaches to fostering student learning and development outside the classroom.* San Francisco, CA: Jossey-Bass.

Kuh, G. D., & Umbach, P. D. (2005, Winter). Experiencing diversity: What can we learn from liberal arts colleges? *Journal of Higher Education, 91*(1), 14–21.

Kuh, G. D., & Whitt, E. J. (1988). *The invisible tapestry: Culture in American colleges and universities* (ASHE-ERIC Higher Education Report, 17[1]). San Francisco, CA: Jossey-Bass.

McLeod, W. B. (2003). *Linking retention and academic performance: The freshman year initiative.* Retrieved August 25, 2006, from the Fayetteville State University, Office of the Chancellor web site: www.uncfsu.edu/chanoff/FYI01.HTM

Miller, M. T., Kuh, G. D., Paine, D., & Associates. (2006). *Taking student expectations seriously: A guide for campus applications.* Washington, DC: National Association of Student Personnel Administrators.

National Center for Higher Education Management Systems. (2004). *Do DEEP institutions spend more or differently than their peers?* Boulder, CO: Author.

National Survey of Student Engagement. (2000). *The NSSE 2000 report: National benchmarks of effective educational practice.* Bloomington, IN: Indiana University, Center for Postsecondary Research.

National Survey of Student Engagement. (2001). *Improving the college experience: National benchmarks for effective educational practice.* Bloomington, IN: Indiana University, Center for Postsecondary Research.

National Survey of Student Engagement. (2003). *Converting data into action: Expanding the boundaries of institutional improvement.* Bloomington, IN: Indiana University, Center for Postsecondary Research.

National Survey of Student Engagement. (2004). *Student engagement: Pathways to collegiate success.* Bloomington, IN: Indiana University, Center for Postsecondary Research.

National Survey of Student Engagement. (2005). *DEEP practice briefs.* Retrieved August 25, 2006, from the Indiana University, NSSE Institute web site: http://webdb.iu.edu/Nsse/?view=deep/briefs

Pascarella, E. T. (2001, May/June). Identifying excellence in undergraduate education: Are we even close? *Change, 33*(3), 19–23.

Pascarella, E. T., & Terenzini, P. T. (1991). *How college affects students: Findings and insights from twenty years of research.* San Francisco, CA: Jossey-Bass.

Pascarella, E. T., & Terenzini, P. T. (2005). *How college affects students: A third decade of research* (Vol. 2). San Francisco, CA: Jossey-Bass.

Peters, T. J., & Waterman, R. H., Jr. (2004). *In search of excellence: Lessons from America's best run companies.* New York, NY: HarperBusiness Essentials.

President's Commission on the Undergraduate Experience. (2002). *The second chapter of change: Renewing undergraduate education at the University of Michigan.* Retrieved August 25, 2006, from the University of Michigan, Office of the President web site: www.umich.edu/pres/undergrad/pdf/UndergradReportUM.pdf

Schroeder, C. C. (1993, September/October). New students: New learning styles. *Change, 25*(4), 21–26.

Senge, P. M., Kleiner, A., Roberts, C., Ross, R., Roth, G., & Smith, B. (1999). *The dance of change: The challenges of sustaining momentum in learning organizations.* New York, NY: Doubleday.

Shulman, L. S. (2004). *Teaching as community property: Essays on higher education.* San Francisco, CA: Jossey-Bass.

Tagg, J. (2003). *The learning paradigm college.* Bolton, MA: Anker.

Appendix A: Summary of the NSSE Clusters of Effective Educational Practice

Level of Academic Challenge

Challenging intellectual and creative work is central to student learning and collegiate quality. A number of questions from NSSE's instrument *The College Student Report*, correspond to three integral components of academic challenge. Several questions represent the nature and amount of assigned academic work, some reflect the complexity of cognitive tasks presented to students, and several others ask about the standards faculty members use to evaluate student performance. Specifically these questions are related to:

• Preparing for class (studying, reading, writing, rehearsing)
• Reading and writing
• Using higher-order thinking skills
• Working harder than students thought they could to meet an instructor's standards
• An institutional environment that emphasizes studying and academic work

Active and Collaborative Learning

Students learn more when they are intensely involved in their education and have opportunities to think about and apply what they are learning in different settings. And when students collaborate with others in solving problems or mastering difficult material they acquire valuable skills that prepare them to deal with the messy, unscripted problems they will encounter daily during and after college. Survey questions that contribute to this cluster include:

• Asking questions in class or contributing to class discussions
• Making class presentations
• Working with other students on projects during class
• Working with classmates outside of class to prepare class assignments
• Tutoring or teaching other students
• Participating in community-based projects as part of a regular course
• Discussing ideas from readings or classes with others

Student Interactions With Faculty Members

In general, the more contact students have with their teachers, the better. Working with a professor on a research project or serving with faculty members on a college committee or community organization lets students see firsthand how experts identify and solve practical problems. Through such interactions teachers become role models, mentors, and guides for continuous, lifelong learning. Questions in this cluster include:

• Discussing grades or assignments with an instructor
• Talking about career plans with a faculty member or advisor
• Discussing ideas from readings or classes with faculty members outside of class
• Working with faculty members on activities other than coursework (committees, orientation, student-life activities, and so forth)
• Getting prompt feedback on academic performance
• Working with a faculty member on a research project

Enriching Educational Experiences

Educationally effective colleges and universities offer many different opportunities inside and outside the classroom that complement the goals of the academic program. One of the most important is exposure to diversity, from which students learn valuable things about themselves and gain an appreciation for other cultures. Technology is increasingly being used to facilitate the learning process and, when done appropriately, can increase collaboration between peers and instructors, which actively engages students in their learning. Other valuable educational experiences include internships, community service, and senior capstone courses that provide students with opportunities to synthesize, integrate, and apply their knowledge. As a result, learning is deeper, more meaningful, and ultimately more useful because what students know becomes a part of who they are. Questions from the survey representing these kinds of experiences include:

- Talking with students with different religious beliefs, political opinions, or values
- Talking with students of a different race or ethnicity
- An institutional climate that encourages contact among students from different economic, social, and racial or ethnic backgrounds
- Using electronic technology to discuss or complete assignments
- Participating in:
  - Internships or field experiences
  - Community service or volunteer work
  - Foreign language coursework
  - Study abroad
  - Independent study or self-designed major
  - Cocurricular activities
  - A culminating senior experience

Supportive Campus Environment

Students perform better and are more satisfied at colleges that are committed to their success and cultivate positive working and social relations among different groups on campus. Survey questions contributing to this cluster describe a campus environment that:

- Helps students succeed academically
- Helps students cope with nonacademic responsibilities (work, family, etc.)
- Helps students thrive socially
- Promotes good relations between students and their peers
- Promotes good relations between students and faculty members
- Promotes good relations between students and administrative staff

11

Making a "Great 'Engaged' University" Requires Rhetoric

Richard A. Cherwitz, E. Johanna Hartelius

The movement to create engaged public research universities, while laudable for its enthusiasm and passion, seems rooted in ideals and principles with which few would disagree (Boyer, 1990, 1996; Cherwitz, 2005c; Gibbons, 2001; Kellogg Commission, 2001). For example, who would dispute the notion that public universities ought to serve the public good or educate and support rigorous scholars and ethical citizens? Who would argue with the claim that public universities, because they are "public," have a mandate—unlike their private counterparts—to become engaged with society and their communities? While these calls for change are encouraging, inevitably one must wonder how to realize such visionary, inspiring, and obvious-sounding principles. As noted in Chapter 1 of this book, implementation is the tricky part.

Why have public research universities failed to implement engagement fully? Perhaps part of the explanation is that, when contemplating implementation, our initial instinct is to become preoccupied with logistical issues. Among the first questions often asked: What specific mechanisms and structures has an institution put in place to achieve engagement? What infrastructure does it need to support these initiatives and what source will fund them? How does campus planning incorporate engagement? What incentives and rewards will ensure compliance with the university charge for engagement from departments, colleges, and their faculty? Finally, how will the institution measure and evaluate these engagement efforts?

These are vitally important issues, but they miss the real challenge. Ascertaining how to implement an idea as complex as engagement, precisely because it is not a mainstream tradition within the academy, cannot begin with logistics. A logically necessary prior step, we argue, is to develop a rhetorical strategy—a way of thinking and talking about engagement—that creates within the academic culture an acceptance of engagement. This rhetoric, in turn, enables universities to address effectively the logistical dimensions of implementation. Without a notion of engagement as essential to the academic enterprise, trying to figure out the logistics of implementation inevitably will prove futile. This situation of engagement, we surmise, is the current and frustrating state of affairs on most campuses.

Readers should not be surprised, therefore, to learn that this chapter offers little in the way of logistical insights into achieving the engaged public research university. We do not make recommendations about budgets and programs, nor do we offer advice about infrastructure, compliance, and assessment. Instead, our objective is to analyze the rhetorical side of implementation, recommending that public research universities alter their discourses for talking about engagement. The primary question posed in this chapter is: What rhetorical strategies are required to mainstream engagement within the academic routines of public research universities? It is our belief that if such strategies can be devised (i.e., if the rhetorical portion of implementation is sound), then logistical challenges will be far less onerous. After all, a major reason why engagement has not been fully implemented is that universities are stymied by beginning with logistical questions. Advocates of engagement have assumed erroneously that these considerations will solve larger attitudinal problems within the academy.

Logistical solutions rarely have the capacity to change philosophies or worldviews. Equipped with a rhetoric that mainstreams engagement, however, logistical issues would be just that—matters of nuts and bolts rather than efforts in and of themselves to remove the long-standing cultural obstacles preventing engagement.

In a similar vein, this chapter refrains from the temptation to propose a template for creating yet another program or initiative for engagement. Such separate entities popping up like administrative mushrooms around campus ultimately are counterproductive (Cherwitz, 2005b). They contribute to the problems of fragmentation that this book addresses. Instead, we explore the rhetoric and mindset of engagement. In our view, the engaged university will result from reconstituted thinking; this, in turn, will transpire when the language through which we understand the role of the academic is changed. To be a scholar is to "follow the knowledge" and be motivated by questions—to be what later in this chapter we call *intellectual entrepreneurs,* faculty who create and are accountable for their scholarly products (Cherwitz & Sullivan, 2002; Hildebrand, 2005). This process requires risk-taking and ownership, and leads to a multitude of products adapted for a variety of venues and audiences. When faculty members' quest to follow the knowledge is viewed as an entrepreneurial pursuit, it is our contention that distinctions among academe's three pillars—research, teaching, and service—appear less rigid. This entrepreneurial concept enables universities to become more fully engaged.

To make this case, this chapter advances two arguments. First, we contend that a scholarly and technical understanding of rhetoric, one of the most venerable academic disciplines, informs our ability to devise and implement an effective philosophy of university engagement. We claim that current efforts to create an interdisciplinary and engaged public research university have not attained maximum impact in part because they have emerged from an institutional rhetoric best described as separate and inherently unequal. Second, we suggest how the language of intellectual entrepreneurship (and the related notion of citizen-scholars) offers an alternative rhetoric. This shift has the potential to make engagement and interdisciplinary learning more central to the academic routines of public research universities, thus offering administrators a stable foundation from which to broach logistical questions about implementation. The concept of a faculty "contract" provides one illustration of a specific mechanism for implementing engagement emerging from this alternative rhetoric.

What Is an Engaged University and What Is Required to Achieve It?

Throughout this chapter, the phrase *engaged university* designates an institution embracing and acting on the assumption of enormous value of intellectual capital. In this case, intellectual capital refers to faculty expertise and creativity, which largely stems from a university's capacity to harness, integrate, and leverage knowledge for social good. To be engaged means recognizing that a university's collective knowledge is among its most precious assets—anchored to, but not in competition with, basic research and disciplinary knowledge.

Becoming engaged requires that universities address two fundamental challenges. First is the considerable task of making transdisciplinary (cross-disciplinary) learning and research endemic to the academic culture. Social problems and academic questions in this century are increasingly complex, hence defying solution by any one discipline or sector. Working across disciplines requires language and institutional structures that successfully integrate the knowledge housed in separate departments and colleges. An engaged university is one that routinely complements the specialist's knowledge with the generalist's perspective, a state of affairs demanding explosion of the academic myth that specialists deserve the highest respect (Gregorian, 2004). Engagement entails production of specialized knowledge, but also a concurrent encouragement of renaissance thinking (Cherwitz, 2005c) and the dialectical interaction between these two ways of knowing.

A second challenge involves the covenant described by the Kellogg Commission: Engaged universities are driven by and accountable for their partnerships with the public. Being an engaged university thus means working with government, businesses, and nonprofit agencies to respond to community needs. It requires faculty members who are not content with being sequestered in or protected by the ivory tower. This dimension of engagement is a two-way street. A genuine collaboration between universities and the public represents more than increased access to a university's intellectual assets. It offers more than knowledge transfer—the exportation of neatly wrapped solutions rolling off the campus conveyer belt. Collaboration demands mutual humility and respect, joint ownership of learning, and co-creation of an unimagined potential for innovation—qualities that move universities well beyond the typical elitist sense of service (Cherwitz, 2005b; Cherwitz, Sullivan, & Stewart, 2002).

Whether by design or effect, most universities have attempted to meet these challenges by developing an array of programs scattered throughout the institutional landscape. Unfortunately, if universities continue to expand and feed a network of separate and disconnected programs that vie for limited resources, the kind of engagement described above will remain unfulfilled. If, on the other hand, engagement becomes mainstreamed and viewed as a naturally integral value for both professors and students, separate initiatives will be superfluous. The point we are making is that the language used to describe the place for engagement in public research universities will determine whether engagement becomes part of academic convention. Breaking the binaries that populate academe—teaching/research, research/service, theory/practice, basic/applied research (Stokes, 1997)—is a matter of considerable rhetorical effort. In order to honor the social contract between universities and the public, we must devise a language wherein academic curiosity serves the common good. Curiosity, after all, is the university's raw material and intellectual capital.

Academics' strength is to ask questions and pursue answers with intellectual integrity and methodological rigor. The key to integrating engagement into the academic culture is to draw on that strength. To be clear, engagement ought not appear in opposition to the sort of hard-nosed science for which researchers strive. Professors are already frustrated and overwhelmed by the amount and variety of demands made by their universities: to amass a sustained record of publication in refereed journals, to achieve and document excellence in teaching, to procure substantial extramural funding, and to participate in the governance of one's academic unit and university (O'Meara & Rice, 2005). A surefire way of alienating faculty from the idea of engagement is to turn it into another obligation—an additional item on their already full plates. Instead, the language of engagement must establish the natural and inherent synergies among the discovery, propagation, and use of knowledge.

Allowing engagement to become another separate obligation for faculty, moreover, dooms it to a peripheral status. So viewed, engagement will always remain supplementary and additive, competing for time and energy. Professors will inevitably perceive it as nonacademic, less rigorous, and less valued by peers and academic decision-makers who grant tenure and promotion and other university rewards. However, if those leaders view engagement as a natural part and extension of research and teaching, it becomes a matter of ownership and self-efficacy—something chosen and deliberately executed as part of a scholarly agenda. What we are suggesting, then, is that engagement should be driven by faculty functioning as intellectual entrepreneurs, agents empowered to own and be accountable for their enterprise. It should not be superimposed by administrators endeavoring to respond to political concerns.

The Rhetorical State of Engagement

As rhetoricians, we are sensitive to the role symbolic influence plays in cultural, social, and political change. In this section, we insist that a technical account of rhetoric and rhetorical perspectives is key to understanding why public research universities are not fully engaged. Introducing research pertaining to rhetoric may at first blush seem odd or even tedious to those who are accustomed to the vocabulary of higher education assessment and wish to know more about engagement. From these readers we ask indulgence. Because a scholarly analysis of rhetoric reveals the enormous capacity of discourse to create meaning, shape policy, and impact implementation (whether in politics or academe), the following pages discuss rhetorical theory. They underscore some of the more important lessons that set up our analysis of the failed discourses of engagement.

Rhetoric: Describing Reality and Creating Possibilities

One of the oldest academic disciplines, dating back to antiquity, rhetoric studies human persuasion. Whether defined as "the rationale of informative and suasory in discourse" (Bryant, 1953, p. 404), "the nature of speech is in fact to direct the soul" (Plato, 1995, p. 73), the application of "reason to imagination for the better moving of the will" (Bacon, 1957, p. 177), "the study of all those arts involving symbolic inducement" (Ehninger, 1972, p. 3), or "the art of describing reality through language" (Cherwitz & Hikins, 1986, p. 62), the discipline of rhetoric has as its subject matter the ways in which discourse influences attitudes, beliefs, and values, and ultimately instigates actions.

Rhetoricians have long recognized that language serves not only an important managerial function but one of invention as well. In recent decades, for example, some have argued that in addition to being a vehicle for transporting and propagating ideas, rhetoric simultaneously serves as a method of discovery. Put differently, we now understand that rhetoric is more than embellishment—more than impulse added to truth or an inherently propagandistic device. After a long history of defending rhetoric against the charge that it is mere ornamentation at best and corruptive deception at worst, rhetoricians declare: Language is not just wrapping! Language does not transport meaning from one mind to another. Rather than use language to deploy ready-made mental constructs, humans use language to generate such constructs. Invention, both intra- and inter-subjectively, is a linguistic activity. Moving beyond pejorative and pedestrian accounts, theorists have articulated the "epistemic" power of rhetorical discourse. Rhetoric is instrumental to the discovery and creation of knowledge and new ways of thinking and acting (Cherwitz, 1980; Cherwitz & Hikins, 1986; Scott, 1967).

Based on these theoretical insights, rhetorical critics have examined individual discourses, discerning how rhetoric both describes and simultaneously imagines or creates reality. We know that the ways in which ideas are rhetorically couched constrain not only what can be thought and done in the present but also what might be possible in the future, that is, what is enabled and prescribed or disenabled and proscribed. For instance, identifying American foreign relations in the Middle East as a "war on terror" rather than an "invasion" or a change of international relations has profound material consequences.

It prescribes that the country responds to an urgent matter with patriotism, fortitude, and perseverance. It further aligns the conflict with other historical experiences the United States has had with war. "War" as a rhetorical construct denotes a time of crisis in which citizens must rally behind their leader against an enemy, whether the enemy is a foreign nation or a domestic threat created by problems such as drugs or poverty. The language also powerfully determines who is considered most germane to the conversation and will therefore be at the table. In this case, "war on terror" suggests that military experts will be the major players in shaping United States policy in the Middle East.

Remarkably, rhetorical effects of this sort often are more pronounced because they are insidious, occurring subconsciously. Audiences, frequently without being aware of it, adopt and internalize a speaker's language. And, as noted by rhetoricians and sociologists, the adoption of language carries with it much more than the mimicking of words and phrases. When audiences internalize a speaker's language, they implicitly take on a set of values and pre/proscribed behaviors.

This is why the power of rhetoric supersedes language practices in creating particular views of reality. These views continue to reproduce themselves beyond the communicator's original efforts. Consistent with Aristotle's concept of the "enthymeme" (a rhetorical syllogism—a truncated syllogism whose missing premise is supplied by the audience), linguistic internalization may also result in audiences completing a speaker's argument, using their own examples and experiences to bolster, amplify, or move beyond the speaker's thesis. A speaker's language thus has an impressive shelf life, chaining out as the public internalizes it and adopts it as his or her own. Put bluntly, language-in-use (Cherwitz, 1980) may be one of the most significant effects of rhetoric, since it is symptomatic of and leads to other substantial affective and behavioral responses.

What research in the discipline of rhetoric reveals, then, is that institutional and cultural changes require deliberate and strategically crafted language. Just as in politics, an academic institution's rhetoric is far more than a vehicle for transmitting and publicizing its core values, policies, and day-to-day operations—what rhetoricians term *disposition*. Institutional rhetoric also and perhaps ultimately serves as the engine for discovering, defining, and shaping the values of its constituents and determining the manner in which those values are brought to fruition—what rhetoricians call *invention*, Additionally, whether intended or not, a university's rhetoric ultimately chooses who will design programs and address the mechanics of implementation. Our success or failure at creating an engaged university, therefore, may be as simple yet challenging as devising and implementing the appropriate rhetorical vocabulary.

From this perspective, faculty and university administrators must begin to recognize that the discourses of engagement translate into more than a public relations campaign. There is nothing more pragmatic and concrete than a rhetorical choice. Institutional discourses have enormous policy implications, all of which bear on how engagement is understood, valued, and implemented. Rhetoric, after all, is a critical tool by which an institution discovers its brand and the best methods available to maximize fulfillment of its objectives. For example, the creation of a new university culture, which, as we alluded to earlier, may be requisite to engaged universities, will be driven at least partially by our language choices. What universities need are effective rhetorical strategies designed not merely to cater to external constituencies (to prove to them that universities are indeed engaged) but those adapted to the academic players who must define, own, deliver, and be accountable for the engaged university. An institution's rhetoric directly determines whether the challenge of implementation is met, for it impacts how professors understand the role of the engaged university and influences whether they take ownership and responsibility for it.

In the pages that follow, we argue that institutional rhetoric may account for why current efforts to create engaged public research universities have not been as effective as desired and in some cases have been counterproductive.

The Discourses of Engagement: Separate and Unequal

The call for engaged universities is a movement whose presence is now palpable on nearly every campus across the nation. Phrases like *public scholarship, applied research, service-learning, community and civic engagement,* and *outreach* are ubiquitous buzzwords. Ubiquity, contrary to popular belief, is not equivalent to general acceptance and integration into the culture. These catchphrases, nevertheless, are symptomatic of the quest to constitute a new language, a way of talking and thinking about the engaged university. Despite the skepticism that it occasionally receives, the proliferation of such language does indicate a genuine desire for engaged universities and for developing mechanisms that bring the vision of engagement to fruition.

Good intentions and a noble cause notwithstanding, an overly restrictive institutional rhetoric has foiled most efforts to create engagement. The result is a wide array of separate and disconnected programs that vie for attention and resources. Although sharing basic ideals, these initiatives remain ineffective, representing tiny points of light, insufficient to generate the sort of heat that the engagement ideal demands for a university-wide reinvention.

A lack of systemic support is part of the problem. The inefficiency that plagues many current engagement efforts ought not to be attributed to a want of commitment or sense of what needs doing. Criticizing those who tirelessly devote themselves to the goal of engagement is not our intention. To the contrary, we fully acknowledge that career centers, continuing education and lifelong learning programs, community outreach offices, and similar units (e.g., the dozens of faculty-run institutes promoting engagement that are tied to academic disciplines) have an extraordinarily lucid understanding of what engagement means. They inform both professors and students about ways to make intellectual and academic work more socially relevant and how academic and professional commitments might be structured in more mutually reinforcing ways. Unfortunately, as long as these programs operate without a strong network supported by the central administration, the challenge to combine efforts and integrate services will be considerable. When one center's version of and formula for engagement competes with another's for attention, funding, and institutional priority, the success of each is limited and the collective impact of engagement remains untapped. What we are suggesting is the downside of allowing the engagement wheel to be reinvented by so many offices and academic units.

But the problem runs much deeper than university geography and administrative infrastructure. It resides with the discourses that present and invent engagement. The language choices that create opportunities can just as easily limit them: "Every way of seeing is a way of not seeing" (Burke, 1965, p. 49). Institutional rhetoric, we contend, reflects and perpetuates a view of engagement best described as separate and inherently unequal. Drawing on the earlier discussion of rhetoric, consider the significance of the current language of engagement and how it potentially stymies implementation.

- Regardless of intent, *community and civic engagement* suggests an activity that is not distinctively academic and one without a unique scholarly component. As modifiers of *engagement,* the words *civic* and *community* evoke a notion of "service" in the traditional sense of volunteerism, where engagement means doing something beyond and apart from one's primary professional responsibilities. This language offers a clear enthymematic invitation to view engagement as benevolent—what human beings, regardless of career or expertise, do out of a moral sense of obligation and duty (and in the case of academics, perhaps to balance and justify the resources that we consume and are privileged to receive from society). The rhetorical effect of this image renders difficult, if not impossible, an understanding of engagement as an organic part of scholarship and thus a professional obligation of academics.

- *Interdisciplinary* entails that which is not the same as or equal to disciplinary knowledge—the academic gold standard of educational institutions and learned societies. Instead, the term conjures up a kind of knowledge or expertise that sits outside of disciplines. Because it is on the edges or margins, interdisciplinary scholarship is less rigorous, "soft," and perhaps even antidisciplinary. One is either disciplinary or interdisciplinary, and to engage in the latter is to appear "off mission" within a research institution.

- *Service-learning* denotes a separate and distinctive kind of learning, one segregated from and viewed as less valuable than the academic and intellectual kind. It also implies that learning takes place in the context of engagement only when it is classified as service-learning—learning, it is assumed, does not happen from service alone.

- *Outreach* sets up a dichotomy between insiders and outsiders—an "us" and a "them." The insiders are the intellectuals, the researchers who "reach out" into the community and "transfer" their expertise. The outsiders are those with insufficient expertise who rely on and need the knowledge produced by academics. The term *outreach,* moreover, implies a unidirectional line of influence, inhibiting the two-way interaction and collaboration that is characteristic of effective engagement.

- *Applied research* reveals that there is another option for researchers, namely to be "not applied." It implies a false dichotomy between kinds of research that perhaps are better represented on a continuum. This dichotomy rhetorically sets up a value judgment: Since applied research is less scholarly and less rigorous than basic research and theory, it is a less valuable commodity of the academy. Furthermore, while the counterpart to applied research is not explicitly labeled *nonapplied*, that is a logical and rhetorically appropriate inference. Hence consistent with this language is the risk of viewing basic research as necessarily and inherently an end rather than a means—a prospect allowing scholarship to be an exclusively self-serving enterprise. To be clear, we are not arguing that all scholarship must be applied or have an applied dimension. Though an application is yet unknown, the work still may be vitally important and academically significant. Nevertheless, the ivory tower criticism against academe is warranted when research lacks a sense of self-reflexivity. As the Kellogg Commission notes, the covenant between the public and the public university demands a contribution from researchers. There is a multitude of ways, however, to view such contributions and different timelines for evaluating the extent to which they have been made. Our point is simply that the language of applied research is limiting and prejudices the case, making realization of an engaged university more onerous.

• The same interpretation holds for phrases like *public scholarship* and *public intellectual*. The underlying assumptions of this language must be exposed. By what standards is scholarship deemed to be "public" rather than "academic"? Is the implication that a public intellectual is distinguishable from an intellectual proper only by employment and title? The language here is highly normative, suggesting that public intellectuals—because they write for a larger and more general audience rather than for specialized readers of peer-reviewed academic journals—are not proper intellectuals. As with prior examples, the public intellectual and public scholarship language, though not intended that way, prejudices the case for university engagement.

In addition to language, the absence of academic ethos provides another rhetorical explanation accounting for our inability to achieve fully engaged public research universities. At research universities, for better or worse, some have it and some don't. Faculty consider administrative offices and nonacademic units as external to the intellectual life of the university. Because they operate outside the institution's academic departments (where the real work supposedly gets done), these offices and their staff are not in a position to advise faculty on matters related to original research. Yet these offices are the ones calling for engagement. Not surprisingly, many scholars dismiss these pronouncements precisely because they come from those without the appropriate scholarly ethos and intellectual motivation. For some faculty, engagement is the rallying cry or diatribe of failed scholars.

This dismissal of engagement is reminiscent of the movement in prior decades to improve university teaching and give it greater institutional priority. As important as teaching is, it frequently is not elevated to a high priority at research institutions. Why does this occur? Perhaps it is because teaching and its advocates (who often are not publishing scholars) seem disconnected from the more primary research mission of universities. What we have is an extension of the mentality that "those who can't do research, teach." The same pattern now may be repeating itself with the movement toward engagement. As long as it is heralded by those not viewed as the university's best, or at least archetypal, scholars, why would we expect faculty commitment to university-wide implementation of engagement?

Our claim about the rhetoric of engagement cannot be overstated. When it is presented to faculty members as an activity external to and separate from their research, and when it is couched as an administratively imposed obligation, engagement inherently remains a second-class, auxiliary assignment. Confining engagement to the traditional language of "service" or other peripheral duties is severely limiting. Nothing could be less appealing to faculty—or graduate students—than another obligation that detracts from time and energy spent on "the real stuff"—rigorous research and publication in prestigious journals. Faculty occupy themselves with prized and rewarded activities—those judged consistent with the primary mission of the university as rhetorically captured and disseminated by the institution's administration. In view of the current rhetoric of engagement, therefore, it is hardly shocking that stepping outside the laboratory and archives or away from the quiet contemplation associated with research and scholarship is by definition "a detour." In addition to being off mission, such detours often seem pointless and unattractive to professors since they come as requests from "outsiders"—administrators and external constituents who are not active researchers and who appear motivated more by a political than a scholarly agenda.

Engagement terminology and the accompanying administrative discourse and dissemination create for faculty a mixed message at best, that is to say, along with building a successful record of scholarship, engagement is a desirable practice. Professors can easily read between the lines: Participating in engagement is laudable but, at the end of the day, it is research that counts and brings rewards. Faculty learn quickly that engagement is not the principal currency of research institutions, no matter how much supplemental rhetoric is generated by administrators calling for universities to contribute to society. They understand full well that although they will be commended for their engagement activities, in the end such work and the accolades handed out for it pale compared to the punishment (e.g., denial of promotion, less merit salary increases, being tagged as a "second-class" faculty member, etc.) received for not keeping one's head down and producing the coin of the realm, research.

What we are suggesting is that engagement must become a way of thinking to which faculty ascribe rather than merely an administrative imposition. Moreover, as revealed by the above rhetorical analysis, engagement must be a way of thinking and speaking that dissolves rather than invites and reinforces the traditional binaries of research/engagement or research/teaching. In order to establish this mindset, universities should allow professors to be professors by asking what lines of inquiry truly inspire academics and then encouraging them to pursue and own those questions.

In the final section of this chapter, we argue that genuine engagement will be achieved when there are discourses allowing it to be seamlessly integrated into universities' academic and scholarly routines. We do not claim to have a detailed map of the ways by which this will occur since, as noted earlier, the logistics of implementation are beyond the scope of our argument. Nevertheless, the following examples from the University of Texas's Intellectual Entrepreneurship Consortium illustrate what is possible if the discourse of engagement is substantially altered.

Intellectual Entrepreneurship: A New Discourse of Engagement

Intellectual entrepreneurship (IE) rests on the belief that intellect is not limited to the academy and entrepreneurship is not restricted to business. IE began in 1996 as a program in the Office of Graduate Studies at the University of Texas–Austin. The program enrolled in classes, workshops, internships, and other activities more than 4,000 students in more than 90 academic disciplines involving every college and school on campus. Since 2003, IE has been transformed from a program into an inter-collegial consortium. This shift was driven by the fundamental philosophy of its participants: that university engagement must be integral rather than peripheral, that engagement is a mindset and not a program.

IE informs the thesis of this chapter. It offers academic institutions one—and certainly not the only—example of a rhetoric extricating us from the less than successful approach to engagement detailed earlier. Drawing on IE as a philosophy of education, this section provides a glimpse into how academic engagement might rhetorically become a part of the culture of public research universities and what specific mechanisms for implementation emerge as a result.

The Intellectual Entrepreneurship Philosophy_____

The language and philosophy of IE fundamentally alters the separate and unequal status under which the quest for engagement has languished. That is its strength: IE is a way of changing academe's rhetorical practices. The mission of IE is to educate citizen-scholars. These scholars are living proof of what it means to take ownership of one's work and intellectual capital—personally, professionally, and academically. Citizen-scholars use their capital as a lever for social good through meaningful contributions to disciplinary knowledge. They realize that when the personal/professional dichotomy is erased, we spawn change from the ground up. Like Demosthenes, citizen-scholars understand that speech (scholarship) without action is empty and idle.

It is a common academic misconception that all entrepreneurs are necessarily businesspersons. To the contrary, the language of intellectual entrepreneurship is not a covert move to import carte blanche the corporate model into universities. We believe that public universities are and indeed should be subject to different rules and expectations than businesses in the private sector. In order to retain their unique identity as places to discover and disseminate knowledge, return on investment must remain a different and distinctive concept for universities. Yet as the Kellogg Commission reports, times are changing. If anything, the push to adopt a corporate model of intellectual capital in universities will come in a much more subtle package than one labeled *intellectual entrepreneurship*. Though it may sound like a cliché, academics must now become the agents of change lest they become its casualties. Being the vanguards of institutional and social change, we argue, is a task well suited for the citizen-scholar.

Engagement and ownership go hand in hand for citizen-scholars. More specifically, they function as mutual prerequisites. To assume ownership of one's work is to assume accountability for all phases of the process: questions, methods (invention), implications, audience adaptation (disposition), and implementation. Ownership entails more than accountability to an "other"; it also means accountability to one's self. Researchers who own their work are able to view themselves as distinct from more conventional faculty members. Citizen-scholars are not cogs in the university machinery. Because these researchers are creative agents of their own practices and products, engagement becomes one of the most natural extensions imaginable of academic scholarship.

Citizen-scholars require certain basic conditions to thrive. Most important is the kind of institutional support that can come only from rhetorical strategies departing from current ones. With the language of IE, we suggest, engagement is a natural part and extension of one's scholarly agenda, rather than a separate and inherently unequal venture. Moreover, the language of IE empowers faculty to own and be accountable for their scholarship, thus rendering them more in control of their professional futures and that of their institutions. In other words, the language of IE liberates us from starting with and incessantly talking about "products" (e.g., publications, grants, awards, etc.). Instead, the language of IE allows faculty to direct attention to the scholarly enterprise itself—an enterprise and way of thinking potentially generating many products, all of which are a fundamental part of scholarship. By focusing on and starting with "process" (how we configure and deploy intellectual resources), rather than "products" (the desired goals and outcomes), IE language fosters ownership, integration, and collaboration—three necessary ingredients of an engaged university.

The citizen-scholar is not a product of IE imagination; she exists. Dr. Martha Norkunas has been at the University of Texas–Austin since 1994. She is the founder of the Project in Interpreting the Texas Past (ITP). Norkunas, a public historian, grounds her research in local sites, employing a variety of methodological approaches in both teaching and research. The ITP project, developed in 1999 in collaboration with the IE program, is based on the IE philosophy of interdisciplinary and community-based education. By organizing graduate training around a particular historical site of public interest, Norkunas integrates theoretical and applied knowledge, offering graduate students a genuine experience in engaged scholarship. This experience affords an opportunity to reflect on the potential outcome of dissolving traditional distinctions among teaching, research, and service—precisely the sort of mechanical distinctions that make engagement less likely.

History admittedly is one of the most traditional disciplines in the academy. In recent times, it has been criticized for harboring many of the qualities that render academic knowledge troubling. Conventional historical scholarship is interested in the story of the past as written by the victors. The losers, left at the margins of society, are rarely invited to tell their story. Over the past few decades, oral historians such as

Norkunas and other scholars of collective memory have partially changed this state of affairs. Her research is an attempt to enrich the public record with the greatest possible diversity of voices.

Norkunas and her students are beginning to reinvent what it means to do history. They are restoring it to its local communities. Rather than imposing their expertise on audiences (what we earlier described as the knowledge transfer model of engagement), they listen and collaborate with local communities to tell jointly important, often untold, stories in new ways. The resulting citizen scholarship not only brings scholars and communities together, but it produces new and more vibrant local histories.

Each year, Norkunas's classes focus on a different historical site or museum. Students survey the site in the fall, asking critical questions about the discipline of history and its methodologies. Because sites often lack resources, their interpretations can be outdated. Students analyze the site's historic presentation in interdisciplinary teams and then develop project proposals to improve it. One of these proposals is then funded. During the spring, students learn interviewing, fieldwork, and documentation skills. In the end, what is produced are local histories—stories contributing importantly to academic knowledge of history and to the needs of communities endeavoring to preserve and bring alive the past.

The success of the ITP project lies in its groundbreaking approach: connecting with society, putting research to work, and making education more responsive and accountable. As universities and communities struggle to better collaborate, initiatives like ITP are blueprints for a new academic model and language of engagement. These citizen-scholars are part of a growing body of intellectuals whose research adds both to academic disciplines and to society. While perhaps differing from traditional conceptions of scholarship, these undertakings hold real and substantive value: they provide a useful way of thinking about engagement and entrepreneurship as part of the scholarly enterprise.

For example, the intellectual curiosity on which Norkunas's research is premised supersedes and thereby "smudges" conventional categories. As a citizen-scholar, she lets curiosity move her seamlessly between different disciplines; in addition, her work simultaneously speaks to different audiences inside and outside academe. By adopting a different rhetorical approach, Norkunas endeavors to circumvent the university's institutional obstacles preventing engagement.

This project, however, exposes an irony: While public research universities are searching for ways to implement engagement, they may be failing to recognize a powerful rhetorical model for obtaining it in their very midst. As previously noted, citizen-scholars do currently exist. Their research is forming a new way of being in the academy. In various departments across campuses, engaged scholars are finding ways to be intellectual entrepreneurs, to make disciplinary contributions that simultaneously speak to community needs. ITP, in particular, is a successful instance of engaged scholarship precisely because it is sustained by a unique discourse. ITP does not invoke a language that perpetuates the usual distinctions between theory and application (service). The ITP project operates on the assumption that historians are intellectual entrepreneurs and hence theoretical and applied knowledge are not at opposite ends of a continuum; they are necessarily concurrent.

Professors are not the only ones who thirst for a sense of ownership and personal/professional coherence. This is true for graduate and undergraduate students as well. They too feel torn between a multitude of different and often conflicting demands. It is not uncommon for undergraduates, in addition to their coursework, to be involved in several extracurricular activities, to work at least part-time, and to be enrolled in professional internships during their college tenure. Increasingly, students search for ways to integrate these different experiences, using them in pursuit of a more focused goal. For example, one student might seek a way to bring together her major in political communication, her internship at the state capitol, her volunteer work in a local nonprofit organization, and her office in a student organization. Where, she wonders, is the language and subsequent structure to express and validate the natural connections that exist among these endeavors?

One aspect of the IE consortium that addresses this concern (both in language and philosophy) is the Pre-Graduate School Internship. It connects talented undergraduate students with graduate student mentors and faculty supervisors in their proposed field of graduate study. The goal of the internship is to offer undergraduate students the opportunity to explore and reflect on those aspects of graduate education that make it different from the undergraduate experience (conducting research, writing for scholarly audiences, participating in seminars, serving as teaching and research assistants, becoming members of scholarly organizations and learned societies, etc.).

Logistically, the internship takes a variety of different forms; each undergraduate intern registers to receive course credit but the "contract" that he or she and the mentor/supervisor formulate together is almost entirely a result of collaboration. Some interns conduct research, writing essays similar to those published in scholarly journals or presented at academic conferences. Other interns are exposed more generally to the culture of graduate education, being encouraged to interrogate (much as an anthropologist would) the academic community they are observing. In other words, these internships are an exercise in entrepreneurship, operating with a high degree of flexibility and deliberately avoiding centralized control. The best way to serve the intern's interest has been and continues to be letting each own the experience, a hallmark of the IE philosophy of education.

This IE Pre-Graduate School Internship constitutes a major rhetorical and structural deviation from the typical academic experiences of undergraduate students attending large public research universities. Students at these institutions are intimately familiar with the process of meeting degree requirements. Successfully completing a major can be a matter of mindlessly checking items off a list of predetermined requirements. This illustrates a product—rather than process-oriented system of public higher education and its assumption that a certain number of semester credit hours translates into and entitles a student to a baccalaureate degree.

By contrast, the IE Pre-Graduate School Internship is a practice in invitational rhetoric. The tables are turned for students participating in this initiative. Accustomed to coming to their instructor for advice on how to complete an assignment, pre-grad interns must function as entrepreneurs. Instead of receiving explicit and ready-to-follow guidelines from their mentors/supervisors, interns are challenged to answer many of their own questions: To what purposes do you personally and professionally aspire? What *questions* must be answered to attain your objectives and what are the best strategies for seeking answers? As an entrepreneur, what is your personal, professional, and academic identity? The invitational rhetoric of this approach provides students with a sense of agency that most never have had before. The entrepreneurial language in which the internship is couched is an invitation for one to own their education. When ownership is a deliberate choice, undergraduate education becomes less of a product and more of a process. Putting all the pieces together—coursework, activities, memberships, and jobs—is a way of getting beyond a mechanistic view of education.

The IE Pre-Graduate School Internship is a powerful illustration of the new way of thinking and talking about engagement. Just as different rhetorical practices make it natural and possible for faculty to work as citizen-scholars, contributing to both their social and intellectual communities, so too is it possible for interns. Once interns escape the language of division and start to think more dynamically about what they want to achieve, transitions between different kinds of work, distinct audiences, and different forms of collaboration become much more natural. Interns are asked: What do you want to know and whom will you work with to find out? Who will benefit from your expertise and whose experience will inform your own work? Wrestling with these issues moves education beyond the transfer model of service-learning, setting the tone for the sort of two-way interaction that characterizes genuine engagement.

One of the most exciting outcomes of the entrepreneurial way of thinking associated with the Pre-Graduate School Internship is achievement of an unintended consequence, that is, greater diversity (Cherwitz, 2005a; Raspberry, 2005). As noted by the Kellogg Commission, the underrepresentation of minorities in graduate education is troubling. Why do minority students choose not to pursue graduate studies? Might it be because academic disciplines are perceived to be insular and out of touch with the real world? For those minority students who feel strongly compelled to give back to their community, to be engaged, graduate education in fields other than law, medicine, and business simply may not be attractive. The current model of education is thus likely to remain unappealing, despite the valiant efforts by public research universities to actively recruit minorities. Supplanting the apprenticeship-certification-entitlement metaphor and method of education with one that encourages discovery-ownership-accountability necessitates, as we have documented throughout this chapter, rethinking the university's rhetorical habits.

The language sustaining the IE internship offers some hope. When minority students are invited to view themselves as citizen-scholars, they are no longer "just students" working to complete degree requirements. Nor are they helpless outsiders needing paternalistic guidance, as is sometimes the rhetorical implication of recruitment and outreach policies that focus almost exclusively on statistical outcomes. When the language bifurcating research and theoretical inquiry from "the applied" is expunged, students become intellectual entrepreneurs, creating and owning their scholarly identities. The result is that they may begin to view their research as simultaneously contributing to disciplinary knowledge and serving the larger community to which they belong. It is not hard to envision how in this way of thinking engagement is integral rather than supplemental to students' educational choices and areas of expertise.

Intellectual Entrepreneurship: Implementing Engagement _____

These examples from Texas's Intellectual Entrepreneurship Consortium illustrate the possibility for change emerging from a shift in language. Faculty and students alike can be citizen-scholars whose work both relies on and validates a new discourse of engagement. So how, one might ask, does this rhetoric make a difference when it comes to the logistics of implementation? Recalling our earlier claim that logistical considerations cannot change philosophy and thus may be doomed to failure without a transformation of the academic culture of research universities, the answer should be apparent. No longer trapped in the binary of research versus engagement, or disciplinary versus interdisciplinary knowledge, or applied versus basic research, professors and administrators will be in a stronger position to discuss issues of academic geography, reward systems, and budgets.

The logic of our argument here is based on a seemingly self-evident fact: The most difficult logistical challenges confronted by universities (and for that matter all organizations) are those where implementation and compliance involve practices that are seen as less than endemic to the organization. Where there is not a natural and inherent tendency to behave in certain desired ways, administrators often struggle to come up with detailed plans to induce artificially such behavior. In the end such plans may fail if the desire is disingenuous (sometimes, it must be admitted, a university's talk of engagement is just that) and/or there is not a natural proclivity for the behavior in the first place. As we have argued, this is the current plight of efforts to achieve engaged public research universities.

If our contention is correct, that is, that the introduction of a new language (like IE) can reenvision academe, providing new ways of thinking about teaching, research, and service, then the logistics of implementation will emerge more readily. While it may be premature if not presumptuous to prescribe how each individual institution will/should implement engagement, we confidently assert that with a solid foundation in place, logistical issues will take care of themselves.

Consider the following example. Assuming a public research university begins to internalize the language of IE, one possible mechanism for implementing engagement that might materialize is a faculty "contract." By contract, we do not mean the sort of legal document used by unionized institutions. Instead, we are referring to a process by which faculty, in consultation with their departments and colleges, negotiate, and then over the course of time, renegotiate their work product.

In view of the IE philosophy, which involves vision, ownership, and accountability, the contract would not begin with a discussion of product. It would commence with professors articulating a scholarly vision and agenda, and explaining how that agenda comports with their larger personal and professional commitments. In addition, the burden would be on the faculty members to document how their scholarship aligns with the mission of the institution and academic unit to whom they report. The next step would be negotiation (or renegotiation) between faculty members and the relevant administration (e.g., department chair, departmental personnel committee, college dean, etc.) regarding the products and outcomes naturally occasioned by the stated scholarly vision and agenda. These work products, once agreed upon, would serve as the metrics for evaluating faculty performance. Thus faculty would be treated consistently and, at the same time, differently.

What this approach suggests is that while all professors at public research universities are expected to be scholars, each has a different scholarly program and therefore should be evaluated uniquely depending on the work products most befitting their chosen pursuits. The contract mechanism and the IE philosophy spawning it also emphasize that the professional vision and scholarship of professors constantly evolve, change, and mature over the course of an academic career. Flexibility in defining outcomes is necessary to ensure that faculty members are energized and innovative, and that they remain resilient and productive. From an IE perspective, the key is creating regular and formalized opportunities for professors to reflect on their professional vision, subsequently articulating it to their academic units and incorporating it into negotiations of acceptable performance.

The contract method of implementing engagement will not create two classes of faculty citizens. Flexibility does not provide a license for faculty members to deviate from the mission of the university and academic unit, to decide arbitrarily and unilaterally about what counts as work product, or to become lazy. Rather, it adds reflection followed by open deliberation to the process, allowing faculty greater ownership of their scholarship and an ability to participate in the definition of appropriate work products. In short, the IE rhetoric and philosophy enable the construction of innovative logistical methods—such as the contract—as a means for implementing the engaged university.

A related implication of our argument is that perhaps the time has come for public research universities to rethink their philosophy for hiring academic administrators. This suggestion applies particularly to those whose portfolios contain issues—such as engagement and inter-disciplinary learning—demanding thoughtful consideration of whether and how to change the academy's longstanding practices. In view of our claim that to implement a concept like engagement requires it to be seen as the academic coin of the realm and defined and disseminated by those with appropriate academic ethos, perhaps universities should select leaders based more on their academic credentials, intellectual creativity, and entrepreneurial skills than their penchant for being good day-to-day administrators. Such a personnel-based approach to change (which, of course, is a major IE theme) provides a better guarantee that concepts like engagement will be effectively implemented, instead of being seen as administrative efforts to impose what is not a natural part of the enterprise.

What we are recommending is that public research universities should jettison the current philosophy of "if you (administrators) build it we (faculty and students) will come." In its place should be put the philosophy "if we (faculty and students) are committed to and own engagement as a part of scholarship, we will be motivated to partner with you (administrators) to make it happen." This is precisely what was meant earlier in the chapter when we suggested that if one is equipped with a rhetoric that mainstreams engagement, logistical issues will take care of themselves—that they will be just that, matters of nuts and bolts rather than attempts to remove longstanding cultural and philosophical obstacles preventing engagement.

Conclusion

To trustees, central administrations, and university governance leaders, we make the following recommendation: Rather than starting and becoming preoccupied with practical ways to solve those problems preventing engagement, work with and empower faculty to rethink the concept of scholarship and define its many natural venues. As argued in this chapter, by devising a thoughtful rhetoric (one with intellectual substance and the requisite academic ethos), public research institutions will inevitably and more effectively serve the public good, thus becoming great sites of engaged learning in the 21st century. While IE is but one example, it underscores our larger claim regarding the centrality of rhetoric to cultural change within academic institutions. In particular, it illustrates how, armed with a concrete and effective rhetorical strategy for seamlessly integrating interdisciplinary research and engagement into the established practices of the academic enterprise, administrators will be able to tackle the logistical issues (e.g., academic

geography, rewards and incentives, evaluation and assessment, campus
planning, budgeting, etc.) necessary for implementing an engaged public
research university.

References

Bacon, F. (1957). *Of the advancement of learning* (5th ed., W. A. Wright,
Ed.). Oxford, England: Clarendon Press.

Boyer, E. L. (1990). *Scholarship reconsidered: Priorities of the professorate.*
Princeton NJ: Carnegie Foundation for the Advancement of Teaching.

Boyer, E. L. (1996, Spring). The scholarship of engagement. *Journal of
Public Outreach, 1*(1), 11–20.

Bryant, D. (1953). Rhetoric: Its functions and its scope. *Quarterly Journal
of Speech, 39*(4), 401–424.

Burke, K. (1965). *Permanence and change* (2nd ed.). Indianapolis, IN:
Bobbs-Merrill.

Cherwitz, R. A. (1980, February). The contributory effect of rhetorical
discourse: A study of language-in-use. *Quarterly Journal of Speech,
66*(1), 33–50.

Cherwitz, R. A. (2005a, January). Diversifying graduate education: The
promise of intellectual entrepreneurship. *Journal of Hispanic Higher
Education, 4*(1), 19–33.

Cherwitz, R. A. (2005b, July/August). Creating a culture of intellectual
entrepreneurship. *Academe, 91*(5), 69.

Cherwitz, R. A. (2005c, November/December). A new social compact
demands real change: Connecting the university to the community.
Change, 37(6), 48–49.

Cherwitz, R. A., & Hikins, J. W. (1986). *Communication and knowledge:
An investigation in rhetorical epistemology.* Columbia, SC: University
of South Carolina Press.

Cherwitz, R. A., & Sullivan, C. A. (2002, November/December).
Intellectual entrepreneurship: A vision for graduate education.
Change, 24(2), 22–27.

Cherwitz, R. A., Sullivan, C. A., & Stewart, T. (2002, Spring/Summer).
Intellectual entrepreneurship and outreach: Uniting expertise and
passion. *Journal of Higher Education Outreach and Engagement, 7*(3),
123–133.

Ehninger, D. (1972). *Contemporary rhetoric: A reader's coursebook.*
Glenview, IL: Scott, Foresman.

Gibbons, M. (2001). *Engagement as a core value for the university: A consultation document.* London, England: Association of Commonwealth Universities.

Gregorian, V. (2004, June 4). Colleges must reconstruct the unity of knowledge. *The Chronicle of Higher Education*, p. B12.

Hildebrand, D. (2005, Spring). Academics are intellectual entrepreneurs. *Peer Review, 7*(3), 30–31.

Kellogg Commission on the Future of State and Land-Grant Universities. (2001). *Returning to our roots: Executive summaries of the reports of the Kellogg Commission on the Future of State and Land-Grant Universities.* Washington, DC: National Association of State Universities and Land-Grant Colleges.

O'Meara, K., & Rice, R. E. (2005). *Faculty priorities reconsidered: Rewarding multiple forms of scholarship.* San Francisco, CA: Jossey-Bass.

Plato. (1995). *Symposium* (A. Nehamas & P. Woodruff, Trans.). Indianapolis, IN: Hackett.

Raspberry, W. (2005, May 31). Filling the racial gap in academia. *The Washington Post*, p. A17.

Scott, R. (1967, February). On viewing rhetoric as epistemic. *Central States Speech Journal, 18*, 9–17.

Stokes, D. E. (1997). *Pasteur's quadrant: Basic science and technological innovation.* Washington, DC: Brookings Institution Press.

12

Transforming the University of Minnesota Through Strategic Positioning

Robert H. Bruininks

> Sailing a ship across the Pacific is no different from organizing a college or university for performance improvement. In both instances, it is immensely helpful if we can come to some agreement on which way to aim the pointy end.
>
> —Daniel Seymour, *Once Upon a Campus*

In nearly every generation, university leaders have faced changing economic and demographic realities that have warranted the invocation of impending calamity or crisis. Some scholars have cheekily observed that a "crisis" crisis has afflicted higher education and its leadership for many years (Birnbaum & Shushok, 2001). That may be true, but regents, presidents, and other administrators—particularly at public research universities—today appear to be at crossroads. At a recent summit, higher education leaders characterized the current environment as walking a tightrope, shooting Class 5 river rapids, or sitting in a pot slowly heating to boil (Lederman, 2005). Whatever the metaphor, higher education leaders appear to recognize the need for substantial change, and that the easier road of denial is a sure path to decline. Yet as Kenneth Shaw (in press), former president of Syracuse University, points out, if anything "we generally underestimate the degree of change needed in our institutions."

The Need for Change at the University of Minnesota_____

The University of Minnesota's wake-up call came in 2003, when the state cut $185 million, or nearly 15%, of the university's two-year state appropriation. These reductions followed a long-term trend of appropriations that had declined as a percentage of the state budget, as a portion of personal income for higher education operations funded by the state, and as a percentage of the university's budget.[1]

The state cuts were unequivocally detrimental, but they did get the attention of the university community, and thus provided an opportunity to discuss the long-term funding environment in which we were operating. To paraphrase Samuel Johnson, a real cut in resources concentrates an institution's mind quite powerfully.

This chapter summarizes recent efforts to plan, position, and improve the university's quality and impact. Once this process was under way, necessity, enthusiasm, and determination combined to create a momentum that has moved us at a pace and with an efficiency often considered impossible at a university of our size. We are in the third year of this process of change, which we have titled "Transforming the U." We have a long way to go before we achieve our goal of improving the university and becoming one of the top three public research universities in the world, but we are solidly on our way. Although Burton Clark (2001) has wisely observed that "one hundred universities require 100 solutions" (p. 183), this chapter is written with the idea that our experience to date may be useful to other public research universities seeking to embark on a similar transformation.

Personal Investment_____

When I was inaugurated as the University of Minnesota's 15th president in February 2003, I had been at the university for 35 years in a variety of positions—executive vice president and provost, dean of the College of Education and Human Development, and professor of educational psychology. Public education had been my entry to professional success, and then the arena in which I was able to expand the contributions I could make to society. I brought to the presidency a strong personal and professional belief in the value and necessity of public education.

Even before the Kellogg Commission began to release its findings with *Taking Charge of Change* (1996), the University of Minnesota had undertaken many individual efforts designed to improve the student experience, strengthen public engagement, enhance interdisciplinary teaching and research, improve service and efficiency, and align the goals of units, colleges, and central administration for the best use of increasingly limited resources. University presidents since C. Peter Magrath (1974–1984) had foreseen the need for our large university to change in significant ways if we were to remain relevant and successful, and they had found support for these changes among faculty, staff, and students.

Important and successful as the many individual change efforts had been to the university's vitality and academic strength, they lacked the cohesion and broader strategic framework to address the fragmentation characteristic of most research universities, including the University of Minnesota. The competitive environment facing higher education by the time I was president made wholesale change essential. Our challenge was to redress the fragmentation while remaining a truly public university, concerned and involved with public issues at a time when public investment in public education was on the decline.

The Strategic Positioning Process and Kotter's Stages of Change

In addition to my primary interest in educational psychology, I have nurtured throughout my career an avid interest in process and planning. (I had even worked for Minnesota's state planning agency in the early 1970s.) In nearly 40 years of observing change and planning efforts, I have seen so many good ideas fall apart in the implementation phase that I knew we could only achieve the degree of change the university required if the entire community was invested in the process, and if we committed ourselves wholeheartedly to advancing at a pace that built on momentum. Ideas would have to be connected to an action strategy.

Our planning effort has been one of trial and error, in part because we built the process at the same time that it was being proposed. We have learned a great deal about effective change through our successes— and our failures. Only our commitment to success has kept us on track and advancing.

I am a strong believer in the need for a template for change, an articulated process that includes preparing for, undertaking, and implementing major changes in a complex organization. John Kotter's eight-stage process for creating successful major change is in close accord with the ideas I have developed as a longtime observer of change in a large university environment. His 1996 book *Leading Change* was a touchstone for a daylong retreat of the university's Executive Team, and for a second retreat attended by the more than 30 chairs and more than 300 members of our strategic positioning implementation task forces.

In our strategic positioning process, the first four of Kotter's stages of change overlap somewhat. At the same time that we were preparing for change, we were creating the guiding coalition. Similarly, we have been communicating the change vision the whole time we've been developing that vision and a strategy for realizing it. Here are Kotter's stages, with explication that reflects the work we have done at the University of Minnesota:

- *Preparing for change—establishing a sense of urgency.* Through a thorough examination of the current environment, university leaders called attention to future challenges and opportunities.
- *Creating the guiding coalition.* The board of regents directed the president, and the president designated to guide this process a group of respected leaders comprised of the university's Executive Team (vice presidents and chancellors), a working group of other university faculty and administrators, and two preliminary task forces—one addressing academic and the other addressing administrative priorities.
- *Developing a vision and a strategy.* The administration proposed a strategic positioning plan and, soon after, a series of specific recommendations for action and further study that incorporated the regents' and community's input.
- *Communicating the change vision.* The administration presented the vision to the university community and the public.
- *Empowering broad-based action.* The administration moved quickly to implement the specific recommendations adopted by the board through a system of task forces.
- *Generating short-term wins.* The momentum of early wins is an antidote to the cynicism that is a danger to any effort at widespread change. (This is the stage I believe the university is in today.)
- The last two stages await action in the future: *Consolidating gains and producing more change,* and *Anchoring new approaches in the culture* (Kotter, 1996, p. 21).

A Brief Description of Our Strategic Positioning Process _____

The University of Minnesota entered into its strategic positioning process because we recognized that to retain the status quo was, inevitably, to decline. With costs increasing, funding sources flattening out, demands for public accountability increasing, and the need for the best use of resources growing critical, the status quo would mean, in the foreseeable future, that we would not be able to remain competitive for top faculty and students, and our research profile would decline. On the administrative and service side of the equation, inferior facilities and service were no longer excused by the public, our students, or our faculty, and we risked losing public favor and a significant share of potential faculty, staff, and students on the basis of service alone. And academically, we were not taking advantage of our comparative strengths, which were scattered throughout the university.

Fragmentation significantly compromised the university's ability to meet the future. I spent a lot of time talking with the Board of Regents, the University Senate, and the Faculty Consultative Committee (a committee representing the faculty at large rather than individual campuses, institutes, colleges, schools, or departments of the university that serves as the consulting body to the president and as an executive committee of the Faculty Senate), and it was clear that disparate visions, priorities, and values made us vulnerable. The idea of belonging to an institution with clearly articulated values that would be better able to weather difficulties was widely appealing.

There was never any question in my mind that the process would involve faculty, staff, and students as well as central administration. Values cannot be mandated top down; they have to be embraced by everyone involved, and that happens most effectively when those values are articulated and created by those who must ultimately act in accordance with them.

Stages of the University of Minnesota's Strategic Positioning Process _____

Stage One: Preparing for Change and Establishing a Sense of Urgency

Preparing for change. The University of Minnesota is the state's only major research university as well as its primary land-grant institution. It is a multicampus university with four established campuses (Twin

Cities, Duluth, Morris, Crookston), and a developing campus in Rochester. Senior leaders of the Twin Cities campus double as system leaders, eliminating the need for a separate system office (the system-wide president serves as chancellor of the Twin Cities campus). The university also has 6 agricultural experiment stations, a forestry center, 18 regional extension offices, and extension personnel in counties throughout the state. The university's public service programs (e.g., extension service; clinics in medicine, dentistry, and veterinary medicine; and outreach to K–12 education) touch several million people annually.

The University of Minnesota–Twin Cities is the university's largest campus and the nation's second-largest university campus as measured by enrollment. It enrolls 78% or 51,175 students of the institution's 65,489 total students, including a substantial number of graduate and professional students. Across the campuses, 62% of registered students are undergraduates, 23% are graduate students, 6% are professional students, and 10% are nondegree-seeking students.

Organizational advantages held by the University of Minnesota as it plunged into a major strategic positioning process included good relations between the different branches of the university's shared governance system, with a Board of Regents focused squarely on setting policy directions rather than day-to-day operations of the institution; an incentive-based budget model that rewards revenue generation and cost savings at the local level, while paying for common goods at the system/central level; a comprehensive institutional accountability report that tracks dozens of indicators of quality; and the ability to set tuition through autonomy granted by the Minnesota constitution. I believe that the university also enjoys high regard and support among policymakers, civic leaders, and citizens in Minnesota.

My predecessor, Mark Yudof, laid a foundation for change by implementing a formal process to encourage individual units to align their priorities with those of the larger university. This "compact process" entails a yearly review and strategic agreement between central administration and units, and provides incentives such as investment to encourage units to pursue broader university goals.

The university had engaged in a precursor process to "Transforming the U" when we reorganized our extension service. Through this reorganization, the university went from a traditional county-based extension model with more than 90 offices across the state to 18 regional centers with extension educators co-located by field of expertise. The reorganization was prompted by the changing needs of Minnesota's communities, the outlook for funding from federal, state, and county sources, new information technologies that allowed new avenues of public access to the university, and the desire to better connect extension services to the university's unique advantages—that is, its research and advanced knowledge. Despite some controversy surrounding this decision, the reorganization was highly successful, and it has come to be seen as a demonstration of the university's commitment to reform and change while remaining true to its historical legacy of connecting its resources to Minnesota's communities.

Finally, we had the advantage of my many years as a member of the university community, and my having served as executive vice president and provost under President Yudof. The continuity with the Yudof administration, which undertook many of the Kellogg Commission–aligned reforms, provided an important foundation for change, and the relationships and mutual trust I developed over my long tenure at Minnesota were significant assets in managing change. Maintaining consistent contact and communication, especially within units and areas most affected by proposed changes, allowed information to flow back to the central administration, which also allowed us to address concerns before they became major issues. Most other senior academic and administrative officers also had long-term leadership responsibilities at the university.

Establishing a sense of urgency. I date the formal beginning of the university's process of change as summer 2004, when the university's Board of Regents held a retreat with senior leaders of the administration. The university had many recent successes, including record enrollments of students with increasingly impressive academic credentials, a swelling undergraduate applicant pool, more than a billion dollars in capital improvements in the previous decade, a highly successful multiyear fundraising campaign that had generated $1.67 billion in gifts and pledges, and annual sponsored research receipts that consistently topped $525 million. Moreover, the Twin Cities campus regularly ranked in the top three to seven public research universities in the United States on selected measures of productivity, according to TheCenter at the University of Florida (Lombardi, Capaldi, Mirka, & Abbey, 2005; Lombardi, Capaldi, Reeves, & Gater, 2004; Lombardi, Craig, Capaldi, & Gater, 2000, 2002; Lombardi, Craig, Capaldi, Gater, & Mendonça, 2001; Lombardi et al., 2003).

Despite these successes, there was a palpable sense of unease and anxiety about the future at the regents' retreat. Although the troubling state funding trends for the university mirrored those found across the country, this was a relatively new phenomenon for Minnesota, where state support for higher education had traditionally been strong. Minnesota's support for higher education had declined from 6th in the nation in 1978, as measured by tax effort by income, to 26th in 2002 (Peterson & Pfutzenreuter, 2004). Although in 2005 the state restored approximately half the cuts it made to the university in 2003 (ignoring inflationary impact), the prospects for a return to reasonable funding look bleak. The university also faces federal funding concerns similar to those detailed in other chapters.

Students are paying more toward their education, and both tuition and external research dollars will soon eclipse state support as a portion of the university's budget. Although Minnesota's undergraduate financial aid program remains among the most generous in the country, federal funding for student aid programs has failed to keep pace with the rising cost of higher education.

Of equal importance to economic factors are changing demographics. In important ways, Minnesota's population mirrors that of the nation. The population in Minnesota and its adjoining states is aging and becoming more diverse, and the pool of high school age students is expected to level off and decline over the next decade. Within this smaller regional student pool, the university expects to serve an increasing number of students of color, first-generation college students, and students for whom English is a second language (Zetterberg, 2004). Although our state is traditionally known for its educated population, the achievement gap between minority and nonminority students in Minnesota is among the worst in the nation (Education Trust, 2005). Even leaving aside moral considerations, this is an urgent practical problem for higher education institutions, which rely on the ability to build on students' previous academic success. (I am tremendously proud that the university has not been content to lament these challenges to education, but has instead recommitted to addressing the "upstream" challenges faced by Minnesota's schools and young people.)

Finally, our costs (like those of our peer institutions) have grown significantly above the rate of inflation for many years. We face increasing competition—especially from private universities—for top scholars. Costs for buildings, laboratories, technology, and other elements of maintaining a research university are also increasingly expensive; for example, library costs at the University of Minnesota have risen 15% annually in recent years. Utility and energy costs—especially heating costs in a cold-weather state like Minnesota—also continue to escalate. And, as is the case for most employers in our country today, employee health care costs continue to outstrip inflation.

The university was involved with and has been able to leverage outside assessments of our institution and Minnesota's higher education resources. The Commission on Excellence, which was created by the legislature in 2001, reviewed the university's scope and mission and reported that the achievement of excellence would require extraordinary focus and priority setting, greater efficiency, and more aggressive reallocation of internal resources. In 2004, Governor Tim Pawlenty called on the Citizens League, a nonpartisan policy-oriented nonprofit organization, to undertake a study of the state's overall higher education environment. The league's study group had recommendations for both secondary and higher education leaders, including increased academic expectations for high school students and continued enhancement by the university of its role as a public research university.

By leveraging these outside assessments, consistently making the case for the university's importance, and outlining the challenges to the university's current resources and its academic and financial future, the administration was able to establish a sense of urgency. This was no manufactured crisis, but a systematic and sustained effort to highlight the university's current state and its most likely future if current trends continued.

Against this backdrop, the university's Board of Regents and senior administrators resolved that the institution, while healthy, would need to make serious adjustments to serve the state and to maintain academic quality. This resolve ultimately grew into an ambitious plan to reposition the University of Minnesota that is touching every corner of our system.

What I believe distinguishes the University of Minnesota's strategic positioning process is its breadth and its implementation. Rather than face the future with piecemeal, one-at-a-time solutions, "Transforming the U" is a process that encompasses nearly every important aspect of the university's programs and operations. And, two years after the Board of Regents 2004 retreat, our attempt to align our academic and administrative enterprises—to find, in Seymour's (1995) words, some agreement on where to aim the pointy end—has already begun to be implemented.

Stage Two: Creating the Guiding Coalition

Creating internal support. A critical element of our strategic positioning process has been the engagement of the university's Board of Regents and the development of strong internal leadership for the effort. Rather than present a strategic positioning plan to the Board of Regents as a fait accompli, the administration designed the process with the sanction of and according to the board's directions. The internal support we nurtured in Stage One grew naturally into a guiding coalition that has proven extraordinarily effective and efficient.

Leading up to the summer of 2004, the university's Board of Regents had for two years been deeply engaged in discussions about budget challenges, trends in the state's demography and economy, and trends in higher education affecting the University of Minnesota such as academic priorities, costs, and revenue issues.

These discussions were the key to the board buying in to the need for a strategic positioning process and, following recommendations from the administration, it essentially chartered the process. When the board created its work plan for the 2004–2005 academic year, it used the strategic positioning process as its primary organizing idea.

The administration had also engaged for several years in wide-ranging discussions with the Faculty Consultative Committee about the intellectual future of the university, during which the need for a more focused approach to the university's future arose repeatedly. Similar discussions were also undertaken between the administration and the university's employee groups and student representative organizations. Some of the best and most memorable conversations about the university, its present and its future, took place with shift employees in University Services held in the early morning and late evening hours.

The regents, the university's Executive Team, and the provost's university-wide working group described in the next section constituted a guiding coalition that enabled the university to move quickly to create a vision and a strategy for institutional change.

Engaging external constituencies. Between 2002 and 2004, the university administration made extensive appearances in the broader Minnesota community, including at chambers of commerce and Rotary clubs across the state, media opportunities, and events as specialized as FarmFest, the Rural Summit, and the Swedish Dining Society. These kinds of visits are a staple of college presidents everywhere, and their primary purpose during this period was to introduce me, the new president of the university, to the state. But I also used them to highlight the university's role as the state's only research university, with the clear message that the viability of this special type of institution depends on remaining competitive for talent and for funding.

Senior administrators and I maintained close ties with and provided regular updates on the university's planning process to the University of Minnesota Foundation and the Minnesota Medical Foundation, our two main fundraising organizations, and to the University of

Minnesota Alumni Association. The members, boards, and executive leadership of these organizations in turn communicated the need for change at the university to alumni, elected officials, the media, and the general public.

As a new president, I spent considerable time engaging the business community, even joining, by invitation, the board of the Minnesota Business Partnership, a group of CEOs of the state's largest companies. The university's connection to the regional business community had improved significantly under Mark Yudof, but a sense of distance and disengagement from the university still remained among many CEOs. I sought to strengthen relations with business leaders not only to facilitate new collaborations and better commercialization of technology, but also to help establish credibility with a new Republican governor and a Republican majority in the Minnesota House of Representatives, leaders for whom the business community was a particularly influential constituency.

Stage Three: Developing a Vision and Strategy

Developing a vision. In September 2004, after the administration presented the Board of Regents with our template for how we would engage the board and other constituencies in creating the strategic plan, Tom Sullivan, senior vice president for academic affairs and provost, gathered a working group of university leaders and support staff from throughout the university that developed statements of the mission, vision, values, framing principles, goals, culture, and broad strategies, along with an environmental scan, that formed the basis for discussions with the board about the next stages of the strategic positioning process.

Through these highly collaborative discussions between the board and the university's faculty and staff leaders, a framework of values and planning principles for developing goals, reviewing programs, and setting priorities was reviewed, revised, and affirmed, including the reaffirmation of the mission statement the board had adopted in 1994. This was a critical step in achieving early consensus on the values and criteria that would set priorities and evaluate whether programs or services should be expanded, maintained at current levels, reduced, or eliminated. These criteria included centrality to mission; quality, productivity, and impact; uniqueness and comparative advantage; enhancement of academic synergies; demand and resources; efficiency and effectiveness; and development and leveraging of resources (University of Minnesota, 2005c). I credit this early consensus around mission, values, and operating assumptions for our ability to reach Kotter's fifth stage. When such critical issues are introduced too late, a strong tendency to move prematurely to tactical issues will undermine the success of the process.

Another important discussion during this period included a dialogue on the university's long-term budget strategy, led by Richard Pfutzenreuter, vice president and chief financial officer, and me, with the goal of developing a flexible and adaptable model to help the board and university leaders assess alternative courses of action as they guide the institution toward its strategic objectives.

At the regents meeting held in February 2005, Provost Sullivan and I presented *Advancing the Public Good* (University of Minnesota, 2005d), a strategic positioning plan drafted by the provost's working group and incorporating the directions articulated by the Board of Regents throughout fall 2004. In the plan, we named our aspiration to become one of the top three public research universities in the world. That boldness was critical in gaining attention and commitment to the plan, and it is worth noting that this goal grew directly out of the consultative process. We had initially proposed the less specific goal of becoming "one of the best public universities," but university constituencies were clear that the specific, audacious goal was the challenge they wanted to meet.

Among the plan's most important contributions were the five action strategies it detailed. These have been key to moving the university from good ideas to implementation:

- Recruit, educate, retain, and graduate outstanding students.
- Recruit, mentor, and retain outstanding faculty and staff.
- Promote an effective organizational culture that is committed to excellence and responsive to change.
- Enhance and effectively utilize our resources and infrastructure.
- Communicate clearly and credibly with all our constituencies and practice engagement responsive to the public good. (University of Minnesota, 2005d, pp. 23–27)

Developing a strategy. Anticipating the need to build on this plan if it were approved, Provost Sullivan and I had previously named two university-wide task forces, one academic and one administrative, to develop recommendations in support of the vision and strategies articulated in the report. The goal of these initial task forces was to look closely at the design and priorities of the university, how we organized and supported programs, and what issues we would likely face in the future. Their charge reflected our strong belief that the strategic positioning process had to be comprehensive and systemic in nature, addressing the academic mission of the university as well as its service and administrative systems. It also reflected our conviction that the widest possible community participation was essential to ensure the success of the strategic positioning process.

On March 30, 2005, these two initial task forces submitted their recommendations for the next steps of strategic positioning. The Academic Strategic Planning Task Force submitted a 59-page report that included 31 recommendations in four key areas—undergraduate admissions, enrichment, and support; faculty culture; coordinate campuses; and design of the university—including the first college consolidations in living memory on the Twin Cities campus (University of Minnesota, 2005a). The Administrative Strategic Planning Task Force made seven broad recommendations to improve the university's service and administrative culture and operations (University of Minnesota, 2005b).

Following extensive consultation with all university constituencies, the action report I submitted for the board's review in May contained 39 recommendations in three broad categories: recommendations for integrating colleges, which needed the board's specific approval; endorsed academic recommendations; and endorsed administrative recommendations, including the administration's commitment to save approximately $20 million from these recommendations and reallocate it to more urgent academic priorities over a three-year period. The report, called *Transforming the University* (Bruininks, 2005), tied these 39 recommendations together through the vision of transforming the university into one of the top three public research universities in the world by supporting our key strengths and comparative advantages.

Taken as a whole, the recommendations clearly and strongly articulated our direction for the future, addressing all aspects of the university, both academic and administrative. The strategic positioning plan and the subsequent recommendations communicated a clear identity for the university and our role in the state, and reflected the importance of a vital and vigorous research university to a regional economy. They reflected and encouraged ownership by all university constituencies, built on the pride developed during the Yudof administration, and reiterated the urgency for change to keep the university from being shut out of a vital, viable future. The more than three dozen recommendations flowed directly from the vision the board and the university community helped to create, and resulted in the subsequent widespread acceptance of major changes to the university's direction, structure, and management. Further, the action-oriented process to date signaled a serious commitment to enacting the recommendations and improving the university's programs and operations.

Stage Four: Communicating the Change Vision

Communicating the vision of change. The university's vision was created through an iterative process that engaged both the internal and external communities of the university. From the very beginning, the administration took great care to ensure that the process was highly interactive and rich in communication so that, in effect, we began communicating the vision at the same time that it was being shaped.

Throughout our process, the administration spent considerable time and effort garnering the input of the internal University of Minnesota community. Our administration regularly updated and requested input from the university community, held town hall meetings, and solicited comments regarding the draft/working strategic positioning documents via a carefully maintained strategic positioning web site. We also reported on the process frequently to the University Senate and the Faculty Consultative Committee.

In April 2005, after the two initial task forces had given me their recommendations, the administration consulted with the university's governance and advisory groups (14 in all), student groups (5 in all), and campus and collegiate groups that would be affected if the strategic positioning recommendations were implemented (9 in all). I attended and led all of these meetings along with other academic officers.

Naturally, the most significant pockets of resistance were in the colleges the plan proposed to consolidate, particularly the smaller colleges that were perceived as being "absorbed" by larger ones. For me, it was important to engage affected college faculty and students directly to explain the reasoning behind the task forces' recommendations and to offer a vision for the university in the future that still overlapped with those of faculty, staff, and students in these colleges. I tried to avoid the pitfall described by veteran college leader Kenneth Shaw (in press), that "many change efforts fail because leaders neglect the affect that goes with major change. They interpret denial as institutional stupidity and anger as directed to them personally."

The discussion about change pervaded our joint governance structure. The University Senate, over which I usually preside, conducted an animated two-hour debate in which the faculty asked me to sit down and listen (a rare event at the University of Minnesota!) as they conducted this debate. This was one of the most vigorous, passionate, considered, and challenging discussions about the future of the University of Minnesota that I had ever experienced. Just the same, when in late April the University Senate voted 120–3 in support of the strategic plan and positioning process with its extensive recommendations for reform, I was surprised by the unprecedented near-unanimity of the vote. This widely shared feeling of astonishment was best articulated by David Metzen, then chair of the Board of Regents, who said he doubted the University Senate would vote to support a 25% increase in its own salary by a vote of 120–3! Many factors contributed to the faculty's overwhelming support of the strategic positioning process and plan, but I believe the most important of these was the recognition that the faculty and departments on their own could not adequately respond to the societal and demographic changes that are affecting every discipline at every university.

Throughout the first year of the strategic positioning process, I and other senior university administrators actively sought public venues in which to discuss the process and its evolving goals, principles, and action strategies. These included significant and regular media interviews, meetings with civic, business, and community groups, and numerous town hall meetings, as well as over the web through the strategic positioning web site. We also took special care to continue to engage the governing boards of the university's associated organizations—the University of Minnesota Alumni Association, the University of Minnesota Foundation, and the Minnesota Medical Foundation—in every phase of the planning process.

The public release of the two initial task forces' recommendations (on March 30, 2005) took place at a news briefing on campus that was well covered by the state's major media outlets, and this event was emblematic of the very public consultation process that followed. I was interviewed more than 20 times regarding the strategic positioning process and the recommendations that were on the table during April and May.

By intention, the strategic planning and positioning process has been highly visible, with a rich and varied communications strategy designed to engage both internal and external constituencies. Its agenda would not have been accepted within or outside the university community without these efforts to publicize our work. In hindsight, although I think we performed admirably, if we had it to do again I would commit even more time and resources to visibility and communications, especially in efforts to engage senior officers, professors, staff, and students of the most affected units.

Stage Five: Empowering Broad-Based Action

Implementation. At the June 2005 regents meeting, the board voted 11–1 in favor of the action plan I submitted to them in May, approving the academic recommendations that required formal board action and endorsing the remaining academic and administrative recommendations.

To maintain momentum and because it was important to me that the strategic planning and positioning process have an accompanying review and action strategy, our administration moved immediately to a comprehensive implementation strategy that we brought to the board at its retreat in summer 2005 and its September 2005 meeting. I believe that the success of the planning and positioning process depended on a carefully developed, swiftly enacted, and publicly accountable implementation strategy.

Our implementation structure consisted of 34 task forces involving more than 300 people, whose work began with a retreat for the task force chairs and members held in mid-September 2005. The task forces are organized into four separate categories (although some tasks are in more than one category): Academic Task Forces (Twin Cities focused); System-Wide Task Forces; Academic Health Center Task Forces; and Administrative Service and Productivity Task Forces.

The 34 task forces were created to either implement the changes recommended to and approved by the regents or to make more preliminary studies of other topics addressed in the recommendations. They were comprised of faculty, students, staff, alumni, and members of the public, and overseen by a Strategic Positioning Executive Team of eight senior university administrators. In each of the four categories listed above, the chairs of each task force, outside faculty and student representatives, and the overseeing senior administrator also met periodically as teams to coordinate their work. A Resource Alignment Team drawn from staff throughout the university supported the task forces and ensured the alignment of implementation across different areas.

The large number of people involved reflects both the high level of interest in the task force issues and the overall strategic positioning process. I felt that the broad sweep of the change effort necessitated equally broad involvement in its implementation and the inclusion of faculty, staff, and students most affected by the strategic positioning recommendations. Keeping task forces on track and coordinated required significant amounts of staff time from the president's office and the offices of members of the Executive Team. In addition, several staff members were hired and/or reassigned to design and organize this process and to staff task forces and coordinating committees.

Approved and endorsed recommendations. Of the 34 task forces, 4 were appointed to design, plan, and implement the consolidation of several Twin Cities campus colleges effective July 1, 2006:

• Departments from the College of Human Ecology were integrated with the College of Architecture and Landscape Architecture to create a new College of Design.
• The College of Education and Human Development and General College were combined to create a new, expanded College of Education and Human Development dedicated to education, training, and human development across the lifespan. (This decision regarding General College, the college that had served as a point of entry to the university for underprepared and nontraditional students, received the most attention from the broader community.)
• The College of Natural Resources was integrated with the College of Agricultural, Food, and Environmental Sciences to create the College of Food, Agricultural, and Natural Resource Sciences, a new, expanded college focused broadly on food systems, environmental science, policy, and renewable resources and with stronger relationships with the School of Public Health and the Medical School.

Examples of academic task force issues include undergraduate and graduate student reform. The Twin Cities campus is building on improvements made over the last decade to the student experience and expanding them to cover graduate students, thereby continuing on a path suggested by the Kellogg Commission. One task force considered the design, planning, and implementation of an improved Twin Cities campus honors program to offer a more coherent honors experience to students in all colleges. Another task force designed and planned the implementation of expanded and strengthened student support services, including expanded one-stop service centers; improved coordination of existing services, including those in academic programs; and strategies to improve student outcomes and retention and graduation rates. A third Twin Cities task force designed and planned the implementation of a strengthened writing strategy. Two task forces worked to create a strategic plan for identifying, recruiting, retaining, mentoring, advising, and graduating world-class graduate and professional students in a timely way, and to plan for world-class graduate programs and education with particular emphasis on emerging and evolving disciplines. Other academic task forces included Faculty Culture; Future Design of the University of Minnesota–Twin Cities; Research; Diversity; PreK–12 Education; International University; Coordinate Campuses; and Academic Health Center.

Examples of administrative task forces are a task force that addressed reducing administrative duplication by enabling the University of Minnesota's campuses, colleges, departments, and units to operate more effectively and efficiently as a single enterprise; and a Metrics and Measures task force, because I believe that great organizations measure what they value. Other administrative task forces included Culture; Administrative Structure; Best Practice Management Tools; Customer Service; Human Resources; and Resource Optimization. These task forces were created to help us clarify our aspirations and assess our progress toward achieving them.

Stage Six: Generating Short-Term Wins

Our most experienced staff and professors have seen ambitious plans for change come and go; early wins provide tangible proof that *this* effort will be different.

When students returned to the Twin Cities campus in fall 2006, we were able to share signs of progress with the entire university community. Enrollment in our newly combined colleges indicated student interest that exceeded our expectations in areas ranging from design to family social science to environmental sciences, policy, and management. Planning was well under way for a new system-wide Institute on the Environment that will allow greater interdisciplinary work on complex challenges such as global warming and creating sustainable energy sources. We also welcomed new Twin Cities faculty with an improved, multiday orientation that facilitated a smoother introduction to the day-to-day administrative operations of the university, such as how to obtain an email account or purchase equipment; the orientation also allowed us to better introduce the idea of broader university citizenship to these new members of our community. These and other early wins helped maintain interest in strategic positioning, and signaled that the process—its aspirations and its strategies—would continue to be front and center at the university.

Later Stages of Change: Initial Considerations

Today, I would place the university's strategic positioning process at Kotter's sixth stage. Here are some preliminary thoughts about the remaining two stages:

Stage Seven: Consolidating Gains and Producing More Change

I believe that the answer to one of the questions posed by Joe Burke, the editor of this book—namely, How can large public universities pursue common goals?—lies partly in the design of the institution and partly in the less tangible change of attitude. Although we will remain quite decentralized compared to other large organizations, and many members of our community will remain focused on their disciplines rather than the institution, our intention is to "centralize" an outlook, attitude, or philosophy that supports reform and the continued pursuit of excellence. This is a considerable challenge, but we are banking on meeting it.

Stage Eight: Anchoring New Approaches in the Culture

We are on our way to greater success, but we still have a long way to go. Yet no community can sustain an unlimited focus on transformation—the added planning and implementing structure requires too much effort for that at all levels, particularly from middle and senior leadership. One important measure of our success will be the extent to which "Transforming the U" becomes a part of the cultural fabric of the university.

Anticipating this need to integrate change into the culture of our institution, the Office of Service and Continuous Improvement was created in 2003 with the idea that many avenues for improved productivity do not impinge on the university's mission or values, and that every dollar saved in administrative costs is another freed up for investment in academic excellence. Equally important to the idea of continuous improvement is a focus on improved service—from college to student, from central administration to college, from system to campus, and so on.

More generally, by focusing on the development of a culture of continuous improvement, we articulate our recognition that change must be an ongoing process. The University of Minnesota will never reach a time when it does not have to minimize administrative costs in order to invest more of its resources directly in academic strengths. The excitement of the university's process of strategic positioning is also one of its most daunting challenges: We have entered an era of change. There is no turning back.

Lessons Learned

Today the University of Minnesota is still in the midst of transformational change, and there are many challenges ahead: in the structure and operations of our institution and the culture that pervades it. That said, our experience does suggest some lessons for other leaders and institutions looking to embark on a similar process.

   1) Overprepare and overemphasize the case for change, both internally and externally.

Leaders in institutions of all kinds tend to underestimate how often we must repeat ourselves to be heard. In academia, in particular, we are used to making our point once or twice in a conference or a paper and assume that we've been heard and understood by our well-attuned and highly educated colleagues. What I have found is that the preparatory steps to an effective change process bear more resemblance to a political campaign than an academic exchange. Leaders must repeat the case for change many times, and often to the same audiences.

   2) Engage the governance structure throughout the process—not just at the beginning and end of the process.

By incorporating the values and criteria that the people within the internal and board governance structures articulate early on and through regular progress reports and opportunities for input, leaders can more easily make the case later for what may prove to be controversial actions.

   3) Set high aspirations and develop a plan of action and strategy for implementation.

The creation of the process should involve not just planning but clear action strategies that can be adapted to further influence the development of a culture. In this way, one can avoid the pitfall that Shaw (in press) describes as "having a thousand ideas and no focus or follow-through." At the University of Minnesota, our process involved the establishment of values, criteria, and action strategies.

   The strategic positioning report, *Advancing the Public Good* (University of Minnesota, 2005d), formulated by respected university leaders—faculty as well as administrative—and approved by the board, set the policy directions and created the foundation for the detailed actions described in *Transforming the University*, which came before the board two months later (Bruininks, 2005). Our process involved linking the broad strategic plan and directions to a comprehensive plan recommending specific actions and reform initiatives. To heed Shaw's warning, we took on a great many ideas, but also a systematic process to study and enact them.

4) Spend political capital in order to make significant change.

If you've established trust and rapport with different constituencies within and outside the institution you lead, you have to be prepared to rely on these intangibles in order to bring the conflicted or ambivalent along with you. Our administration had to put everything on the line at several points during this process. It was an uneasy position, but it was absolutely necessary to keep our broad aims from falling prey to individual details or disputes. It is equally true that you cannot take resistance or pushback personally; all change is accompanied by conflict. It is a leader's duty to engage people and find resolution, but it is also a leader's obligation to remain true to an aspirational vision and to avoid being unnecessarily waylaid, delayed, or paralyzed by opposition and differing views.

5) Appoint strong, hands-on leadership to drive the process.

Although there was vigorous debate and discussion, the board, administrative Executive Team, faculty leaders, and the other governance groups noted earlier gave sustained attention to this process and its success. A corollary derives from this time effort. Leaders and staff will expend a great deal of time and energy on the change process, and these efforts will be in addition to what are usually already quite heavy workloads. The hiring of additional staff or reallocation of current human resources may be necessary to manage the increased workload.

6) Develop a comprehensive communication strategy and a clearly articulated scope of change.

An oft-heard refrain throughout this process was that everything was on the table: that the university would be looking at all aspects of its work—from aspirations to operations. As an administration, we have considered it essential to communicate the scope of change as well as the progress of the strategic positioning process to our internal community, our governing board, and our stakeholders in the community (see Figure 12.1). Yet capturing the attention of busy faculty, staff, and students—not to mention members of the broader public—is a continuing challenge.

7) Seek alignment between academic directions and administrative and financial strategies.

It may be true that research universities such as the University of Minnesota will always encounter costs that increase above "normal" rates of inflation, but it is also true that institutions like ours have been

Figure 12.1
Timeline

Summer 2002–2004	University of Minnesota (U) Board of Regents (BOR) engaged in in-depth discussions about the higher education landscape and the future of the U
Summer 2002–2004	Extensive community visits by new U President Bruininks
Fall 2002–2003	Reorganization of U Extension Service
February 2003	President Bruininks formally inaugurated
Spring 2003	State cuts U's two-year appropriation by nearly 15%
Summer 2004	BOR retreat; BOR endorses need for strategic plan
August 2004	Provost Sullivan emails university community about strategic positioning: "Building Coherence Through a Coherent Vision"
September 2004	Administration presents BOR with template for creating strategic plan
October 2004	BOR meeting; reaffirm mission statement adopted by BOR in 1994
	Email from Provost Sullivan to faculty, staff, and students with strategic positioning update and invitation to participate
November 2004	BOR meeting; testimony from Minnesota state demographer and state economist outlining possibilities for state's demographic and economic future
	Emails from Provost Sullivan inviting university community to town hall meetings and to faculty requesting comments
	Three strategic positioning town hall forums
December 2004	BOR meeting; discussion about U's long-term budget strategy
	Update email from Provost Sullivan to faculty, staff, and students
January 2005	Provost-led committee presents president with draft of *Advancing the Public Good*, the strategic positioning plan
	Anticipating BOR approval of directions articulated in *Advancing the Public Good*, provost and president appoint two U-wide task forces to develop recommendations regarding the vision and strategies articulated in the report
	Update email from Provost Sullivan inviting comments on the draft strategic positioning report posted on the new strategic positioning web site
February 2005	BOR meeting; *Advancing the Public Good* presented to the BOR
	Update email from Provost Sullivan to faculty, staff, and students
	Two strategic positioning open forums held
March 2005	BOR meeting; BOR unanimously approves *Advancing the Public Good* and its call to action
	Task forces named in January commence their work
	Update email from President Bruininks to faculty, staff, and students

March 30, 2005	Academic and administrative task forces deliver their reports, including 39 recommendations for action, to the president
April 2005	Administration consults with 14 governance and advisory groups, 5 student groups, 9 campus and college groups, and 3 U-associated organizations
	Outreach to public through newspapers, radio, and television
May 2005	BOR meeting; president presents *Transforming the University*, the strategic planning action recommendations, to BOR
June 2005	BOR meeting; BOR votes 11–1 in favor of *Transforming the University*
Summer 2005	BOR retreat; administration brings comprehensive implementation strategy to BOR
	Implementation structure enacted, creating 34 task forces involving more than 300 people
September 2005	Retreat for task force chairs and members begins implementation phase
Fall 2005	Task forces meet regularly and solicit input from faculty, staff, students, alumni, and public via surveys, open meetings, and web site to develop implementation plans
	BOR considers possible future sources of new revenue
December 2005	Task force reports due and submitted from 11 of the 34 task forces; reports posted on the Transforming the U web site for public comment period
February 2006	Task force reports due and submitted from 7 of the 34 task forces; reports posted on the Transforming the U web site for public comment period
March 2006	Task force reports due and submitted from 16 of the 34 task forces; reports posted on the Transforming the U web site for public comment period
July 2006	Newly consolidated College of Food, Agricultural, and Natural Resource Sciences, College of Design, and College of Education and Human Development launched
August 2006	Administration presents Strategic Positioning progress report to BOR
	Final combined recommendations of seven administrative task forces are issued
October 2006	Administration presents comprehensive program report to BOR

far too complacent in addressing cost issues; we have been too slow to foster an academic culture that emphasizes the best use of resources and continuous improvement. I felt strongly that our scope of change had to include both the academic and administrative aspects of the university's work, and the detailed recommendations accepted by the regents in June 2005 reflect these wide-ranging ideas for transformation.

8) *Assess successes and limitations throughout the process.*

We could have done a better job early on in engaging students and some selected academic leaders in the change process; today there are student representatives helping to oversee the implementation teams in all aspects of the strategic planning process. On another note, one part of our process that surprised me—a limitation—was the uneven reaction from middle tiers of academic leadership. This has required a redoubled effort to bring these leaders along in the implementation phase of this process, which might have been avoided by earlier and more intensive engagement.

Conclusion

The implementation of the university's strategic plan is moving quickly, but its pace matches the energy and excitement it is breathing into both our academic and administrative enterprises. The changes we are already making and our holistic approach to the challenges we face now and in the future will, I believe, position us well to leverage the strengths and comparative advantage of the university. Our goal—to become one of the top three public research universities within a decade, with similar aspirations for our coordinate campuses according to their strengths and comparative advantages—was adopted in the midst of "moving goalposts," the rapidly changing higher education environment that demands the university make progress in academic quality in order to retain its standing relative to other universities. From all indications, the alternative would be a slow decline in quality, one that, instead of encouraging synergies between departments and colleges, would exacerbate what one of my colleagues has playfully called "antergism," in which an institution's whole is less than the sum of its parts, and its breadth is a drag on productivity and progress rather than an asset.

The strategic positioning process itself strengthened us and helped our community prepare for change. We have had to articulate and develop the investment of all our constituencies. Students, faculty, staff, legislators, alumni, the business community, and supporters throughout the world—all are more informed about the university's critical role in and contributions to our state and region. The sense of buy-in that we cultivated has resulted in a widespread sense of ownership and a new level of pride, although pockets of opposition and resistance remain.

With so much time, effort, and expense at stake, a question that Kenneth Shaw (in press) raises must be directly addressed: Is this change worth the cost? I think it most definitely is. But I also often think of Washington Irving (1824/2004), who wrote: "There is certain relief in change. . . . As I have often found in traveling in a stagecoach, that it is often a comfort to shift one's position, and be bruised in a new place" (p. 7). Change can be rough and tumble, and it can be bruising. At the risk of mixing my transportation metaphors, change is usually well worth the cost if you can find broad agreement on your institutional direction—on where to aim the pointy end.

Author Note

This chapter is based in part on discussions I had with colleagues at the conference titled "The New Balancing Act in Higher Education," held at the TIAA-CREF Institute in November 2005. Reflecting the collaborative nature of the strategic planning and positioning process at the University of Minnesota, this chapter was written with extensive contributions from many members of the university community. In the Office of the President, Dan Gilchrist drew from conversations, speeches, and planning documents to help draft and research this chapter, and Eve Wolf provided extensive and valuable editorial assistance. For their contributions to the planning process, I would like to thank the University of Minnesota's Board of Regents; senior administrative officers, in particular Senior Vice Presidents Frank Cerra, E. Thomas Sullivan, and Robert Jones; Vice Presidents Kathleen O'Brien, Linda Thrane, and Kathy Brown; Executive Associate Vice President Al Sullivan; the Faculty Consultative Committee chaired by Professor Marvin Marshak; and the University Senate for their help and leadership in this as yet unfinished strategic planning and positioning process. Finally, I would like to thank my predecessors, including former University of Minnesota Presidents C. Peter Magrath, Kenneth H. Keller, Nils Hasselmo, and Mark G. Yudof, whose work laid the foundation for the success of the strategic positioning process currently under way.

Endnotes

1) The university's appropriation went from 8% to less than 5% of the state budget from 1971 to 2003; the portion of personal income for higher education operations funded by the state is down by 20% from 1.0% in 1980 to 0.8% in 2003; the state appropriation's portion of the state budget declined from 48% of "current funds: education and general" in 1994 to 35% in 2004 (Peterson & Pfutzenreuter, 2004, p. 24).

References

Birnbaum, R., & Shushok, F., Jr. (2001). The "crisis" crisis in higher education: Is that a wolf or a pussycat at the academy's door? In P. G. Altbach, P. J. Gumport, & D. B. Johnstone (Eds.), *In defense of American higher education* (pp. 59–84). Baltimore, MD: Johns Hopkins University Press.

Bruininks, R. (2005). *Transforming the University of Minnesota: President's recommendations.* Retrieved August 24, 2006, from the University of Minnesota, Transforming the U web site: www1.umn.edu/systemwide/strategic_positioning/pdf/umn_pres_rec.pdf

Clark, B. R. (2001). The entrepreneurial university: New foundations for collegiality, autonomy, and achievement. *Higher Education Management, 13*(2), 9–24.

Education Trust, Inc. (2005). *Data from eighth graders on the 2005 National Assessment for Educational Progress-math and reading.* Washington, DC: Author.

Irving, W. (2004). *Tales of a traveler* (G. G. Crayon, Ed.). Whitefish, MT: Kessinger. (Original work published 1824)

Kellogg Commission on the Future of State and Land-Grant Universities. (1996). *Taking charge of change.* Washington, DC: National Association of State Universities and Land-Grant Colleges.

Kotter, J. P. (1996). *Leading change.* Boston, MA: Harvard Business School Press.

Lederman, D. (2005). The "crisis" in higher ed financing. Retrieved August 24, 2006, from http://insidehighered.com/news/2005/11/04/tiaa

Lombardi, J. V., Capaldi, E. D., Mirka, D. S., & Abbey, C. W. (2005). *The Top American Research Universities.* Gainesville, FL: University of Florida, TheCenter.

Lombardi, J. V., Capaldi, E. D., Reeves, K. R., Craig, D. D., Gater, D. S., & Rivers, D. (2003). *The Top American Research Universities.* Gainesville, FL: University of Florida, TheCenter.

Lombardi, J. V., Capaldi, E. D., Reeves, K. R., & Gater, D. S. (2004). *The Top American Research Universities.* Gainesville, FL: University of Florida, TheCenter.

Lombardi, J. V., Craig, D. D., Capaldi, E. D., & Gater, D. S. (2000). *The Top American Research Universities.* Gainesville, FL: University of Florida, TheCenter.

Lombardi, J. V., Craig, D. D., Capaldi, E. D., & Gater, D. S. (2002). *The Top American Research Universities.* Gainesville, FL: University of Florida, TheCenter.

Lombardi, J. V., Craig, D. D., Capaldi, E. D., Gater, D. S., & Mendonça, S. L. (2001). *The Top American Research Universities.* Gainesville, FL: University of Florida, TheCenter.

Peterson, D., & Pfutzenreuter, R. (2004). *University of Minnesota 2004 strategic positioning: Environmental scan.* Retrieved August 24, 2006, from the University of Minnesota, Academic Administration web site: www.academic.umn.edu/img/assets/17505/3-1.1%20Environmental Scan.pdf

Seymour, D. (1995). *Once upon a campus: Lessons for improving quality and productivity in higher education.* Phoenix, AZ: American Council on Education/Oryx Press.

Shaw, K. A. (in press). Institutional change: The why and how. In R. L. Clark & M. d'Ambrosio (Eds.), *The new balancing act in the business of higher education.* London, England: Edward Elgar.

University of Minnesota. (2005a). *Academic task force report and recommendations: Academic positioning.* Retrieved August 24, 2006, from the University of Minnesota, Transforming the U web site: www1.umn.edu/systemwide/strategic_positioning/pdf/SP_Acad_ Task_Force_Report.pdf

University of Minnesota. (2005b). *Administrative strategic planning task force: Report to the president.* Retrieved August 24, 2006, from the University of Minnesota, Transforming the U web site: www1.umn.edu/systemwide/strategic_positioning/pdf/SP_Admin_ Task_Force_Report.pdf

University of Minnesota. (2005c). *Strategic positioning executive summary.* Retrieved August 24, 2006, from the University of Minnesota, Transforming the U web site: http://www1.umn.edu/systemwide/ strategic_positioning/summary.html

University of Minnesota. (2005d). *The University of Minnesota: Advancing the public good.* Retrieved August 24, 2006, from the University of Minnesota, Transforming the U web site: www1.umn.edu/sys-temwide/strategic_positioning/pdf/Strategic_Positioning_Report.pdf

Zetterberg, P. (2004). *University of Minnesota 2004 strategic positioning: Environmental scan.* Retrieved August 24, 2006, from the University of Minnesota, Academic Administration web site: www.academic. umn.edu/img/assets/17505/3-1.1%20EnvironmentalScan.pdf

13

A Targeted Path Toward Academic Excellence at The Ohio State University

Karen A. Holbrook

Providing direction while preserving decentralization at The Ohio State University differed from the tasks faced by Presidents Bruininks at the University of Minnesota and Maidique at Florida International University. They both planned and implement the strategic plans for their universities. At Ohio State, this task so far has stretched over three presidencies. My predecessors, Gordon Gee, who served from 1990 to 1998, and later, William Kirwan, who served from 1998 to 2002, launched a series of initiatives that came together in an Academic Plan. That plan provided a vision of making Ohio State the best land-grant institution in the country, priorities to achieve this goal, and the criteria to judge the extent of achievement.

When I became Ohio State's president in October 2002, everyone asked, "What is your plan?" I gave my response in my investiture address:

> I am frequently asked about <u>my agenda</u> for Ohio State's future and my standard answer is: "We have a <u>university agenda</u>, the "Academic Plan," a clear and thoughtful collective vision to enhance our academic quality, diversity, and stature as a world-class research university for the people of Ohio." How we emphasize, prioritize, apply resources, and measure our progress in implementing the plan will frame a near-term agenda and the strategies for long-term gain. (Holbrook, 2003a)

My role as president today is in part to focus my leadership agenda to implement our Academic Plan via efforts that help respond to the Kellogg Commission's Challenge for Change: to bring land-grant universities to the highest standards of excellence in research, teaching, and engagement so that they can better serve their students, states, and society. While we strive to be the best research university we can be, the Kellogg Commission reminds us that we must be the best teaching and publicly engaged university as well. For institutions such as Ohio State, the Kellogg Commission reminds us that a strong focus on research does not diminish any other part of the land-grant mission, but rather informs and improves the mission as a whole.

This chapter carries many messages about the academic and budgetary initiatives that provided direction for our public research university, but two are critical. First, plans setting institutional directions are not presidential prerogatives to be changed with each successor to that office. Second, as noted in Chapter 1, great plans fade without careful and continuous implementation.

Fragmentation: Different Positions, Different Perceptions

The perception of the university as a cohesive or fragmented organization depends largely on one's position, role, and longevity at an institution. It also reflects how the university itself has worked to foster coherence through its programs and initiatives designed to position itself among its peers, both current and aspirational.

Undergraduate students tend to have a broad view of the university as a whole. They are often less differentiated in their interests, sample more of the academic disciplines through general education courses, and are involved in the multitude of activities and social experiences characteristic of college life. Ohio State's undergraduates play a more inclusive role in the university than ever before, from participation in research to involvement in outreach activities, studying abroad and in other special environments away from the campus. They are likely to know how their university is positioned among other universities, in the region and athletic conference, through its national rankings (e.g., *U.S. News & World Report*), and certainly through the rankings of the athletic programs. They have learned how to influence and modify the direction of the university. In short, undergraduate students are often fully involved in and have a cohesive view of the university.

Graduate and professional students typically join the institution because of a desire to work in an outstanding program with a renowned professor, because of a unique facility, or because it offers another opportunity to prepare them for their futures. Of less concern to them is what goes on around them in unrelated colleges, programs, and even campus activities that are distant from their disciplines. The student government Inter-Professional Council and the Council of Graduate Students, however, engage students who work to inform and involve themselves in the life of the campus and to have a voice in university-wide decisions.

The faculty, especially junior faculty, may unknowingly contribute to the sense of a fragmented, or certainly a decentralized, university because they focus on their own development within their discipline. Their academic success and tenure will depend on how good they are and how well known they become in their fields, and thus they contribute most of their efforts to their students, departments, colleges, and national professional organizations. Though they have pride in their institution—especially if it continues to improve in stature—they often feel a greater allegiance to their colleagues within the discipline than to the university as a whole. This is not a critical statement about the faculty, but simply an observation based on personal experience as a long-time faculty member.

Involvement in interdisciplinary work, however, can bring faculty more into the realm of the whole university, and involvement of professors in all-university activities such as senate, search committees, general topic committees assembled to develop a strategic plan or consider revision of the undergraduate curriculum, and institutional accreditation activities helps promote a broader understanding and perspective of the university.

It is essential for an administrator to see the university as a whole, how the parts come together—or if they do not come together, how to integrate them to assure upward mobility of the whole university. Each member of the central administration has the responsibility of sharing relevant information with all members of the administration about the university, as seen from within his or her domain of responsibility, in order to inform the decisions that benefit the whole.

Differences Between Fragmentation and Decentralization

An important difference exists between a university that is fragmented and one that promotes decentralization. Fragmented implies that something, once whole, has been broken, shattered, and disconnected, and that those pieces that remain may no longer fit together. In such an environment, the campus community is unlikely to rally around a common purpose and be trustful about future direction. It is also more likely they will be without the connections and reciprocal relationships that can provide mutual benefit.

On the other hand, decentralized implies that there are "pieces" that have some autonomy and manage various aspects of their own enterprise independently. It does not necessarily mean they see themselves as separate. Units will have various allegiances to the central core of the university—perhaps related to how many services they perceive they need for their own well-being. They will also have alliances with each other through overlapping areas of research and teaching as well as participation in centers and institutes and interdisciplinary projects. Professional schools may see themselves as "independent" and often speak of "them" and "us." In such cases, both sides must work to prevent this situation.

Universities typically support a combination of decentralized and centralized activities. They encourage units to take ownership and leadership in building their own disciplinary futures based on the differences and distinctiveness of their colleges, and the university may often provide the resources for them to do so. Universities also work hard to develop the kinds of activities that build consensus, continuity, and enthusiasm for the institution among students, faculty, and staff as well as external constituents, from alumni, donors, and friends to legislators and governors. The challenge is to develop the positive aspects of independence along with efforts to advance the university as a single comprehensive whole.

Missions and Sagas as Unifiers

All universities refer to their constituents collectively as the "university family," united by a range of factors that include core values, mission and purpose, traditions and culture, campus landmarks and master plan, a capital campaign focused on university-wide priorities, membership in the athletic conference, and a sense of competition, success, and pride. A crisis can also bring a campus together. On the more proactive side, we at Ohio State University develop campus-wide initiatives that provide opportunity for all units, and we find champions across campus for their support. Such initiatives create the sense of wholeness. Campus constituents generally greatly value the sense of belonging to a longstanding, revered institution. Over time, these feelings become university sagas that bring unity to the institution.

Stronger Units Make a Stronger University_____

We continually work to develop pride in the institution through accomplishments that, in turn, influence ranking and reputation. But pride in the university as a whole does not just happen. Largely independent academic units—whose independence we help create by assigning them more autonomy and providing incentives for making their own strategic decisions and setting their own priorities—work to improve their unit rankings and reputation, which are necessary for improving the university ranking. Ohio State has taken the position that stronger units will result in a stronger university. It has co-invested resources with the units in targeted areas through central initiatives that will also prove most effective in expediting the success of the entire institution. These university activities succeed only when the academic units adopt the same priorities. Investing new resources in areas that units want and that the university needs helps gain that support.

Initiatives Providing Direction While Protecting Decentralization_____

Ohio State's process to meet the objective of the Kellogg Commission reports beginning in the mid-1990s involved a series of initiatives and plans. They coalesced in the Academic Plan (Ohio State University, 2000a) that has furthered the university's teaching, research, and service, with a resultant improvement in various rankings and in the perception of the institution by students, alumni, state leaders, and the public.

To promote Ohio State's overarching goals of achieving academic excellence, improving its position as a leader among public research universities, and better serving our students through teaching and our community through outreach and engagement, the central administration has established several initiatives. Over the last 10 years, the university invested funds strategically, deliberately, and creatively in selected academic units and programs, typically matched to varying levels with unit funds. These investments stem from initiatives proposed by the Commission on Research, the 20/10 Plan, Selective Investment, Academic Enrichment, the Academic Plan, Diversity Action Plan, and the newest plan, Targeted Investment in Excellence. All these initiatives focused on institutional priorities, balanced an institutional agenda with college and departmental perspectives, promoted cohesion within the university, moved the university to higher levels of achievement and distinction, and enabled it to serve better its students and citizens in Ohio, the region, and the country.

Although each initiative showed some differences in the areas targeted for action, all had basically the same goals and objectives outlined in the Kellogg Commission reports—to unify our research, teaching, and service into a cohesive whole that best serves the tripartite land-grant mission. I share these as an example of how the underlying challenges of the commission existed in all the planning that has taken place during the past three administrations of Ohio State University presidents. In my mind, the university's planning serves as a road map of achieving the vision outlined by the Kellogg Commission. Successive plans, highlighted below, often incorporated or replicated elements of previous initiatives but with a slightly different emphasis. As a result, they have had a connected and continuous impact. The timing of the various plans shows the sequential as well as confluent nature of effort.

The Commission on Research: Improving Research Capacity

In 1997, President E. Gordon Gee established a Commission on Research—broadly representative of the campus community—to assess university investment in research internally and comparatively with competitive institutions. Its charge also called for recommendations of strategic areas for future investment and development and design measures of performance. The president expected the commission work to coincide with the planned restructuring of the university's budget allocations.

First, to begin the research study, selected senior faculty and administrators from peer institutions participated in a roundtable with a group of Ohio State professors and administrators. The discussions revealed a number of tactics used by peer universities to improve their position in research and scholarship, but investing in the faculty constituted the number one strategy that produced unanimous agreement. That strategy combined recruiting professors carefully, retaining them selectively, setting expectations for them that were aligned with university goals, and providing them with competitive administrative and financial support that allowed them to perform optimally.

Second, the commission undertook a comprehensive benchmarking study to reveal Ohio State's position among its peers on faculty quality, graduate program strength, research infrastructure, current funds revenue, and university fundraising. An accompanying situational analysis helped the university understand its own position across its units and identify areas that it could improve immediately.

The commission submitted its report after a year and a half of work to new President William "Brit" Kirwan and his provost for review by various university constituencies prior to adoption. It recommended ways to move Ohio State to a position among the top 10 research universities, in line with the university's research mission.

As one might anticipate, strategies for success began with the goal of building an excellent faculty and attracting the best students. They also called for planning and providing for a competitive research infrastructure and for facilitating and promoting interdisciplinary/multidisciplinary activities in research, and in graduate and undergraduate programs. The report also recommended working with a broad range of internal and external constituencies to enhance the nation's recognition of our research capacity and outcomes.

The second element of the report included suggestions for investment and generating new resources. The university would need to improve the existing economics of sponsored research (e.g., facilities and administrative rate [F&A], larger grants, etc.), restructure some of the existing investments in research and reallocate to priority areas, enhance the university's investment in development activities, establish research alliances, and secure additional dollars from the state. The report still showed optimism that the downward trend of state funding could be reversed if only the state legislature recognized a greater value of the institution's impact on the state's economy. Subsequent reports have given up on this strategy. The university's Academic Plan in 2000 later reiterated and reformed many of the objectives and strategies presented in the Research Commission Report.

This highly detailed and thorough report set forth the problems and requirements for success. It identified the barriers, highlighted the rewards for professors who invest effort in entrepreneurial activities, identified areas for investment in research where the impact would be measurable, and presented the required resources necessary for Ohio State to gain greater visibility and an enhanced image in research. The current research record demonstrates the successful implementation of the Research Commission Report. Today, Ohio State ranks among the top 10 public universities based on total research expenditures during 2003, the most recent national data currently available (National Science Foundation, 2005). The Research Commission Report was Ohio State's first major effort to address the challenges of the Kellogg Commission.

The 20/10 Plan: Promoting Academic Disciplines Poised for Excellence

Reputation is a key factor in moving an institution to a higher level in ranking among its peers. The 20/10 Plan evolved from a university goal of having 10 academic programs ranked in the top 10 of their respective disciplines and an additional 20 among the top 20 of public universities by 2010. It sets forth a clear measurable benchmark that continues today, supported by special funding, that emphasizes the strategy of investing in top programs to enhance the university's research, teaching, and outreach enterprises. Strategies to achieve this goal are best exemplified by the Academic Enrichment and Selective Investment initiatives, detailed next.

Academic Enrichment: Emphasis on Value-Added Centers and Programs

The Academic Enrichment program (1995–2001) provided an annual investment of cash funds from central resources and matching dollars from academic units to enhance or create centers and programs that would have an immediate impact on the university. Typically, the support rewarded innovative interdisciplinary activities on the cutting edge of disciplines that would expand the learning experience of undergraduate students. In many cases, this funding was the first substantial commitment of resources to promising new programs.

Nearly identical criteria existed for Academic Enrichment, and its successor and overlapping Selective Investment program, discussed next. Some $175 million of central university investment—with unit matches—funded multiple new teaching and outreach programs in all the colleges, the Graduate School, the honors program, the libraries, academic advising, international studies, and the Office of Research.

The Academic Enrichment program expanded the curriculum and research through new interdisciplinary programs in such areas as the life sciences, aging/geriatrics and gerontology, computational linguistics, political psychology, preventative medicine, engineering, and environmental engineering. Projects, for example, provided facilities to promote teaching and research in food technology, electron optics, and super high field magnetic resonance imaging, a classic case of direction to encourage collaboration while continuing unit decentralization. The Microscopic and Chemical Analyses Center is used today by 10 colleges and 25 departments.

This program also created policy centers to disseminate research outcomes to the community, initiated seminar series, launched new graduate and professional specializations, and committed dollars for graduate recruitment grants and competitive graduate fellowships. Campus funds leveraged state dollars for research and for new industry partnerships. And, importantly, the effort encouraged faculty to invest in new efforts to revitalize the urban neighborhood surrounding the university through education, landscape improvement, housing, adult library services, and health care, to name just a few examples.

Other funds went to the most important goal of investing in recruiting and retaining professors to enhance our teaching, research, and service. The university gained 85 new professors, often with joint appointments to support and bridge new interdisciplinary activities.

Selective Investment in Academic Excellence: Promoting Departmental Success

Initiated in 1997, with awards made to 13 units in the three succeeding years, Selective Investment in Academic Excellence was designed to identify outstanding departments that had a clear vision for, and the best opportunity to achieve, excellence in research, teaching, and service, and to provide them with $500,000 in continuing funds, matched by an equal amount from the departments and colleges. The goal, in line with the Kellogg Commission challenges, was to enhance the academic experience for our students and to stimulate and expedite the department's upward progression toward top ranking in research and outreach.

Faculty committees that were broadly representative of the university were established in each of the three years to evaluate proposals, applying the following criteria for selection that insisted the department must:

- Be central to the academic teaching and research missions of the university
- Promote interdisciplinary activities
- Build on existing strengths and hold promise of substantial future benefit
- Present a realistic strategic plan and appropriate benchmarks for monitoring progress and evaluating achievement
- Contribute to outreach efforts with business, industry, and the community

Selective Investment had a broad impact on the university. The departments receiving the awards housed 17% of the tenure-track faculty and generated 31% of all student credit hours. Further, these departments resided in six colleges that included more than 60% of the tenure-track faculty, 70% of the sponsored research, and 50% of undergraduate and graduate degrees awarded. The units invested their funds in ways that they determined would make the greatest difference to their future success in terms of teaching, research, and engagement.

All departments hired new faculty members, with a resulting immediate impact on the caliber of the university's research and teaching. In some cases, they recruited senior professors with established records of distinction and significant research funding. For example, materials science and engineering hired two members of the National Academy of Engineering, and physics hired a renowned expert on the subject of black holes and string theory. Mathematics recruited a member of the National Academy of Science, who established the NSF Mathematical Biosciences Institute. Such senior faculty immediately boosted several measures of quality within their units, and helped attract top students, other high-quality teaching, and research faculty and research funding. Departments also added junior faculty to build an investment in the future.

Additionally, funds were used to support graduate students (physics, chemistry) and new professional master's programs, strengthen new programmatic areas (materials science and engineering), enhance technology support, and intensify research collaboration in multidisciplinary areas.

The most recent review of the impact of funding on the Strategic Investment departments has been highly encouraging. The university reviews and periodically benchmarks all these investment programs, even after the new investment dollars have ceased. University committees such as the Research Commission reviewed the progress toward goals proposed in the research report; the Deans Learning Technologies Committee reviewed the development and delivery of technology-enhanced teaching; the Central Investment Review Committee reviewed Selective Investment and Academic Enrichment and other centrally funded programs. Finally, an annual Strategic Indicators report compares current with past institutional data and benchmarks our success against peer institutions.

The Academic Plan and Leadership Agendas: A Strategic Plan—A Road Map to Success_____

All the initiatives just described built up to Ohio State's Academic Plan, whose development began in the summer of 1999 (Ohio State University, 2000a). It sought to improve the university's teaching, research, and service, with the goal of raising what many believed to be a less-than-stellar reputation; an underperforming research enterprise; low numbers of minority faculty, staff, and students; and unacceptable student graduation and retention rates. As with many effective strategic plans in the wake of the Kellogg Commission reports, it attempted to fill the absence of a clear central vision and aspirations to help position Ohio State among the top American public universities. The Academic Plan remains today a framework, a point of reference, and a source of confluence and grounding for all colleges and programs when seeking direction for their own unit-specific strategic goals.

The process began with working committees that developed different segments of the plan. Its developers designed a template that encompassed the strategic statement, performance objectives, program initiatives, and implementation and evaluation mechanisms. The directive from then-President Kirwan challenged participants to think big, emphasize excellence, identify required resources, and focus on students and the faculty. A retreat engaged deans and trustees in the planning process. Shortly thereafter, a draft plan was broadly circulated to the campus for comment.

The faculty, department chairs, and faculty, student, and staff committees embraced the idea and improved the document with specific and constructive criticism. A second retreat pared back and focused the initiatives to the final 14 that are in place today. The turning point in developing a strong and meaningful document came when a planning group met with author and consultant Jim Collins, who asked the simple question, "What are your values?" The plan was subsequently redrafted with a new university vision, purpose, overarching goals, and a set of core values reflective of the land-grant university of the new millennium:

• Pursue knowledge for its own sake.
• Produce discoveries that make the world a better place.
• Ignite in our students a lifelong love of learning.
• Celebrate and learn from diversity.
• Open the world to our students.

President Kirwan released the Academic Plan in its final form in October 2000, and the Board of Trustees approved it that December. It forged a road map for Ohio State to be among the world's truly great universities, with a price tag of $750 million for completing the objectives. The plan presented six strategies, all of which relate to the Kellogg Commission challenges:

- Build a world-class faculty.
- Develop academic programs that define Ohio State as the nation's leading public land-grant university.
- Enhance the quality of the teaching and learning environment.
- Enhance and better serve the student body.
- Create a diverse university community.
- Help build Ohio's future.

Leadership Agendas

Recognizing the broad sweep of objectives and the importance of maintaining it as a dynamic plan that grows and evolves with the institution, I now lead the development of a leadership agenda each year that allows us to identify smaller pieces of the Academic Plan for near-term accomplishment and to assign responsibility for each of the initiatives. Annual Leadership Agendas assess and report the previous year's accomplishments on an academic scorecard using standard measures. The scorecard compares our progress in each of the six strategic areas and benchmarks our position with our direct and aspirational peers. We have made progress, but not as much as would have been possible had state funding for the plan been available in the amount recommended.

The Diversity Action Plan: Stressing a More Inclusive Campus

Recognizing a diverse environment at Ohio State as central to its land-grant mission to serve all Ohioans, the university charged a Diversity Action Committee in January 1999 to develop a plan to make Ohio State one of the most welcoming universities in the nation through a commitment to "real and measurable change." The committee circulated a draft plan for discussion and considered the feedback. That plan, enacted in October 2000, became a first step in a long-term commitment to create a culture of inclusion in its broadest meaning.

Budget Restructuring: Aligning Priorities With Resources

Universities have clearly discovered that strategic plans and institutional direction seldom work without budget support. Ohio State designed its budget restructuring as a multiyear process to improve resource allocation for the entire university. It became an essential tool for implementing the Academic Plan, to support college strategic plans as aligned with the institutional plan, and to sustain programs already targeted through Academic Enrichment and Selective Investment.

Budget restructuring helped determine what should be funded centrally and which responsibilities were better met locally. The intent was to reconcile unit workload with its resources, as well as reflect unit quality, potential, and centrality to Ohio State's mission. It gave increased flexibility to the colleges to use their resources to improve and reward units selectively based on their performance. It was believed that a budget that more equitably rewards teaching, research, and service could ultimately help unify those equally important missions.

The university began earlier to collect the required data on revenues earned and expenditures generated, but it did not outline the first steps in the budget-restructuring plan until February 2001. By that time, the provost had met with each dean to share budget data, and had appointed an ad hoc University Senate Oversight Committee on Budget Restructuring and other campus consultants to develop a series of principles to guide the process, which led to three components:

- The general fund revenue budgets of the colleges would be rebased.
- Marginal revenue from tuition, state subsidy, and indirect cost dollars would be shared.
- Funds would be allocated to the responsible units for central costs for student services/student affairs (based on number of undergraduate degrees per college), physical plant costs (based on assignable square feet for utilities, custodial service and maintenance), research administration, residential graduate fee authorization, and a central tax to support the president's and provost's functions and certain aspects of business and finance units.

The central administration would retain portions of the F&A calculated for libraries and renovation and rehabilitation of research space. Differential fees enacted would go to the respective college and only residential fees would be considered. Special subsidies were outside these calculations. Budget restructuring represented a classic version of unit decentralization of resources, with provision for university direction and priorities. It represented Ohio State's version of responsibility centered budgeting, a decentralized system adopted by many public and private research universities.

Rebasing favored a focus, as university administrators said, on opportunities of the future instead of decisions of the past, and positioned colleges to contribute to the institutional Academic Plan. It created unit incentives to generate and receive resources for developing new programs, courses, and collaborative initiatives that support student learning, and to eliminate those activities not in synch with institutional needs and goals. Implementation first adjusted base budgets for changes in reporting lines and added summer enrollment incentive funds. Rebasing then determined how closely each unit's generated funds aligned with its budget requirements. The calculation showed some colleges as net receivers of funds and others as net contributors, along with the extent of these subsidies and contributions. Rebasing occurred in those colleges where revenues deviated 10% or more from their budget requirements—in either direction.

The budgeting plan sorted the colleges into three groups: traditional core colleges with Selective Investment programs, traditional core colleges without Selective Investment programs, and the professional colleges. Selective Investment colleges were grouped to ensure that the university sustained its commitment to their support. No Selective Investment college would receive a budget reduction as long as the level of teaching and research stayed the same or improved.

Rebasing did not automatically redirect funds based on the above formula. Units with formula base adjustments had to state how they would use redirected funds to meet their faculty and enrollment needs and improve the quality of the learning environment in support of the goals of the Academic Plan. Three colleges that constituted net receivers of 20% or more of their resources had to begin planning for reduced university funding to become more self-sufficient over a five-year transition period.

The cross-subsidies in rebasing also considered a college's relevance to the academic and land-grant mission of Ohio State. For example, medicine and public health received subsidies from the hospital and used hospital space for their operations, veterinary medicine is the only college of its kind in the state, and dentistry the only public college.

Rebasing also considered inherent advantages and disadvantages of the various units. Some colleges have more opportunity for fundraising; others receive the bulk of the F&A dollars associated with sponsored research. Some are more effective in outreach activities; others receive state subsidies and line-item dollars to support their activities. Rebasing the budgets did not constitute a zero-sum game since the total transfer "to" units amounted to almost $10 million over the five-year period and transfers "from" reached only slightly more than $1.4 million. Various central sources would have to make up this deficit.

As might be expected, a good deal of skepticism arose about this level of change in resource distribution, and many professors and administrators feared that the system would emphasize quantity of instruction over quality of teaching. In general, however, the fears that budget restructuring would push quantity over quality appear unfounded. Small-sized honors courses have increased. Proliferation of graduate programs to capture more of the subsidy did not occur, nor did graduate enrollment decline out of fear that dollars for student stipends would be reduced and redirected. The number of tenure-track faculty did not decline; the quality of programs remained, and course quality was not down or duplicated to capture more funds. Instead, the result has helped Ohio State better unify its teaching, research, and outreach with the dollars related to each of those efforts.

Targeted Investment in Excellence: Investing for Excellence and Impact

Today, Ohio State continues its commitment to academic excellence with further initiatives that follow on, enhance, and augment those of the past. They maintain the crosscutting goals while taking a somewhat different tangent than the former programs. The leadership agenda for 2005 evaluated the university's status five years after adoption of the Academic Plan, then focused on defining the big ideas that would shape Ohio State's goals for the next five years within the Academic Plan—new or continuing—that build on current college-specific or cross-college programs. This planning focuses on both institutional and college goals that raise university and unit reputations and improve their performance and service to students and the state in terms of teaching and outreach.

The provost announced the Targeted Investment in Excellence initiative whereby the central administration would commit $10 million per year for each of the next five years to support high-profile programs that would bring distinction to the colleges and university. The money consists of one-time cash, lines of credit, and continuing funds to be matched equally by the colleges for a total investment of $100 million during the five-year period.

The program placed no limit on the number of applications submitted. However, all applications for central funding must pledge that the unit will begin the program even if not awarded central dollars. The college must be prepared to divert internal resources to start the program. Central support will simply speed up the program, broaden it, or take it to a higher level. Forty-six proposals were submitted for review by multiple groups of faculty and administrators using excellence (recognition as top in the field) and impact (on university stature) as the primary criteria for selection. The program made clear that central funds would likely support only a few programs of the highest quality rather than a large number of fields. Final decisions were made at the end of spring quarter 2006, when the next fiscal year budget began.

Campus-Wide Reviews and Redesign

Two other campus-wide initiatives on program redesign, review, and update targeting specifically the Academic Plan strategy to "enhance and better serve the student body" are also under way.

A committee on graduate education is reviewing our graduate programs, particularly doctoral education. Programs recruit and admit students without central oversight of the graduate school and thus vary significantly in quality. No financial benefit exists for increasing the quality of graduate students admitted, since the current fiscal model rewards only credit hours generated. The faculty committee has designed criteria for measuring excellence and is reviewing the formula funding for graduate education and the role of the graduate school in supporting a top-quality graduate experience. As in all cases, the group seeks campus-wide feedback before implementing a campus-wide plan.

A second faculty committee focused its attention on the undergraduate teaching curriculum. No comprehensive review of this curriculum has occurred since 1988. Over this 18-year period, the student body has changed dramatically in academic preparation, achievement, and aspirations, and Ohio State must tailor today's curriculum to match our commitment to diversity, interdisciplinarity, personalized and relevant experiences, and outreach. It must offer students an integrated, coherent educational experience that permits flexibility to meet their wide-ranging interests. The general education curriculum and number of credit hours required for graduation constitute critical questions for committee consideration. Feedback on this plan is being collected broadly to influence the next iteration of the plan before being accepted. The hope is to begin implementation in fall 2007.

Conclusion

In my state of the university address in 2003, I noted that "It is exceptionally rare for an institution the size of Ohio State to share a unity of vision—and this is our great advantage" (Holbrook, 2003b). New initiatives and development and planning during the terms of three presidents have provided both university direction and unit decentralization. All of them made extensive effort to engage all constituencies in the process of planning and programming. That participative process

has allowed the university to accomplish a large number of very important initiatives, all focused on improving academic quality with the primary goal of fulfilling our land-grant mission of better serving our students, our state, and society. Shared governance has been essential on
many issues; it has been a weighted partnership on others. Shared governance provided important opportunities for faculty, staff, and students to work with trustees and through various campus governing and
leadership organizations. Participation by all these groups in the
process of developing university plans and programs has contributed to
moving this institution forward as a cohesive body.

The successes to date suggest our strategies are effective. At Ohio State,
we are beginning to see the tangible results of our planning efforts, through
improved rankings, as well as through a higher perception of us by our
colleagues and all Ohioans, including students, parents, and legislators. In
specific areas of the land-grant mission, our plans have led to improved
retention and graduation rates reflective of better teaching, a research
enterprise that is more fully attached to outcomes, and professors and
students who are committed to serving and improving our communities.

We have proven, most importantly to ourselves—as I quoted in
remarks at the ceremony installing me as president—that Ohio State has
met the Kellogg Commission challenge: We are "good enough to lead,
strong enough to change, and competent enough to be trusted with the
nation's future" (Holbrook, 2003a; Kellogg Commission, 1996, p. 5).

References

Holbrook, K. A. (2003a). *Investiture address.* Retrieved August 21, 2006,
from The Ohio State University, Office of the President web site:
http://president.osu.edu/speeches/investiture.html

Holbrook, K. A. (2003b). *State of the university address.* Retrieved August
21, 2006, from The Ohio State University, Office of the President
web site: http://president.osu.edu/speeches/sou_10_09_2003.html

Kellogg Commission on the Future of State and Land-Grant Universities.
(1996). *Taking charge of change.* Washington, DC: National
Association of State Universities and Land-Grant Colleges.

National Science Foundation, Division of Science Resources Statistics.
(2005). *Academic research and development expenditures: Fiscal year
2003* (NSF 05–320). Retrieved August 21, 2006, from
http://www.nsf.gov/statistics/nsf05320/pdfstart.htm

Ohio State University. (2000a). *Academic plan.* Retrieved August 21,
2006, from The Ohio State University, Academic Plan web site:
www.osu.edu/academicplan/Acad_Plan.pdf

14

Florida International University: A Top Urban Public Research University

Mayra E. Beers, Paul D. Gallagher, Modesto A. Maidique

Florida International University (FIU) has grown and developed at a record pace during its 35-year history. It was initially designed as a bookend to South Florida's two-year junior college system and limited to upper-level classes and a handful of graduate programs; now, three decades later, it has achieved Carnegie Research University status and admission to the ranks of Phi Beta Kappa. The physical growth of the university, from the initial 5,667 students to nearly 39,000 and the implementation of more than 200 academic programs, has been meteoric—a testimony to its ability to meet community needs in programs and access while embracing excellence. However, managing the momentum and growth has tested the traditional higher education governance structures and provided ways for Florida International to establish an innovative strategic planning paradigm that respects the traditional while incorporating innovative approaches.

The initial burst of enthusiasm and excitement about the creation of a brand-new "people's" university under President Charles (Chuck) Perry was almost overwhelmed by the need to conform to the norms of academia in order to be able to "play the game." However, for nearly two decades, under the leadership of President Modesto (Mitch) Maidique, Florida International University has exercised the privilege and opportunity of realizing the dream—making what seemed impossible happen. Nevertheless, the building process has not been without detours and pitfalls, including, as the Kellogg Commission commented, the fragmentation inherent in creating a public research university.

Fragmentation is arguably a vital part of what we call the academy.

Academic debate, the race to discovery, and communication of knowledge all hinge on independence of thought and action fostering the multi-versity phenomenon at many institutions. To nurture a successful uni-versity, it can be argued, decentralization must play a significant role; the integrity and development of disciplines, schools, and colleges mandates it. For decentralization to work, however, a clearly articulated and shared vision must exist, and it must be consistently and effectively communicated in a multitude of ways. Just as important, it is necessary to have solid control systems in place to ensure the shared vision and philosophy are being implemented by individual units. Florida International University's unique history and its development, especially over the last two decades, in part exemplify the evolution of decentralization with strategic focus.

Perhaps one of the best illustrations of the concept of decentralization with strategic focus was the establishment of our first professional schools. The push to create a School of Architecture at Florida International University was met with much resistance beyond South Florida, but with resolute and unflagging support from within and across the university and the community at large. The vision of what professional schools could mean to the university, well beyond discipline-specific benefits, ignited broad-based support. Students chartered buses to the state capital to influence the legislature and the state's higher education governing board, the Board of Regents; local newspapers and civic organizations rallied and vocalized their support, and the faculty was united in championing a school that was seen as a service and benefit for students, alumni, and community members alike. While administrative personnel worked through the official processes, it was the phenomenal groundswell of grassroots support that was perhaps most effective. Years later, the support for the establishment of a School of Law was even bigger and broader. As a result, our community, our alumni, our students, and our university have reaped the benefits.

Recalling his dependence on the work of Galileo and Kepler, Isaac Newton wrote to his colleague and sometimes antagonist Robert Hooke, "If I have seen further [than certain other men] it is by standing upon the shoulders of giants." Since 1986, we have worked with a similar perspective to engage all members of the university community in a shared vision of excellence for Florida International and to carry on a legacy of strategic planning inclusivity and university-wide engagement.

Historical Background: Tabula Rasa_____

In 1969, the Florida Board of Regents appointed 32-year-old Charles "Chuck" Perry as the first president of Florida International University. He envisioned a new kind of university, one that was responsive to the needs of the community and that would establish a novel paradigm of university governance. Clearly, for the first time in many years, strategic planning for a university could begin with a kind of tabula rasa, unencumbered and uncluttered by the constraints and traditions of a storied past. Working together, the initial group crafted the university's first strategic plan, *The Birth of a University . . . And Its Plans for Development, 1970—1980.* That document was the basis for subsequent strategic planning efforts, setting the precedent for constant change and growth based on three principles: 1) education for students through programs based in the academic disciplines but which will also enable students to improve their social and economic status, 2) service to the community by serving as a resource in the solution of public problems, and 3) developing greater international understanding, by fostering the unique position and potential of Miami and South Florida as international cultural and economic centers.

The following decade, in 1979, Gregory Wolfe, Florida International University's third president, took the helm and commissioned a self-study that once again focused the university's energies on improving curriculum offerings and eventually developed a lower-division curriculum that would make FIU a full-fledged member of the traditional higher education community. In 1981, the Florida Senate passed Higher Education Bill 986, which opened the door for FIU to finally become a four-year university.

When Modesto A. Maidique accepted the position of university president in 1986, he was charged with taking Florida International to the next plateau, with accomplishing what the Kellogg Commission has called for in American higher education: the creation of a great student-centered and publicly engaged research university, as well as a research-oriented university. It was clear that if Florida International was to fulfill its mission, it had to have the right people in the right jobs, endowment must grow, contract and grant funding had to meet potential, numerous additional Ph.D. programs were needed, and it was time to look at the development of several professional schools, including architecture, law, and medicine. The new vision eventually moved Florida International from its primary emphasis on teaching to a more balanced approach that included research. The focus would be on strategic planning, accountability, quality assurance, and internal reporting; the challenge lay in how to articulate and shape that vision effectively and how to rally all the disciplines in its support.

Two avenues for development were possible. One looks to a growth strategy—a by-the-numbers approach—where the bottom line determines the ability of a program or service to remain as part of the institution's inventory. In this scenario, however, lack of cohesion often undermines the organization's strengths and the survival instinct can overshadow the overall mission of the institution. In the long term, this approach alone probably could not be successful at Florida International. A second option adopts the informal approach to managing an organization—one that is more hands-off in operational matters and that allows for a participative strategy coupled with persistent and effective communication of the overarching vision. This method allows the chief executive to provide initial leadership and feedback to new ideas used to implement the vision, and in a participative fashion to analyze the results after an agreed-upon time. With a modified version of this second approach, we began the process by systematically collecting and analyzing information about the university across a broad spectrum of constituencies and sources.

The Process: Providing Direction

Since 1986, collaborative strategic planning has been the hallmark of Florida International University. At first, "strategic planning" was done on the fly. The president literally fleshed out his ideas on the back of an airline ticket and on borrowed scraps of paper; planning sessions with university staff and faculty were held in airports, restaurants, and assorted meeting rooms. After a few months of evaluating the situation, from outside and within, it became evident that systematic and organized planning was the key to unleash Florida International's potential. In spite of the difficulties inherent with transition, such as apprehension about culture change, personnel shifts, and funding, the university community was open to a paradigm shift.

In 1988, the university underwent a self-study in preparation for reaffirmation of accreditation by the Southern Association of Colleges and Schools in 1990. One of the recommendations of the study strengthened President Maidique's conclusion that ongoing planning and self-evaluation were essential for institutional development. As a result, he appointed a Strategic Planning Advisory Committee. Consisting of faculty, staff, and administrators, this group was charged with providing oversight to annual planning cycles that would fine-tune the long- and short-term goals of the university. These planning cycles and accompanying open discussion forums were seen as consensus builders providing regularly recurring venues for broad and intense discussions throughout the university. A resultant strategic plan was first issued in draft form in 1995 and solicited additional feedback from across the university community, allowing us to further refine and fortify our strategic themes, goals, and focus. A five-year plan, *Reaching for the Top* was circulated in 1996 (FIU, 1995).

By fall 1999, Florida International began crafting a second strategic plan. While *Reaching for the Top* focused on growth in enrollment, degree programs, and services to the community, the president's vision was that the new plan should have a strong emphasis on quality and effectiveness. The 10-year *Millennium Strategic Plan* (FIU, 2003a) would serve as the rudder to establish Florida International as a research university for the new millennium. Although built on past accomplishments, the plan began with a participatory review of university goals, philosophies, themes, and challenges, relying on an extremely broad base of contributors and participants, from students and general staff, to faculty, administrators, and the community. Preplanning activities by the advisory committee were followed by Presidential Millennium Forums where feedback was elicited from a variety of constituencies on the structure of the process upon which the university would embark.

As recorded on the plan's web site (FIU, 2003a), the process was designed in three stages. Stage One was discovery, through developing answers to three questions:

1) Who are we?—our core values
2) Where do we want to go?—our vision for the future
3) Where are we now?—the external and internal factors that would impact our future

Stage Two, the analytical stage, examined how we could achieve our desired future by aligning institutional goals with the strategies. Stage Three was operational and looked at the development and implementation of action plans to realize the vision.

At the onset of the process, the Strategic Planning Council (SPC) replaced the Strategic Planning Advisory Committee as the key group in the planning process. The president appointed members with input from the provost, vice presidents, deans, the faculty senate, and the Student Government Association. The council was composed of representatives from each of the university's executive areas. Additionally, the Foundation Board of Directors (our only local university "governance" body at the time) and the Council of 100 (a community advisory board) each appointed a representative. The SPC, chaired by the provost/executive vice president, had the overall responsibility for the design and implementation of the strategic planning effort. SPC members provided a direct link between their constituents and the process; each was responsible for providing updates and information to the group they represented, collecting feedback, and sharing it with the council at its regularly scheduled meetings.

Throughout the preplanning process, the goal was to understand as completely as possible both the internal and external context in which Florida International University would grow and operate during the first and second decades of the 21st century. We found that 1) our core values reflected our community's focus on excellence, respect (for the individual and the environment), diversity, and integrity; 2) our vision was to be among the nation's leading urban public research universities; but also that 3) we were facing significant challenges in infrastructure support, funding, and state governance issues. Thus two priorities emerged: 1) developing an institutional values statement as a unifying theme, and 2) generating insights concerning the university's external context to better understand community needs and challenges.

The initial version of the values statement was drafted by the SPC and circulated via email, web access, and hard copy to all university constituencies. The many comments received and debated were weighed and the final document reflected a fusion of ideas:

- As an institution of higher learning, Florida International University is committed to freedom of thought and expression; excellence in teaching and in the pursuit, generation, dissemination, and application of knowledge; respect for the dignity of the individual; respect for the environment; honesty, integrity, and truth; diversity; strategic, operational, and service excellence. The values statement is a prominent feature of our university web site and copies are posted in offices across campus.
- The Strategic Planning Council organized environmental scanning sessions for community advisory boards; convened a values identification session with university staff and faculty; and sponsored a critical success factors forum to gauge the community's needs. The process included steps for the assessment and prioritization of opportunities, threats, strengths, and challenges of the successful 21st-century university. As a result, the SPC prepared preliminary recommendations concerning goals, challenges, strategic issues, and strategic success fac-

tors. At each step, the findings were circulated, recommendations by constituents reviewed, and the plan adjusted as necessary. These efforts focused on understanding the university's current performance through external and internal scans.

• The external scanning process was carried out by three teams of faculty and staff identified and appointed by the Strategic Planning Council and the president. Their work led to the citation of six factors as critical to the development of general society and higher education during the early decades of the 21st century. Subsequently, the council created six external environmental scanning teams to address each of the critical higher education and Florida International priorities: Health, International, Urban, Environment, Arts and Culture, and Learning Opportunities.[1] The themes did not focus on disciplines or programs, but rather on areas of opportunity where the university and the South Florida community could successfully invest for the future.

The approach used to conduct internal scans represented a modified version of the balanced scorecard model developed by Kaplan and Norton (1996). Our institution-specific model included five performance areas: 1) outcomes/results, 2) academic processes, 3) support service processes, 4) financial processes, and 5) institutional learning and improvement. Five teams composed of faculty and staff carried out the internal scanning activities for each of the five performance areas. The work of the five teams resulted in a comprehensive report, *Assessing Our Capacities* (FIU, 2001), which identified key performance areas for each of the five major components of the model and presented details concerning institutional strengths, opportunities for institutional improvements, and implications for university performance. The teams found that while students were very satisfied with the education they received and the caliber of the faculty, there was a challenge in institutionalizing a performance assessment system. Additionally, they found that state funding issues and the exponential growth of university offerings and enrollment would be hard pressed to ensure future development. During the next months, the internal and external scan results were used to review and make changes to the existing university mission and vision statements, institutional goals, strategic themes, and management philosophy. The resultant documents were shared with the university community and other local constituencies and feedback was elicited.

Participation in the feedback process was insured through both structured and informal methodologies. Two primary vehicles for strategic planning participation were used.

1) *The Millennium Strategic Planning web site* (FIU, 2003a) (more formal and institutional). In the very early stages of the process, three key feedback devices were created. First, a Millennium Strategic Planning web site was established to keep the university community up-to-date on the planning process and to collect feedback in real time. Members of the university community were notified regularly of new postings for the plan sections and were encouraged to submit suggestions and comments. Second, interactive web sites were used to encourage the community to provide insight and opinions directly to the Strategic Planning Council. Third, the "What do you think?" link solicited feedback from anyone on any topic—whether directly about the plan or not. Prominently positioned on the university's home page, the link became so popular that after the publication of the *Millennium Plan*, it ran for several months. These electronic forums served as invaluable tools in collecting information to fine-tune the planning process, administer surveys, conduct assessments, and coordinate a variety of activities.

2) *The Millennium Meetings* (more informal and fluid). To provide a broader base of participation that allowed every member of the university community an opportunity to engage in the process, at every stage of the process, from preplanning to implementation, the president convened Millennium Meetings. In total, more than two dozen meetings were held. Scheduled for a minimum of two hours, the meetings were widely publicized and all members of the university community were encouraged to participate. Departments were encouraged to release staff in order for everyone to have the opportunity to attend, and student meetings were scheduled at strategic times of the day. We even provided bag lunches when time appropriate and light refreshments for the rest of the meetings. Also, we hosted meetings that invited the general public to participate in the process. The format was simple: The president delivered a five- to ten-minute introduction explaining the purpose of the meeting; the floor was then open for questions, discussion, or comments from anyone on any subject of concern to them.

The success of the Millennium Meetings may be gauged, in part, by the participation: more than 2,000 attended and in excess of 600 comments were logged. A general feeling existed that any issue could be brought to the table. These meetings produced invaluable information from many "grassroots" employees who expressed their thoughts on key issues such as infrastructure support, salary, working conditions, and job security, to name a few. Students spoke about advising, campus life, and the availability of classes. Members of the South Florida community focused on cultural enrichment, access, career development, and lifelong learning experiences. The Millennium Meetings provided important material for the Millennium Plan and prompted the realignment of some priorities. In addition, many issues that could be resolved immediately were addressed in follow-up sessions with the president's staff. Without question, attendees left the meetings knowing that their concerns had been heard and that their voices would have an impact on the overall strategic planning process and resultant plan. The meetings always closed with a visual reminder of the president's personal email address and a request that additional comments, questions, or concerns be sent directly to the president.

In part, the *Millennium Plan's* deliberative process led to a change in the traditional annual state of the university address to a more participatory gathering. At least twice each year, the president addresses the university community in a town hall-type meeting that engages faculty, staff, and students on the issues that most concern them. A shortened version of the traditional address is delivered so that a good share of the meeting is taken up with the audience's questions and concerns. At times the exchange can be far from a love fest, with support staff feeling unappreciated for their behind-the-scenes work or professors from one discipline disgruntled about being "slighted" in strategic funding. However, these instances have been few and usually handled through effective and frequent communication, fostering understanding and alignment of goals among constituencies that reduces the them-versus-us divisions. Having top administrators attend every meeting also facilitated answering questions and enhancing communication. Although the process proved time intensive at Florida International, we found that consensus can only be built on the foundation of shared vision, which has been collectively developed and persistently communicated.

Cornerstone Vision

Ultimately, the Millennium Strategic Planning process allowed Florida International to crystallize the vision for the future into five words that would resonate across campus and around which we could focus our energies and resources no matter the school, college or program: Florida International would be a Top * Urban * Public * Research * University (TUPRU)[2]:

• *Top:* To be recognized in national rankings as one of the top urban public research universities.

- *Urban:* To address metropolitan and community issues and contribute through teaching, research, and service to the economic growth and cultural richness of the region. Students, faculty, staff, and alumni reflect the diversity of the urban region.
- *Public:* To be known for the breadth and quality of academic programs, affordable tuition, and engagement with local communities, industries, and governments.
- *Research:* To be recognized as contributing to the discovery, invention, and reinterpretation of knowledge as well as for the innovative application of knowledge and techniques that contribute to the enhancement of human understanding and to the promotion of artistic accomplishment.
- *University:* Magistorum et scholarium: To be dedicated to teaching, scholarship, and service while offering a full range of programs from baccalaureate to doctoral level with professional schools and programs for professional development and lifelong learning. TUPRU served as the cornerstone of the *Millennium Strategic Plan* published in 2000. The plan and every step of the process were and remain posted on the web for easy access (FIU, 2003b).

Executing the Plan

To execute effectively the *Millennium Strategic Plan*, the SPC and the provost also appointed 17 Cross-Functional Action Planning Teams that involved more than 200 faculty and staff, with the charge to focus on the goals, themes, and critical issues identified within the plan. Membership of these cross-functional teams ranged from 8 to 17, including top-level administrators and a broad range of faculty and staff identified by the vice presidents and deans, with recommendations from the faculty senate. For example, the largest group, the Undergraduate Education Team—charged with student learning, institutional culture and enrollment management—included a vice president, an associate vice president, two deans, four directors, two staff positions, and the balance consisting of professors and associate professors from disciplines ranging from architecture to philosophy. The teams identified strategic initiatives within the context of the plan and developed action plans providing detailed operational answers to how the university would achieve its goals. These plans addressed the following types of questions in each of the 17 areas: 1) What, how, and when will the work be completed? 2) What resources will be needed? 3) How will success be measured? Each team developed a standardized matrix positing answers to these questions (FIU, 2003b).

The Success Factor: Leadership _____

Throughout the work of the SPC, the Millennium Meetings, and all the forums, the president's leadership was a key component. It was no less important after the plan was developed. In making TUPRU the university's shared vision, we took every opportunity to articulate clearly and consistently that vision to the university community, area residents, legislators, and anyone who would listen. Today, the acronym resonates clearly across the campus, is used by community leaders in a variety of venues, and is even heard in the state legislature.

Since the development of the *Millennium Plan*, a new governance structure for public higher education has been put in place in Florida. For the first time, we have a local Board of Trustees for Florida International. This recent development coincided with the publication of the *Millennium Plan* and has allowed yet another forum to promote shared vision. Among the board's 13 members sit the chair of the university's Faculty Senate and the student government president along with 11 appointed members of the community, representing our immediate constituencies. The board has added a new dimension to the shared vision, weighing in on numerous planning issues, including expansion of new Ph.D. programs, budget, facilities, and, most recently, the intense planning in preparation for a School of Medicine.

In addition, in 2003, the state of Florida established a statewide Board of Governors with the mandate to operate, regulate, and manage the entire state university system. This body has also developed a statewide university strategic plan requiring alignment of university priorities and initiatives, adding still another layer of input and feedback to the local universities' planning process (State University System of Florida, 2005).

While noting that participatory governance requires a high degree of patience, understanding, and maturity by all members of the community, one must also recognize and appreciate that ultimately the president bears the final responsibility for major decisions. Because frequent leadership shifts may result in lackluster initiatives and stunted development of an institution, one of the assets that Florida International has enjoyed is a long tenure under a single president. Organizational leadership research has found a direct correlation between tenure of university presidents and university performance in a number of areas. One recent study, which tracked presidential tenure at 200 of the nation's leading research universities, found that it has been steadily declining in average length since the 1960s (Padilla & Ghosh, 2000). The report noted that the intense social and political pressures exerted on the modern public research university often lead to shorter and shorter tenures. In turn, shorter tenures generally mean the playing out of new and sometimes dramatically different leadership styles, with little time for effectively communicating shared vision (Padilla & Ghosh, 2000).

In contrast to most public universities, Florida International has had consistent leadership for two decades. This longevity has enabled the vision of the emergence of a great research university to permeate the organization. Using all available resources, including the counsel of deans, faculty, and students, the president's vision-centered leadership has focused efforts and sustained long-term results. It has also allowed time and provided space for individual schools and colleges to align priorities to the overall shared strategic vision.

The Challenge: Implementation

Throughout this concerted effort to implement the new plan, there are, nevertheless, two fundamental difficulties inherent in strategic planning within a university context. The first is the inability to fund properly strategic initiatives because of shortsighted or ineffective budgeting—which can bring any strategic planning effort to its knees. This problem is especially critical for public urban institutions that are significantly dependent on legislative largesse for their base budgets. Second, because university offerings are often so different and interests so disparate, attempts at strategic planning run the risk that an initiative may alienate one faction of participants, which can cripple or diminish the momentum of even the best plans.

The modern research university resembles a huge nonprofit holding company, where individual components have a value that exceeds their individual contributions to the financial success of the organization. Unlike a business concern, part of a higher education institution's core values is commitment to academic freedom, administrative respect for faculty opinions, and commitment to the tenure process. However, extremely limited resources, especially for public higher education, do not allow for egalitarian allocations that please every academic unit. For example, what university would not want classicists on its faculty? Yet it would be difficult to argue that classicists provide avenues for the growth of university funding or depth of research in the same way that the twin wheels of biotech and information technology might. Thus if research is important, then faculty must acknowledge, for example, that if the chemistry program is a leading research entity, then the university is fulfilling its mission if it apportions funding to develop chemistry options over those of another area. When all is said and done, for strategic planning to work, constituents must 1) understand and buy in to the university's overall mission and the accompanying budgetary priorities, and 2) dissent (and there will be dissent) must be handled with transparency and effective communication.

Budgeting

Although there are universities where unit aspirations are largely misaligned with the overall strategy, they may still manage to survive for some time. However, such institutions have, at best, only modest efficiency in the use of their resources. The center usually cannot force strategic resource alignment of the periphery. The decline of state funding demands an increase in self-generated income, which comes largely from the activities of departments, schools, and colleges. Therefore, fostering entrepreneurship of academic units is an essential part of an implementing strategy. A key component of success becomes not allowing units to live exclusively off the institution's primary resources, largely from the state. Instead, the university must provide incentives and opportunities for each to generate resources for their own success in alignment with institutional priorities. Proposals produced by the periphery should be funded as they align with the overall mission and strategy of the university.

Florida International follows a decentralized budgeting model where each unit submits its budget through the executive area budget managers to the executive area vice president. The baseline generally remains equal to that of the previous year and any unit may request additional funds for strategic initiatives. These requests are rolled up at the university level and tied to available revenues. For the 2005 fiscal year, each college, school, and executive area was given the opportunity to submit projects tied to the plan's strategic initiatives. After allocation of the base budget, each proposal received consideration for funding. Though academic affairs gets the largest cut of the budget, budget constraints restrict additional funding beyond base budgets to strategic initiatives. Professors submit proposals to deans who in turn winnowed the list before submission to the provost. The Division of Human Resources submitted their initiatives for personnel orientation, recruitment, retention, and assessment as they aligned with the identified university priorities. And the same process exists for each executive area. In each case, final proposals were meticulously scrutinized and debated during two all-day meetings of the president and the executive team.

The key question asked of every proposal is how it ties in to the overall strategy, to the Millennium Plan, and to state higher education planning. After consensus is reached, final budgets are allocated to the individual units. The faculty senate is not officially part of the budgeting process, but each year the chief financial officer and provost present the budget and its rationale to the members of the senate and provide a forum for questions and answers.

Another area of budgeting to ensure the success of the strategic plan encouraged development of a faculty funding model. How would new and replacement positions be funded to align with strategic goals? While it is still being refined and expanded, we have developed a matrix using national benchmarks for urban public institutions, state enrollment indicators, and Carnegie I standards (McCormick, 2000). Academic programs receive faculty lines that meet their measurable, benchmarked criteria. For example, a department working within the strategic model and with a 30 to 1 student-to-faculty ratio where the benchmark is 20 to 1 most likely would be placed at the forefront for available faculty positions. While the matrix is far more complex than this example, it is nevertheless enrollment and strategy driven. The goal of the model is not to be arbitrary, but instead to create a funding framework that ties funding for faulty positions to strategic issues while being transparent. Because of its scarcity and its pivotal role in achieving institutional goals, funding must be structured around dynamic measures and devoted to key strategic and mission-driven initiatives. Providing a clear process and articulate guidelines for funding lays out the rules of the game and levels the playing field for all areas of the university.

Dissent

Dissent can undermine any strategic plan and any strategic plan will produce dissent. Therefore, effectively dealing with dissenting factions becomes critical to any planning effort. While our experience has been that a well-articulated and communicated vision helps diminish dissent, not everyone can or will be happy with a strategic direction. Streamlining programs to align with strategic priorities and their effects on faculty and staff members often provokes the most visible forms of dissent. The president, provost, or senior administrator must address the issues head on, meeting with those involved and listening to their concerns. Program closure proposals have on occasion been cancelled or delayed as a result of meetings with students, and staff positions reinstated or expanded as a result of compromise or adjustments.

As with most things "new" to the academy, the implementation of new budgeting guidelines more closely tied to strategic initiatives recently caused severe rumblings of discontent. The chief financial officers and the provost had to meet with the faculty senate, deans, administrators, and ad hoc faculty committees, explaining and dialoguing with small groups across campus. This process, though time consuming and labor intensive, is essential in a university setting. Having the support—or at least the acquiescence—of those most affected by the changes strengthens everyone's commitment to the strategic plan. Nevertheless, in any discussion, the focus must remain on the long-term accomplishments of the institution, not its short-term comfort.

The Next Strategic Plan: Recommendations_____

There is always a cost associated with success, and failures are the normal consequences of growth. For decentralization with focus to be most effective, it is imperative to have depth of expertise and experience in key positions. There is no substitute for competent, well-trained professionals who understand the processes and are equipped to do the right thing. For example, while university-wide financial controls may exist, allowing specific areas to exercise autonomy permits the area head to make decisions quickly and more efficiently. Nevertheless, when an administrator with minimal experience is permitted to exercise control—without depth of training and experience in the number two or three position in the unit—failure is almost certain. Even if one has the authority, not possessing the competence to "turn on the safety switch" in a specific area has a significant institution-wide impact. Yet, such "bumps" should be viewed as teachable moments. When these setbacks occur it is important that the organization address the deficiency quickly and decisively, and once again define clearly the rules of play in order to better align all the players.

Some difficulties are institution specific and can be addressed in house; others, however, are almost beyond the institution's ability to control or correct. In Florida, there have been (at least) two major higher education governance shifts at the state level since 2001: from centralized statewide governance and reporting to local autonomous governance, and recently to a "shared" governance and reporting structure. The administrative and reporting changes were compounded when the state financial system was changed from a centralized operation to one that mandated each state university and college to implement and manage all financial and human resource operations. The transition from the statewide system created a hard "bump" for FIU as we embarked on a new strategic plan. In addition, the decentralization coincided with the implementation of a new information technology system at Florida International that allowed us to modernize and standardize university processes. As with most technology, the acceptance of the new system and the difficulties in training and implementation were still another bump at a critical juncture in the strategic plan implementation process. These counterpoints have slowed and shifted the implementation somewhat, but the plan's resiliency and ability to adapt have allowed us to continue to make progress—if at a somewhat slower pace.

There are perhaps two key issues that Florida International may address differently the next time in strategic planning. First, the planning process for the *Millennium Plan* was lengthy; three years was perhaps too long. Cutting that time in half, without sacrificing the key components that produced a successful plan, would be optimal. The nature of the academy is such that discussion and debate will continue until someone calls for a stop—and, as has been noted, there is nothing better than deadlines to improve debate. Therefore, it is important to set a timeframe that will allow the process to play out effectively while keeping the interest of the participants. Second, the process should identify flexible resources early. Having at least a general understanding of the nature and availability of funds that might be leveraged allows planners to develop realistic goals and keeps the plan focused and on task. Dreams that cannot happen often lead to disappointment and disillusionment that permeates the entire plan.

Some critics will always argue that strategic planning regiments the academy and its flexible academic spirit. Ultimately, in strategic planning the end result is less important than the process by which it is produced. For a university, especially a public research university, the process is one of educating the people involved, promoting the exchange of ideas, fostering collective learning about the institution and its sociocultural environment, and continually providing clear direction. This strategy provides the framework and guidelines that define the rules by which we can participate, contribute, and execute in the most efficient and effective way. Clear direction and continuous, effective communication of the vision in measurable ways make the vision come alive; that is a key role of the visionary president.

Recommendations

Planning sets goals and, with aligned budgeting, helps fix the fragmented university. Nevertheless, implementing a comprehensive strategic planning process in large, complex universities is a difficult task and the barriers to success are numerous. In our experience, there are a number of things that can assist in making the process successful.

- *Leadership.* A leader with vision is essential. He or she must also be an able and effective communicator. While a great deal of the burden of developing and implementing a strategic plan falls on the provost/academic vice president, it is critical that the president play a major guiding and visible role. The leader's vision must guide the process to successful completion. His or her visible participation (as in our Millennium Meetings chaired by the president) shows the university community that the top leadership is totally behind the process. The leader must also take the final responsibility for setting the university priorities.
- *Feedback.* There cannot be too much emphasis on allowing time and providing venues for feedback. Holding meetings open to the entire university community proved critical for the buy in that we wanted. Encouraging attendance at the open forums and allowing everyone to leave their work to participate left staff in particular with the feeling that what they had to say was important.
- *Actionable vision.* Any road will get you to your destination if you do not know where you are going. A clearly articulated vision that is effectively communicated motivates all sectors of the university to work together to achieve a shared goal. It also empowers divisions and departments to refine their own vision and initiatives in alignment with institutional goals.
- *Communication.* In real estate, a key phase is "location, location, location." To implement successfully a university strategic planning process, the key phrase is "communicate, communicate, communicate." At every stage of the process, it is important to communicate the status of the strategic planning process. We found that the more we communicated, the more people provided feedback and the hungrier they got for information. The key is to allow adequate time for feedback and to use multiple methods and venues of communication including meetings, open forums, the web, written documents, and formal and informal interviews.
- *Participation.* Providing a broad spectrum of venues and methods for the exchange of ideas is vital for participants to buy in to the process and the plan. Utilize the town hall meeting, brown-bag lunches, every form of media available, formal surveys, and informal conversations while walking the halls—the more people that experience the process, the greater the buy-in; the more ideas and feedback processed, the stronger the final plan. In short, create a system where no one can say, "No one asked me!"

- *Transparency.* Every step of the strategic planning process and its implementation must be candid, honest, and open. It is imperative to lay out the steps in the process and identify the key players in an easily accessible and understandable format. People will be more involved if they can believe that the "administration does not already have the plan." Diligently work to assure faculty, staff, and students that there are no hidden agendas. During the implementation phase and especially the budgeting phase, ensure that the measures and guidelines are clear and consistent across disciplines and executive areas.
- *Data.* Hard data should play a major part in the process. First, rely on your institution's internal research team (in the case of Florida International, the Office of Institutional Research) to provide reliable data for the decision-making processes. Second, consult national studies and benchmarks for similar institutions. Third, while it is important to examine data from as many sources as possible, it is even more important that the data be reliable. Allow space for individual units within the university to crosscheck the data as it relates to each area.
- *Measurable criteria.* "What gets measured gets done." Set appropriate benchmarks for determining success—both long and short term. Establish cycles of annual reviews for university entities including reviews of academic programs and strategic issues to determine how well the execution of the plan is going and how far the institution has moved in achieving its stated goals.
- *Timeline.* The strategic planning process should have a beginning and ending time. It must be long enough to allow for the development of a workable plan but not so long that people will lose interest. If the process goes on for too long, conditions (budgetary or others) change and what might have been appropriate at one time is no longer viable.
- *Implementation plan.* If vision identifies strategic goals, implementation determines the plan's success. It is critical that the implementation process be part of the plan. Implementation should address issues such as budgeting and the allocation of resources for strategically aligned personnel and program decisions. It is also important to provide transparent and accessible guidelines for measuring progress and success at each step of the process.
- *Evaluation plan.* Every strategic plan must have an evaluation plan as one of its major components. Institutionalize an annual review process for the plan, adjusting as necessary. Establish benchmarks to guide the plan's evaluation. Make sure the plan maintains momentum

and remains flexible and open to changing environments, especially if it is a long-term plan that may necessitate revisions of goals and strategies.

Conclusion: A New Strategic Plan

Since its founding, Florida International University has been guided by a strategic planning paradigm that provided direction and the ideal of becoming and remaining a student-centered and publicly engaged university. Strategic planning has been the key factor in focusing the institution's attention on the shared vision, mission, and goals, while empowering individual areas to excel and grow under the shared rubric. We have worked to use transparent processes that allow for collaboration in acquiring and using the best information and data available. We have been committed to providing ample and varied venues for discussion and debate on the architecture, content, and implementation of each plan. This process has also engaged the community at large by incorporating the needs, concerns, and challenges of the external environment as part of the strategic plan. Finally, there has been no time to rest on laurels. The planning process remains animate, energetic, and ongoing.

As Andrew Carnegie once noted, teamwork is "the ability to work together toward a common vision; the ability to direct individual accomplishments toward organizational objectives; the fuel that allows common people to attain uncommon results." In spring 2006, the university was successful in securing state approval for a College of Medicine. A College of Medicine means a new Strategic Planning Council will be designated, a round of Millennium-style meetings will be organized, data from new external and internal scans will be collected, a new strategic plan will be developed and implemented, and the cycle will be reborn. Once again, Florida International University will be marshaling its ability to work together toward a common vision, one that will ensure that it continues on a trajectory to become one of the nation's Top Urban Public Research Universities.

Endnotes

1) These six priorities were subsequently distilled to five: Health, International, Urban, Environment, and Information.
2) The acronym was first used in Reaching for the Top (FIU, 1995) but was modified and became the hallmark of the *Millennium Plan* (FIU, 2003a).

References

Florida International University. (1995). *Reaching for the top*. Miami: FL: Author.

Florida International University. (2001). *Assessing our capacities*. Miami, FL: Author.

Florida International University. (2003a). *Millennium strategic plan*. Retrieved August 22, 2006, from the Florida International University, Planning and Institutional Effectiveness web site: www.fiu.edu/~pie

Florida International University. (2003b). *Millennium strategic planning: Identifying strengths and weaknesses*. Retrieved August 22, 2006, from the Florida International University, Planning and Institutional Effectiveness web site: www.fiu.edu/~pie/snwcommittee.htm

Kaplan, R. S., & Norton, P. D. (1996). *The balanced scorecard: Translating strategy into action*. Boston, MA: Harvard Business School Press.

McCormick, A. C. (Ed.). (2000). *The Carnegie classification of institutions of higher education, 2000 edition*. Menlo Park, CA: Carnegie Foundation for the Advancement of Teaching.

Padilla, A., & Ghosh, S. K. (2000, Winter). Turnover at the top: The revolving door of the academic presidency. *The Presidency, 3*(1), 30–37.

State University System of Florida, Board of Governors. (2005). *Board of Governors State University System of Florida strategic plan*. Miami, FL: Author.

15

The Kellogg Commission: Glancing Back, Looking Forward

C. Peter Magrath

In the mid-1990s, supported by the W. K. Kellogg Foundation, 25 university presidents and chancellors representing primarily large public state and land-grant universities, but also urban, regional, and tribal colleges, organized themselves under the conviction that major changes in the social and economic environment were impacting American higher education. They believed that as university leaders they should "take charge of change."

The Origins and Purposes of the Commission

The Kellogg Commission on the Future of State Universities and Land-Grant Colleges remained active for five years. As president of the association representing state and land-grant universities, it struck me forcefully in the early 1990s that major changes were impacting and would continue to impact in significant ways American higher education, and most certainly research-extensive universities. With this thought in mind, following discussion with a few knowledgeable colleagues, including officials at the Kellogg Foundation (to my mind the "land-grant foundation"), I felt that the time was at hand for a high-powered commission of university presidents. Joined by lay advisors, such a commission ought to take a candid look at what our research universities were doing, what changes needed to be made, and how public trust and credibility could be restored where necessary and in any event strengthened as cultural, economic, and social circumstances were changing.

I also broached the idea of such a commission as one that should be inclusive of the great private research-extensive universities along with the public ones. This general concept was presented to the Association of American Universities, which represents both public and private universities. While the idea was warmly received by the public universities, the reception by private university leaders was, if not frigid, certainly very cool. They believed that opening up a discussion of the strengths and weaknesses of American universities to public discussion would invite unwelcome government and public intrusion into their operations. As a consequence, I concluded that this effort would focus on public universities, which are clearly the major part of American higher education.

After further discussion and helpful insights from public university presidents and leading officials of the Kellogg Foundation, including its president, Bill Richardson, the commission was generously funded and organized. It issued six reports—as calls to action—on some of the major issues impacting American public higher education. The commission's presidents and chancellors analyzed trends and public needs, and recommended changes both in practice and attitude along with specific illustrations of changes that were, at least partially, under way in some of the participating institutions. The commission met with a group of lay advisors, including business and civic leaders and university trustees; it had a small staff led by its executive director, John V. Byrne, president emeritus of Oregon State University, and was assisted by Jim Harvey, an educational writer and consultant.

The Kellogg Commission came together at a time when various surveys had shown then, as they do now, that the American public and its leaders were generally quite satisfied with American higher education. But they were troubled by a belief that undergraduate students were too often ignored and neglected, and that the costs of supporting higher education were higher than they should be because of inefficiencies and lax fiscal controls. The commission presidents shared the view that major changes were on the horizon and that, inevitably, financial challenges would be front and center. They believed that leadership mattered, and that if they as chief executives "in the saddle" (not just as theoretical commentators) tried to lead, they could make a positive difference.

But the presidents were realists, and they fully understood that the commission could not mandate campus changes—that depended on the campuses and their leaders. Yet they believed they could encourage needed changes and chart directional guidelines to stimulate reforms. All the five major Kellogg Commission reports used as a theme the title

"Returning to Our Roots"; they addressed five issue areas: *The Student Experience* (1997); *Student Access* (1998); *The Engaged Institution* (1999a); *A Learning Society* (1999b); and *Toward a Coherent Campus Culture* (2000b). A final statement was titled *Renewing the Covenant: Learning, Discovery, and Engagement in a New Age and Different World* (2000a). Because the commission did not want simply to issue reports with an active shelf life of a few days, it asked presidents and other leaders at public universities to examine seriously the reports and their meaning for their institutions. It also organized a series of regional meetings involving faculty and staff, students, and civic and community leaders to consider its recommendations and their implications for their university and region.

Despite its diversity of institutions, the commission was dominated by research universities who implicitly came to the conclusion that, as much as we all saw research as a fundamental obligation of American universities, we would not issue a report calling for more research support. In part, perhaps, the operative assumption was that research was such a powerful driver within universities (as well as in the broader society that loves the fruits of research in food, medicine, engineering, and many other areas) that it would take care of itself. Even more, there was an explicit assumption that typically large and complex universities had to address the issue of students and their needs as a first priority.

Put another way, it is not that the commission devalued research, but that it wanted to emphasize the need for more student-centered, more outward-looking and outwardly responsive universities. One of the key assumptions was that presidents from research-extensive universities would have the greatest credibility in arguing for more attention to students, to public engagement as part of the core mission of a university, and to lifelong learning. (For those whose memories go back a way, this was in political terms a bit like the reality that it had to be Richard Nixon and not Hubert Humphrey who opened the door to renewed American relationships with China. And moreover, the China opening demonstrated that significant change requires leadership and clear messages from the top.)

It is worth noting that, just as research was not the explicit topic of a commission report, neither were a number of other clearly significant issues. For example, the commission, while discussing in its reports needed linkages between K–12 and university education, the need for strong student assistance programs, or the value of diversity in our universities, did not issue separate reports on these topics. Similarly, the great opportunities that involve American universities in international education were noted but not featured in a special report. In 2004 however, the National Association of State Universities and Land-Grant Colleges issued a major statement very much in the spirit of the Kellogg Commission: *A Call to Leadership: The Presidential Role in Internationalizing the University.* This report, which has specific and practical guidelines for university presidents, could well have been a commission report. This, then, is the background on the origins and purposes of the Kellogg Commission.

What It Accomplished

The opening paragraphs of this section draw on a survey conducted by John Byrne (2006), who served as the Kellogg Commission's executive director, and quote extensively from comments he has prepared for his forthcoming report to the Kellogg Foundation and the National Association of State Universities and Land-Grant Colleges.

More than five years after the commission's final meeting, it is instructive to address the impact that it had on higher education reform. John Byrne's (2006) assessment of its influence is based on responses from 34 presidents, chancellors, and friends of public higher education, including many of the institutions that were formally represented on the commission. The respondents were asked to give their views of the effectiveness of the commission and to share examples, if possible, related to significant changes on their campuses based on its recommendations.

Not surprisingly, perhaps, the respondents all made positive comments about the general value of the commission in creating an awareness of the need for higher education reform. Several said that it had stimulated and shaped discussion nationally and had stimulated action on their campus. In some cases the respondents suggested that the commission had validated changes already under way or that were being implemented at their university. Many, in commenting on its importance, used such phrases as "provided a wake-up call," "generated an important national discussion," "accelerated the process of transformation," "provided a clear articulation of issues," "improved an understanding of academic issues," "emphasized the importance of 'learning, discovery, and engagement,'" and "served as a guide for reform" (Byrne, 2006, p. ii). Several respondents called for an ongoing Kellogg Commission-type effort to continue to stimulate reform.

These campus leaders pointed out that the primary areas of change influenced by the commission included engagement with society; internationalization of the campus, with particular attention to overseas opportunities for students; holistic learning, including residential and in-service learning; undergraduate research opportunities; and distance and lifelong learning (Byrne, 2006). A number of campuses had revised their curricula with specific attention to the general core and to capstone in-service experiences. Several institutions reviewed and revised their guidelines for promotion and tenure in keeping with academic changes and greater engagement with society. Many indicated greater emphasis on diversity and attention to campus culture in general.

In summary, the respondents all claim that at "their" university significant changes are under way; some, apparently, are clearly innovative, while many indicated that they had adopted changes already being implemented at other universities. All respondents suggest that they are striving more to meet the educational needs of the 21st century, needs that they are pledged to serving. And they indicate that the Kellogg Commission's work, whether directly or indirectly, has been a benefit to them personally and to higher education. Obviously, some of their expressions may be rhetorical wishful thinking or cheerleading that is typical of virtually all of us who have served as university presidents. Nevertheless it would be unfair to dismiss these observations as meaningless. At the very least, and this indeed is considerable, the Kellogg Commission laid out a road map, with directions, for significant changes in American public higher education that many chancellors and presidents see as needed and most worthy objectives.

Obviously, precise statistical data on the accomplishments of the Kellogg Commission are impossible; the Byrne survey is based on impressions, self-reporting, and personal observations. But there is no doubt that the commission attracted considerable attention and provoked dialogue and discussion by university leaders in state and land-grant universities. It reinforced their desire to promote better education for students; a recognition of the critical importance of access for America's increasingly diverse population; the growing importance of lifelong, or continuous, learning as a major part of the future of higher education in the 21st century; and the necessity for universities to be fully engaged in partnership with their communities and regions.

Interestingly and perhaps tellingly, the commission's third report, *The Engaged Institution* (1999a) was its "bestseller" in terms of requests for copies and hits on the Internet from around the world. It of course reflected some of the historic roots of the land-grant universities and their commitment to "service" in the agricultural arena through their extension function going back to their origin. But it went far beyond that, because all universities, whether private or public, have a broad commitment to being of use and value to their society. *The Engaged Institution* report, which also was one of the most explicit and specific in recommendations on how engaged partnerships between universities and their communities and regions could be implemented, spoke to a deep impulse. It owed much to the fact that education and research or discovery needs to be applied to be socially and economically useful. It is also a way for universities to engender support politically and financially by being seen as vital and useful to their communities—not just as so-called ivory towers located within defined campuses and, somewhat mysteriously, doing good things in cloistered ways.

I believe it can be fairly argued that, while student needs and interests still deserve more attention, both public and private universities are today far more self-conscious to the interests of their students for flexible learning, for personal attention, and for learning opportunities throughout their lives for both vocational and personal improvement reasons. At the leadership level of provosts, academic vice presidents, deans, and indeed many professors, there is a renewed appreciation of the importance of being as responsible as possible to students and their needs and interests. In summary, while hardly accomplishing all its lofty intentions, the Kellogg Commission improved understanding within universities of changes that need to be made. And it provided a climate for new efforts to improve student learning and bring the fruits of the university and its research and other talents into collaborative partnerships with communities and groups throughout their regions.

What It Did Not Accomplish_____

No one associated with the Kellogg Commission imagined that its various recommendations and policy guides would automatically be implemented. Universities are complex organisms with many participants, internal and external interests, and cultures that are resistant, though not necessarily impervious, to change and adaptation. Moreover, the commission was never conceived of as an implementing body or organization—how could it be?—but as a hopefully influential, well-connected group of university leaders whose collective voice would make an impact on American public higher education. The idea was that, working as best they could in their complex university environments, they would try to further the goals of the commission.

Although public universities have not become as student centered as the commission hoped, more attention is being given by university leaders both in the public and private sectors to student issues and needs. Universities still have more to do on this front, but their leaders are today far more conscious of the imperative to be responsive to students needs; in the language of the Kellogg Commission, "putting students first." Students are not the only reason for the existence of universities—the research or discovery function is absolutely essential to American society. But without students who are being taught well, learning to learn, and, at their best, enjoying the thrill of participating in the discovery of knowledge, there is no true university.

As any seasoned observer of universities understands, changing internal cultures within complex organizations at the collegiate and departmental level is extraordinarily difficult. Indeed, the commission's report *Toward a Coherent Campus Culture* understood very well that there are many cultures within universities. We phrased it this way:

> An academic culture, made up primarily of faculty and students, fragmented into its own subcultures organized around disciplines, self-governing departments, and professional schools; a distinct and entire separate student culture, with a bewildering diversity of aims and interests, from fraternities and sororities to student associations and research clubs; an administrative culture that tends to be separated from that of the faculty and sometimes in competition with it; and an athletic culture, perceived to be autonomous and beholden to commercial interests. (Kellogg Commission, 2000b, p. 10)

Universities, after all, reflect an individualistic modus operandi in which faculty have enormous discretion and power in shaping the curriculum, the methods of teaching, and the research projects that are undertaken. The commission fully understood the working realities of American higher education. It directed its main recommendations to chancellors and presidents in leadership positions—recognizing that penetration into "the woodwork" of universities at the collegiate and departmental level is a slower, longer-range process. But over time there could be changes as presidents and provosts pushed for them, aided by such factors as the competition among universities to attract students, along with public expectations for high-quality undergraduate education.

This individualistic focus, to repeat, is the reality of American higher education. It is hardly surprising that the Kellogg Commission recommendations have not yet led to fundamental changes in the internal cultures of our universities. Yet internal cultures within complex organizations can, and do, change when external forces (such as changing economic, financial, and political realties) become irresistible. As the consequences of not "changing" become clearer and clearer—especially the loss of financial resources—leading participants within organizations become realistic and accept the need for change, especially if strong leaders state the case and show the way. Today, most presidents of American universities, both public and private, are articulating publicly, as well as internally within their universities, that the economic and social forces affecting American higher education are markedly different from what they were 20 or even 10 years ago.

Gradual change is possible. And it is probably the only kind that endures and lasts without destroying the fabric of enterprises, such as American universities, that have been extraordinarily successful. It is increasingly being promoted by trustees and presidents who consistently state the need for attention to student interests as well as to the imperative of access and diversity within the American society. Moreover, skillfully applied, budgetary incentives can be used to achieve desired objectives. President can utilize at least a significant portion of budgetary resources to support those departments and colleges that reflect the kind of balances proposed by the Kellogg Commission in the teaching or learning and research or discovery responsibilities of universities. Such funding can also encourage the role of universities in being engaged in economic, social, and cultural partnerships in their communities.

Those who have worked within universities understand that the reward and recognition structure for faculty is critical to bringing about needed changes. Incentives of a financial sort can be given to departments and programs that commit themselves in practical, not just rhetorical ways, to the outreach and engagement responsibilities of universities and to serving student needs. One might also remember that most American professors are not ideologically hostile (quite the contrary) to service and engagement, if their work is recognized and rewarded. The overwhelming majority of professors also consciously care about students. In fact, during the commission's lifetime, a number of universities reviewed and revised their promotion and tenure policies because they recognized the changing roles and expectations surrounding universities. There has been some progress, even as more is needed.

It also deserves recognition that there is a significant schizophrenia (a harsher word might be *hypocrisy*) on the part of the dominant forces in American life regarding universities: The external world—the funding sources, the political and civic leaders, and the media—bestows huge prestige on research and its accomplishments, not only in medicine, but in virtually all arenas. The public and its representatives may sincerely care about the education and learning processes of students, but the dominant forces in society reward and recognize those American universities that are leaders in research—and the American research university has been extraordinarily valuable to our economy and society. In truth, the internal and external roles of universities substantially reflect the political realities of the broader public. And this needs to be understood as efforts are made to adapt and bring changes into the internal workings and reward systems of our universities as defined by the Kellogg Commission.

Looking Forward

Just as the internal dynamics of America's public universities still need to change to fulfill the vision and recommendations of the Kellogg Commission, so too is there a continuing challenge on the larger issue of the informal social compact between universities and the American society, a topic addressed in the final Kellogg Commission report. Radically changing financial circumstances confront public universities, and it is highly unlikely that decreased state investment in public higher education will be reversed. The commission suggested a Higher Education Millennial Partnership Act, intended to promote a truly close working linkage between public higher education and elementary and secondary education as a critical need to a knowledge society in which all elements of education ought to be collaborating closely. The thought was that new federal legislation could be promoted which would have the kind of dramatic impact that eventually resulted from the original land-grant acts of the 19th century. That of course has not happened, although a component of that thought is reflected in proposals still being promoted for federal action that would focus heavily on information technologies and how they can be used creatively to link and form partnerships between all segments of American education. In fact, in 2003, the Business–Higher Education Forum, an organization of educational and business leaders, produced a clear and focused statement and set of recommendations in a report titled *Building A Nation of Learners*, which provides a road map to move in that direction. This effort is still a work in progress, but the core idea is sound and speaks to many, if not all, of the needs of the United States for a truly integrated educational system that serves the competitive demands of a knowledge society and economy.

But the Kellogg Commission's hope for a formal new compact between the state and federal governments has not happened. This result is partially a consequence of the financial problems of the 21st century, and in part because it now seems clear that any kind of new compact will emerge informally—and not as a conscious piece of legislation. Moreover, when we view circumstances realistically, it is clear that the federal government will always be vital in terms of its financial support for student assistance and research but will not become a substitute for the erosion of state dollars. These factors have pushed American higher education into more entrepreneurial relationships, higher tuition charges, and intensified private fundraising campaigns. Put most bluntly, the federal government will not substitute federal dollars for the eroding state dollars.

As one assesses the educational landscape, it is good to emphasize a strength of American higher education. In both the public and private sectors, universities enjoy relative autonomy and decentralization compared to the far more centralized educational systems typical of universities in Europe and many other parts of the world. Interestingly, significant changes are being pursued in Europe, led and organized by ministers of education. They are working to harmonize the educational systems of European countries, to reorganize their credit and degree-granting structures, and to attract increased investments in university research. These efforts, generally speaking, flow out of a movement known as the Bologna Process—a movement of a kind unthinkable in the United States because it is led by government ministries and the European Union.

Any new social understanding or compact that emerges in the United States in the years ahead inevitably will be informal and probably somewhat messy. Yet it may well lead to new understandings and arrangements even if they are not officially stamped with formal government approval. A major initiative under the coordination of the American Council on Education seeks to provoke public discussion and understanding of the benefits that derive from a well-educated citizenry. These include a stronger economy, better health, more engaged volunteerism and community involvement, enhanced global understanding and competitiveness, along with the many fruits that flow from university-based research. This initiative aims to be a structured national, state, and local effort in which colleges and universities work with civic and corporate groups to communicate the national interest in a strong and competitive American system of higher education. Along with the economic and social circumstances of this new century, this effort over time may stimulate further progress toward the kinds of outcomes proposed by the Kellogg Commission.

Moreover, even as reference has been made to the power—indeed the tyranny—of cultures within complex organizations such as universities, cultures can change. They can change when threats as well as opportunities exist—and both are there for American higher education. University budgets, which ultimately reflect the true priorities of institutions, can be made to reflect even more than they do today the objectives of university presidents. Exercised skillfully and artfully, budgetary authority—the power of the purse—can penetrate into departments and their colleges in order to promote the kind of changes recommended by the Kellogg Commission. Incentives work among human beings, and budgetary incentives can be used to bring about changes within academic departments. Departments will remain as a fundamental unit of American universities even as inter- and multidisciplinary studies and relationships become increasingly significant in research-extensive universities. While it is tempting to suggest some kind of a new Kellogg Commission report titled something like *"Restructuring the Culture and Workings of American Universities,"* that is probably not in the educational cards. But forces are at work on behalf of needed changes. In the years ahead, a modified academic culture could emerge. It would recognize departments as useful entities furthering the ascendancy of interdisciplinary and multidisciplinary work, and engagement as the wave of the future that reflects the true needs of a knowledge society.

Obviously, this is speculative; the future will be what unfolds. But public universities, even if they receive less public money, can still operate under an ethos and mission that are unequivocally public. The leaders, however, must promote understanding that education is both a private and a public good, and that there is a compelling practical need for a highly educated citizenry that is creative (discovers and applies knowledge) and serves the needs of a diverse society in a highly competitive, interconnected world. The public clearly wants access to higher education, at least in the traditional sense of students being educated, acquiring skills, and receiving meaningful degrees. American business desires access for our diverse population that requires the skills of an educated workforce. Moreover, business and the public, when properly approached, appreciate the fruits of research and its valuable application for social and economic needs.

This ethos of service to the public is central to America's state and land-grant universities. Critics and naysayers to the contrary, I have no doubt that this is the land-grant ethos, and it applies not only to those universities that are technically land grant, but virtually to all public universities. It is alive and well, despite funding challenges and the complex circumstances of American society and its educational system in a highly competitive world.

My perspective is inevitably influenced by a personal involvement with the Kellogg Commission. But I believe its vision and directions still ring true, even if implementation of many of its ideals and recommendations are still a work in progress. Optimistically and hopefully, perhaps the implementation strategies being discussed and proposed in this book by its knowledgeable contributors can help provide guidance of practical value that brings needed changes to our universities.

Finally, to those who believe that change, even if gradual and partial, is impossible, consider this question: What are the alternatives to educational leaders trying and striving for change? Do we simply give up, saying that it is status quo yesterday, today, and forever? Can we be comfortable with a drift in which public universities will be governed and unduly influenced by external pressures and influences? Or, rather, do we continue to promote a vision for socially and economically more responsive universities? For me the answer is clear: We continue to try to pursue various strategies and tactics to implement needed changes in a valuable educational system that needs to reform and adapt in a world that continues to change.

Author Note

This chapter was prepared with the assistance of John V. Byrne, president emeritus of Oregon State University, who served as executive director of the Kellogg Commission.

References

Business–Higher Education Forum. (2003). *Building a nation of learners: The need for changes in teaching and learning to meet global challenge.* Washington, DC: Author.

Byrne, J. V. (2006). *Public higher education reform five years after the Kellogg Commission on the Future of State and Land-Grant Universities.* Retrieved August 22, 2006, from www.nasulgc.org/Kellogg/KCFiveYearReport.pdf

Kellogg Commission on the Future of State and Land-Grant Universities. (1997). *Returning to our roots: The student experience.* Washington, DC: National Association of State Universities and Land-Grant Colleges.

Kellogg Commission on the Future of State and Land-Grant Universities. (1998). *Returning to our roots: Student access*. Washington, DC: National Association of State Universities and Land-Grant Colleges.

Kellogg Commission on the Future of State and Land-Grant Universities. (1999a). *Returning to our roots: The engaged institution*. Washington, DC: National Association of State Universities and Land-Grant Colleges.

Kellogg Commission on the Future of State and Land-Grant Universities. (1999b). *Returning to our roots: A learning society*. Washington, DC: National Association of State Universities and Land-Grant Colleges.

Kellogg Commission on the Future of State and Land-Grant Universities. (2000a). *Renewing the covenant: Learning, discovery, and engagement in a new age and different world*. Washington, DC: National Association of State Universities and Land-Grant Colleges.

Kellogg Commission on the Future of State and Land-Grant Universities. (2000b). *Returning to our roots: Toward a coherent campus culture*. Washington, DC: National Association of State Universities and Land-Grant Colleges.

National Association of State Universities and Land-Grant Colleges. (2004). *A call to leadership: The presidential role in internationalizing the university*. Washington, DC: Author.

16

Returning to Their Roots: Putting Unity, Students, and Public Back Into State Universities

Joseph C. Burke

The Kellogg Commission challenged presidents and chancellors of public universities to take charge of three critical changes: to fix the *fragmented university* and create campuses as *student centered* and *publicly engaged* as they are research focused. The real problem for public research universities on the eve of the 21st century was not what they should do, but how to do it. The Kellogg Commission never claimed originality. It echoed existing concerns about campus priorities and problems. As Peter Magrath observes in Chapter 15, the novelty of the Kellogg Commission came not from the issues raised, but from the challenge issued to campus colleagues to take charge of change—to return to their roots by putting unity, students, and public back into state universities.

Five years after the last commission report, what does the record suggests about results? In a survey of university leaders, Byrne (2006) found increasing awareness of the need for reform and implementation of some of the Kellogg recommendations on individual campuses. Presidential speeches, mission statements, and strategic plans proclaim the importance of becoming student centered and publicly engaged, but the reality on most campuses still falls short of the rhetoric. More public research universities did begin setting institutional priorities that coupled campus capabilities with shifting demands, but mostly because external forces gave them little choice.

When the Kellogg Commission met in 1996, external developments already demanded institutional direction as well as continuing decentralization. Falling state funding as a percentage of university budgets necessitated self-generated income that came mostly from departments, schools, and colleges with burgeoning demands from student majors and sponsored research (see Chapters 3 and 6). Responding to market forces required institutional direction to realign university priorities, reallocate resources, and at times to reorganize academic units. Growth in multidisciplinary research also demanded institutional initiatives to achieve cooperation among academic units. As one university commission later declared, "Interdisciplinary research and teaching at a major research university . . . are not just nice things to do from time to time; they are essential for its success" (Ohio State University, 2004, p. 1). Cooperation increasingly called for combining some departments, schools, and colleges, instead of creating additional independent institutes and centers.

The earlier model of university organization favored dividing and decentralizing, creating new departments, schools, and colleges and devolving authority to the lowest possible level. By the late 1990s, the momentum shifted to collaborate and combine to control costs and respond to changing markets. President Timothy White's letter transmitting Oregon State's strategic plan said it plainly: "For all organizational changes, the guiding principle is that organizational form follows desired function such that effectiveness is improved, that we gain efficiencies whenever possible, and encourage entrepreneurial efforts" (Oregon State University, 2003, p. 3).

At the same time, the requirement of self-generated revenue split the faculty and the departments into "haves" and "have-nots"—those with and those without growing demands for sponsored research and student majors. These trends are transforming the organization, management, and governance of public research universities. Bennis and Movius (2006) claim this split explains the fall of President Lawrence Summers at Harvard University, but it exists in top research universities across the country, public as well as private.

Governance Shift

So long as state funding remained mostly incremental and external demands for majors and research were mostly stable, "the faculty" as a whole could claim common interests or at least ignore differences. By the 1990s, the decline in state funding per student, the shift in sponsored research to multidisciplinary fields, and the change in demand for undergraduate majors from some of the liberal arts and traditional sciences to business and professional fields splintered faculty unity at the university level. If the previous situation supported stability, the new condition called for change. It united the interest of entrepreneurial professors with entrepreneurial presidents and provosts in pushing for market responsiveness, reordered priorities, reallocated resources, and academic reorganizations. All these shifts demanded institutional direction while preserving decentralization.

The wide adoption of various forms of Responsibility Center Management encouraged this shift from stability to change (see Chapter 6). It rewarded entrepreneurial colleges and schools by returning most of the income they generated from research and tuition. Professors from less favored fields for research and majors worry that this new form of budgeting puts a premium on generating income, even with the cross-subsidies that most of these plans provide (Whalen, 1991). They fear that markets, not institutional missions or academic values, now drive public research universities.

Revenue generation became the coin of the realm not just in campus management and governance but also in another powerful external force, reputational ratings. The ratings from both the *U.S. News & World Report* and *Top American Research Universities* use many indicators that reflect revenues from sponsored research, fundraising, and student selectivity in undergraduate admissions that permit substantial tuition increases (see Chapter 1). In a competitive age when both funding and prestige depend on taking charge of change, a majority of the faculty at many public research universities could no longer settle for stalemate or deadlock in institutional governance. Increasingly, leading professors, tired of the endless quarrels about which group had the right to decide, remembered that governance "is the means to implementing ideas that either respond to problems or provide new strategies" (Tierney & Lechuga, 2004, p. 1).

A New Form of Shared Governance

The old shared governance saw distinct divisions in the interests of trustees and central administrators on one side and the faculty on the other. Now the demand for self-generated income divided the faculty into those groups that benefited from growing demands for student enrollments and research grants and those units that suffered from declining interests. Pushed by market demands and pulled by peer prestige, the dividing line in many public research universities increasingly becomes, for professors as well as administrators, the attitude toward campus change, not location in governance groups.

Critics claim "managerialism" imported from business by activist presidents and trustees subverted faculty governance at the university level, especially faculty senates (Birnbaum, 2001). In reality, at least part of the shift came from within faculty ranks. The requirement of self-generated income to replace falling state funding resulted in a new form of shared governance. Changing resources and demands increasingly placed faculty or university senates—where professors traditionally hold majorities—in an impossible position on campuses that want to raise their revenues and reputations.

Roger Benjamin points to the problem created for senates because of "the public assumption by the collective faculty of the equality of all fields of knowledge within the university" (see Chapter 4). Although few professors really believe in such equality, they could not assert publicly that any field is less important than other areas. Faculty senates face a dilemma when confronted with institutional initiatives championed by professors in some areas but opposed by colleagues in others. The discomfort becomes especially distressing when these proposals require reallocating resources and at times even restructuring academic units.

Multi- and interdisciplinary proposals represent classic examples of this shift. Faculty senates in the past generally opposed them because of the dominance of disciplinary departments. The reactions of senates to these extradepartmental programs began to change when more professors—especially those with national reputations—started to support them as research problems and grant opportunities required inputs from multiple disciplines. Universities cannot have shared governance without shared values. In many public research universities, the shared values of trustees, administrators, and most of the faculty now appear to favor an entrepreneurial response to market demands for sponsored research and to a lesser extent for academic majors.

Faculty Senates: From Approval to Acceptance or Acquiescence

In these times of tight institutional budgets, self-generated income, and changing demands, faculty senates in some public research universities appear to undergo a quiet reformation. They seem to shift from demanding senate approval of all institutional initiatives in academic areas to acquiescence or quiet acceptance of proposals supported by many departments, schools, and colleges and opposed by only a few. The rhetoric of faculty senates in these universities continues to claim the right of "approval," but in reality they quietly move to acceptance or acquiescence on initiatives that many professors support but others, always a distinct minority, oppose.

In such cases, the litmus test for faculty senates shifts to judging the participative process rather than the proposal's substance. Faculty senates have always tended to stress process over product, but funding and multidisciplinary shifts that divide the faculty make insisting on right of participation rather than the right of approval the safer course. Senates return to the one factor in university-wide governance that still unites the professoriate—faculty participation. This approach continues to protect academic freedom, which focuses largely on process. It also preserves the right to disapprove administrative proposals that provoke widespread, or at least substantial, faculty opposition.

Acquiescence or acceptance occurs not only on issues where shared governance traditionally gives primacy to central administrations and boards of trustees, such as institutional mission and strategic planning, but also in academic areas affecting the organization of departments, schools, and colleges. Senates do insist on retaining approval of academic programs and personnel policies, actions closely related to faculty expertise and interests.

The reaction of the University Senate at the University of Minnesota to President Bruinink's strategic positioning proposal (see Chapter 12), which recommended reducing by three the number of colleges and schools, offers a classic case of acquiescence. Though the University Senate adopted a set of resolutions on strategic positioning with 122 for, only 3 opposed, and 6 abstaining, the resolutions did not endorse closing the General College and merging two schools (University of Minnesota, 2005). Rather than approving these specific reductions and reorganizations, the resolution stated, "The University Senate recognizes that reconfiguration of academic units may be necessary to achieve the University's strategic goals" (University of Minnesota, 2005). In contrast, the senate did specifically approve the creation of an Honors Program and a Writing Center, which were hardly controversial. Not surprisingly, the strongest resolve urged full participation of the faculty in further actions under strategic positioning, particularly from groups negatively affected by proposed changes.

Oregon State University entered earlier into a planning process similar to Minnesota's. Oregon State also produced plans endorsing consolidations of colleges, schools, and departments. The first version of the plan produced by an ad hoc commission went to the president for approval, with briefings for the Faculty Senate but apparently without a formal review (Oregon State University, 2003). The appointment of a new president led to the creation of a new strategic plan, *A Strategic Plan for the 21st Century* (Oregon State University, 2004). The new president, Edward Ray, had served as provost at Ohio State University during development of its academic plan (Ohio State University, 2000a). After talking about the challenges of falling state funding and changing societal demands, he claimed that Oregon State could turn its dreams of becoming a leading land-grant university into reality if it had the will.

> That is the key: Summoning the will. Conversations here have reminded me of earlier experiences in which colleagues asked who would make the hard decisions and who would be held accountable for our success. The truth is that success will depend on all of us. The planning process must be consultative and inclusive so that our statement of aspirations belongs to all of us. We cannot succeed if we are not bound to a common cause and if we are not bound to that cause for the long term. In the last analysis, however, responsibility for making the right hard decisions resides with the president, provost, vice presidents, vice provosts, deans, directors and department chairs. They have the authority to lead and they should be held accountable for doing so. (Ray, 2003)

Six months later, the minutes of the Faculty Senate merely note: "The Strategic Plan is in the final production stage and it is anticipated that it will be shared with the campus over the next 10-14 days" (Oregon State University, 2004a).

Shared Governance for Campus Change

The shift in university-wide governance requires that presidents and provosts become not just more active but also more participative with leading professors in preparing and implementing proposals that respond to market demands while protecting institutional values. Increasingly, as in the case of Minnesota's strategic positioning, presidents and provosts use commissions and task forces to develop strategies on difficult issues with heavy faculty representation. Those commissions composed of respected professors—including from fields favored by external demands—increasingly recommend reallocation of resources and reorganizations of departments, schools, and colleges in response to growing demands for multidisciplinary research and shifting student interests. Their proposals still require the tacit consent of "the faculty," gauged by a sense of general approval coupled with the absence of significant dissent, but only after exhaustive communication and consultation with the faculty and students, and often with external stakeholders.

These commissions resemble the "joint big decision committees" that George Keller (1983) advocated more than two decades ago and reiterated recently: ". . . faculty participation in all-university governance should be largely through special task forces . . . that help solve a major problem or provide advice on a significant issue and then dissolve" (Keller, 2004, p. 173). Many universities have made such representative committees permanent, especially for advice on planning and budgeting (Schuster, Smith, Corak, & Yamada, 1994). President Bruininks of the University of Minnesota used a large number of ad hoc groups in preparing and, especially, implementing Strategic Positioning, and President Maidique relied on both temporary and more permanent groups to develop the Millennial Plan for Florida International University (Chapters 12 & 14). Former President Kirwan also used a commission to develop Ohio State's academic plan (Ohio State University, 2000a), as do many other public universities.

Presidents and provosts at Ohio State (2004, 2005), Michigan (University of Michigan, 2000, 2004; see also Chapter 3), and many other universities also used such commissions for preparing initiatives in areas such as undergraduate education, interdisciplinary teaching, campus technology, research directions, public engagement, and priority budgeting. The academic plan of the University of North Carolina–Chapel Hill (2003) claims that it built on the foundations of a series of commission and task force reports, on intellectual climate, research and graduate studies, access and diversity, and Native Americans. These commissions represent the "strengthened 'central core'" that Burton Clark (1998) advocated for entrepreneurial universities where ". . . academics trusted . . . by their peers served on central councils and took up responsibility for the entire institution" (p. 137). Later, to correct a mistaken impression that he favored administrative dominance, Clark (2001) coined the phrase *collegial entrepreneurialism*.

At the request of the University Senate at Ohio State, then-President Kirwan appointed a commission to recommend how to improve the senate's effectiveness (Ohio State University, 2000b). The commission report noted the complaints about ad hoc commissions and task forces but also recognized the reasons for their growing use.

> Various constituencies . . . have expressed concern
> that when the need arises for a group to focus on an
> important University problem, central administra-
> tion often looks past existing Senate committees and
> instead creates a new ad hoc group outside the Senate
> structure. The reasons for this practice are under-
> standable. First, it allows the administration to make
> a bold public statement about the importance of the
> problem or task to be addressed. Second, it permits
> the selection of committee members who have special
> expertise in the area of concern. Third, it produces
> quicker results than might be expected from a Senate
> committee. (Ohio State University, 2000b, p. 29)

Instead of recommending the end to such ad hoc committees, the
report urged consultation with the senate leaders on their creation and
membership and more use of university senate committees.

That commission studied senates at peer institutions: Arizona,
Illinois, Michigan, Minnesota, Texas-Austin, Washington, Wisconsin,
Penn State, and UCLA. It reported a practice of shared governance that
appeared much less faculty focused than that conveyed in the American
Association of University Professors' Statement of 1966.

> Most senates have some legislative role focusing on
> academic programs and personnel issues. They make
> recommendations to the President/Chancellor who
> reviews, acts, and where appropriate, sends them for-
> ward for action by the trustees/regents. The other
> major role for these Senates is advisory. They indicate
> that they have a good working relationship with the
> central administration. (Ohio State University,
> 2000b, p. 21)

A New Model of Governance

The classic tripartite models of university-wide governance described
by Baldridge and Curtis (1977) of *bureaucratic, collegial,* and *political,*
and a fourth, *symbolic,* added by Birnbaum (1991), now appear to have
a fifth, the *entrepreneurial* model. It allies entrepreneurial professors
and administrators with a shared interest in change in response to shifting markets for sponsored research and undergraduate majors. Rhoades
(2003) deplores this trend but concedes its dominance. These efforts

are bureaucratic in the sense that presidents and provosts identify crucial challenges and opportunities; collegial in the participation of professors on commissions and task forces preparing proposals; and political in the process of persuading internal constituents and external stakeholders of the necessity for change. President Bruininks calls communicating and consulting on strategic positioning more of "a political campaign than an academic exercise" (see Chapter 12). President Maidique's "Millennium" campus and town meetings also show similar characteristics (see Chapter 14).

This new version of university-wide governance shifts from a fixation on who *decides* questions to the extent and depth of *communication* and *consultation* and to a *sense of consent* from constituents, especially from the faculty, with only *minimal dissent*. The shift occurs because the *who decides* has in practice become more complex and less clear, given the participation on commissions of administrators, professors, and students, and the breadth and depth of the consultation. Trustees and presidents may officially have the final word, but they can only decide by the acceptance or acquiescence of the faculty, students, and at times even outside stakeholders. Communication, consultation, and consent have become not distinct actions but interconnected parts of a seamless process. Both Bruininks and Maidique insist that the extensive process of communication and consultation in their university planning efforts led to changes and improvements in the initial proposals (see Chapters 12 and 14).

Consultation must allow academic units and faculty groups—disadvantaged by reorganization proposals—a full and fair opportunity to defend their positions. Presidents neglect this critical consultation at their peril. The president of the University of Georgia proposed creating three new colleges by shifting academic departments and then a reorganization of the College of Education, cutting the number of departments from 18 to 10 (University of Georgia, 2004). Though the University Council, the faculty governance body, approved the reorganizations, complaints about consultation with disaffected groups, especially in education, soured administrative and faculty relations and led to the development of a detailed proposal on dissolutions and reorganizations (Dendy, 2004). Even the most popular reorganizations require attention to process, especially in relation to faculty units that are negatively affected.

Instead of attacking faculty or university senates as the source of delays and deadlocks, perhaps it is time to clarify this new avenue of university-wide governance that allows institutional action without undermining faculty collegiality, and to connect it to faculty and university senates. Presidents should do the following when creating commissions and task forces:

- Consult senate leaders for reaction to the purpose and membership of proposed commissions.
- Consider and respond to senate comments on commission recommendations.
- Submit with their recommendations to boards of trustees both senate comments and presidential responses along with the commission reports.

Clearly, university commissions and task forces are here to stay. The above principles allow the body representing the collective faculty to permit difficult changes while preserving collegiality, protecting participation, and retaining the right to review recommendations that affect the academic operations of the universities. Although boards of trustees have in theory the power to decide, they would certainly consider carefully commission recommendations that received critical comments from faculty or university senates. This shift in governance alters the roles of the trustees, presidents, and the faculty.

The Participants

Trustees, administration, and the faculty constitute the traditional participants in university-wide governance. Though the role of students is now recognized, the extent of their participation and impact in university-wide decision-making remains less clear. Although students should become much more active and their participation deserves more study, this book has focused on trustees, presidents, and the faculty participation in decision-making at the institutional level.

Trustees

Trustees today seem to run to extremes, either inactive or intrusive, and lately more of the latter. Tom Ingram (see Chapter 2) sees the strategic role of trustees as helping their universities steer that difficult course between public needs and campus concerns, market demands and campus values. Trustees should have standing in both camps, appreciating external and internal interests. This chapter, written by a former long-time president of the Association of Governing Boards of Colleges and Universities (AGB), argues for a balanced role for university trustees.

He criticizes activist trustees who advocate a political or ideological agenda as well as inactive ones who merely cheerlead for their campus and its athletics. His chapter urges trustees to take advantage of their natural position by acting externally as critical advocates and internally as friendly critics of their universities. This balancing act requires that public governing boards again become a buffer against undue influence from governors and legislators. AGB advocates blue-ribbon nominating commissions that recommend candidates for trustees to governors, which would enhance their stature and their independence (see Chapter 2).

Ingram contends that trustees succeed not so much by the actions they take or the decisions they make as by the questions they ask and the answers they provoke. By asking tough questions about institutional priorities and performance, they can ensure that university missions and goals are not just for public consumption or state compliance but direct campus activities. Along with presidents, trustees are the only university officials that have responsibility for the entire institution. Given that perspective, they have a vested interest in fixing the fragmented university by ensuring implementation of institutional priorities. Their special concern for responding to public needs should also support their advocacy of undergraduate education and public engagement.

Presidents

James Duderstadt (Chapter 3) once complained that the presidency of research universities represents "a mismatch between responsibility and authority which is unparalleled in other social institutions" (Duderstadt & Womack, 2003, p. 137). Yet his chapter is not a paean to presidential power. It is more nuanced than expected from a former president who helped produce considerable change at the University of Michigan during difficult times. He calls for continuity as well as change for public research universities, and for caution as well as action from their presidents.

Duderstadt insists that dramatic developments in society—such as globalization, technology, social diversity, and knowledge economies—combine to demand cultural changes in public universities that presidents must lead. Yet his chapter has an ambivalent ring about presidential activism. Changing campus culture in response to societal needs and market demands requires presidential leadership, says Duderstadt, but presidents must remember, "First, to do no harm" (see Chapter 3). Yet worries about doing no harm can lead to inaction, for launching any critical change on campus carries inevitable risks. Courage and caution seldom come in combination. Duderstadt claims that the critical contribution of presidents is to reinforce the university saga of values and traditions and relate it to the campus changes required for a challenging future.

President Bruininks of the University of Minnesota and President Maidique of Florida International University (FIU) favor a more activist role in producing change. But they also are participative in involving leading professors in the process of developing and implementing directions for their universities. They acted to change campus culture to respond to new imperatives, but continued the institutional sagas that inspire loyalty not only from the alumni, but also from students, professors, and state officials. President Holbrook also champions the importance of the university saga.

The size and diversity of today's public research universities do pose challenges to continuing institutional sagas. After all, Burton Clark (1992)—the champion of sagas—wrote about their force in three small liberal arts colleges: Antioch, Reed, and Swarthmore. Still size need not suppress saga. When President Bruininks mentions "The U" in speeches, which he frequently does, it evokes the image of a venerable university to many Minnesotans, alumni, students, and professors. His 34 years as professor, dean, provost, and president at the University of Minnesota add weight to his interpretation of what that saga suggests about the "U" of the future. Governor La Follette and President Van Hise are long gone, but the "Wisconsin Idea" lives on and evolves, even though the University of Wisconsin–Madison now serves much of the world as well as its home state (University of Wisconsin–Madison, 2003). The saga need not be long in the making. FIU's climb in just 35 years from a small two-year upper division college to a large urban research university has already become a saga of a university on the move against all odds. The long tenure of President Maidique of nearly two decades has become part of that saga.

In entrepreneurial universities, visions that incorporate sagas of enduring values may represent the major counterweight to market forces. They evoke enduring images of memorable courses with favored faculty members, public engagement of students and professors working on community projects, or of universities repeatedly turning challenges into opportunities. But today, the visions of public research universities too often fixate on climbing toward the top of the national rankings. Unfortunately, those ratings give no points for sagas, or contacts between professors and students, engagement with the community, or anticipating long-term challenges.

Presidential visions are both indispensable and dangerous. They can hold the hope of the exciting possibility of actualizing an attractive image of what could be. But visions can also represent impossible dreams—seeing something that is not there and never could be.

Realistic and inspiring are rarely compatible. Public university visions must reflect more than aspirations. They must convey a compelling combination of institutional saga, campus capabilities, competitive advantages, and public needs, funded with special budget support. As Duderstadt observes, the faculty tend to dismiss visions not backed by budgets.

Is presidential leadership possible in the fragmented university? Though presidential leadership is not the only ingredient required for fixing the fragmented university, success is unlikely without it. Many of the reactions to the resignation of Lawrence Summers as Harvard president seemed to accept the conclusions that presidential moves to fix fragmented universities, whether public or private, will inevitably fail because of faculty opposition. Those interpretations tend to underplay presidential personality and overplay faculty resistance to campus changes. Bold actions, however desirable, pushed by arrogant leaders seldom work in universities.

The winds may be changing on campus as well as in society. The best and brightest scholars and students are beginning to demand an end to fragmentation. Sponsored research increasingly goes to faculty teams that collaborate across disciplines to address societal and theoretical problems. The best undergraduates are avoiding narrow specialization that limits their perspectives and career opportunities. Graduate and undergraduate education is becoming inquiry-based and problem- rather than discipline-centered. Increasingly, the best jobs are going to graduates who can work well in multidisciplinary teams to solve problems. A growing band of students and professors supports presidential plans that encourage collaboration and cooperation across disciplines.

In short, more students and faculty are beginning to support changes that bring more unity to the university and make it more student- and society-focused. The lesson current and aspiring presidents should learn from the "Harvard affair" is not to back off from changing the fragmented university but to become better collaborative leaders.

Reviving Faculty Senates

Roger Benjamin notes the declining influence of faculty senates and offers a bold proposal for their revival (see Chapter 4). He believes senates became dormant because they have insisted on dealing with the full range of academic issues, most of which have become too diverse for university-wide policies and better belong to faculty governance at the college, school, or department levels. For this reason, Benjamin urges senates to devote less attention to research and graduate studies and to revive their power and prestige by taking charge of an academic area that only the collective faculty can address—general education and assessing student learning.

Benjamin has a series of answers for skeptics who question why the faculty and its senates would take charge of areas most of them have assiduously avoided for years. He argues that professors in senates might do this to avoid a more frightening prospect—a governmental mandate dictating the details of general education and learning assessment. Benjamin also contends that this move could regain the lost prestige of the liberal arts and sciences on campus.

Though acceptance of Benjamin's challenge, as he concedes, would involve an amazing change in attitudes, it is hard to imagine a single suggestion that would do more to provide direction for the fragmented university than putting unity back into general education. An accreditation review of one public university declared, ". . . concern about the core experiences of the General Education program is one of the few pieces of glue holding universities together, yet there doesn't appear to be a strongly articulated role for general education in the undergraduate experience" (Western Association of Schools and Colleges, 2003, p. 9). No other change would respond more to the complaints of state and federal officials and business and civic leaders.

Integrating the Institution

Research universities, public and private, have available a range of programs that could put unity back into the university. They include strategic planning, priority budgeting, assessing institutional effectiveness, institutional accrediting, and internal performance reporting. None of these programs alone can cure fragmentation. They work best in combination.

Strategic Planning

The danger of the entrepreneurial university is that it becomes market dominated and values deprived. Zemsky, Wegner, and Massy (2005) argue that universities must be mission focused as well as market smart. Successful universities must balance markets and missions, linking public demands and needs with institutional values and capabilities. That collection of requirements presents the classic case for strategic planning, which links external opportunities and needs with internal capabilities and values. Daniel Rowley and Herbert Sherman insist that strategic planning must protect decentralization while providing direction (see Chapter 5). They worry about top-down planning and the lack of faculty participation, but the rise of the entrepreneurial university, as noted earlier, gives both professors and administrators a stake in identifying trends that will affect research and enrollment.

It is no coincidence that the presidents of both Florida International University and the University of Minnesota—two leaders interested in transformational change—chose to center their chapters on strategic planning in a book on fixing the fragmented university. These two universities planned from far different positions, which led to different approaches. FIU climbed during its short history from an upper-division college to an urban research university by adding schools, such as architecture, law, and now medicine. The University of Minnesota—already a leading research institution with a full complement of colleges and schools—prepared for a challenging future by combining some of these units to build multidisciplinary strengths in developing fields, to control costs, and to reduce weak areas.

President Bruininks—recognizing strategic planning is all about changing campus direction—modeled his strategic positioning on Kotter's (1996) eight stages of change. The first two stages, *preparing for change* and *creating the guiding coalition,* closely coincide with Rowley and Sherman's critical "planning to plan phase," which also includes establishing a sense of urgency for change and creating a committee that includes not just top administrators but a representative group of respected professors along with student leaders. They contend that "crisis" conveys a sense of urgency, but demands swift action that prevents careful planning and campus preparation. They favor a period of "well-understood challenges" rather than an impending crisis as the best time to launch strategic planning.

The University of Minnesota and FIU also stress the third Kotter stage of *developing a vision and a strategy.* Minnesota envisioned becoming one "of the top three public universities in the world" and FIU a "Top Urban Public Research University." Though diverse goals, each reached for the "top," underscoring the point that the vision has to inspire internal constituents and external stakeholders. Ohio State's academic plan also reached for the top: "Develop academic programs that define Ohio State as the nation's leading public land-grant university" (Ohio State University, 2000a, p. 10). Rowley and Sherman stress the importance of devising an inspiring vision and developing a strategy tailored to each institution rather than copied from another university. The current president of Ohio State, Karen Holbrook, calls for a "distinctive," not an imitative, university.

We must be distinctive as an institution. All AAU universities believe they are excellent, forward-looking, student-centered, accountable, critical in thought, and nimble—and all of us who are not in the Top 10 aspire to be. We must identify the signature elements that make Ohio State unique and enhance our upward mobility. (Holbrook, 2003)

Presidents Bruininks and Maidique see the fourth stage, *communicating the change vision,* as vital. No vision, however inspiring, sells itself. Others can chair the planning committee, but presidents must communicate the vision. Despite their incessant efforts to communicate both on an off campuses, through meetings, speeches, writings, and web sites, both President Bruininks and Maidique say if they had to do it over, they would devote even more attention to communication. They stress not just selling the vision and strategy, but also listening to reactions, particularly from professors, staff members, and students negatively affected.

The purpose of planning is Kotter's fifth stage, *empowering broad-based action.* If vision is the means, action is the end. The two presidents preach broad-based transformational change through strategic planning, but Rowley and Sherman seem more comfortable with incremental movement. Minnesota's strategic positioning through 2005 had not gone beyond Kotter's stage five. FIU has fulfilled stage six, *generating short-term wins,* by achieving approval for law and medical schools and a rating as a research-extensive university. It has not yet reached stages seven, *consolidating gains and producing more change,* and eight, *anchoring new approaches in the culture.*

All these authors suggest that rapid shifts in societal demands and needs will force frequent external and internal scans. Rowley and Sherman, while recognizing the necessity of strategic planning, stress its problems. The two campus presidents accent its possibilities. The former voices the need for considerable time to prepare, communicate, and implement strategic planning. President Maidique observes that the planning process can lose momentum if it takes too long. He would cut the three-year time span in half, if redoing FIU's strategic plan. Bruininks would overemphasize the necessity for change, recognizing that it takes a titanic necessity to get attention in a huge research university. The traditional conclusion is that the process is more important than the product in planning. Strategic positioning at Minnesota and Millennium planning at FIU seem to merge process and product, with each of equal importance.

The planning efforts at FIU and the University of Minnesota conflict with Ingram's belief that university governance should define more clearly proposals requiring communication, consultation, or decision-making, depending on the issues and the varying authority of trustees, presidents, and the faculty. The planning process at both universities does the opposite. Their approach transforms *communicating, consulting,* and *decision-making* into a stream of simultaneous messages, exchanges, and decisions. It suggests that credible decision-making comes not at a point of time usually at the end, but in serial fashion at various stages in the planning process. They do follow Rowley and Sherman's admonition that the process should build trust by convincing the faculty that the administration and trustees have not already made up their minds. For example, strategic positioning left most of the details to more than 34 representative committees. The experiences of the University of Minnesota in strategic positioning and FIU in Millennium planning suggest a new approach to decision-making for a new age, one involving a broad range of participants, mostly on but also off campus.

Karen Holbrook faced a different situation on becoming president of Ohio State University in 2003. As she noted in her investiture remarks, the university already had strategic priorities identified in its academic plan (Ohio State University, 2000a). Her chapter makes two critical points. "First, plans setting institutional directions are not presidential prerogatives to be changed with each successor to that office. Second, as noted in Chapter 1, great plans fade without careful and continuous implementation" (see Chapter 13). Every new president should heed her advice. Great universities are not the product of a single president at a particular point in time. They come from the continuous and collaborative effort of the academic community and their external supporters over time. Holbrook's chapter illustrates how three presidents linked their strategic initiatives over time with the goal of making Ohio State the best land-grant university in the country.

Strategic Budgeting: Decentralization With Direction

According to William Massy, "budget-making is a method—some would say *the* method—for steering the institution" in both good and bad times. It is a "prime tool for fighting fragmentation" (see Chapter 6). Both Massy and Duderstadt (see Chapter 3) accept the principle that institutional budgets should provide both direction and decentralization. As noted earlier, many public research universities have adopted variations of Responsibility Center Management (RCM) to encourage raising revenues and controlling cost. This system permits colleges and schools to keep most of their income but also to cover most of their costs. RCM also allows presidents and provosts to retain sufficient revenue to support central services and institutional priorities and to provide cross-subsidies to valued programs with limited revenues. Both authors reject the concept of "every tub on its own bottom," which returns all the revenues to the unit that raised them.

Massy and Duderstadt insist that presidents and provosts must have sufficient income, acquired by retaining a portion of state funding and taxing income from colleges and schools. As Massy observes, taxing by colleges and schools creates discontent, for no one likes taxes. Taking discretionary funds off the top of state appropriations for institutional priorities and cross-subsidies seems less controversial. State funding, which runs several hundred million dollars a year for the top public research universities, represents a declining portion of their revenues, but it can help fund institutional priorities that provide direction. Cross-subsidies create controversy from the income generating units. Duderstadt offers a practical—and Massy a conceptual—defense of them. Duderstadt declares that the University of Michigan's RCM—by keeping some state appropriations and taxing unit revenues heavily—leaves even colleges and schools with the highest income in need of subsidies. Apparently, the best defense for subsidies is to make every unit need them. Massy takes the high ground by insisting that cross-subsidies distinguish public benefit organizations from for-profit businesses.

> Do away with cross-subsidies and one has a for-profit business. For-profits are driven by market forces and only market forces, whereas not-for-profits seek to balance values and market forces. The balancing of values and market forces is what it means to steer the university and/or its constituent parts. (see Chapter 6)

Massy is critical of full-blown RCM, fearing it will increase fragmentation. But his biggest objection is that it ignores "what should be a sine qua non for all universities: education quality, especially for undergraduates" (see Chapter 6). He advocates a combination of decentralized and centralized budgeting. This combination would devolve revenues in areas where markets can help ensure quality, such as in research with peer review, and use central grants to reward quality in areas, such as undergraduate education, where markets respond to prestige not performance (e.g., Zemsky, 2005). Massy also believes that university budgets should reward desired results. "Budget-making without performance measures amounts to flying blind without a compass . . ." (see Chapter 6).

One wonders whether presidents and provosts, by accepting RCM, also sought to avoid conflict with colleges, schools, and departments over budget allocations. When senior administrators allocated funding from centralized budgets, they received the blame for what the faculty and the units considered bad budgets. By decentralizing budgets to academic units based on their revenue generation, the fault for funding shortfalls shifted from presidents and provost to deans and chairs.

Assessing Institutional Effectiveness

Assessing institutional effectiveness, says Volkwein, should help to unify the fragmented university and make it more student centered (see Chapter 7). Connection is the key. He argues that the linkage of strategic planning, priority budgeting, internal reporting, and assessing student learning at the class, program, and institutional levels can align institutional and unit priorities and performance. But Volkwein concedes that assessing undergraduate education—especially general education—is seldom a high priority at public research universities. A Commission on Undergraduate Education at the University of California–Berkeley suggests a range of reasons for this slighting that easily fits other elite public universities.

> Some say that the size and decentralization of Berkeley, and the notoriously independent minds of the faculty, make it difficult to come to consensus. . . . Others cite the allegiance of faculty to their disciplines and departments, and by extension their preoccupation with majors. . . . Still others point to the persistent sense of competition amongst three priorities— undergraduate education, graduate education and research—and the pervasive fear that we can emphasize the first only at the expense of the other two. (University of California–Berkeley, 2000, p. 6)

Benjamin thinks senates should take on this task, but the past record is not promising for future success (see Chapter 4). The response of a faculty senate committee on general education at Louisiana State University to a recommendation from a committee calling for a goals-based general education program suggests the difficulty.

> The General Education Committee does not believe that a complete restructuring of General Education

> courses into a program is necessary. Furthermore, the
> General Education Committee does not want to be
> in a position of dictating instructional approach and
> course content to faculty. (Louisiana State University,
> 2002, p. 1)

Administrators can push planning and budgeting reforms, but
general education and learning assessment are clearly a faculty responsibility that requires broad participation and a university-wide program. A number of public research universities have praised the
inquiry-based approach to undergraduate education advocated in the
Boyer Commission (1998) report (see also University of
California–Berkeley, 2002). But the most detailed recommendation in
that useful report——one championed by the Kellogg Commission and
many campus reforms—urges involving undergraduates in research.
Volkwein views the research initiative as a worthy objective, but sees it
as no substitute for identifying undergraduate learning goals and assessing their achievement. He applauds the Boyer Commission's criticism
of the lack of an effective general education program in research universities and its argument for an inquiry-based program. Volkwein
champions the knowledge and skills for undergraduates proposed by
the Association of American Colleges and Universities, advocated by
business and civic leaders, and now endorsed by regional and program
accrediting agencies (see Chapter 7).

Presidents, provosts, and faculty leaders of public research universities complain about college ratings, such as *U.S. News & World
Report's* based on the inputs of students, resources, and faculty. But they
fail to respond to those ratings by developing an alternative approach
that assesses the quality of undergraduate education. Absent an accepted method for measuring the quality of undergraduate learning outcomes, the default position is to count inputs, not assess results. These
input judgments make achieving quality easy for universities, for they
treat the excellence of undergraduate education like that of computers
as mostly a matter of good-in, good-out. It is time for leaders of public research universities to champion student learning assessment,
which examines results rather than resources and reputations. Massy
makes the point:

> No area in public research universities is more in
> need of steering than the quality of undergraduate
> education . . . The lack of robust value-added metrics
> limits the market's ability to distinguish between stu-

dent intake quality . . . and the quality of the education itself. (see Chapter 6)

Volkwein acknowledges that developing methods for assessing
undergraduate learning at the individual, program, or institutional levels
is not easy. Yet he believes the failure of most public research universities
to develop such assessment stems more from a lack of will than a shortage of ways. He proposes that program accreditation extend to general
education as well as specialized majors. He hopes to give well-designed
and implemented general education programs the same visibility and
recognition that flow from accreditation of specialized programs.
Though this proposal might have such effects, it could also lead to
institutional accreditation paying less attention to general education
and assessment. Moreover, program accreditation is voluntary for single departments, while general education should be mandatory for the
collective faculty led by the faculty in the arts and sciences.

Accreditation

Institutional accreditation would seem a perfect fit for fixing the fragmented university and ensuring that it becomes more student centered
and publicly engaged as well as research focused. After all, accreditation
uses outside peers to examine institutional missions and performance
in teaching, research, and service. Unfortunately, regional accreditation
has not been as successful as desired in assessing the quality of undergraduate education, says Ralph Wolff (see Chapter 8). The fault stems
not from the intent of accreditation agencies or the willingness of their
teams to write critical reports. The problem is that the administrators
and the faculty of top public research universities, knowing their
accreditation is secure, have often been less than responsive to the
accreditation reports criticizing them for slighting general education
and learning assessment.

The Council for Higher Education Accreditation (2003) claims,
"Accrediting organizations are responsible for establishing clear expectations that institutions and programs will routinely define, collect,
interpret, and use evidence of student learning outcomes" (p. 1). The
report continues: ". . . accreditors should: Ensure that using evidence
of student learning outcomes plays a central role in determining the
accredited status of an institution . . ." (p. 2). Yet an accreditation self-
study at UC Davis conceded candidly,

> We have . . . good means of measuring our effectiveness
> in research in the form of grants and of ratings on
> national surveys. Where we need work, *as does virtually*

every other major research university, is . . . assessing the
effectiveness of undergraduate education. Faculty have
not been quick to respond positively to the suggestion
that we should be developing instruments besides the
ordinary grading process to determine how well we are
succeeding in educating undergraduates. (University of
California–Davis, 1996)

To remedy this situation, institutional accreditors should concentrate even more of their reviews on the capacity of research universities
to assess undergraduate learning, particularly in general education.
Program accreditation can better evaluate performance in academic
majors, graduate studies, and faculty research, which exhibit too much
diversity for credible evaluations by institutional reviews. Institutional
accreditation should focus on student learning assessment in general
education. It is the area of greatest complaints about public research universities and the one often cited as in need of reform by regional accreditation reviews. Moreover, it constitutes the one academic area that must
remain a common responsibility for the institution as a whole.

The regional accrediting agencies deserve credit for moving toward
assessing institutional performance results rather than resource inputs,
and especially for their increasing emphasis on student learning outcomes (see Chapters 7 and 8). The problem is that repeated reviews
demonstrate that these agencies will not deny accreditation to a leading
research university, public or private, because it has not implemented
an effective assessment program. Accrediting agencies have only two
options. They will not use the "nuclear option" of denying accreditation; and re-review remains only an irritant and unlikely to occur more
than once during an accreditation cycle.

Two steps might get the attention of university leaders. First, no
institution could opt for a focused accreditation review, which they
largely select, if it had left unaddressed a major criticism from the last
accreditation review. Second, regional accreditors should publish summaries of accreditation team reports. Research universities are most
protective of their external reputations and might well move to make
improvements to avoid public criticism. Their administrators and professors would take criticisms on general education and student learning
assessment more seriously, if the accrediting bodies published at least a
summary of their recommendations. Confidentiality of accreditation
reviews supposedly encourages more candid self-study reports, but confidential candor becomes useful only when it leads to institutional
action to remedy acknowledged shortcomings. Wolff urges institutions

to put accreditation documents in accessible places on their web sites and use them to encourage dialogue, especially on improving general education and learning assessment (see Chapter 8).

Departmental Reporting

The fundamental problem with the fragmented university is that university priorities seldom get down to departments and departmental plans seldom get up to central administrations. As Chapter 1 claims, the answer to the problem is neither a top-down nor a bottom-up approach, but one that provides direction with decentralization. The real goal is to make institutional planning and performance reporting have internal meaning rather than remain as routine exercises done mostly for external consumption. Chapter 9 achieves this result by linking the institution and its colleges, schools, and departments in performance loops that convey information on institutional priorities reflecting societal needs and on academic unit performance according to common and unique indicators. The loops feed back not only information about unit performance but also the knowledge acquired through program reviews, academic audits, and outcomes assessments. Each college, school, and department not only receives the information about university priorities but also revises its plans in response and suggests potential changes to institutional priorities. The goal is to couple— as the title of this book proposes—decentralization with direction. The key to performance reporting is linkage, or as the next section suggests, connections.

The Key to Institutional Integration Is Connection____

The ties that can bind the public university are clear. Although strategic planning, priority budgeting, and institutional accreditation are more developed than undergraduate learning assessment and departmental performance reporting, most public universities have all these tools in some form. Nearly every one has something called a strategic or academic plan. All have annual budgets that fund units, programs, and activities. All have accreditation reviews that concentrate on institutional priorities and performance. Most of them have some type of program that assesses undergraduate learning—or at least are working to develop an approach for the next regional accreditation review. Most universities require reports from academic departments, though largely on inputs of funding, students, and professors, not performance results on institutional priorities. The problem in most public universities is that these programs are not connected.

An accreditation report for the University of California–Davis, says it all:

> Connect the Pieces: UC Davis needs to better coordinate, synthesize, and integrate all its separate educational initiatives under the strategic plan. We see added value to UC Davis by pulling these threads together creating a more cohesive internal action agenda and external public image. (Western Association of Schools and Colleges, 2003, p. 42)

Figure 16.1 presents this connection as a feedback loop. The loop begins with *Planning* that examines both external needs and opportunities and internal capabilities and values to set realistic institutional priorities. *Budgeting* provides special funding for those priorities at the institutional, college/school, and department levels and encourages goal alignment, rewards quality, and hopefully improves performance. *Assessing* uses student learning assessment, program review, academic audit, and accreditation at the program and institutional levels to evaluate performance results. *Reporting* transmits the information gathered about performance at the college, school, and department levels, especially on institutional priorities, and feeds the results back to *Planning*, which reviews and reconsiders priorities based on these internal reports and external changes. Florida International University has operationalized such a linkage (see Chapter 9 and the FIU planning and effectiveness web site at www.fiu.edu/~opie/main.htm).

Figure 16.1
Feedback Loop

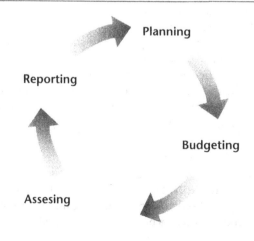

Student Centered and Public Engaged_____

The Kellogg Commission challenged public universities to become as student centered and public engaged as they are research focused. Peter Magrath claims correctly that presidents and provosts often speak of their universities becoming more student centered and public engaged. Yet the reality is that institutions pulled by prestige and pushed for revenues have continued to focus on the climb up the national-rankings rungs by stressing graduate studies and research and student selectivity. Indeed, reading the annual addresses of presidents at research universities leaves the impression that raising their national rankings represents the only shared goal on many campuses. To repeat Mark Yudof's (2003) question and answer on that topic: "How many Top 10 or Top 50 universities can there be? . . . If you believe all the university generated press releases, the answer seems to be something like 200."

The Student-Centered University

Need for tuition income and reliance on national ratings that consider the quality of undergraduate education as mostly a matter of good-in, good-out makes public research universities seem more interested in attracting than educating undergraduates. Given the absence of accepted and comparable methods for assessing quality results in undergraduate education, universities have engaged in an "arms race" of physical and social amenities to attract undergraduate students (Weinberg, 2005).

George Kuh—drawing on results from the National Survey of Student Engagement (NSSE) and a study Documenting Effective Educational Practices (DEEP)—insists that the way to become more student centered is to arrange programs, activities, and environments to encourage students to become more engaged with their studies and campus life (see Chapter 10). *Student engagement* suggests a shared responsibility of the university and the student for student success, while *student centered* implies only institutional effort. Kuh distinguishes between the *espoused* mission—what the university says about its undergraduate education—and its *enacted* mission—what undergraduates actually experience. An engaged university focuses on student learning and improvement and lays out the steps required for student success, inside and outside the classroom.

The NSSE approach represents a major move from the inputs of the national ratings by pushing campus processes that encourage student engagement. But NSSE, though a major development, is merely a valuable halfway house on the road from inputs to outcomes for it focuses on processes that encourage student engagement rather than on the results of student learning. Still, NSSE is a tremendous advance that could improve student learning in all colleges and universities, including public research universities. Indeed, advocates would argue that the only way for universities to change outcomes is to change the processes that produce them.

The good news is that increasing numbers of public research universities are participating in NSSE and using the comparison of their scores on the student survey of the presence of good practices with the combined average of peer institutions to spur improvements. Unfortunately, the insistence of participating institutions that results must remain confidential means that NSSE results cannot provide a counterweight to national ratings such as *U.S. News & World Report's.*

Public Engagement

Peter Magrath notes that the Kellogg Commission document on public engagement received the most attention of all its reports (see Chapter 15). Presidential speeches often tout public engagement, especially in universities with a land-grant tradition. Richard Cherwitz and Johanna Hartelius (see Chapter 11) add an important element to the effort of engaging pubic universities more with their communities and society. They claim this goal requires a persuasive rhetoric for professors, which presents public engagement as a rigorous scholarly activity. Success demands voluntary commitment, they insist, rather than the administrative mandate. For this reason, their approach is faculty centered rather than community focused.

Though rhetoric is often viewed as putting a favorable face on an unpleasant reality, Cherwitz and Hartelius believe developing an academic rhetoric for public engagement is the only way to change a campus culture where most professors see such activity as a refuge for "failed scholars" (see Chapter 11). Their chapter provides a rhetoric that seeks to elevate public engagement by making the problems of society worthy subjects for both scholarship and learning.

These authors are undoubtedly correct that making research universities more publicly engaged requires a more faculty-friendly rhetoric that stresses teaching, research, and engagement as simultaneous rather than separate activities and sees university involvement in community issues, problems, and initiatives as mutually beneficial to both parties. The Intellectual Entrepreneurship Consortium created at the University of Texas–Austin by Cherwitz turns the rhetoric into a reality by offering exciting opportunities for public engagement combined with research and learning for faculty and undergraduate and graduate students (see https://webspace.utexas.edu/cherwitz/www/ie/index.html).

Presidents, provosts, and deans must also make public engagement a consideration in hiring, rewarding, promoting, and tenuring professors. Magrath makes the point that "most American professors are not ideologically hostile (quite the contrary) to service and engagement, *if* their work is recognized and rewarded" (see Chapter 15).

Recommendations

The authors of this book offer specific recommendations for fixing the fragmented university or making it more student centered or publicly engaged, depending on their topics. What follows are some suggested ways that participants, programs, priorities, and principles can contribute to achieving those goals.

Participants

• *Trustees* should balance public needs and campus concerns by asking strategic questions about institutional priorities and performance and insisting on persuasive answers.

• *Presidents* should become both more active and more participative in pushing for strategic changes and by articulating a collaborative and inspiring vision that links their university's saga to the changes required by a challenging future.

• *Academic deans* should champion university direction as well as unit decentralization in their colleges and schools, and *provosts*, who appoint them, should insist that they perform both duties.

• *Faculty participation* at the university level should focus more on participating on commissions and task forces that propose strategic directions and university priorities.

• *Faculty and university senates* should have the opportunity to propose participants and comment on commission recommendations, and *presidents* and *trustees* should consider senate comments before acing on commission reports.

• *Faculty and university senates* and the arts and *sciences faculty* should take charge of developing programs in general education and assessing undergraduate learning—academic areas that represent a collective faculty responsibility.

Programs

• *Strategic planning* conducted by representative committees of administrators, professors, and students should identify an inspiring but realistic future, with institutional priorities based on state and student needs and on competitive advantages and campus values.

- *Strategic budgeting* should be decentralized to encourage income generation, cost control, and faculty innovation, but centralized to retain funds for institutional priorities and cross-subsidies and to reward departments for quality performance results.
- *Institutional accreditation* should focus more on the quality of general education and assessment of student learning, and publicize summaries of team reports.
- *Departmental performance reports* should encourage direction and decentralization by identifying a common set of performance indicators for academic units based on institutional priorities, by reporting performance results from these units, and by revising institutional plans based on those results.
- *Student engagement* should encourage a joint responsibility of the university and the student for undergraduate learning and growth, and universities should further these goals by administering the National Survey of Student Engagement and by comparing their results with those from peer institutions to improve campus performance.
- *Public engagement* requires a rhetoric that underscores for the faculty the rigor of problem-centered research and teaching focused on community and societal issues; universities should make public engagement a positive factor in hiring, merit, and promotion and tenure decisions.

Principles
- *Connection* among the above programs is the key to providing university direction, for they work best in coordination.
- *Process* in decision-making, contrary to the cliché, is not more important than the *product*, which would make means more important than ends. Each is equally important, for one cannot succeed for long without the other.
- *Vision* is the means, but action is the end of strategic planning.
- *Market smart and mission centered* means creating not imitative universities chasing changing markets but distinctive universities based on institutional values and competitive advantages.
- *Great universities* are not the product of a single president, but the continuous, collaborative creation of the academic community over time.

Conclusion

The Kellogg Commission challenged presidents and chancellors to fix the fragmented university and create campuses as student centered and public engaged as they are research focused. Many public research universities appear on the way to the first goal. In many ways, they had no choice. History does repeat itself. Clark Kerr (1963) said it nearly 50 years ago: "Universities . . . have been moving in clear directions. . . . But these directions have not been set as much by the university's visions of its destiny as by the external environment . . ." (p. 122). Two external forces, which once appeared contradictory to academics, now combine to provide direction for public research universities: market forces and national ratings. Market forces drive sponsored research and undergraduate majors; national ratings, by linking resources with reputation, reinforce market demands.

Pushed by market forces, pulled by peer prestige, and funded mostly by self-generated income, these universities are losing their sense of public purpose. The Kellogg Commission challenged them to become what the public wants most—undergraduate centered and publicly engaged universities. Those challenges have produced rhetoric from presidents but have not changed the reality in many universities and in most departments, schools, and colleges. The reason is clear. These two goals get little response from external markets and no points on national ratings. To recapture their public character, public research universities must become not only market smart but mission centered, which means making undergraduate learning and public engagement equal partners with graduate studies and research. Though worthy goals for all universities, they are mandates for those that call themselves public.

The Kellogg Commission (2000) asked the right question and gave the right answer. "What . . . does the term 'public university' mean today? The irreducible idea is that we exist to advance the common good" (p. 9). For institutions to return to their roots requires that trustees, presidents, and professors put unity, students, and the public back into state universities. The good news is that the knowledge society and the best scholars and students are beginning to demand it.

References

American Association of University Professors. (1966). *Statement on government of colleges and universities.* Retrieved August 9, 2006, from www.aaup.org/statements/Redbook/Govern.htm

Baldridge, J. V., & Curtis, D. V. (1977). Alternative models of governance in higher education. In G. L. Riley & J. V. Baldridge (Eds.), *Governing academic organizations: New problems, new perspectives* (pp. 1–25). Berkeley, CA: McCutcheon.

Bennis, W., & Movius, H. (2006, March 17). Why Harvard is so hard to lead. *The Chronicle of Higher Education,* p. B20.

Birnbaum, R. (Ed.). (1991). *New directions in higher education: No. 75. Faculty in governance: The role of senates and joint committees in academic decision-making.* San Francisco, CA: Jossey-Bass.

Birnbaum, R. (2001). *Management fads in higher education: Where they come from, what they do, why they fail.* San Francisco, CA: Jossey-Bass.

Boyer Commission on Educating Undergraduates in the Research University. (1998). *Reinventing undergraduate education: A blueprint for America's research universities.* Retrieved August 20, 2006, from the Stony Brook University web site: http://naples.cc.sunysb.edu/Pres/boyer.nsf/673918d46fbf653e852565ec0056ff3e/d955b61ffddd590a852565ec005717ae/$FILE/boyer.pdf

Byrne, J. V. (2006). *Public higher education reform five years after the Kellogg Commission on the Future of State and Land-Grant Universities.* Retrieved August 22, 2006, from www.nasulgc.org/Kellogg/KCFiveYearReport.pdf

Clark, B. R. (1992). *The distinctive college: Antioch, Reed, and Swarthmore.* New Brunswick, NJ: Transaction.

Clark, B. R. (1998). *Creating entrepreneurial universities: Organizational pathways of transformation.* Oxford, England: Elsevier Science.

Clark, B. (2001). The entrepreneurial university: New foundations for collegiality, autonomy, and achievement. *Higher Education Management, 13*(2), 9–24.

Council for Higher Education Accreditation, Institute for Research and Study of Accreditation and Quality Assurance. (2003). *Statement of mutual responsibilities for student learning outcomes: Accreditation, institutions, and programs.* Washington, DC: Author.

Dendy, L. B. (2004). *Committee will consider procedures for reorganization of academic units.* Retrieved August 26, 2006, from the University of Georgia, Office of Public Affairs web site: www.uga.edu/columns/041213/news-ucouncil.html

Duderstadt, J. J., & Womack, F. W. (2004). *The future of the public university in America: Beyond the crossroads.* Baltimore, MD: Johns Hopkins University Press.

Holbrook, K. A. (2003a). *Investiture address.* Retrieved August 21, 2006, from The Ohio State University, Office of the President web site: http://president.osu.edu/speeches/investiture.html

Keller, G. (1983). *Academic strategy: The management revolution in American higher education.* Baltimore, MD: Johns Hopkins University Press.

Keller, G. (2004). A growing quaintness: Traditional governance in the markedly new realm of U.S. higher education. In W. G. Tierney (Ed.), *Competing conceptions of academic governance: Negotiating the perfect storm* (pp. 158–76). Baltimore, MD: Johns Hopkins University Press.

Kellogg Commission on the Future of State and Land-Grant Universities. (2000). *Renewing the covenant: Learning, discovery, and engagement in a new age and different world.* Washington, DC: National Association of State Universities and Land-Grant Colleges.

Kerr, C. (1963). *The uses of the university.* Cambridge, MA: Harvard University Press.

Kotter, J. P. (1996). *Leading change.* Boston, MA: Harvard Business School Press.

Louisiana State University, Faculty Senate Committee on General Education. (2002). *Comments on the recommendations from the General Education Learning Outcomes and Assessment Committee.* Baton Rouge, LA: Author.

Ohio State University. (2000a). *Academic plan.* Retrieved August 21, 2006, from The Ohio State University, Academic Plan web site: www.osu.edu/academicplan/Acad_Plan.pdf

Ohio State University. (2000b). *Report from the Presidential Commission on University Governance: A review of the governance structure of the University Senate and the effectiveness of its role in shared governance.* Retrieved August 26, 2006, from The Ohio State University, Faculty Council web site: http://facultycouncil.osu.edu/GovernanceReport.pdf

Ohio State University. (2004). *Report of Committee on Barriers to Interdisciplinarity.* Retrieved August 26, 2006, from The Ohio State University, Office of the University Senate web site: http://senate.osu.edu/Reports/FCEC/InterdiscRptfinal.pdf

Ohio State University. (2005). *The Ohio State University academic plan 2005 update.* Retrieved August 26, 2006, from The Ohio State University, Academic Plan web site: www.osu.edu/academicplan/2005index.php

Oregon State University. (2003). *The plan for a path of distinction.* Retrieved August 26, 2006, from the Oregon State University, Administrative Leadership web site: http://oregonstate.edu/leadership/strategicPlan.pdf

Oregon State University. (2004a). *Faculty senate minutes.* Retrieved August 26, 2006, from the Oregon State University, Faculty Senate web site: http://oregonstate.edu/dept/senate/min/2004/20040205.html

Oregon State University. (2004b). *A strategic plan for the 21st century.* Retrieved August 26, 2006, from the Oregon State University, Administrative Leadership web site: http://oregonstate.edu/leadership/strategicplan/StrategicPlan.pdf

Ray, E. J. (2003). *Challenges in advancing our land grant mission.* Retrieved August, 26, 2006, from the Oregon State University, University Day web site: http://oregonstate.edu/events/universityday/2003/presidentsAddress.html

Rhoades, G. (2003). *Democracy and capitalism, academic style: Governance in contemporary higher education.* Retrieved August 28, 2006, from the University of Southern California, Rossier School of Education web site: www.usc.edu/dept/chepa/gov/roundtable2003/rhoades.pdf#search

Schuster, J. H., Smith, D. G., Corak, K. A., & Yamada, M. M. (1994). *Strategic governance: How to make big decisions better.* Phoenix, AZ: American Council on Education/Oryx Press.

Tierney, W. G., & Lechuga, V. M. (Eds.). (2004). *New directions for higher education: No. 127. Restructuring shared governance in higher education.* San Francisco, CA: Jossey-Bass.

University of California–Berkeley. (2000). *Commission on Undergraduate Education: Final report.* Retrieved August 26, 2006, from the University of California–Berkeley, Commission on Undergraduate Education web site: http://www-learning.berkeley.edu/cue/final/CUE_Final.pdf

University of California–Berkeley. (2002). *UC Berkeley strategic academic plan.* Retrieved August 26, 2006, from the University of California–Berkeley, NewsCenter web site: www.berkeley.edu/news/media/releases/2003/05/sap/plan.pdf

University of California–Davis. (1996). *UDC in the mid-nineties: Responses to the 1991 accreditation visit of the Western Association of Schools and Colleges.* Retrieved August 26, 2006, from the University of California–Davis, Office of the Vice Provost web site: http://undergraduatestudies.ucdavis.edu/wasc/WASC96.htm

University of Georgia. (2004). *University Council Executive Committee minutes.* Retrieved August 26, 2006, from the University of Georgia, University Council web site: http://regapp.reg.uga.edu/web/committees/index.php?page=anon_display_meetingagenda&mid=133

University of Michigan. (2000). *Two commissions formed to study university issues.* Retrieved August 26, 2006, from the University of Michigan, News Service web site: www.umich.edu/~newsinfo/Releases/2000/Jan00/r012000a.html

University of Michigan. (2004). *Presidential task force on multidisciplinary education and team teaching*. Retrieved August 26, 2006, from the University of Michigan, Office of the President web site: www.umich.edu/pres/committees/team_charge.html

University of Minnesota. (2005). *Resolution on strategic planning*. Retrieved August 26, 2006, from the University of Minnesota, University Senate web site: www1.umn.edu/usenate/resolutions/strategicplan ningres.html

University of North Carolina–Chapel Hill. (2003). *Academic plan*. Retrieved August 26, 2006, from the University of North Carolina–Chapel Hill, Office of the Provost web site: www.unc.edu/provost/news/aca_planOct03.pdf

University of Wisconsin–Madison. (2003). *Connecting ideas: Strategies for the University of Wisconsin–Madison*. Retrieved August 26, 2006, from the University of Wisconsin–Madison, Chancellor's Page web site: www.chancellor.wisc.edu/strategicplan/

Weinberg, A. (2005, September 2). An alternative to the campus as Club Med. *The Chronicle of Higher Education*, p. B13.

Western Association of Schools and Colleges. (2003). *UC Davis educational effectiveness review: Team report*. Retrieved August 26, 2006, from the University of California–Davis, Western Association of Schools and Colleges web site: http://wasc.ucdavis.edu/WASC_FinalReport2003.pdf

Whalen, E. L. (1991). *Responsibility center budgeting: An approach to decentralized management for institutions of higher education*. Bloomington, IA: Indiana University Press.

Yudof, M. (2003). *Remarks by Mark G. Yudof*. Retrieved August 10, 2006, from the University of Texas System, Office of the Chancellor web site: www.utsystem.edu/cha/speechesarticles/AGBFlorida1-22-03.htm

Zemsky, R. M. (2005). The dog that doesn't bark: Why markets neither limit prices nor promote educational quality. In J. C. Burke & Associates, *Achieving accountability in higher education: Balancing public, academic, and market demands* (pp. 275–295). San Francisco, CA: Jossey-Bass.

Zemsky, R., Wegner, G. R., & Massy, W. F. (2005, July 15). Today's colleges must be market smart and mission centered. *The Chronicle of Higher Education*, p. B6.

Index

Printed in the United States
By Bookmasters